Studying Speaking to Inform
Second Language Learning

SECOND LANGUAGE ACQUISITION
Series Editor: Professor David Singleton, *Trinity College, Dublin, Ireland*

This new series will bring together titles dealing with a variety of aspects of language acquisition and processing in situations where a language or languages other than the native language is involved. Second language will thus be interpreted in its broadest possible sense. The volumes included in the series will all in their different ways offer, on the one hand, exposition and discussion of empirical findings and, on the other, some degree of theoretical reflection. In this latter connection, no particular theoretical stance will be privileged in the series; nor will any relevant perspective – sociolinguistic, psycholinguistic, neurolinguistic, etc. – be deemed out of place. The intended readership of the series will be final-year undergraduates working on second language acquisition projects, postgraduate students involved in second language acquisition research, and researchers and teachers in general whose interests include a second language acquisition component.

Other Books in the Series
Age, Accent and Experience in Second Language Acquisition
    Alene Moyer
Age and the Acquisition of English as a Foreign Language
    María del Pilar García Mayo and Maria Luisa García Lecumberri (eds)
Effects of Second Language on the First
    Vivian Cook (ed.)
Fossilization in Adult Second Language Acquisition
    ZhaoHong Han
Learning to Request in a Second Language: A Study of Child Interlanguage Pragmatics
    Machiko Achiba
Portraits of the L2 User
    Vivian Cook (ed.)
Silence in Second Language Learning: A Psychoanalytic Reading
    Colette A. Granger

Other Books of Interest
Audible Difference: ESL and Social Identity in Schools
    Jennifer Miller
Context and Culture in Language Teaching and Learning
    Michael Byram and Peter Grundy (eds)
Cross-linguistic Influence in Third Language Acquisition
    J. Cenoz, B. Hufeisen and U. Jessner (eds)
Developing Intercultural Competence in Practice
    Michael Byram, Adam Nichols and David Stevens (eds)
English in Europe: The Acquisition of a Third Language
    Jasone Cenoz and Ulrike Jessner (eds)
How Different Are We? Spoken Discourse in Intercultural Communication
    Helen Fitzgerald
Language Learners as Ethnographers
    Celia Roberts, Michael Byram, Ana Barro, Shirley Jordan and Brian Street

Please contact us for the latest book information:
Multilingual Matters, Frankfurt Lodge, Clevedon Hall,
Victoria Road, Clevedon, BS21 7HH, England
http://www.multilingual-matters.com

SECOND LANGUAGE ACQUISITION 8
Series Editor: David Singleton, *Trinity College, Dublin, Ireland*

Studying Speaking to Inform Second Language Learning

Edited by
Diana Boxer and Andrew D. Cohen

MULTILINGUAL MATTERS LTD
Clevedon • Buffalo • Toronto

Library of Congress Cataloging in Publication Data
Studying Speaking to Inform Second Language Learning/Edited by Diana Boxer and
Andrew D. Cohen.
Second Language Acquisition: 8
Includes bibliographical references and index.
1. Language and languages–Study and teaching. 2. Oral communication–Study and
teaching. 3. Discourse analysis–Study and teaching.
I. Boxer, Diana II. Cohen, Andrew D. III. Series.
P53.6.S78 2004b
418'.0071--dc22   2003024056

British Library Cataloguing in Publication Data
A catalogue entry for this book is available from the British Library.

ISBN 1-85359-721-X (hbk)
ISBN 1-85359-720-1 (pbk)

Multilingual Matters Ltd
UK: Frankfurt Lodge, Clevedon Hall, Victoria Road, Clevedon BS21 7HH.
USA: UTP, 2250 Military Road, Tonawanda, NY 14150, USA.
Canada: UTP, 5201 Dufferin Street, North York, Ontario M3H 5T8, Canada.

Typeset by Florence Production Ltd.
Printed and bound in Great Britain by the Cromwell Press Ltd.

Contents

Bio-statements

The Editors

Diana Boxer is Professor and Chair of the Linguistics Department at the University of Florida. She is the author of *Applying Sociolinguistics: Domains and Face-to-face Interaction* (John Benjamins, 2002) and *Complaining and Commiserating: A Speech Act View of Solidarity in Spoken American English* (Lang, 1993). She has published in the areas of discourse and pragmatics, sociolinguistics, gender and language, and second language acquisition in such journals as *The Annual Review of Applied Linguistics, Discourse and Society, ELT Journal, Journal of Pragmatics, TESOL Quarterly, Text,* and *Women and Language.*

Andrew D. Cohen, Professor in the MA in English as a Second Language Program, University of Minnesota, Minneapolis, also directs the National Language Resource Center at the Center for Advanced Research on Language Acquisition (CARLA) at the University. He is author of *Assessing Language Ability in the Classroom* (Heinle & Heinle, 1994), co-editor with Lyle Bachman of *Interfaces Between Second Language Acquisition and Language Testing Research* (CUP, 1998), and co-editor with Elaine Tarone and Susan Gass of *Research Methodology in Second-language Acquisition* (Lawrence Erlbaum, 1994). He has also published books on language learning and use strategies (*Language Learning: Insights for Learners, Teachers, and Researchers,* Newbury House/HarperCollins, 1990; *Strategies in Learning and Using a Second Language,* Longman, 1998).

Contributing Authors

Kathleen Bardovi-Harlig, Professor of TESOL/Applied Linguistics at Indiana University, is widely published in the areas of second language acquisition, interlanguage pragmatics, and the intersection of language acquisition and pragmatic development. She is author of *Tense and Aspect in Second Language Acquisition: Form, Meaning, and Use* (Blackwell, 2000), and editor, with B. Hartford, of *Beyond Methods: Components of Language Teacher Education* (McGraw Hill, 1997).

Leslie M. Beebe is Professor of Linguistics and Education and Director of the Applied Linguistics Program at Columbia University Teachers College. A former President of the American Association for Applied Linguistics, she is Editor of *Issues in Second Language Acquisition: Multiple Perspectives* and co-author of *English in the Cross-cultural Era*. She publishes widely in the areas of sociolinguistics, second language acquisition, and cross-cultural and acquisitional pragmatics.

Annie Brown has been a Research Fellow in the Language Testing Research Centre at the University of Melbourne since 1990. At the Centre she has been involved in language test development, postgraduate teaching about testing, teacher in-servicing, language test research, and the evaluation of language programs. She is also a frequent contributor at major conferences and reviewer for *Language Testing*. She has taught English as a Second Language in Australia and around the world.

Dan Douglas is Professor in the TESL/Applied Linguistics Program, English Department, Iowa State University. His major research interests include language testing, language for specific purposes, and second language acquisition. He has taught and conducted research in Botswana, Hawai'i, Scotland, England, Sudan, and Japan. He is the author of *Assessing Languages for Specific Purposes* (CUP, 2000), and Co-editor of the journal *Language Testing*.

Helena Halmari is Associate Professor in the Department of English, Sam Houston State University. Her publications focus principally on codeswitching from the point of view of its syntax, discourse, and pragmatics. She is the author of *Government and Codeswitching: Explaining American Finnish* (John Benjamins, 1997) and the co-editor, with Tuija Virtanen, of *Persuasion Across Genres: A Linguistic Approach* (John Benjamins, 2004). Her articles have appeared in such journals as *Linguistics, Applied Linguistics, Issues in Applied Linguistics, Journal of Pragmatics, Journal of Finnish Studies*, and *Neuphilologische Mitteilungen*.

Heidi Hamilton is Associate Professor in the Department of Linguistics, Georgetown University, where she teaches courses in discourse analysis and applications of interactional sociolinguistics. Her research interests focus on issues of language and Alzheimer's disease, language and aging, medical communication, and second language acquisition. Her books include *Conversations with an Alzheimer's Patient* (Cambridge University Press, 1994), *Language and Communication in Old Age: Multidisciplinary Perspectives* (Garland, 1999), *Glimmers: A Journey into Alzheimer's Disease* (RiverWood Books, 2003), *Handbook of Discourse Analysis* (with Schiffrin and Tannen) (Blackwell, 2001) and *Linguistics, Language, and the Professions* (with Alatis and Tan) (Georgetown University Press, 2002).

Joan Kelly Hall is Professor of Applied Linguistics and Education at the Pennsylvania State University. Her work is based on a sociocultural perspective of language and learning and is organized around two over-arching goals. The first is to understand the conditions by which language learners' involvement in the various constellations of their classroom practices is shaped, and how such involvement affects both what is learned and how it is learned. The second is to use this understanding o help create effectual classroom communities of language learners. Her most recent publications include *Teaching and Researching Language and Culture* (Pearson, 2003) and *Methods for Teaching Foreign Languages: Creating a Community of Learners in the Classroom* (Prentice-Hall, 2002).

Koji Konishi is Professor at Matsuyama University in Japan. His research area is applied linguistics and TESOL, and his current research interest focuses on communication strategies. He was a Visiting Professor at the University of Minnesota between 1999 and 2000, where he carried out research on communication strategies with Elaine Tarone.

Anne Lazaraton is a faculty member in the MA ESL Program at the University of Minnesota. Her research interests include discourse analysis of NS-NNS and NNS-NNS interaction, oral language assessment, and applied linguistics research methodology. Her work has appeared in *Language Testing, Modern Language Journal, Research on Language and Social Interaction, SYSTEM,* and *TESOL Quarterly. A Qualitative Approach to the Validation of Oral Language Tests,* her new book, was recently published by Cambridge University Press.

Carsten Roever is an academic staff member in the Department of Linguistics and Applied Linguistics at the University of Melbourne. He received a Ph.D. in Second Language Studies from the University of Hawai'i at Manoa. His research interests include second language teaching and learning, interlanguage pragmatics, and second language assessment.

Tom Salsbury is the Director of Foreign Languages and Philology and a Professor of English as a foreign language at the Monterrey Institute of Technology in Mexico City. He received his doctorate in Linguistics from Indiana University, Bloomington, in 2000 and has published in the area of interlanguage pragmatics and discourse as well as the acquisition of L2 English modality.

Elaine Tarone is Professor in English as a Second Language at the University of Minnesota. There, she is also Head of the Program in English as a Second Language, and Director of the Center for Advanced Research on Language Acquisition (CARLA). She has published research on second language acquisition since 1972, and is particularly interested in the way in which social forces and communicative contexts influence cognitive processes of second language acquisition. She is currently studying acquisition processes in immigrant populations in the US.

Carrie Taylor-Hamilton is Assistant Professor of English and Linguistics at the University of the Incarnate Word in San Antonio, Texas. She holds a doctorate in linguistics from the University of Florida. She has taught ESL/EFL in the United States, Greece, France, Malaysia, Japan, and the United Arab Emirates.

Hansun Zhang Waring is Assistant Professor of Speech Communication at Mercy College and Adjunct Assistant Professor of Linguistics and Education at Teachers College, Columbia University. Her research interests are discourse and conversation analysis, interlanguage pragmatics, and second language acquisition. Her writings have appeared in scholarly journals such as *Language in Society*, *Issues in Applied Linguistics*, *Research on Language and Social Interaction*, *Journal of Pragmatics*, *Discourse Studies*, and *Discourse & Society*.

Part I: Theoretical Issues

Chapter 1

Studying Speaking to Inform Second Language Learning: A Conceptual Overview

DIANA BOXER

This chapter provides a conceptual overview of the intersection of two sub-fields of Applied Linguistics: Discourse Analysis and Second Language Acquisition. I review several theoretical perspectives on how the analysis of spoken discourse can inform what we know about the various processes of language learning and testing. Three frameworks are discussed herein: (1) Language Identity; (2) Language Socialization; and (3) Sociocultural Theory. Moreover, a major focus of this introduction is an overview of methodological approaches to studying spoken discourse in language learning contexts. The 12 chapters that comprise the present volume are placed into their theoretical and methodological frameworks.

Introduction

The past 30 to 40 years have witnessed the emergence of the field now known as Applied Linguistics. Indeed, in this relatively short time, we have seen the birth and growth of the sub-field of Applied Linguistics known as Second Language Acquisition (SLA),[1] now in its adolescence. At the same time, there has been an enormous proliferation of literature in the realm of Discourse Analysis (DA), including the ethnography of communication, or speaking (ES), Interactional Sociolinguistics (IS), Conversation Analysis (CA), and Critical Discourse Analysis (CDA). These two strands of research, discourse studies and SLA research, have only recently begun to intersect. This fact holds true despite the belief held by many that SLA and DA can and should inform each other. While it is true that some recent research in SLA has begun to glean insights from the various approaches to the analysis of spoken discourse, there is much more to be studied that can lend theoretical illumination and practical applications to second language (L2) learning and pedagogy. By studying how language users employ their language(s) in a variety of contexts, with a variety of types of interlocutors, and on a variety of topical issues, students, teachers, and scholars can create curriculum, materials, and assessment instruments based on something more substantive than the intuitions of mother tongue users. Given the state of affairs of a highly developed DA and a highly developed body of research in SLA, it is timely to put forth a collection of articles that closely connects these two thrusts in Applied Linguistics. In so doing, we demonstrate the value of studying spoken discourse as it can be applied to language learning contexts. Such is the intention of this volume.

Background

It would be unfair and indeed untrue to categorically state that spoken interaction has been overlooked in the relatively brief history of research in L2 studies. A fair amount of early SLA research as well as more current investigations have studied speaking to ascertain the *interactional* features so important to language learning (e.g. Gass & Varonis, 1985; Hatch, 1978; Long, 1983; Pica, 1988; Swain, 1985). This research thrust views conversation from the perspective of negotiated interaction, either between native speakers and learners (NS-NNS) or between two or more learners (NNS-NNS). This kind of interaction encourages language learners to stretch their linguistic abilities in L2 by means of checking their understanding of the discourse until mutual competence is achieved.

Studies in negotiation of input and production of comprehensible output have been taken by some as a narrowly defined psycholinguistic approach to acquisition. A notable example of this stance is Firth and Wagner (1997). At a colloquium that took place at the International Association of Applied Linguistics (AILA) meetings in Jyväskylä, Finland, in 1996, Alan Firth and Johannes Wagner opened up a very interesting and controversial debate on this very issue, in which they called for a reconceptualization of SLA in order to address what they saw as an imbalance biased toward a cognitive perspective on SLA that neglected social interactional perspectives. Their major claim is that SLA research has by and large viewed L2 development from a purely psycholinguistic point of view, with learners traversing an "interlanguage" continuum that has, at its hypothetical end point, the abstract notion of the idealized "native speaker." Movement toward the "target" proceeded along the linguistic dimensions of phonological, morphological, syntactic, lexical, and semantic growth. Pragmatic considerations have been studied in terms of "interlanguage pragmatics," a concept viewing the acquisition of norms of appropriate speech behavior largely through a lens of movement from L1 norms to L2 norms, with particular attention to pragmatic transfer. Few would deny the usefulness of these perspectives in amassing a body of knowledge on how additional languages are developed, with attention to the various levels of linguistic competencies.

However, since the beginning of this rich body of research in Applied Linguistics amassed over the past 40 years, the world has become a very different place. While it remains true that English continues to be the world's lingua franca with regard to commerce, trade, and diplomacy, it is now the case that communication in the English language occurs, more often than not, among speakers none of whose first language (L1) is English (see McKay, 2002, for a good overview of this phenomenon). The issues of "native speaker," "learner," and "interlanguage" have consequently changed from how they were seen in early SLA research.

Given this proliferation of "Englishes," Firth and Wagner proposed three major changes in SLA research, including: "(a) a significantly enhanced awareness of the contextual and interactional dimensions of language use, (b) an increased *emic* (i.e. participant-relevant insider perspective) sensitivity towards fundamental concepts, and (c) the broadening of the traditional SLA data base" (Firth & Wagner, 1997: 286). The proposal caused quite a stir among applied linguists, giving rise to rebuttals by such SLA researchers as Michael Long, Gabriele Kasper, and others. In fact, the *Modern Language Journal*, one of the foremost venues publishing cutting-edge theoretical and data-driven work in the field, took the debate to print by publishing papers on both sides of the issue in 1997, following the 1996 panel presentations and debate in Jyväskylä. Because the theoretical perspectives on how to best study L2 learning remain controversial, it is worth taking up some of the principal arguments here that relate to how the study of spoken discourse can lend insight into the process of second language learning (see the *Modern Language Journal*, Vol. 81, No. 3, 1997 for a complete overview of the debate).

Regarding SLA research dating back some 20 years, to the 1980s, it is true that much of what was studied as "interactional" had, at its core, a psycholinguistic basis. Note that I use the term "basis" and not "bias," as did the strong oppositional perspective of Firth and Wagner. I take the point of view here that SLA, as a relatively young field, has grown dramatically since its early days. Most researchers in the field would not now deny that there are advantages in taking multiple perspectives on how the acquisitional process occurs. Michael Long, in his strong rebuttal of Firth and Wagner, conceded that multiple perspectives can certainly benefit the field: ". . . clearly it would be dangerous and counterproductive to succumb to a single paradigm at this early stage in the field's development" (Long, 1997: 319).

While it may be true that the groundbreaking work on studying the spoken discourse of negotiated interaction had its roots in the psycholinguistic sphere, other early work in SLA did indeed take into account more sociolinguistically relevant points of view: Labovian sociolinguistic perspectives on SLA (see, for example, the early work on variation and SLA of Tarone, 1985, 1988), accommodation theory perspectives on SLA (e.g. Beebe & Giles, 1984; Beebe & Zuengler, 1983), acculturation theory perspectives (e.g. Schumann, 1978, 1986), and classroom discourse and interaction perspectives (e.g. Kramsch, 1985; Mehan, 1979; Stubbs, 1983).

The arguments in defense of psycholinguistic perspectives on SLA research are cogently outlined in Kasper's rebuttal (1997) in which it is clear from the title of her piece that " 'A' stands for acquisition." Kasper takes up Firth and Wagner's critique of the three fundamental concepts in SLA research noted above: (1) native speaker, (2) learner, and (3) interlanguage. She argues that dropping the "A" in SLA results not in study about the developmental process of language learning but in the study of language "use" as opposed to "acquisition." Kasper states:

> If the "A" of "SLA" is dropped, we are looking at a much wider field of second language studies, which spans as diverse endeavors as intercultural and cross-cultural communication, second language pedagogy, micro- and macrosociolinguistics with reference to second languages and dialects, societal and individual multilingualism, and SLA. (Kasper, 1997: 310)

It is difficult to take issue with this perspective. Indeed, the wider arena of L2 studies incorporates research that diverges from the cognitive and psycholinguistic and ventures into the realm of studying contexts of language interaction in which, in Kasper's own words, learners ". . . construct their own identities and those of their respective others . . ." (p. 311). Kasper points out that the field of SLA has indeed seen more and more research of an ethnographic nature that clearly analyzes language learning in context and from an *emic* point of view. These studies, however, are not about the acquisitional process from a cognitive perspective but are about L2 issues that focus on identity, insider–outsider perspectives, and issues of what it means to be a language user in a world of increasing globalization.

There are many applied linguists who have argued for a broadening of perspectives on SLA to include increased social interactional and contextual points of view. These researchers and the work that they represent continue to press for a body of work in the field that takes into account what are now well-developed approaches stemming from the analysis of spoken discourse. Rampton (1997) is one important voice among this group whose arguments in the debate are both philosophical and sociopolitical. Consistent with Firth and Wagner's outlook, Rampton sees the current state of world globalization as necessitating new perspectives on what it means to be a language "learner" and "user." For him globalization presents an opportunity to take a postmodern view on issues such as communicative competence and speech community.

Indeed, language learning can no longer be seen as a purely cognitive phenomenon, as the issue of the native speaker is obfuscated in a shrinking planet (cf. Boxer, 2002b). When we speak about the acquisition of English as a second or foreign language, for example, we can no longer view it as an interlanguage with some "target" in mind. In his rebuttal of Firth and Wagner, Long also agrees with this inarguable fact when he states, "there are, however, of course, numerous multilingual settings in which most, even all, L2 users that a learner encounters will be other NNSs" (Long, 1997: 320). The issue, then, becomes, what it means to be a member of a "community of practice" (Le Page & Tabouret-Keller, 1985), rather than what it means to become or be a member of any particular "speech community." Rampton states:

> in the discourses that one can call "postmodern," there is now much more of a preoccupation with fragmentation, contingency, marginality, transition, indeterminacy, ambivalence, and hybridity. . . . In particular, it is now quite often suggested that being marginal is actually a crucial experience in late modernity . . . [and] there are now many more scholars interested in how people negotiate and reconcile themselves both to *otherness* and *incompetence*, and this has implications for research on the teaching and use of additional languages. (Rampton, 1997: 330)

Thus, Rampton calls for a view of L2 research that departs from the earlier goal of SLA as guiding learners to become competent members of a new speech community. This perspective turns more traditional approaches to SLA research on their heads: "[SLA research] has generally shown very little interest in the context-sensitive, value-relevant, interpretive methodologies that fit more comfortably with late modern assumptions" (1997: 330). Given this state of affairs and change in the air, if we construe SLA not as a question of striving toward some "target," the endeavor of L2 learning becomes transformed from the way in which it was previously seen. This new perspective is congruent with a view of the world as it presently exists: one of transnationalism and globalization. Given these arguments, the question facing applied linguists presently is: "How can we weave together a new view of talk-in-interaction research that can adequately inform L2 learning?

Theoretical Frameworks for Spoken Discourse and Language Learning

In order to adequately analyze the best means for applying findings on spoken language to SLA, we must assess the usefulness of existing theories, models, and frameworks for the processes involved in the development of spoken language ability in both first and second/additional languages. Three theoretical models offer fairly compatible insights into these processes: (1) Language Identity, (2) Language Socialization, and (3) Sociocultural Theory.

Language Identity

In the past several years there has been an increasing interest among applied linguists in the relationship between identity and second language development (e.g. Boxer & Cortes-Conde, 2000; McKay & Wong, 1996; Norton, 1997; Norton-Pierce, 1995; Pavlenko & Lantolf, 2000). These scholars have been interested in studying how incorporating an additional language and culture impacts on one's sense of who one is in the world. For immigrants, the issue of taking on a new and/or changed identity is a hallmark of one's linguistic and cultural development in the context of immigration. Even for those learning an L2 for more instrumental purposes, as the case with ESL/EFL as the world's lingua franca, adding a second language to one's verbal repertoire necessarily entails modifying one's self perception in relationship to others in the world. From this basic premise stems the relatively new heightened interest among applied linguists in Language Identity.

In their emphasis on "agency enhancement" and "identity enhancement," McKay and Wong (1996) focused on the importance of fluid and changing individual and social identities and their relation to multiple discourses (e.g. immigrant, minority, academic, gender). In this view, the identity of an individual in the process of second language learning is an extremely important consideration for such learning, affecting agency, a concept that differs from the traditional view of motivation. Agency enhancement derives from identities that afford learners a sense of power over their environment and thereby their learning.

In a somewhat parallel view, Norton (cf. Norton, 1997; Norton-Pierce, 1995) highlighted the importance of "investment enhancement" in her discussion of identity and its relation to language learning. Her 1995 piece described investment as the relationship of social identity to power differences between learners and mother tongue speakers: "An investment in the target language is also an investment in a learner's own social identity, which changes across time and space" (Norton, 1997: 411). In a similar vein, Pavlenko and Lantolf (2000) describe the process that immigrants go through when they confront and either appropriate or reject linguistic and cultural "affordances" of the new language and culture. Here, "affordances" refers to aspects of the new language and culture that have the potential to transform one's sense of self.

Boxer and Cortes-Conde (1997, 2000) put forth the concept of "relational identity" (RID), which differs from both individual and social identity. Relational identity is displayed and developed between and among specific interlocutors in their interactions over time. For language users and learners, relational identity reflects the comfort to build on sequential interactions that rest on rapport and solidarity. This relationship built between interlocutors leads naturally to further interaction and, consequently, increased opportunities for scaffolding and thus language development.

It seems likely that the first and foremost resource of those involved in additional language learning is social and interactional, involving face-to-face spoken discourse. Individuals involved in acquiring additional languages must grapple with fluid and shifting identities – individual, social, and relational – and come to terms with the power relations inherent in them. Whether or not those in the position of taking on new linguistic and cultural identities choose to appropriate or reject the "affordances" of the new language/culture may depend largely on the lived histories of the individuals, the contexts of their interactions, and the power relationships inherent in these contexts.

Language Socialization

The Language Socialization framework of studying linguistic and cultural development emanates most notably from the work of linguistic anthropologists Bambi Schieffelin and Elinor Ochs (e.g. 1986). In this early work, language is viewed as the symbolic means by which humans appropriate knowledge of norms and rules of verbal and non-verbal behavior in particular speech communities. These researchers have studied socialization from the perspective of children's L1 development in little-known speech communities (e.g. Samoa). For children, language and behavior are modeled by those more expert in the acceptable patterns and usages (e.g. parents, teachers). Much of the transmission of linguistic and cultural knowledge is thus accomplished implicitly; however, for L1 as well as L2 development, explicit metalanguage is also used in the socialization process. Studies in language socialization repeatedly offer examples of child L1 acquisition in which parents/teachers/other experts make explicit references to what ought to be said or done (e.g. "What do you say?" "Say 'thank you' " . . . "Say 'I'm sorry' "). Becoming a competent member of any speech community for children in L1 and for learners of L2 essentially entails taking on the appropriate behaviors of the community.

Language Socialization is somewhat different when we take the context of socialization as a community of practice rather than a speech community as our focus of analysis. Since communities of practice are not fixed in a society, but fluid and ever-changing, Language Socialization must been seen in this context as taking on the norms of how to fit into a group in order to achieve insider identity. Such a perspective on socialization give us a clearer picture of how identity and Language Socialization are intertwined.

The applications of a Language Socialization model to second language learning have been most notable in studies focusing on second language classrooms as communities of practice. Socialization practices of such communities are reflected in the classroom discourse and interaction of second language classes in which talented teachers take on the role of socializing agent, much in the fashion of adults vis-à-vis children for L1 acquisition (see Ohta, 2001, for an excellent example of how this is done in Japanese L2 classrooms).

Indeed, there are multiple studies of second and foreign language learning in which teachers socialize students into norms and rules of turn-taking, participation structures, and speech behavior generally. Hence, the applications of socialization theory to SLA are principally in the realm of discourse and pragmatic development (see Kasper, 2001 for an overview of this research).

Both frameworks, those of Language Identity and Language Socialization, are compatible with each other. Indeed, they are overlapping in the theoretical standpoints they take and in the methodological frameworks that lend themselves to their investigation.

Sociocultural Theory

A contingent of applied linguists spearheaded most notably by James Lantolf has been actively engaged in adopting the theoretical perspectives of Russian psychologist Lev Vygotsky to second language studies. Specifically, Vygotsky's work, published posthumously, on *Mind in Society* (1978) and *Thought and Language* (1986) is taken as the basis for viewing the acquisition of language (first and subsequent) as a sociocultural phenomenon linking the social/interactional with the cognitive. Sociocultural Theory (SCT), in contradistinction to the Language Identity and Language Socialization models described above, specifically connects the role of language as a mediating tool between social interaction and the development of higher order mental processes.

Indeed, Vygotsky's seminal work has been taken up as a call for elucidating the connection between internal, mental representations of learning and language development stemming from interactions between and among interlocutors of differing levels of expertise. Lantolf (2002) clearly explains:

> At its core, the theory proposes that mental functioning such as memory, attention, perception, planning, learning and development, come under the voluntary control of individuals as they internalize culturally constructed artifacts, including above all culturally organized forms of human communication. The theory argues that social relationships are transformed into psychological processes as taken control of by individuals as a means for mediating their own mental activity. (p. 1)

Vygotsky's notion of "Zone of Proximal Development" (ZPD) is useful in envisioning just how the expert/novice paradigm of sociocultural interaction leads to new mental representations in learners:

> Children learning to master their own psychological behavior proceed from dependency on other people to independence and self-regulation as a consequence of gaining control over culturally fabricated semiotic tools. (Lantolf & Appel, 1994: 6)

Those who espouse Sociocultural Theory as a lens through which we can view more clearly both tutored and untutored second language development call for a careful analysis of the social setting of such development. Joan Kelly Hall cogently explains the connection drawn by Vygotsky between psycholinguistic and sociolinguistic spheres of interaction:

> Individual development begins in the social relationships both framing and framed by extended participation in our communicative practices and proceeds from these to the psychological, i.e. from intermental to intramental activity. (Vygotsky, 1981 as cited in Hall, 1997: 302)

Hall explains that the concept of "scaffolding" here is one in which the interlocutor possessing expertise guides the novice through a series of interactions in which the expert gradually cedes and the novice takes on increasing responsibility. This scaffolding occurs through the various configurations of social interaction between the two, including modeling and training by the expert and observing and imitating by the novice. Gradually, then, the novice becomes more adept, and that which began as an inter-mental, socially mediated activity becomes an intra-mental, cognitive developmental process. As such, Sociocultural Theory is one way of viewing any learning process, and specifically for our purposes, the language learning process, as one which connects sociolinguistic with psycholinguistic contexts and outcomes. Thus, in contrast to a more traditional SLA view of the learner as a "deficient version of an idealized monolingual expert in linguistics" (Hall, 1997: 303), a sociocultural theoretical view of SLA treats the learner as "an active and creative participant in what is considered a sociocognitively complex task" (1997: 303).

The three frameworks described above, Language Identity, Language Socialization, and Sociocultural Theory, are not methodological approaches to the study of second language development. They are frameworks or theoretical perspectives on how such development takes place and on what counts as important foci in the study of the development of additional languages. It seems clear that any analysis of speech activity in communities of practice and of interactions within the ZPD lend themselves to close, contextualized, *emic* analyses of communicative practices.

> In sociocultural and language socialization theory alike, the acquisition of language and culture and the development of cognition critically depend on social interaction in concrete sociohistorical contexts. (Kasper, 2001: 523)

In order for the reader to have a clearer picture of how the chapters in this volume reflect the three frameworks discussed above, I offer the following chart. Please note that many of the studies included herein touch upon all three frameworks, while some highlight one more than the others. Since language assessment of any sort involves emerging L2 identities and socialization, the three chapters in the section on assessment of oral language reflect an interest in these two frameworks. Moreover, assessment studies necessarily omit reference to SCT, as assessment and evaluation contexts preclude experts guiding novices to greater development. The chapters are listed in the order they appear in the volume:

	Language Identity	Language Socialization	Sociocultural Theory
Douglas			X
Lazaraton	X		
Hall	X	X	X
Hamilton	X	X	X
Halmari	X	X	X
Taylor-Hamilton	X		
Konishi and Tarone		X	X
Bardovi-Harlig and Salsbury		X	X
Beebe and Waring		X	
Brown	X	X	
Roever	X	X	
Cohen	X	X	

Let us turn now to an overview of methodological possibilities for studying speaking and its relationship to second language learning.

Methodological Perspectives

Spontaneous spoken data approaches

There is a growing body of literature on Native Speakers (NS) discourse and language learner discourse deriving from various contextually rich methodological approaches to perspectives on language use. Some of these methods of data collection and analysis have lent important insights into language *use* for decades. Their applications to language *learning* contexts, however, are more recent. The studies included in this volume are examples of the recent call for more highly contextualized studies on second language development. For the purposes of this volume we eschew the term "qualitative" in describing methodologies of data collection and analysis. The term, as differentiated from "quantitative," suggests that studies which count items or tokens, or that test for statistical significance, necessarily omit qualitative insights. We know this not to be true. Nowadays it is increasingly problematic to "pigeon-hole" methodologies as we have in the past, as applied linguistics research is increasingly a confluence of approaches. Therefore, we attempt here to refrain from simplistic divisions. What we do offer here, however, are a dozen contextually rich analyses of talk-in-interaction that reveal important information about language learning. Let us turn to a brief overview of three of these approaches – the ethnography of speaking, conversation analysis, and interactional sociolinguistics.

The ethnography of speaking

The ethnography of speaking (ES), first proposed by Hymes (1962), has offered unique perspectives on how members of speech communities go about their day-to-day interactions in all of the domains of life. ES is the uniting of the classic anthropological approach to research, ethnography, with linguistic analysis; thus, ES is an important way of studying language as it is used in a variety of contexts. Ethnographic research is holistic and *emic*, as it takes into account a variety of contexts as well as insider knowledge. The meaning of speech for particular speakers in specific social activities is a central concern for ES; thus, it is particularly suitable for the study of spoken language and its application to second language learning. Indeed, ethnographers know that some of the socio-cultural knowledge affecting speech behavior in particular contexts is below the level of consciousness of community members. This is precisely the argument for taking such a research perspective in the study of norms of interaction and their relationship to language learning contexts. Given that our intuitions about how we actually use language are inherently unreliable, we must first study spoken language *in situ* before we can write curriculum and materials from which we teach languages, particularly regarding discourse and pragmatic norms of interaction.

One of the primary goals of ES is to look at the functions that particular speech behaviors have in a speech community and the way in which community members use various types of speech to fulfill these functions. ES is concerned with community members' perceptions and representations of their own culture; therefore, it must be able to describe everyday, ordinary functions of language. For this very reason it is a potentially very powerful methodological approach to language learning data. While its insights are often limited in generalizability, an ES approach offers applied linguists deep insights into what counts as "acceptable" for any mother tongue speaker of a language, and thus in turn what is acceptable for any novice language user.

Conversation analysis

Conversation analysis, as a distinct methodological approach to the collection and analysis of discourse data, offers much to the applied linguist in terms of teaching spoken language to the L2 learner (cf. Lazaraton, 2002; Markee, 2000). With its emphasis on managing the sequential organization of talk, CA perspectives have given applied linguistics important insights into many aspects of talk-in-interaction. It has concentrated on several phenomena critical to the explanation of the work that everyday interaction entails: turn-taking systems, inter-ruptions and repair, adjacency, conversational openings and closings, and topic organization, to name but a few of the foci of existing CA studies. CA approaches take the point of view that analyses of talk must grow out of examinations of transcriptions that include small details (e.g. fillers, gaps) that might be relevant to the unfolding interaction. Like ES, CA attempts to take an "unmotivated looking" (Lazaraton, Chapter 3, this volume) without preconceived hypotheses. For both CA and ES, research questions are not taken a priori but rather emerge from the data. The goal is to study talk in interaction in order to learn something about social practices as they take place. Thus, CA tends to analyze single cases or "deviant cases" of some interactional phenomenon, building evidence through the compilation of such cases (Lazaraton, Chapter 3 this volume).

ES and CA diverge specifically in their distinct notions of context. While for ES the sociolinguistic variables of gender, social distance, status and power, age, and class are taken as indexical to the analysis, for CA what is in the transcription of the interaction is what counts as important. Likewise, the participant perspective is not considered useful, as it is in interactional sociolinguistics (described below). Thus, while both CA and ES are important contextualized thrusts in discourse research, they differ in what is construed as relevant contributing factors to the realization of speech behavior. Notwithstanding this distinction, both CA and ES researchers are hesitant to claim universality for their findings. While the key ES concept of "speech event" and the constituent factors that characterize speech events are regarded as universal, cultural traditions differ in how they are defined and how they function. Likewise, for CA researchers the categories of adjacency, repair, and turns, for example, are universal; however, the way in which these phenomena are realized varies from conversation to conversation, and thus constitutes an impor-tant focus of analysis. These two research traditions share an interest in analyzing stretches of talk (some long and some short) that are recorded and serve as retrievable data capable of close and careful analysis.

Lazaraton's chapter in this volume offers an overview of Conversation Analysis. I direct you to that chapter for a closer consideration of the potential value of contributions of CA-oriented research to second language studies.

Interactional Sociolinguistics (Micro-ethnography)

Work in the tradition of Interactional Sociolinguistics (IS) (e.g. Chick, 1985; Gumperz, 1982) takes as its focus developmental bilingualism and cross-cultural miscommunication between and among different linguistic/ethnic groups. IS unites some of the tenets of ES and CA, but typically employs triangulation techniques in order to tap into the participants' own perspectives on the interaction under analysis. This sort of *emic* consideration can lend critical insights into miscommunication and misperceptions between interlocutors of different cultural and linguistic backgrounds. With retrievable audiotaped or videotaped data and triangulation, participants in the interaction are able to reflect on the interaction as it naturally occurred to lend insights into what they meant by what they said, what they were trying to achieve, and how they felt about their own language use and that of the other participant(s) in the moment-to-moment unfolding of the exchange. As such, IS offers rich analyses of talk in interaction that have important potential implications for the application of the study of spoken language to SLA contexts.

ES, CA, and IS are highly contextualized methodologies for studying language use. Moreover, their usefulness for studying second language development has long been overlooked. Many of the chapters in the present volume are excellent examples of these approaches to second language studies (e.g. Lazaraton and Brown for CA approaches; Hamilton, Hall, Taylor-Hamilton, and Halmari for ES and IS approaches).

Elicited data

Discourse Completion Tasks

Elicited data is quite distinct from the sort of spontaneous data used in ES, CA, and IS. One of the most widely employed elicitation techniques for researching speech behavior, particularly speech act[2] realization, has been the Discourse Completion Task (DCT) (see, for example, Kasper & Dahl, 1991; Kasper & Rose, 1999). The DCT is a specific type of questionnaire whose typical use is in response to the following challenges: (1) rarely occurring speech acts/events and possible responses (e.g. rude remarks, see Beebe & Waring, this volume); (2) Speech acts that readily occur but which are difficult to capture as recorded data (e.g. work on requests as in the CCSARP project carried out by Blum-Kulka *et al.*, 1989); and (3) Speech acts that may not readily occur in two languages (e.g. work on apologies by such scholars as Andrew D. Cohen & Elite Olshtain, 1981). DCTs can be open-ended in that they set up a situation and then leave a blank for the speech act to be supplied; or they can be of a second type that provides a situation, gives a first turn, a blank space for a turn from the subject, and then a second and even a third turn for the fictional interlocutor. DCTs manipulate the sociolinguistic variables (e.g. status, age, distance, gender) in order to ascertain the subject's reaction to them. Current efforts have been made to construct DCTs that offer multiple turns in order to make them more interactive in nature (e.g. Cohen & Shively, 2002).

Much discussion has taken place over the years about other advantages and disadvantages of this type of instrument (see, for example, Beebe & Cummings, 1996). A criticism of the DCT is that it is an instrument that makes *a priori* decisions about the sociolinguistic variables that are deemed to be the most important in constraining speech in a given situation. Nonetheless, good studies employing DCTs use them to ascertain the canonical patterning of speech acts. Thus, numerous researchers have collected focused and valuable information on speech acts through the use of DCT instruments (e.g. Cohen & Olshtain, 1981, on apologies; Beebe *et al.*, 1985, on refusals). Many studies employing DCTs use such instruments to find out more about a speech behavior after first studying the speech via a more spontaneous method of data collection. For example, Beebe's prior work on rudeness (1995) stemming from more ethnographically collected examples of rude remarks and responses to such remarks, was the starting point for the study contained herein on novice L2 users' responses to rudeness. Hence, DCT instruments have a place in applying findings on spoken interaction to language learning contexts.

Interviews and role-plays

Interviews and role-plays can be used effectively for studying speaking to inform second language learning. Several of the studies reported here employed face-to-face interviews or role-plays in their data collection (e.g. Bardovi-Harlig & Salsbury, Konishi & Tarone, Taylor-Hamilton). In certain contexts such data are similar to spontaneous spoken data, with the caveat that the researcher is able to set up a context for studying speaking. Many types of role-play tasks and interviews are useful for research that has the potential to inform second language learning. The sociolinguistic interview is akin to ordinary social conversation; however, unlike everyday talk, the researcher directs the conversation through a series of questions designed to elicit talk, or narratives, on specific topics (see Schiffrin, 1994). Somewhat different is the ethnographic interview, in which the researcher sets up a topic for discussion with a consultant/ informant who gives the researcher an *emic* perspective on a particular speech behavior through providing what an insider knows about that behavior. In the ethnographic interview the researcher does not have a fixed agenda of questions; questions emerge from the narratives of the informants. Thus, it is important to build a rapport with individuals who play this role in the interview process, for the goal is to make the interviewee feel comfortable being the "expert" and conveying this expert knowledge to the researcher (for more complete reading on this type of interview, see Boxer, 1996; Spradley, 1979).

Interviews, role-play tasks, and discourse completion tasks have been and continue to be important methodological approaches to collecting discourse data that has the potential to inform second language learning, pedagogy, and assessment. We give primary importance to research methodology in this volume since the quality of research on speaking as it relates to second language learning is in large part determined by the quality of the research methods used to collect the speaking data.

Applying Baseline Information to Language Learning

While there is now a considerable body of rich, highly contextualized research on how speakers carry out their daily communicative practices, few scholars have applied what we know about norms of spoken discourse in communities around the world as a *baseline* to SLA. The little that has been applied to language learning contexts has been by and large applied to the English language and to ESL/EFL contexts. Nessa Wolfson (1986, 1989), an early protégée of Dell Hymes regarding application of his theories of communicative competence to educational linguistics (1972), was one of the first to propose that, before we can study what language "learners" do in spoken L2, we need to know, from empirical evidence, how languages are actually used in face-to-face interaction by members of communities. While much of this knowledge is intuitive, we have no way of really knowing what we do in conversation as community members until we systematically study these speaking practices (cf. Boxer & Pickering, 1995).

Recall in the discussion above that the world has begun to be transformed into one in which language users, employing languages from their linguistic repertoires other than their L1s, quite frequently interact in these languages with other speakers who are also *not* mother tongue users of those languages. Firth and Wagner made this case strongly, and Rampton eloquently elaborated on it. No one would deny the truth of the present state of affairs in linguistic usage, especially that of English as a lingua franca around the world. Here we move beyond the social domain and enter domains of language use that are transactional as well as inter-actional. Thus, the issue of comprehensibility in such cross-cultural interactions is more critical now than at any other time in history. Even if we eschew the concepts of "native-speaker," "learner," and "interlan-guage," we are still left with the nagging question of whose burden it is to make a message comprehensible in any linguistic interaction (see Boxer, 2002b for a more complete discussion of this issue). Having said this, it is important to take into account norms and rules of any commu-nity of practice in order to be able to guide and train novice language users into increased expertise.

Once we have knowledge of what members of discourse communities successfully do in spontaneous spoken discourse, we can then apply these findings to situations in which novice language users are acquiring and employing an L2 in any domain and in variously configured communities and interactions. Such varied contexts include: bilingual language prac-tices such as code alternation and switching; sensitivity to the constraints of the sociolinguistic variables (e.g. gender, social distance, social status) in the L2; sensitivity to domains of usage (e.g. workplace, education, social interaction); and understanding how to carry out transactional and inter-actional discourse (cf. Brown & Yule, 1983), to take some examples.

Thus, highly contextualized, *emic* approaches to applied linguistics research are increasingly critical in current analyses of spoken discourse, now not necessarily only within native speech communities, but in multi-lingual contexts of interaction as well. Critical Discourse Analysis is an important thrust in such analyses, since issues of power and dominance necessarily come into play.[3] Yet we are still left with nagging questions of how best to view language acquisition as well as use, and ethnographic, conversational analytic, and interactional sociolinguistic perspectives have only recently begun to lend insights into these questions.

It will become clear, in reading the following chapters, how method-ological considerations play an important role in the types of data that researchers are able to collect, and thus the kinds of analyses that each procedure enables. The following chart gives an overview of data approaches referred to or used by contributors to the present volume. Douglas's chapter is theory-driven rather than data-driven; therefore, it does not appear in the following categorization. Note that some studies, using a combination of methodologies, are placed in more than one category:

ES	CA	IS	DCTs	Interviews/ Role-Plays
Hall	Lazaraton	Halmari	Roever	Konishi and Tarone
Hamilton	Brown	Hall	Beebe and Waring	Bardovi-Harlig and Salsbury
Taylor-Hamilton			Cohen	Taylor-Hamilton

Organization of this Volume

The intention of this collection of articles is to pull together cutting-edge research that offers perspectives on the study of spoken language that in turn inform second language studies. Taken as a whole, the chapters included herein offer a renewed understanding of the connection between oral interaction in various contexts – classroom, immersion, interviews, role-plays, spontaneous conversation – and the development and assessment of language proficiency. Thus, our intention is to connect the sociolinguistic with the psycholinguistic, the interactional with the cognitive. The indirect benefit is to lead applied linguists to insights for the development of curriculum and materials, pedagogical techniques, and evaluation instruments.

Consistent with the aim of having this volume focus on methodological issues, the book's sections are organized around research methodologies. The studies described here take a variety of approaches to analyzing discourse – from ethnographic, conversational analytic, and interactional sociolinguistic, to more controlled methods such as discourse completion tasks and task-inspired role-play interviews. Detailed explications of how the data for the studies were collected and analyzed offer critical insights into their application to the field of SLA. This focus on research tools will assist readers in evaluating the applicability of the findings to their own areas of interest. The contributing authors of this volume discuss in detail the procedures they employed in collecting and analyzing their data. As such, the volume offers an interweaving of perspectives.

Following this introductory chapter, this book proceeds with a theoretical contribution by Dan Douglas focusing on the notion of "discourse domains" and how they fit into the cognitive context of speaking. Douglas builds on his earlier work on defining the relationship between context of interaction and internal, cognitive representations. His chapter delineates how language novices appropriate the ability to participate in the various discourse domains through building a schemata for such participation.

The volume continues with chapters divided into three additional parts: (II) studies on the development of additional languages based on the collection of spontaneous spoken data (Lazaraton, Hall, Hamilton, Halmari); (III) studies based on elicited data such as interviews, role-plays, and discourse completion tasks (DCTs) (Bardovi-Harlig & Salsbury, Beebe & Waring, Konishi & Tarone, Taylor-Hamilton); and (IV) studies focusing on the assessment of spoken discourse in language learning that incorporate various methods in their data collection and analysis (Brown, Roever, Cohen).

The goal of this book, from its inception to its publication, has been to put together an up-to-date, systematic overview of the current state of research at the crossroads of Discourse Analysis and second language studies.

Notes

1. Throughout this volume we use the term "learning" synonymously with "acquisition" to denote both tutored and untutored second and foreign language development.
2. *Speech acts* are patterned, routinized utterances that speakers use regularly to perform a variety of functions such as apologizing, complaining, requesting, refusing, and complimenting. A speech act is an utterance with a basic or propositional meaning (e.g. "I am hot" = the speaker is feeling hot) and an intended effect or illocutionary meaning (e.g. "I am hot" = the speaker is requesting that someone open the window).
3. For a thorough overview of Critical Discourse Analysis, see Fairclough, 1989, 1992, 1995.

References

Beebe, L. (1995) Polite fictions: Instrumental rudeness as pragmatic competence. In J. Alatis, C. Strahle, B. Gallenberger, and M. Ronkin (eds) *Georgetown Roundtable on Languages and Linguistics* (pp. 154–168). Baltimore, MD: Georgetown University Press.

Beebe, L. and Cummings, M. (1996) Natural speech act data versus written questionnaire data: How data collection method affects speech act performance. In S. Gass and J. Neu (eds) *Speech Acts Across Cultures* (pp. 65–86). Berlin: Mouton.

Beebe, L. and Giles, H. (1984) Speech accommodation theories: A discussion in terms of second language acquisition. *International Journal of the Sociology of Language* 46, 5–32.

Beebe, L. and Zuengler, J. (1983) Accommodation theory: An explanation for style-shifting in second language dialects. In N. Wolfson and E. Judd (eds) *Sociolinguistics and Second Language Acquisition* (pp. 195–213). Rowley, MA: Newbury House.

Beebe, L., Takahashi, T., and Uliss-Weltz, R. (1985) Pragmatic transfer in ESL refusals. In R. Scarcella, E. Andersen, and S. Krashen (eds) *On the Development of Communicative Competence* (pp. 55–73). Rowley, MA: Newbury.

Blum-Kulka, S., House-Edmonson, J., and Kasper, G. (eds) (1989) *Cross-cultural Pragmatics: Requests and Apologies*. Norwood, NJ: Ablex.

Boxer, D. (1996) Ethnographic interviewing as a research tool in speech act analysis: The case of complaints. In S. Gass and J. Neu (eds) *Speech Acts Across Cultures* (pp. 217–239). Berlin: Mouton.

Boxer, D. (2002a) *Applying Sociolinguistics: Domains and Face-to-face Interaction*. Amsterdam: John Benjamins.

Boxer, D. (2002b) Discourse issues in cross-cultural pragmatics. *Annual Review of Applied Linguistics* 22, 150–167.

Boxer, D. and Cortes-Conde, F. (1997) From bonding to biting: Conversational joking and identity display. *Journal of Pragmatics* 27, 275–294.

Boxer, D. and Cortes-Conde, F. (2000) Identity and ideology: Culture and pragmatics in content-based ESL. In J. K. Hall and L. Verplaste (eds) *Second and Foreign Language Learning Through Classroom Interaction* (pp. 203–219). Mahwah, NJ: Lawrence Erlbaum.

Boxer, D. and Pickering, L. (1995) Problems in the presentation of speech acts in ELT texts. *ELT Journal* 49 (1), 44–58.

Brown, G. and Yule, G. (1983) *Discourse Analysis*. Cambridge: Cambridge University Press.

Chick, K. (1985) The interactional accomplishment of discrimination in South Africa. *Language in Society* 14 (3), 299–326.

Cohen, A. D. and Olshtain, E. (1981) Developing a measure of sociolinguistic competence: The case of apology. *Language Learning* 31 (1), 113–134.

Cohen, A. D. and Shively, R. L. (2002) *Pre-departure and Post-study Abroad Speech Act Measures (Peninsular Spanish, South American Spanish, and French Versions): Maximizing Study Abroad Through Language and Culture Strategies*. Minneapolis, MN: Center for Advanced Research in Language Acquisition, University of Minnesota.

Fairclough, N. (1989) *Language and Power*. London and New York: Longman.

Fairclough, N. (1992) *Discourse and Social Change*. Cambridge: Polity Press.

Fairclough, N. (1995) *Critical Discourse Analysis: The Critical Study of Language*. London and New York: Longman.

Firth, A. and Wagner, J. (1997) On discourse, communication, and (some) fundamental concepts in SLA research. *Modern Language Journal* 81 (3), 285–300.

Gass, S. and Varonis, E. (1985) Variation in native speaker speech modification to non-native speakers. *Studies in Second Language Acquisition* 7 (1), 37–57.

Gumperz, J. (1982) *Language and Social Identity*. Cambridge: Cambridge University Press.

Hall, J. K. (1997) In response to Firth and Wagner: A consideration of SLA as a theory of practice. *Modern Language Journal* 81 (3), 301–306.

Hatch, E. (ed.) (1978) *Second Language Acquisition*. Rowley, MA: Newbury House.

Hymes, D. (1962) *The Ethnography of Speaking*. In T. Gladwin and W. C. Sturdevant (eds) *Anthropology and Human Behavior* (pp. 15–53). Washington, DC: Anthropological Society of Washington.

Hymes, D. (1972) On communicative competence. In J. J. Gumperz and D. Hymes (eds) *Directions in Sociolinguistics: The Ethnography of Communication* (pp. 35–71). New York: Holt, Reinhart and Winston.

Kasper, G. (1997) "A" stands for acquisition: A response to Firth and Wagner. *Modern Language Journal* 81 (3), 307–312.

Kasper, G. (2001) Four perspectives on L2 pragmatic development. *Applied Linguistics* 22 (4), 502–530.

Kasper, G. and Dahl, M. (1991) Research methods in interlanguage pragmatics. *Studies in Second Language Acquisition* 13 (2), 215–247.

Kasper, G. and Rose, K. (1999) Pragmatics and SLA. *Annual Review of Applied Linguistics* 19, 81–104.

Kramsch, C. (1985) Classroom interaction and discourse options. *Studies in Second Language Acquisition* 7 (2), 169–183.

Lantolf, J. (2002) Sociocultural and second language learning research: An exegesis. Paper presented at the Ninth Annual Sociocultural Theory Workshop, Tallahassee, Florida, November.

Lantolf, J. and Appel, G. (eds) (1994) *Vygotskyan Approaches to Second Language Research*. Norwood, NJ: Ablex.

Lazaraton, A. (2002) *A Qualitative Approach to the Validation of Oral Language Tests*. Cambridge: Cambridge University Press.

Le Page, R. B. and Tabouret-Keller, A. (1985) *Acts of Identity*. Cambridge: Cambridge University Press.

Long, M. (1983) Native speaker/non-native speaker conversation and the negotiation of comprehensible input. *Applied Linguistics* 4 (2), 126–141.

Long, M. (1997) Construct validity in SLA research: A response to Firth and Wagner. *Modern Language Journal* 81 (3), 318–323.

McKay, S. (2002) *Teaching English as an International Language: Rethinking Goals and Approaches*. Oxford: Oxford University Press.

McKay, S. and Wong, S. (1996) Multiple discourses, multiple identities: Investment and agency in second language learning among Chinese adolescent immigrant students. *Harvard Educational Review* 66 (3), 577–608.

Markee, N. (2000) *Conversation Analysis*. Mahwah, NJ: Lawrence Erlbaum.

Mehan, H. (1979) *Learning Lessons: Social Organization in the Classroom*. Cambridge, MA: Harvard University Press.

Norton, B. (1997) Language, identity, and the ownership of English. *TESOL Quarterly* 31 (3), 409–429.

Norton Peirce, B. (1995) Social identity, investment, and language learning. *TESOL Quarterly* 29 (1), 9–31.

Ohta, A. (2001) *Second Language Processes in the Classroom: Learning Japanese*. Mahwah, NJ: Lawrence Erlbaum.

Pavlenko, A. and Lantolf, J. (2000) Second language learning as participation and the (re)construction of selves. In J. Lantolf (ed.) *Sociocultural Theory and Second Language Learning* (pp. 155–177). New York: Oxford University Press.

Pica, T. (1988) Interlanguage adjustments as an outcome of NS-NNS negotiated interaction. *Language Learning* 38 (1), 45–73.

Rampton, B. (1997) Second language research in late modernity: A response to Firth and Wagner. *Modern Language Journal* 81 (3), 329–333.

Schieffelin, B. and Ochs, E. (1986) Language socialization. *Annual Review of Anthropology* 15, 163–191.

Schiffrin, D. (1994) *Approaches to Discourse*. Cambridge, MA: Blackwell.

Schumann, J. (1978) The acculturation model for second language acquisition. In R. Gingras (ed.) *Second Language Acquisition and Foreign Language Teaching* (pp. 27–107). Arlington, VA: Center for Applied Linguistics.

Schumann, J. (1986) Research on the acculturation model for second language acquisition. *Journal of Multilingual and Multicultural Development* 7, 379–392.

Spradley, J. (1979) *The Ethnographic Interview*. New York: Holt, Reinhart and Winston.

Stubbs, M. (1983) *Discourse Analysis: The Sociolinguistic Analysis of Natural Language*. Chicago: University of Chicago Press.

Swain, M. (1985) Communicative competence: Some roles of comprehensible input and comprehensible output in its development. In S. Gass and C. Madden (eds) *Input in Second Language Acquisition* (pp. 235–257). Rowley, MA: Newbury House.

Tarone, E. (1985) Variability in interlanguage use: A study of style-shifting in morphology and syntax. *Language Learning* 35 (3), 373–403.

Tarone, E. (1988) *Variation in Interlanguage*. London: Edward Arnold.

Vygotsky, L. S. (1978) *Mind in Society: The Development of Higher Psychological Processes*. Cambridge, MA: Harvard University Press.

Vygotsky, L. S. (1981) The genesis of higher mental functions. In J. Wertsch (ed.) *The Concept of Activity in Social Psychology* (pp. 144–188). Armonk, NY: M. E. Sharpe.

Vygotsky, L. S. (1986) *Thought and Language*. Cambridge, MA: MIT Press.

Wolfson, N. (1986) Research methodology and the question of validity. *TESOL Quarterly* 20 (4), 689–699.

Wolfson, N. (1989) *Perspectives: Sociolinguistics and TESOL*. Boston, MA: Heinle and Heinle.

Chapter 2

Discourse Domains: The Cognitive Context of Speaking

DAN DOUGLAS

In discussing the context of communicative language use, I have argued for a view of context as a psychological construct, influenced by physical and linguistic contextualization cues (Douglas, 2000). In this view, what really counts in the communicative performance of a language user is not the external context per se but how the speaker interprets the contextualization cues present in the communicative event. Thus, we are compelled toward an internal view of context as a construct created by language users for the interpretation and production of language. Douglas and Selinker (1985a, 1985b) use the term discourse domain to refer to the internal interpretation of context, and define the concept as a cognitive construct created by a language learner as a context for interlanguage development and use. In this chapter I elaborate the notion of discourse domains, attempting to update and specify the definition more concretely, to review current research, and to suggest research yet needed to more fully understand the influence of context on speaking in second language learning and use.

Introduction

> *. . . people construct the world in which they learn languages.*
> Undergraduate student, Iowa State University,
> March 2002

Few, I think, would deny that context influences the way we use language, that we adapt our speaking style to the setting, participants, purpose, topic, and content of the communicative event we are engaged in. At the same time, however, the influence of context on language *learning* is a different and more contentious matter altogether. There are serious questions about whether context affects the acquisition process and/or the resulting interlanguage grammar at all (Tarone, 2000).

Selinker and Douglas proposed the term "discourse domains" to help us talk about how context influences both second language acquisition and use. The paper most often associated with the origin of the term, Selinker and Douglas (1985), focused on acquisition, defining discourse domains as "internally-created contexts, within which . . . IL structures are created differentially" (p. 190).

The second of our two 1985 papers (Douglas & Selinker, 1985) focused on language use in a restricted context, that of language testing: "each test taker creates for him- or herself an internal context within which he [*sic*] renders the text intelligible" (p. 206). In that paper, we defined the concept of discourse domain more elaborately:

> A discourse domain is a personally, and internally created "slice" of one's life that has importance and over which the learner exercises content-control. Importance is empirically shown by the fact that in interaction one repeatedly talks (or writes) about the area in question. Discourse domains are primarily dynamic and changing, and may become permanent parts of a learner's cognitive system. Some domains may be created temporarily for particular important purposes. The concept also has a discontinuous aspect to it in that a domain can be taken up, dropped, left dormant and revived. Such domains are usually thus not fixed for life but may change with one's life experience – and often do. (Douglas & Selinker, 1985: 206)

Thus, in our earliest thinking about discourse domains, we viewed them as possessing a number of characteristics. The following features were intended to characterize discourse domains:

- they are personal;
- they are internal to the language learner;
- they are related to important aspects of life as demonstrated by the learner communicating about the aspects repeatedly;
- they are related to specific content over which the learner exercises some measure of control;
- they are dynamic and changing but may become permanent;
- they may be created temporarily for certain specific purposes;
- they may be discontinuous – dropped, left dormant for a period, and then revived;
- the temporary domains may change as life circumstances change.

In the years since 1985, we and others have attempted to refine the concept of discourse domains and specify it more concretely, but have not really succeeded, as Long (2003) points out, using such adjectives as "vague" and "nebulous." He is right, for we are attempting to deal with context, a notoriously difficult concept to get a handle on, as well as the equally imprecise concept of cognitive constructs, and if we have been vague and somewhat nebulous, it is because we have been struggling to conceptualize a very thorny issue; I hope in this chapter to clarify the notion of discourse domain and show how it is important to our understanding of speaking in a second language.

I would like to review some terminology surrounding the concept of discourse domains before turning to the development of the concept of discourse domain and its bearing on our understanding of speaking in second language learning, on the way attempting a better understanding of discourse domains, and I will provide some suggestions later in this chapter for how the concept of discourse domains can be applied in the classroom. Finally, I will discuss some possible research directions for the future.

Terminology

The terms *domain* and *discourse domain* are used in fields allied to second language acquisition. Fishman (1972) discusses the concept of *sociolinguistic domain*: ". . . societal constructs derived from painstaking analysis and summarization of patently congruent situations . . . all of which are commonly associated with a particular variety or language" (p. 248). Fishman lists such domains as school, church, professional worksphere, and government as affecting language choice and topic (see Boxer, 2002, for an application of the concept of sociolinguistic domains to the study of face-to-face spoken interaction). In the field of computational linguistics, the term discourse domains is used to mean semantic categories of language (http://www.ima.umn.edu/multimedia/fall/m1.html). While both the above usages are related to the meaning intended by Selinker and Douglas, we have a more specific meaning in mind: a discourse domain is a cognitive construct created in response to a number of factors, including semantic category, but also to other features of situational and linguistic context. For example, when we enter a room where a conversation is going on, we of course pay attention to the topic of the talk, but we also take note of a number of other features of the situation, including the physical setting, who the participants are, what the purpose of their conversation appears to be, whether the conversation seems to be businesslike, friendly, or angry, what features of language the participants are using, and what relationship they appear to have with each other. Depending upon our analysis of the situation in terms such as these, we might feel that this is a situation we are familiar with and would feel comfortable joining; in other words, as Douglas and Selinker would say, we possess a discourse domain for dealing with this communicative situation.

For us, the term discourse domain refers to an interaction between a language learner/user and the situational context in which communication takes place. Zuengler (1989) reminds us of the interactional nature of the concept: "Discourse domain can provide an explanation for a nonnative's extent of participation in an interaction, but only if it is viewed as not strictly a *cognitive* construct. It must also be viewed as an *interactionally-negotiated* one" (p. 242; emphasis in original). I agree but would argue that, ultimately, even an interactionally negotiated construct is a cognitive one: what counts is the language learner/user's interpretation of the context, including its interactional characteristics. I return to this point later in this chapter.

I have made the link between discourse domains and situational and linguistic context most explicit in the context of specific purpose language testing:

> ... providing clear, appropriate, and sufficient contextualization cues to help ensure the engagement of the intended discourse domain is of paramount importance in specific purpose language testing. (Douglas, 2000: 46)

As the above quote suggests, discourse domains are developed or engaged in response to signals in the situational and linguistic environment which interlocutors attend to in interpreting (indeed, creating) context:

- *physical*: setting, participants;
- *phonological*: voice tone, pitch, tempo, rhythm, volume;
- *semantic*: code, topic;
- *rhetorical*: register, style, genre;
- *pragmatic*: purpose, interactional salience;
- *paralinguistic*: posture, gesture, gaze, facial expression. (Based on Hymes, 1974; Gumperz, 1976; Douglas & Selinker, 1985a)

The above list is not intended to be exhaustive and there are no doubt other types of contextualization cues, but it does give the reader a sense of the types of information available to language learners/users in communicative situations.

I have also argued that discourse domains are developed within the strategic component of communicative language ability, in which language learners (indeed, all language users) assess a communicative situation, engage an appropriate discourse domain, plan a communicative response to the situation, and then execute the response (Douglas, 2000). In this sense, the term is more closely related, perhaps, to a number of other terms used in applied linguistics, including *genre*, *text type*, and *register* (see Lee, 2001, for a fuller discussion of these terms).

Perhaps the closest conceptualization to discourse domains is that of *schema theory*, in which a schema (plural, *schemata*) is a hypothetical mental structure for representing generic concepts stored in memory – a sort of framework, plan, or script. Schemata are abstract and generic, associated with varying degrees of control over content, individual importance, and interactional involvement. As we will see below, discourse domains are also characterized by varying degrees of control, importance, and involvement.

In my own thinking about discourse domains, I have been heavily influenced by Widdowson's *Learning Purpose and Language Use* (1983) in which he discussed schema theory in a most practical way. Widdowson (1983) defined schemata as ". . . cognitive constructs or configurations of knowledge which we place over events so as to bring them into alignment with familiar patterns of experience and belief " (p. 54), noting that they are "derived from instances of past experience" (p. 37). It is easy to see the connection between this view of schema and the Selinker and Douglas view of discourse domain as a cognitive construct within which interlanguages are acquired. Widdowson went on to illuminate the relationship between language knowledge and schemata, arguing that ". . . the language itself does not convey information: what it does is to provide a set of directions for which a schemata [*sic*] in the user's mind is to be engaged" (pp. 35–36). This notion is now a familiar one in Widdowson's work (see Widdowson, 2001).

Widdowson's use of schemata appears, however, to give linguistic context a primary place in communication. I would argue that language is but one part, albeit an important one, of what leads to the engagement of discourse domains: situational context is the other. Widdowson does point out that ". . . schemata do not tell us the whole story of language use. . . . Interpretative procedures are needed to exploit schematic knowledge and bring it to bear on particular instances of use" (p. 40). The purpose of these procedures is the alignment and adjustment of interlocutors' schemata so that they are close enough to each other for each interlocutor to be satisfied that understanding has been achieved. Sometimes, when interlocutors share cultural norms, very little procedural work may be called for; at other times, when, for example, the interlocutors are from quite different cultural backgrounds, a great deal of procedural work may be needed. Again, I see this as important background to my own thinking about discourse domains in the context of second language acquisition, and much of the reconceptualization of the notion that follows is owed to Widdowson's insights. First, however, I will discuss a bit more background of the development of the discourse domains hypothesis.

Before leaving the topic of terminology, note that I have sometimes referred to *language learners* in the context of discourse domain and sometimes to *language users*. While this chapter is primarily concerned with speaking in the context of second language learning, it should be clear that the notion of discourse domains may be applied to all language use. I use the term "language learner/user" to capture this idea.

Background

Previous work on discourse domains

Douglas and Selinker (1985a) initially proposed that criteria for recognizing discourse domains include importance to the learner, interactional salience, and control of content, and in our early research (Selinker & Douglas, 1986, 1987a, 1987b, 1988a, 1988b; Douglas & Selinker, 1985b, 1986, 1988, 1989, 1992a, 1992b, 1993, 1994b) we often found that our research subjects would name the relevant discourse domains for us. Some examples of discourse domains that have been proposed in the literature include "life story" and "life history" domains (Selinker & Douglas, 1985; Whyte, 1992), "work" domain, "family" domain (Whyte, 1991), "studies" and "academic major" domains (Whyte, 1992, 1995), "test taking" domain (Douglas & Selinker, 1985a, 1992b; Martin Halliday, 2002), "being a teaching assistant" domain (Douglas & Selinker, 1986), "being an international professor" domain, and "telling stories about Poland in English after a few vodkas" domain (Selinker & Douglas, 1988b). Most recently, Selinker and Kinahan (in progress) have identified a domain of "international news speak" used primarily by politicians and celebrities.

The research methodology (Selinker & Douglas, 1988a; Douglas & Selinker, 1994a) for recognizing and distinguishing discourse domains has been primarily one of recording communicative events (either naturally occurring or experimentally contrived) which differed in a small number of contextual variables, most notably those of participants and topic, and then asking the participants to review the recordings and comment on their communicative performance. It was in these "play-back sessions" that subjects would sometimes name the domain for us, but we sometimes imposed our own analysis on the data and named domains ourselves, based on observed rhetorical/grammatical differences in the recorded texts. There is no doubt that we found language variation associated with different contexts, but to really know that this variation was associated with different *discourse domains*, we clearly need evidence that the participants themselves recognized internally that they were engaging different domains in the two situations (Tarone, 2002). In the cases where the subjects named the domain themselves, we have such evidence, I think; in those cases where we imposed an interpretation on the data, we cannot be so sure. This is an avenue for future research, it seems to me. Discourse domains are all about language learner interpretations of context and their consequent organization of their communicative response to it. As I have argued:

> A further aspect, and a crucial one, of the notion of context is the following: what really counts in the communicative performance of a language user is how that individual *interprets* whatever contextualization cues are present in the communicative event. Thus, we are compelled ... toward an internal view of context as a cognitive construct created by language users for the interpretation and production of language. (Douglas, 2000: 45; emphasis added)

Are there observable features of discourse domains such that researchers can tell what domain language learners/users are engaging in a given communicative task? I think not: as a cognitive construct, a discourse domain is by definition unobservable except indirectly by interpreting performance. Context is also nebulous in the sense that it is dynamic and constantly changing and thus hard to pin down: A context is not simply a collection of features imposed upon the language learner/user, but rather is constructed by the participants in the communicative event. A salient feature of context is that it is dynamic, and constantly changing as a result of negotiation between and among the interactants as they construct it, turn by turn.

As I noted above, our research strategy has been to locate or set up situations so different from each other that we felt safe in the likelihood that participants would in fact engage domains differentially (Douglas & Selinker, 1994a). We have tended to confirm our categorization of domains through secondary data, mainly by retrospective interviews with the participants. I think this will continue to be the best way forward for research on context and discourse domains – we need not only to observe differences in production in different contexts, but also to attend to participants' commentary on their perceptions of these performances so as to learn more about their understanding of the domain they were engaging.

The most comprehensive attempt, independent of Selinker and Douglas, to define discourse domains and study their effect on the creation of discourse to date (but see Martin Halliday, 2002) is that of Whyte, whose formulation specifies a cognitive dimension, an affective dimension, and an interactive dimension:

> A discourse domain is a topic area that is characterized by extensive knowledge (for which speakers possess an elaborated schema, and which they control completely), by important knowledge (which is central to speakers' networks of schemata, and in which they are invested), and by current knowledge (which speakers use frequently in interaction, and with which they are familiar). (1995: 158)

This formulation is illustrated in Whyte's diagram (p. 159), reproduced as Figure 2.1. For each dimension, there are two continua associated with topic characteristics and speaker characteristics. Discourse domains can thus be seen as specialized schemata in which the language learner/user has maximal content control of an elaborated schema, which is of central importance in her life, and about which she speaks or writes frequently. I think Whyte errs in giving too much prominence to "topic area" as a defining characteristic of discourse domains, as I will discuss below, but much is owed to her for her elaboration of dimensions, thus allowing for the notion that domains may vary in strength and need not be thought of as "all or nothing" constructs.

Whyte found only partial support for her formulation: speakers who demonstrated all three of the above dimensions performed better on both turn taking structure and episodic structure than speakers who were less invested in the topic. On the other hand, speakers who were neither experts in the topic nor affectively invested did show enhanced performance on the measures of discourse organization under conditions of topic currency. Young (1999) suggests that this partial support for Whyte's formulation may be due to a failure to account for the influence of the speakers' interlocutors – the effect, in other words, of the interaction on the development of the discourse domain. Giving more prominence to the interactive nature of discourse would speak to Zuengler's concern that discourse domains should be viewed as interactionally constructed and not just cognitive constructs (see also McNamara, 1997, on interaction in language performance).

Whyte's framework does include an interactional dimension – her *currency of knowledge* dimension – although she does not specifically

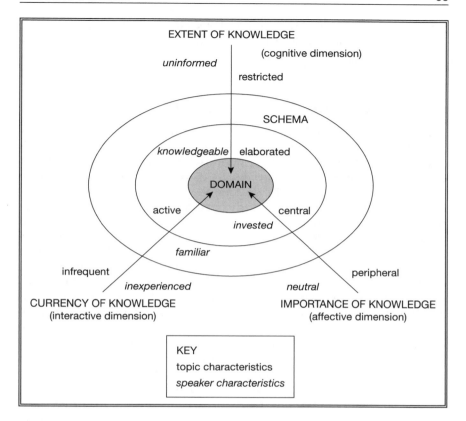

Figure 2.1 Whyte's formulation (1995: 159)

allude to the possible influence of co-construction of the discourse on the creation of a discourse domain. The notion of co-construction certainly fits with the view of context as dynamic, constantly changing, involving attention to contextualization cues provided in part by an interlocutor, as noted above. Discourse, even monologic discourse, is always interactional in that the speaker is strategically involved in trying to communicate with an audience, whether that audience is present or not. Nevertheless, I think the key feature of this dimension is not interaction per se but rather, as Whyte has suggested, *currency*, the degree to which the interaction is a current part of the life of the language learner/user, rather than something she may know about and have an interest in but which is at the moment dormant and not being talked or written about. Still, a greater emphasis on the interactive nature of discourse would shift the focus, I believe, more toward the co-construction of context that McNamara, Young, and Zuengler (see also Chapelle, 1998; Martin Halliday, 2002) have called for.

A Revisionist View of Discourse Domains

There are other problems with the original Selinker and Douglas formulation of the discourse domains hypothesis. Most notable is a lack of clarity about the notion of "temporary" domains. Tarone (2002) has questioned whether "a learner would construct a temporary domain out of nowhere in the amount of time they have: it is more likely that they use another domain they already have, adapted in superficial ways to suit the needs of the moment." I agree that domains cannot be constructed out of nowhere and that the learner/user employs an existing domain, though often modifying it, to cope with new situations. The very notion of temporariness is an important aspect of the way communicative competence develops. As Widdowson (1983) points out, a world in which we had to make do with a limited set of unchanging frameworks for interpretation would be a dull one indeed. Learning and growth are hallmarks of humanity and we are constantly creating new domains to deal with new communicative challenges. However, not all of these newly created domains remain viable, as Widdowson notes: "Sometimes, these creations will be fugitive affairs which last only as long as the discourse in which they appear; but sometimes they will be retained by custom, become conventionalized and placed in schematic store for future use" (1983: 42). This adaptability is the essence of communicative competence – the ability to adapt to new situations, to develop new ways of interpreting the world, and to discard old views and strengthen new ones.

Building on Whyte (1995) as well as on previous work and my current thinking, I now offer a revised definition of discourse domain:

> A discourse domain is a cognitive construct within which a language is developed and used. Discourse domains are developed in relation to context, as defined by setting, participants, purpose, content, tone, language, norms of interaction, and genre. They are created as part of communicative competence along three dimensions: the *extent* of content knowledge, its *importance* in the life of the user, and the *currency* of the knowledge in interaction. Discourse domains are dynamic and changing, and vary in strength depending on the amount and quality of experience associated with particular communicative situations.

This definition maintains the earliest views of Selinker and Douglas of the cognitive nature of discourse domains as interpreters of external context, influenced by multiple features of context, not simply topic; it incorporates Whyte's insight that domains have dimensions, allowing for the concept of varying strengths of domains; it incorporates Young's and Zuengler's call for giving the notion of interaction a more prominent place in the formulation of domains; and it elaborates the idea that domains are dynamic and changing, as argued for by Widdowson and Tarone.

Figure 2.2 illustrates this reconceptualization of discourse domain: The diagram situates the language learner/user within a communicative context. Communication strategies act as mediators between this external context and its internal interpretation, discourse domains. The double-headed arrow is intended to capture the notion that there is a

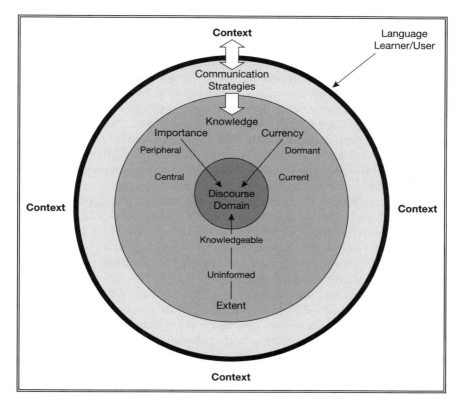

Figure 2.2 Revised discourse domains formulation

two-way interaction between the language learner/user and the context, with the participants in the communicative situation influencing the context in a dynamic way. The strategic component creates discourse domains of varying strength along three dimensions of knowledge about the context: varying levels of content knowledge, the importance of that knowledge to the learner/user, and currency of the knowledge in interaction. Domains are engaged in response to contextual cues (as listed on page 28). Contexts are co-constructed in interaction with interlocutors and discourse domains thus reflect the depth, currency, and importance associated with the setting, participants, purpose, topical content, tone, language, norms of interaction, and genre of the communicative situation.

Research on Discourse Domains and Context

Tarone (2000) has reviewed research on context and its relationship to SLA, including its potential both for producing differential grammars and for affecting changes in the process of acquisition itself. She refers to the discourse domains hypothesis as a way of showing "how social and psycholinguistic processes might be included in a theory of interlanguage" (p. 182). Tarone notes that there is a paucity of evidence owing in part to a split in SLA research – research on cognitive factors and on social factors. Most studies demonstrate "the impact of social factors on interlanguage USE at a single point in time and do not show that these social factors affect the ACQUISITION of SPECIFIC linguistic features of IL over time" (p. 185; emphasis in original; IL = interlanguage). It is difficult to do the longitudinal studies, transcribe long stretches of conversation, and identify the new forms being acquired. We should also note, as shown by Han's (in progress) work on fossilization, that not all SLA phenomena are related to discourse domains. There are certainly many factors that influence the outcome and process of language acquisition; in this chapter I am merely focusing on one of them.

Tarone discusses research evidence with regard to two possible effects of context on language acquisition: changes in the context may either change the grammar acquired or change the process of acquisition. Let us consider the first possibility, whether changing the social setting leads to changes in the IL grammar. Tarone notes that there are two ways to answer this question: (1) a single learner learns different grammars in different settings; and (2) a single learner learns one grammar but uses it variably according to social setting. The first of these Tarone rejects on the grounds that it is unnecessarily complicated; the second she sees as much more plausible. But she offers a third possibility: two learners in different social settings learn different grammars. Research on the nature of input in various settings suggests they do: the target language rules to be learned vary in specific ways from one setting to another; the degree to which native speakers adjust their language for learners differs in different settings; and the amount of overall modeling and collaborative assistance given to learners differs in different settings. Thus, it seems likely that different contexts lead to different grammars.

Even if we cannot go so far as to suggest that different contexts lead to a single learner acquiring different grammars, and I can understand how many teachers and researchers would find the suggestion unacceptable, we are compelled to the conclusion that a learner acquiring a language in a variety of contexts is acquiring a richer, more flexible set of communicative possibilities – a linguistic repertoire that enhances the learner's capacity to adapt to new and varied communicative situations. Chapelle (1998), incorporating the work of Michael Halliday regarding the function of context in language development and use (Halliday, 1979; Halliday & Hasan, 1989), argues that the interaction between context and the cognitive trait of language knowledge changes the nature of both, and I have used this insight to argue for the existence of specific purpose language (Douglas, 2000, and forthcoming). Certainly, this proposal needs research and we need to seek methodologies to help us to determine the systemic effect of different contexts on the acquisition of language knowledge.

Tarone's second possible effect of context on language acquisition is that changing the social setting may change the *way* the learner acquires the L2. Certain types of change in acquisition processes might arise due to different social settings. The first involves error detection and correction. If a learner is correcting differentially in different social contexts to accommodate different interlocutors, then the uncorrected errors will be different in those contexts. Secondly, Tarone points out that a small amount of research suggests that different social contexts impact the sequence of acquisition of phonological, morphological, or grammatical features of interlanguage. If this phenomenon can be shown more robustly, then perhaps we could begin to suggest that the process of acquisition is different in different contexts. Finally, it is likely that social context features such as task type, background knowledge, status differences, familiarity, and gender affect the way meaning is negotiated. There is some evidence that attention to social context leads to differences in noticing/focus on form, another small but significant effect on the acquisition process. In these ways, it seems to me, the concept of discourse domains, in impacting the way learners acquire the second language, will be of interest and practical use to teachers and test developers: as researchers provide findings on differential error correction in different social contexts, on the sequence of acquisition of linguistic features in different contexts, and on how negotiation of meaning in different contexts affects focus on form, teachers and testers will better understand through these findings just how contextual factors in instructional and assessment tasks influence the acquisition process. In principle, this knowledge will allow them to more effectively manage student learning.

Research on the possible effects of context on language acquisition will certainly involve research on the discourse domains hypothesis in the context of speaking. In particular, I would like to emphasize the need to collect and analyze large bodies of data on spoken interaction, such as that reported by Carter and McCarthy (1995), Douglas and Myers (2000), Biber *et al.* (2002), Lawson (2001), and Barbieri (2002). Biber, one of the editors of the monumental *Longman Grammar of Spoken and Written English* (Biber *et al.*, 1999), has noted the importance of situation in language use (*register* in Biber's terms): "one major finding in doing the *Grammar* was the belief that register is so important that there is no such thing as a general use" (Biber, 2002). Corpus-based approaches to the study of speaking offer much to the study of discourse domains and I hope to see more and more corpus studies in the future.

Conclusion

In this chapter, I have outlined and elaborated on the discourse domains hypothesis in the context of speaking in a second language. I have reinforced the idea that a discourse domain is a cognitive construct within which a language is developed and used, a concept that situates the language learner/user within a communicative context. I suggested that communication strategies act as mediators between this external context and its internal interpretation, discourse domains, and argued that there is a two-way interaction between the language learner/ user and the context, which is dynamic and constantly changing, co-constructed in interaction with interlocutors. The speaker's strategic component creates discourse domains of varying strength along three dimensions of knowledge about the context, given the varying levels of content knowledge, the importance of that knowledge to the learner/user, and the currency of the knowledge in interaction. The dynamic nature of discourse domains, particularly the co-constructed aspect of them, can be very frustrating for researchers, teachers, and language test developers, for it means that we can never be entirely sure that the activities we devise for learning or measurement purposes will be associated with the intended discourse domains in the minds of the learners. We must, however, try to understand the nature of the internal context, discourse domains, as best we can, and try to ensure that we provide sufficient contextualization cues in the learning and research tasks we present to our students so that they will, in a profound sense, "know where they are" in using their second language.

There are a number of ways teachers and test developers can help learners and test takers enrich their repertoire of language knowledge to respond to the limitless variety of situations they will encounter. Below are some brief ideas in terms of contextual features referred to earlier in this chapter:

Setting: In classroom learning activities and test instructions, we need to provide the learner with detailed information, by means of oral or written text, realistic drawings or photographs, and even sound effects. Smells might be going a bit too far, but perhaps not – Bachman and Palmer (1996) have suggested the smell of chemicals and exhaust fumes as part of the setting in a hypothetical test for trainee auto mechanics! The temporal setting can be signaled by providing information about the time of day (or night), day of the week, season, and so on.

Participants: Again, teachers and testers must provide information about participants in the communicative situation clearly and in some detail as professor, fellow student, close friend, colleague, including information about age, gender, and personality. In live role-plays, the behavior of the interlocutor(s) can be varied, as well. For example, the interlocutor might play the role of someone who constantly asks for clarification, who shows interest by asking questions, or who shows boredom, and so on. The number of participants is relevant, since performances will vary depending on whether an individual or a large group is involved, for example.

Purposes: A key aspect of language use is the establishment of a clear purpose for communication, in addition to the obvious purpose of language learning or testing. For example, the learner/test taker can be instructed to explain a term in her field in order to convince an interlocutor of its crucial importance to her field, to correct a misunderstanding, to solve a problem she is having, and so on. The goal of identifying purpose here is not to try to make the learner forget that she is engaged in a language learning exercise or a test, but to add another ingredient to the richness of the communicative context, increasing the likelihood that the learner will engage an appropriate discourse domain.

Topical content: That the topic of the communicative situation should be clearly derived from real situations of interest and value to the learner almost goes without saying, but providing an appropriate topic is just one factor in addressing the problem of establishing the context in relation to discourse domain. The topic may be explicitly presented in instructions, but may often be implicit in the interaction itself.

Tone: Engaging in conversation, even in academic discourse, is not the unemotional, dry, objective undertaking that textbook writers and test developers might imagine. Irony, humor, sarcasm, gratitude, authority, and many other indicators of attitude or mood, play a role in all discourse. Sensitivity to tone is an important part of what it means to learn a language. (Munby, 1978, actually lists 51 dichotomous indices of tone!)

Language: Dialect and register vary from situation to situation, even from moment to moment in spoken discourse, and learners must develop a sensitivity to changes in language and enrich their linguistic inventory in response to various contexts. For example, speakers often switch dialects or registers for rhetorical effect – politicians, for example, frequently move from a formal style to a more casual one to demonstrate their down-to-earth, blue-collar roots among "the people" – and sensitivity to this aspect of speaking is indispensable to learners.

Norms of interaction: Expectations for level of formality among interlocutors vary somewhat automatically with the choice of setting and with the status and roles of the participants. Speakers perform differently, in terms of forms of address, topic choice, turn taking routines, interruptions, and politeness forms, when the interlocutor is a professor rather than a fellow student, or when speaking to a medical colleague as opposed to a patient. It is therefore doubly important that instructors and test developers provide sufficient information to learners/ test takers about setting and participants so that they will be able to make appropriate decisions about norms of interaction.

Genre: Learners need to be aware of the formal and pragmatic distinctions between such genres as monologue, interview, lecture, advertisement, panel discussion, and so on. Again, this is a matter of increasing the communicative repertoire of the learners and is an important responsibility of teachers and test developers. Teachers can provide opportunities for learners to engage in a number of different types of speaking activities, such as giving instructions, participating in group discussions, presenting formal research reports, and so on, relevant to their needs and learning purposes. Test developers should likewise vary the types of speaking tasks they provide so that test takers will have opportunities to display their abilities in a number of ways.

The issue of providing sufficient information to learners about contextual variables and how they impact speaking is important if we teachers and testers are to become better at facilitating second language learning, but in addition, we applied linguists, materials writers, and test developers, need to know more about the nature of the second language grammars acquired by learners, including discourse and pragmatic competence, and about the process of acquisition as it is influenced by context. These then are research issues of concern in these fields.

I have discussed a number of research needs, including: (1) understanding more fully the mechanism of domain engagement, such as through retrospective data from learners concerning their recognized engagement in different domains in different communicative situations; (2) understanding the systemic effect of different contexts on the acquisition of language knowledge; and (3) analyzing the frequency and saliency of lexico-grammatical features of spoken language in various contexts through the collection and analysis of spoken interaction using corpus-based techniques. I see these as key areas of future research in the area of discourse domains as we continue to wrestle with context in the teaching and testing of speaking ability in a second language.

References

Bachman, L. and Palmer, A. (1996) *Language Testing in Practice*. Oxford: Oxford University Press.

Barbieri, F. (2002) A corpus-based study of direct speech quotatives in American English conversation. Unpublished Master's Thesis, English Department, Iowa State University.

Biber, D. (2002) Corpus linguistics and the study of English grammar. *Quentin Johnson Lecture*, Iowa State University, February.

Biber, D., Conrad, S., Reppen, R., Byrd, P., and Helt, M. (2002) Speaking and writing in the university: A multidimensional comparison. *TESOL Quarterly* 36 (1), 9–48.

Biber, D., Johansson, S., Leech, G., Conrad, S., and Finegan, E. (1999) *The Longman Grammar of Written and Spoken English*. London: Longman.

Boxer, D. (2002) *Applying Sociolinguistics: Domains and Face-to-face Interaction*. Amsterdam: John Benjamin.

Carter, R. and McCarthy, M. (1995) Grammar and the spoken language. *Applied Linguistics* 16 (2), 141–158.

Chapelle, C. (1998) Construct definition and validity inquiry in SLA research. In L. Bachman and A. D. Cohen (eds) *Interfaces Between Second Language Acquisition and Language Testing Research* (pp. 32–70). Cambridge: Cambridge University Press.

Douglas, D. (forthcoming) Testing languages for specific purposes. In E. Hinkel (ed.) *Handbook of Research in Second Language Teaching and Learning.* Mahwah, NJ: Lawrence Erlbaum.

Douglas, D. (2000) *Assessing Languages for Specific Purposes.* Cambridge: Cambridge University Press.

Douglas, D. and Myers, R. K. (2000) Assessing the communication skills of veterinary students: Whose criteria? In A. Kunnan (ed.) *Fairness in Language Testing: Selected Papers from the 1997 Language Testing Research Colloquium* (pp. 60–81). Cambridge: Cambridge University Press.

Douglas, D. and Selinker, L. (1985a) Principles for language tests within the "discourse domains" theory of interlanguage. *Language Testing* 2 (2), 205–226.

Douglas, D. and Selinker, L. (1985b) The problem of comparing discourse domains in interlanguage studies. Paper presented at the Second Language Research Forum, Los Angeles, February.

Douglas, D. and Selinker, L. (1986) The interlanguage of three teaching assistants: Two domains. Paper presented at TESOL Convention, Anaheim, California.

Douglas, D. and Selinker, L. (1988) The notion of internal context in language testing theory. Paper presented at the Seventh Language Testing Symposium, Academic Committee for Research on Language Testing, Israel, May.

Douglas, D. and Selinker, L. (1989) U.S. vs. NNS TAs: Markedness in discourse domains. *Papers in Applied Linguistics* 1 (1), 69–82.

Douglas, D. and Selinker, L. (1992a) CHEMSPEAK: Measuring speaking ability among international teaching assistants. Paper presented at International TESOL Convention, Vancouver, March.

Douglas, D. and Selinker, L. (1992b) Analyzing oral proficiency test performance in general and specific purpose contexts. *System* 20, 317–328.

Douglas, D. and Selinker, L. (1993) Performance on a general versus a field-specific test of speaking proficiency by international teaching assistants. In D. Douglas and C. Chapelle (eds) *A New Decade of Language Testing Research: Selected Papers from the 1990 Language Testing Research Colloquium* (pp. 235–256). Alexandria, VA: Teachers of English to Speakers of Other Languages.

Douglas, D. and Selinker, L. (1994a) Research methodology in context-based second-language research. In E. Tarone, S. Gass, and A. D. Cohen (eds) *Methodologies for Eliciting and Analyzing Language in Context* (pp. 119–132). Hillsdale, NJ: Erlbaum.

Douglas, D. and Selinker, L. (1994b) Native and non-native teaching assistants: A case study of discourse domains and genres. In C. Madden and C. Myers (eds) *Discourse and Performance of International Teaching Assistants* (pp. 221–230). Alexandria, VA: TESOL Publications.

Fishman, J. (1972) The sociology of language: An interdisciplinary social science approach to language in society. In J. Fishman (ed.) *Advances in the Sociology of Language* (Vol. 1) (pp. 217–404). The Hague: Mouton

Gumperz, J. (1976) Language, communication, and public negotiation. In P. Sanday (ed.) *Anthropology and the Public Interest.* New York: Academic Press.

Halliday, Martin (2002) The discourse domains theory of interlanguage. Unpublished MA thesis, Department of Applied Linguistics, Birkbeck College, University of London.

Halliday, Michael (1979) *Language as Social Semiotic.* London: Edward Arnold.

Halliday, Michael, and Hasan, R. (1989) *Language, Context, and Text: Aspects of Language in a Social-Semiotic Perspective.* Oxford: Oxford University Press.

Han, Z.-H. (in progress) Fossilization: Some conceptual and methodological issues.

Hymes, D. (1974) *Foundations of Sociolinguistics: An Ethnographic Approach.* Philadelphia, PA: University of Pennsylvania Press.

Lawson, A. (2001) Rethinking French grammar for pedagogy: The contribution of spoken corpora. In R. C. Simpson and J. M. Swales (eds) *Corpus Linguistics in North America* (pp. 179–194). Ann Arbor, MI: The University of Michigan Press.

Lee, D. Y. W. (2001) Genres, registers, text types, domains, and styles: Clarifying the concepts and navigating a path through the BNC jungle. *Language Learning & Technology* 5 (3), 37–72.

Long, M. (2003) Stabilization and fossilization in interlanguage development. In C. Doughty and M. Long (eds) *Handbook of Second Language Acquisition.* Oxford: Blackwell.

McNamara, T. (1997) "Interaction" in second language performance assessment: Whose performance? *Applied Linguistics* 18 (4), 446–466.

Munby, J. (1978) *Communicative Syllabus Design.* Cambridge: Cambridge University Press.

Selinker, L. and Douglas, D. (1985) Wrestling with "context" in interlanguage theory. *Applied Linguistics* 6 (2), 190–204.

Selinker, L. and Douglas, D. (1986) Longitudinal variation in interlanguage in two discourse domains. Paper presented at Eastern States Conference on Linguistics, Carnegie-Mellon University, Pittsburgh.

Selinker, L. and Douglas, D. (1987a) Integrating interlanguage use, development, and fossilization with context. Paper presented at the Second Language Research Forum, University of California, Los Angeles.

Selinker, L. and Douglas, D. (1987b) LSP and interlanguage: Some empirical studies. *ESP Journal* 6 (2), 75–84. Special issue.

Selinker, L. and Douglas, D. (1988a) Using discourse domains in creating interlanguage: Context theory and research methodology. In J. Klegraf and D. Nehls (eds) *Studies in Descriptive Linguistics: Essays on the English Language and Applied Linguistics on the Occasion of Gerhard Nickels' 60th birthday* (pp. 357–379). Heidelberg: Julius Groos Verlag.

Selinker, L. and Douglas, D. (1988b) Comparing episodes in discourse domains in LSP and Interlanguage Studies. In A. M. Cornu, J. Vanparijs, N. Delahaye, and L. Baten (eds) *Beads or Bracelet: How Do We Approach LSP?* (pp. 366–378). Oxford: Oxford University Press.

Selinker, L. and Kinahan, C. (in progress) Distance online interlanguage analysis: An aid to language learning or "absence is presence." In S. Fotos and C. Browne (eds) *New Perspectives on CALL for Second Language Classrooms.* Mahwah, NJ: Lawrence Erlbaum Associates.

Tarone, E. (2000) Still wrestling with "context" in interlanguage theory. *Annual Review of Applied Linguistics* 20, 182–198.

Tarone, E. (2002) Personal communication, May 31.

Whyte, S. (1991) Language in context: The effect of personal investment on talk. Unpublished paper, Indiana University, Bloomington.

Whyte, S. (1992) Discourse domains revisited. In L. Bouton and B. Kachru (eds) *Pragmatics and Language Learning Monographs* (Vol. 3) (pp. 81–103). Urbana, IL: Division of English as an International Language, University of Illinois.

Whyte, S. (1995) Specialist knowledge and interlanguage development: A discourse domain approach to text construction. *Studies in Second Language Acquisition* 17 (2), 153–183.

Widdowson, H. (1983) *Learning Purpose and Language Use.* Oxford: Oxford University Press.

Widdowson, H. (2001) Communicative language testing: The art of the possible. In C. Elder, A. Brown, E. Grove, K. Hill, N. Iwashita, T. Lumley, T. McNamara, and K. O'Loughlin (eds) *Experimenting with Uncertainty: Essays in Honour of Alan Davies* (pp. 12–21). Cambridge: Cambridge University Press.

Young, R. (1999) Sociolinguistic approaches to SLA. *Annual Review of Applied Linguistics* 19, 105–132.

Zuengler, Jane (1989) Performance variation in NS-NNS interactions: Ethnolinguistic difference, or discourse domain? In S. Gass, C. Madden, D. Preston, and L. Selinker (eds) *Variation in Second Language Acquisition (Discourse and Pragmatics)* (Vol. 1) (pp. 228–244). Clevedon: Multilingual Matters.

Part II: *Studying* Spontaneous *Spoken Discourse to Inform Second Language Learning*

Overview

This section focuses on four studies that utilize spontaneous spoken discourse data for their primarily qualitative analyses of several important second language learning issues. The first chapter in this section is a study by Anne Lazaraton: "Conversation Analysis and the Nonnative English Speaking ESL Teacher: A Case Study." Lazaraton's focus in this research is on the very relevant issue of teacher identity when the teacher's L1 is a language other than what s/he is teaching. The study is an example of the application of CA to the study of the initiation, feedback, and response (IRF)[1] configuration typical of classroom discourse and its consequences for language use and development. The study of classroom discourse is fertile ground for the analysis of unfolding communities in practice, which in turn provides important insights into issues of identity – relational, individual, and social. Lazaraton provides one of the few in-depth studies of language *learning* (in contrast to language *use*) through conversational analysis, capitalizing on the usefulness of CA tools to analyze *students'* asking of questions. In so doing, the author shows how the IRF pattern is somewhat turned on its head, with student talk creating increased opportunity for interaction and language development. Lazaraton clearly demonstrates how an analysis of unfolding talk-in-interaction in classroom discourse reveals important issues in what it means to be accepted as "expert."

The second chapter in this section is a study by Joan Kelly Hall: "'Practicing Speaking' in Spanish: Lessons from a High School Foreign Language Classroom." Hall analyzes patterns of spoken interaction in a foreign language class over a period of time. Her approach to the data takes a critical sociocultural perspective, with micro-ethnographic, thick description of the specific community of practice being analyzed. As in many studies of classroom discourse and interaction, an important focus here is on teacher talk and its effects on subsequent language learning. In an effort at triangulating the data much in the tradition of micro-ethnography, or interactional sociolinguistics (IS), Hall had the teacher flesh out the transcription. Through micro-analysis of pedagogical inter-action, the study examines the issue of what it means to encourage/ discourage socially meaningful speaking practices in FL classroom discourse, and examines repercussions for the development of abstract concepts in the FL. Hall's finding, that "practicing speaking" in this language class entails neither agency nor investment on the part of the students, has important pedagogical implications. Indeed, the study illus-trates how we must transform our notion of what "practice" means in formal, tutored language learning contexts.

A third chapter in this section is Heidi Hamilton's "Repair of Teenagers' Spoken German in a Summer Immersion Program." This study is also an in-depth analysis of foreign language learning (here the L2 is German). In contrast to Hall's analysis of FL classroom discourse, Hamilton focuses on an FL immersion context in a summer camp environment. She studies feedback mechanisms and expectations for L2 use in such a setting, analyzing adolescent learners in interaction with each other and with an expert, here a "counselor" whose L1 is German. The analysis of talk in the sub-contexts of the immersion setting illustrates the notion of unfolding identities as learners take on the affordances of the new language and culture. Hamilton's methodology is highly ethnographic, offering rich, contextualized descriptions of language use in the various sub-contexts that make up the immersion camp setting. Implications for what can be expected in immersion contexts of this type are offered.

A final chapter in this section is by Helena Halmari: "Codeswitching Patterns and Developing Discourse Competence in L2." The study is a longitudinal, interactional sociolinguistic analysis of the spontaneous spoken language use of bilingual children at play. Halmari's data consist of audiotaped recordings of two siblings over a period of several years. She analyzes changes over time in the children's use of their two codes: L1 Finnish, the language of interaction of the children's family; and L2 English, the language of the larger community. Because the emerging bilinguals are siblings, they have a built-in relational identity, affording them opportunities to scaffold language use for each other. The chapter thus offers us a glimpse of how the interactional practices of novice users with each other can lend insights into developing bilingualism. Halmari's research has the advantage of analyzing a longitudinal corpus to demon-strate changing patterns of code use and alternation.

Note

1. In the IRF pattern of discourse, the teacher initiates with a question or other prompt, the students respond, and then the teacher gives feedback, such as "very good." This pattern is also sometimes referred to as "ERF" or "ERE," denoting "elicitation, response, feedback (evaluation)."

Chapter 3

Conversation Analysis and the Nonnative English Speaking ESL Teacher: A Case Study

ANNE LAZARATON

The relative benefits and drawbacks of the classroom teacher who is a nonnative speaker in the language of instruction continue to be a hotly debated issue in education today. This qualitative, descriptive case study of one pre-service nonnative English speaking teacher (NNEST) of English as a Second Language (ESL) in an intensive English program at a US university investigates the complex relationship between English language ability and classroom teaching skills as they are manifested in audio- and videorecordings of actual classroom discourse. Conversation analysis, a rigorous, inductive approach to examining authentic spoken discourse, is used to analyze one segment of transcribed classroom instruction, where the teacher is required to answer a student question about cheddar cheese. The analysis suggests a rather "ordinary" explanation was achieved; although no firm conclusions can be put forward from the limited analysis of just one segment of classroom data, it is rewarding to find another application of conversation analysis, one which has the potential to inform both our beliefs about and our practices in second language teaching and learning.

Introduction

The pedagogical and sociopolitical issues surrounding the classroom teacher who is a nonnative speaker in the language of instruction continue to be hotly debated in education today. Whether that teacher is a native English speaking foreign language teacher of French in a North American high school, a native Taiwanese speaker teaching a chemistry lab section in English at a US university (an International Teaching Assistant, or ITA), or a nonnative English speaking teacher (NNEST) in the English as a Second Language (ESL) classroom, questions continue to arise about the language ability, the pedagogical skills, and the cultural knowledge of these teachers.

The perspectives, concerns, and interests of nonnative English speaking teachers (NNESTs) are now being voiced in a growing body of work (e.g. Braine, 1999; Liu, 1999; Samimy & Brutt-Griffler, 1999; Saylor, 2000). For one, the terms "native speaker" and "nonnative speaker" continue to be debated in the professional literature (e.g. Cook, 1999; Medgyes, 1992). In addition, a handful of empirical studies have focused specifically on nonnative ESL teachers. For example, Liu's (1999: 100) case study of seven "NNS TESOL professionals" suggests that the impact of the NNEST "is complex and involves the sequence in which languages are learned, competence in English, cultural affiliation, self-identification, social environment, and political labeling." According to Liu, the preoccupation with "nonnative speakerness" (in hiring, admissions, and the like) masks the real issue, the importance of being a "trained TESOL professional" (1999: 100). In fact, as Milambiling (2000) points out, often overlooked by teacher trainers, by researchers, and even by the NNS themselves are the many positive attributes NNESTs bring to the ESL class, not the least of which are their own experiences in becoming bilingual and/or bicultural. Samimy and Brutt-Griffler's (1999) study of a graduate seminar for NNESTs reveals a number of ways that critical reflection on teaching practice can stimulate the process of empowerment. And Saylor's (2000) case study of six NNESTs (three at the University of Minnesota and three elsewhere) suggests that language improvement, cultural awareness, and pedagogical expertise are the primary needs of these teachers. Yet even these data-based studies focus on teacher impressions and reflections (about decision-making processes, practical knowledge, and the like) – data sources which are the standard in second language teacher education (e.g. Freeman & Johnson, 1998; Johnson, 1999) – rather than the discourse produced in ESL classes taught by NNESTs.

Applied linguistics researchers have long been interested in the nature of talk produced in second language (SL) classrooms, especially classes where students are learning English as a Second Language. Chaudron (1988), for example, summarizes literally hundreds of studies (most of which were both experimental and quantitative in nature) that analyzed the amount and type of teacher talk; learner verbal behavior with respect to age, culture, and language task; teacher–student interaction in the SL classroom as shown through questioning behavior and corrective feedback; and the influence of these factors on learning outcomes. Johnson's 1995 book analyzes the ways in which teacher communication patterns influence and in some ways restrict student participation opportunities, and by extension, their acquisition of a second language. And several more recent studies have employed interpretive analytic techniques in analyzing actual recorded and transcribed talk to understand, for example, the nature of helping behaviors bilingual students employ in primary school classes (Klingner & Vaughn, 2000); the ways in which the discourse patterns present in an adult ESL conversation class are influenced by particular instructional goals of the teacher (Ulichny, 1996); and the means by which ESL teachers answer student requests for definitions of unknown vocabulary (Markee, 1995). Yet again, a notable shortcoming of almost all of this second language classroom-based research, however, is its failure to consider spoken language data from teachers who are nonnative speakers of English in ESL classrooms.

In other words, what is missing in all of this work is a direct link between classroom discourse, on the one hand, and the role of the NNEST on the other. More specifically, it is still unclear how the *communicative competence* (Canale & Swain, 1980) of NNESTs interacts with their *pedagogical performance* in this particular classroom setting. Towards this end, the present study is an initial effort to bridge the gap between two seemingly disparate research agendas – describing the nature of discourse and interaction in the SL classroom and understanding the role of the NNEST in this context – in an innovative way by employing the discourse analytic technique of *Conversation Analysis* that has recently been embraced by applied linguists interested in validating oral language tests (Lazaraton, 2002a), in understanding SLA (Markee, 2000), and in teaching oral skills (Riggenbach, 1999). In more concrete terms, this study represents an initial attempt in a long-term research program to shed light on broad questions such as the following:

- What are the parameters of the communicative competence of NNESTs as evidenced by their classroom discourse?
- How is their pedagogical performance influenced by their ability to communicate?
- How can an analysis of NNEST classroom discourse aid in the education of these teachers?
- What unique insights does Conversation Analysis (CA) provide about second language teacher practice?

Methodology

What is Conversation Analysis?

Conversation Analysis (or CA, as it is often referred to) is a rigorous empirical approach to the analysis of oral discourse, with its disciplinary roots in sociology, which employs inductive methods to search for recurring patterns across many cases without appeal to intuitive judgments of what speakers "think" or "mean." That is, unlike other approaches to discourse analysis, the conversation analyst avoids appeal to "speaker intent," since knowledge of the internal states of the participants is as inaccessible to the analyst as it is to the participants: all that is there is the talk, and the talk that has gone before. The purpose of CA is to discover the systematic properties of the sequential organization of talk, the ways in which utterances are designed to manage such sequences, and the social practices that are displayed by and embodied in talk-in-interaction. The basic question facing the analyst is, *"Why this now?"* instead of "that" or instead of "later." The analyst attempts to model the procedures and expectations employed by the participants by proceeding as the talk does: on a turn-by-turn basis. In theory, no feature or observation based on it is too small, too random, or too irrelevant or insignificant. What "counts" can only be determined through a systematic examination of naturally occurring materials. This is one reason why the CA transcription process is so lengthy and detailed: there is no way to know beforehand which features of talk might be important in later analyses. Just as important is the fact that there is no way to know who might be interested in using the data at a later time, and what their research agenda might be. CA, then, is really a process more than a product, because it grows out of the transcription and repeated and prolonged examination of materials.

Very briefly, CA is guided by the following analytic principles:

- *Using authentic, recorded data which are carefully transcribed.*
- *Using the "turn" as the unit of analysis.*

CA insists on the careful collection of authentic spoken interaction, recorded via audiotape, or, preferably, videotape, which are then scrupulously transcribed into turns at talk using a conventional notation developed by Gail Jefferson (see Appendix on pp. 64–65).

- *"Unmotivated looking" at data rather than pre-stating research questions.*

Generally speaking, the conversation analyst does not formulate research questions prior to analyzing data; rather, questions emerge from the data. Consider what Harvey Sacks, one of the co-founders of CA (along with Emanuel Schegloff), has to say about this approach:

> Now people often ask me why I choose the particular data I choose. Is it some problem that I have in mind that caused me to pick this

corpus or this segment? And I am insistent that I just happened to have it, it became fascinating, and I spend some time at it. Furthermore, it is not that I attacked any piece of data I happen to have according to some problems I bring to it. When we start out with a piece of data, the question of what we are going to end up with, what kind of findings it will give, should not be a consideration. We sit down with a piece of data, make a bunch of observations, and see where they will go. (1984: 27)

That is, as Pomerantz and Fehr (1997: 66) point out, CA "rejects the use of investigator-stipulated theoretical and conceptual definitions of research questions." It is not that the analyst approaches any piece of data with no preconceptions whatsoever; rather, s/he tries to keep preconceptions about what will be found, important, etc. to a minimum. The data should generate questions, rather than the reverse.

- *Analyzing single cases, deviant cases, and collections thereof.*

The goal of CA is to build a convincing and comprehensive analysis of a single case, then to search for other similar cases in order to build a collection of cases that represent some interactional phenomenon. Deviant cases are particularly useful, because they may delineate the limits of a phenomenon or point to a new phenomenon altogether.

- *Disregarding ethnographic and demographic particulars of the context and participants.*

Unlike other qualitative research approaches such as ethnography, the conversation analyst places no a priori importance on the sociological, demographic, or ethnographic details of the participants in the interaction (e.g. gender, ethnicity, and class) or the setting in which the interaction takes place. Rather, the analyst, if interested in these issues, attempts to detect their manifestations in the discourse as it is constructed, instead of assuming some sort of "omnirelevance" beforehand; as Pomerantz and Fehr note, "persons who occupy different positions in some status or power hierarchy do not necessarily make that difference the basis for all and every interaction between them" (1997: 66). Strictly speaking, the conversation analyst does not consider the "participant perspective" (accessed by means of retrospective recall, for example) either useful or reliable. If the researcher wishes to make claims about a particular participant identity, these claims conclude, rather than shape, the analysis in question.

- *Eschewing the coding and quantification of data.*

Finally, unlike most sociological research, CA studies rarely report coding, counts, or statistical analyses of data, since the emphasis in CA is understanding single cases in and of themselves, not as part of larger aggregates of data (see Schegloff, 1993, for a cogent argument for this position).

In the thirty or so years that scholars have been engaged in CA, many robust findings about the nature of native English speaker conversation have emerged; for example, the systems of turntaking, repair, and sequence structure are now fairly well understood. The *turntaking system* of English is perhaps the most obvious aspect of conversational organization (Sacks *et al.*, 1974). Turntaking can be described by a set of rules with ordered options that operate on a turn-by-turn basis; this is why turntaking is characterized as a "locally managed" system. It can explain why only one speaker speaks at a time, how next speakers are selected, where and how overlaps (points where two or more speakers talk simultaneously) are placed, and how periods of silence occur within the talk of one speaker (a pause) or between the talk or two or more speakers (a gap). A turn is made up of *turn-constructional-units* (TCUs), which have syntactic, intonational, semantic and/or pragmatic status as potentially "complete." Because a TCU may be a sentence, a clause, a phrase, or a word, syntax matters a great deal for determining completeness. Speakers will initially be allotted one TCU (although most turns are more than one unit) and the turntaking apparatus applies at the end of each such unit, which is known as a *transition relevance place*, or TRP. In fact, we find that the ends of TCUs and turns are highly predictable using the four "completeness" criteria listed above; this is not to say that overlaps do not occur, but that when they occur at TRPs, they are quickly resolved by the turntaking machinery.

A second domain of conversational organization is concerned with the *sequencing rules* which apply to such talk. The basic structural unit is the *adjacency pair* (Schegloff & Sacks, 1973), consisting of a *first-pair-part* (FPP) and an adjacent, conditionally relevant *second-pair-part* (SPP), produced by different speakers. Examples of adjacency pairs include Question–Answer, Request–Acceptance/Denial, Summons–Response, and so on.

The system of *repair* is the major third organizational system, which operates to remedy trouble situations in conversation (Schegloff *et al.*, 1977), specifically problems in speaking, hearing, and understanding. We can differentiate *repair initiation*, where the existence of a problem is acknowledged, from *actual correction*, which is where the trouble is remedied. Repair can be initiated in four different positional "slots": same turn, transition space to possible next turn, next turn, and third turn. In all cases but next turn, there is a preference for self-initiation of repair and for self-correction.

Other systems of conversational organization that have been studied include the system of *preference organization*, which is an important aspect of the sequential organization of talk-in-interaction (Pomerantz, 1984). Not all potential second-pair-parts to the first-pair-part of an adjacency pair are of equal "rank": some are "preferred" while others are "dispreferred." Preference does not refer to psychological or individual preferences of the speakers who produce the talk, but to the structural notion that there are junctures at which participants have alternate but unequal courses of action available to them – at the level of lexical choice, turn type, sequence selection, and so on. *The overall structural organization* of an occasion of talk can be identified by the openings, pre-closings, and closings sections of conversation (Schegloff & Sacks, 1973). An examination of conversation shows that participants orient to these sections in and by their talk and to the work that is accomplished in them. A final organizational system that has received some, but not much, attention is *topic organization*. The simple reason for this lack of focus is that "topical maintenance and shift are extremely complex and subtle matter[s]" (Atkinson & Heritage, 1984: 165). Finally, it should be noted that conversation analysts are now trying to grapple with the role of nonverbal behavior in conversation, the systematic properties of conversation in languages other than English, and the interactional features of talk involving nonnative speakers of English.

In recent years, there has been a growing interest among conversation analysts in what is known as "institutional talk"; that is, interaction in, for example, classrooms, courtrooms, and medical encounters. Talk in the workplace, as one "discourse domain," is also a locus of research in sociolinguistics, as discussed by Boxer (2002). According to Drew and Heritage (1992), there are three salient features of institutional talk. First, it shows an orientation to a set of institutional goals which are relevant to the encounter (e.g. imparting some knowledge in a classroom, obtaining testimony in a courtroom, or formulating a diagnosis in a medical encounter). How and whether these goals are met is a matter that is negotiated by the participants in the course of the interaction. Secondly, it is quite clear that there are constraints on the quantity and quality of contributions that participants make in institutional encounters. Whether these constraints are of a legal sort (as in courtroom testimony) or more informal, as in a classroom setting, conduct is shaped according to these constraints. Finally, the interactional inferences that are operative in conversation may be modified, or even suspended, in institutional talk. For example, a range of behavior common in conversation (expressions of surprise, anger, and the like), if withheld, may indicate rudeness or boredom, whereas in institutional contexts, participants seem to reinterpret these behaviors with the particular institutional goals in mind (for example, being objective).

With respect to classroom interaction, several studies have microanalyzed the organization systems for this institutional context from a CA perspective. Mehan (1985) was the first to propose the basic three-part sequence for the classroom talk of teachers of Initiation-Reply-Evaluation (IRE); McHoul (1990) refers to such sequences as *adjacency triads*, and believes such sequences play an important role in the system of repair he found in an examination of the discourse produced in high school geography classes in Australia. While both the teachers he studied and their students self-corrected, he found a differential distribution of repair initiation and correction for classroom talk, where next turn repair initiations are the right of teachers, and third turn correction is the responsibility of students: "Teachers correct themselves and so do students. But, contrary to what may be a popular image of the classroom, teachers tend to show students *where* their talk is in need of correction, not how the correction should be made" (p. 376). Looking at the same Australian high school data, McHoul (1978: 188) concludes that "only teachers can direct speakership in any creative way." He maintains that "formality" of classroom interaction is evidenced by the fact that teachers and "students-as-speakers," unlike speakers in conversation, have no need for conversational techniques to obtain turns of multiple units, since the classroom uses a "heavily preallocated system" in which "local management" of turntaking is solely the sphere of teachers; there is a "distinct differentiation of participant rights (and obligations) in the classroom" (1978: 209). Lerner (1995), in his study of third grade bilingual children in a language arts classroom, shows how teachers use incomplete turn units to structure subsequent participation in class.

Five analytic tools for doing CA

So how does one actually "do" CA? Pomerantz and Fehr (1997: 71), in a useful introductory article on conversation analysis, present a concise list of analytic "tools" which can assist in CA's stated goal of "illuminat[ing] understandings that are relevant for the participants and the practices that provide for those understandings." Specifically, these tools, and the analysis that they help to generate, should describe a

conversational "practice" and the knowledge that conversational participants employ in conducting the practice. The tools tell the analyst to:

- Select a sequence of interest by looking for identifiable boundaries.
- Characterize the actions in the sequence by answering the question, "What is the participant doing in this turn?"
- Consider how the packaging of actions, that is, how they are formed and delivered, provides for certain understandings.
- Consider how timing and turntaking provide for certain under-standings of actions and the matters talked about.
- Consider how the ways the actions were accomplished suggest certain identities, roles, and/or relationships for the interactants.

These five tools are explained and employed to analyze one data fragment from an ESL classroom taught by a nonnative English-speaking teacher.

The Data

These data come from a one-hour lesson on grocery shopping in an intermediate-level oral skills class in an intensive English program affili-ated with a major US university. This fragment is part of a three-minute section on "how to order food from the deli" in a supermarket. In this section, two students, F2 (a Chinese female) and M1 (a Korean male) have completed a demonstration role-play for the class where M1 orders a pound of cheddar cheese and a half pound of smoked ham from the clerk, F2. The teacher (TE) has just set up the activity for pairs of students to do a similar role-play in lines 1–2.

The teacher is a female in her mid-twenties from Taiwan who was enrolled in an MA TESOL program in the United States, which required a one-semester internship course. As such, she can be considered a pre-service teacher, but she did have some prior English teaching experience in Taiwan. Also, it should be remembered that this was not "her" class, but that of her cooperating teacher.

The verbal data were transcribed by a graduate research assistant, using conversation analysis conventions (see Appendix on pp. 64–65). The researcher checked the transcript and added the information on the TE's nonverbal behavior at a later time.

Note that this fragment was not chosen for any special reason other than it was bounded, as Pomerantz and Fehr recommend (although as a result of analyzing it, I am now becoming interested in these sorts of unplanned explanations, where vocabulary questions arise and the teacher chooses to deal with the question on the spot, rather than through a pre-planned explanation). The specific question I would like to consider while examining this fragment is the following:

> *Is there evidence in this segment that either the teacher and/or the students show attention/orientation to the teacher being a NNEST?*

But in doing so, we are reminded by Schegloff (in an interview with Wong & Olsher, 2000: 125) that we need

> a kind of self-awareness about where this native–nonnative interest is coming from. There's nothing wrong with it as long as you're clear about it so you don't *insist it* into the data, so that you don't insist that the participants be as preoccupied with native/nonnative speakers as you are . . . unless *they* are. If they are, of course, you need to recognize that and trace out the consequences as the way it figures in the way they conduct the interaction. But that's because *they're* preoccupied with it or oriented to it, not because *you* are.

In other words, the analyst only has access *to the talk as it was produced* to figure out what such preoccupations were; the job of the analyst is to uncover and explicate these preoccupations. In "pure" CA, the analyst chooses not to consider speaker perceptions, recalls, and the like, which, even if available, are not thought to be reliable (because the speaker may not know, cannot recall, or says what s/he thinks the researcher wants to hear, for example).

Data analysis

1. Select a sequence of interest by looking for identifiable boundaries

The first step that Pomerantz and Fehr (1997) recommend is to select a boundaried sequence. The data fragment below represents one such sequence; in fact, it is a *side sequence* (Jefferson, 1972), where there is a temporary termination of some talk to deal with some other matter, after which the original sequence is resumed. So, in the following, the directions the teacher gives for a practice role-play in lines 1 and 2 are "suspended" while she deals with a question from a student in line 3; the role-play directions are then resumed in line 44.

TE: a Taiwanese female teacher; her turns are in italics with her non-verbal behavior in bold;

F2: Chinese female who acted as the clerk in the demo role-play;

M1: Korean male who acted as the customer in the demo role-play;

??: unable to identify speaker;

M?: unidentifiable male student.

Cream Cheese

```
1   TE:   so (.) >when you are< doing your role-play you can directly
2         specify (it)=
3   F2:   =[excuse me the <cheeddar> is kind of brea:d?
4   TE:   [moves to F2
5         (.5)
6   TE:   <it's a kind of> cheese.
7         (.5)
8   M1:   chee:se.=
9   F2:   =uh huh
10  TE:   [(yeah)
11        [nod
12  ??:   [cheddar cheese
13  ??:   [cheese
14  TE:   [(it means) a kind of ye:llow right?
15  ??:   [(
16  F2:   like a: (.2) [cream cheese?
17  TE:                [yellow
18  ??:                              ])
19        (.8)
20  TE:   cream cheese is [<whi:te.>
21                        [points to F2
22  M?:                   [%no::!%
23  F2:   other-[other:: (.2) other kind of.
24  M?:         [this (    ) a kind of % (cheese is [something else)
25  TE:                                             [uh::::: hhh (.8)
26                                                  [looks up
27  TE:   [it's other kind. [it's not cream cheese. [cream cheese
28        [looks at F2 [shakes head "no" [right hand in
29        cheese is softer!
30        pinch shape
31        (.)
32  F2:   [mmhmm
33  ??:   [%ye::s%
34  TE:   [and whi:te! (.5) but-! (.8) cheddar cheese is yellow.
35  ??:   (murmur)
36  TE:   %and% (.8)    [hard!
37                      [makes a fist and pounds it
38  ??:   [(    )
39  ??:   [(    )
40  ??:   [(    )
41  TE:   [okay::?
42        [looks down at then points to paper
43        (1.2)
44  TE:   so:- (.8) could you do that (.5) role-play. ...
```

2. Characterize the actions in the sequence by answering the question, "What is the participant doing in this turn?"

Lines 1–2	directions for role-play
Line 3	clarification question (Q1)
Line 6	(unplanned) explanation/answer (A1)
Line 9	continuer/acceptance/comment (C1a)
Line 10	confirmation (C1b)
Line 14	further explanation (more A1)
Line 16	question which displays understanding so far (Q2)
Line 17	repetition of "yellow" (more A1)
Line 20	explanation/answer (A2)
Line 23	display understanding of answer (C2/Q3)
Lines 25–30	explanation/answer (A3)
Line 32	continuer/acceptance/comment (C3)
Lines 34–37	continuation of A3
Line 41	final check of understanding
Line 44	resumption of prior talk about role-play

3. Consider how the packaging of actions, that is, how they are formed and delivered, provides for certain understandings

Line 3 contains a request for clarification about what exactly cheddar cheese is (Q1), prefaced by the "interruptive" marker excuse me, which shows F2's orientation to this turn being an interruption.

In *line 6*, TE structures her "answer" (A1) to F2's question in line 3 (Q1) as both an embedded correction of grammar (is kind of is reformulated as it's a kind of) and of the conceptual misunderstanding about cheddar cheese being a kind of bread. This answer is said slowly and clearly, as shown by the arrows. Notice the TE does not directly correct F2 with "no" or any other negative term.

In *line 9*, F2 claims (at least some) understanding (C1a) with uh huh, although this is not a very strong indication; this functions as the third turn in the classroom I-R-E sequence, although here the roles of speaker and recipient are switched (student asks question and evaluates instead of teacher).

In *lines 10–11*, TE confirms this understanding with what sounds like a yeah and an affirmative head nod (C1b). At this point, the side sequence is potentially complete, pending no further talk on the matter at hand.

In *line 14*, TE elaborates on line 6 (in a continuation of A1) by replacing the noun cheese from line 6 with the descriptor ye:llow (which is emphasized), still using the original (but corrected) structure of the initial question. The tag right? invites a confirmation of understanding.

In *line 16*, F2 displays her understanding of, or at least knowledge about, another kind of cheese, namely cream cheese, with her candidate understanding `like a: cream cheese?` formatted as a question (Q2).

In *line 17*, TE repeats `yellow` in overlap with `cream cheese` in line 16.

In *line 20*, TE "corrects" F2's understanding in line 16 by stating `cream cheese is <whi:te>` (A2), whereas cheddar cheese is yellow, as she said in line 14. Note again, "no" is not used as an explicit correction marker by the teacher, but by another student in overlap with "white" in line 22.

In *line 23*, F2 confirms her understanding that cheddar cheese is `other kind of` cheese, not cream cheese (C2/Q3).

At this point (*lines 25–30*), because TE responds to the prior C2 as if it were a question, I reinterpret line 23 as a question (Q3), although not formatted as such. Here, TE appears to be checking her own conceptualization of the two cheese types with her elongated hesitation (`uh:::`) and her gaze towards the ceiling. She confirms F2's understanding (`other kind of`, in line 23), with the statement `it's other kind` (A3). Then, she more explicitly rejects F2's understanding displayed in line 16, `it's not cream cheese`, at the same time shaking her head no. Then, she makes an additional contrast of cream and cheddar cheese (the first being color, yellow vs. white) by adding a second criterion of difference: consistency. That is, `cream cheese is softer!`, which is accompanied by a pinching hand gesture.

In *line 32*, F2 claims understanding (C3); this overlaps the continuation of TE's turn from line 29.

In *lines 34–37*, TE adds `and whi:te!`, marks the contrast with `but-!` then uses a parallel structure, `cheddar cheese is yellow and hard!`, now accompanied by a hand gesture of a pounding fist (more A3).

A final check of understanding in *line 41* precedes a return to the directions for the role-play activity that were suspended during this side sequence.

4. Consider how timing and turntaking provide for certain understandings of actions and the matters talked about

Just two observations seem relevant to this point. First, the "marvels of split-second turntaking" are present in lines 2–3, where F2 asks her question with no audible gap between it and TE's talk.

Secondly, as McHoul notes, teachers have the (sole) right and responsibility to answer student questions; here it is TE, and TE only who responds with A1 at line 6. After this answer, though, there is a general murmur in the class about cheese. This is replicated with Q2 at line 16, where only TE answers with A2 at line 20; and with Q3 at line 23, where TE answers in lines 25–30.

5. Consider how the ways the actions were accomplished suggest certain identities, roles, and/or relationships for the interactants

First, the participants in this ESL classroom are clearly oriented to their institutional "roles." As was mentioned, the teacher takes the responsibility for answering F2's question, which is characteristic of classrooms. It is also worth noting that the I-R-E structure of classroom interaction is maintained in this fragment, although the roles are reversed because it is a student asking a question (I), the teacher answering (R), and the student commenting (E). Still, the teacher has the final "say" in this sequence (line 41), which again shows how the teacher ultimately controls the turntaking in the classroom.

Now, to the question posed earlier: Is there evidence in *this* segment that either the teacher and/or the students show attention/orientation to the teacher being a NNEST? My initial response, based on the data as transcribed and analyzed, is no. In other words, no feature jumps out as relevant to this question, but in analyzing this fragment, it is unclear to me what such evidence might look like. In other words, how could a teacher (either consciously or unconsciously) "do being a nonnative speaker of English"? Although the pronunciation and fluency of TE are not represented in the transcript, hearing her talk, we would not mistake her for a native speaker. And she makes at least one surface error it's other kind in line 27. But she herself shows no awareness of the error (by a self-correction, for example); perhaps if she had self-corrected or apologized for this error, this might suggest a conscious orientation to the mistake, and perhaps by extension, to her language competence. Clearly, an examination of a larger portion of the classroom discourse would be necessary to draw any conclusions about this identity issue.

On the other hand, one might argue that there are two other places where her "nonnativeness," at least in a sociocultural sense, is on display. The first is in line 14, where the tag appended to a kind of yellow, right sounds tentative and checking; the second instance is her hesitation at line 25 (and the way she looks up as if thinking hard) in differentiating the two types of cheese. But this is speculation on my part, and I must, for the present, remain agnostic on the question posed.

Discussion

I didn't "find" any evidence of "nonnativeness" that the participants oriented to as relevant, nor did I expect to, consistent with CA orthodoxy, in which the analyst refrains from imposing pre-determined "relevancies" on the data. As a first try at looking at ESL classroom data where the teacher is a nonnative speaker of English, this analysis has suggested ways in which I might proceed in the future with similar data. I believe that this approach to understanding second language teacher practice is extremely valuable, because one of the unique strengths of conversation analysis as an analytic tool is its ability to supplement intuitions, retrospective recalls, and third person explanations about sources of data which, as mentioned above, are the standard in research on language teacher education. Furthermore, the results that emerge from CA make sense not just to researchers who undertake them, but to those involved in the interactions and others who have a stake in their outcomes.

Obviously, one such stakeholder is the teacher herself. Although she did not have the benefit of seeing the lesson transcripts and my analysis of them (because they were prepared and analyzed several years after she graduated and returned to Taiwan), she might have been interested in how she constructed her explanation; how teaching is highly unpredictable (who could guess that a learner would think cheddar cheese is a kind of bread?); and how "meaning making" and understanding are progressively and collaboratively constructed. More generally, lesson transcripts have proved useful in fostering the development of second language teachers' skills in asking questions (Cullen, 2001). In fact, I have been advised by graduate students who have taken my discourse analysis seminars that they wish they had been required to record and transcribe some of their own classroom discourse data during their pre-service practicum experience. In any case, it is increasingly clear that conversation analysis provides an innovative tool for understanding second teaching and learning; Riggenbach (1999) discusses many activities that use CA and other forms of discourse analysis for ESL/EFL learners.

Finally, because of the rather "one-dimensional" nature of conversation analytic results, information about teacher beliefs, knowledge, and the like will be collected and then "triangulated" with the transcribed data in a study currently underway. As one of the teachers in a subsequent project (e.g. Lazaraton, 2002b) comments:

> Through introspection, I think I'll be given a chance to reflect on my teaching and teacher beliefs, and through discourse analysis, I'll probably see how my teacher belief is practiced (or not). What a great opportunity for teacher development!

Limitations

Obviously, no substantive claims can be made based on the analysis of one short fragment taken from the classroom discourse involving just one teacher. On the other hand, developing a collection of such instances would help build a persuasive case for these sorts of questions. I am also well aware of the inherent limitations of the CA approach. Aside from a number of theoretical and conceptual objections to CA (see Lazaraton, 2002a), a major obstacle for those wishing to learn and carry out CA is the fact that it is difficult, if not impossible, to learn without the benefit of tutelage under a trained analyst and/or with others. As a result, the number of teacher educators who feel comfortable with and driven to use the methodology will undoubtedly remain small. Related to this is the labor-intensive nature of CA, especially the transcription process, where a 50-minute class can take as much as 20 hours of transcription effort just to represent the verbal behavior. This commitment of time and expertise makes it quite impractical for the conversation analyst to look at the discourse produced by more than a few teachers in any one study.

Another problem with interpretive discourse analysis in general is that it results in copious amounts of transcribed talk but no "hard" statistical data, making it generally difficult for the researcher to find a home in professional dissemination outlets, such as conferences and journals. It is hoped that, when the results of this research can be more widely circulated, argued, and replicated, not only among second language teacher educators but among the larger community of applied linguists, the CA approach to spoken discourse will achieve a more central status in our discipline.

Conclusion

The purpose of this study was to analyze a small fragment of talk in order to begin to understand how language ability and teaching performance interact in an ESL classroom taught by a nonnative speaker of English. The analysis suggests a rather "ordinary" explanation was achieved in the data. Although no firm conclusions can be put forward from the limited analysis of just one segment of classroom data, it is rewarding to find another application of conversation analysis, one which has the potential to inform both our beliefs about and our practices in second language teaching and learning.

Appendix: Transcription Notation Symbols (from Atkinson & Heritage, 1984)

(1) *unfilled pauses or gaps* – periods of silence, timed in tenths of a second by counting "beats" of elapsed time. Micropauses, those of less than 0.2

seconds, are symbolized (.); longer pauses appear as a time within parentheses: (0.5) is five tenths of a second.

(2) *colon (:)* – a lengthened sound or syllable; more colons prolong the stretch.
(3) **dash (-)** – a cut-off, usually a glottal stop.
(4) *.hhh* – an inbreath; *.hhh!* – strong inhalation.
(5) *hhh* – exhalation; *hhh!* – strong exhalation.
(6) *hah, huh, heh, hnh* – all represent laughter, depending on the sounds produced. All can be followed by an (!), signifying stronger laughter.
(7) *(hhh)* – breathiness within a word.
(8) *punctuation* – markers of intonation rather than clausal structure; a period (.) is falling intonation, a question mark (?) is rising intonation, a comma (,) is continuing intonation. A question mark followed by a comma (?,) represents rising intonation, but is weaker than a (?). An exclamation mark (!) is animated intonation.
(9) *equal sign (=)* – a latched utterance, no interval between utterances.
(10) *brackets ([   ])* – overlapping talk, where utterances start and/or end simultaneously.
(11) *percent signs (%   %)* – quiet talk.
(12) *asterisks (*   *)* – creaky voice.
(13) *carat (^)* – a marked rising shift in pitch.
(14) *arrows (>   <)* – the talk speeds up; *arrows (<   >)* – the talk slows down.
(15) *psk* – a lip smack; *tch* – a tongue click.
(16) *underlining or CAPS* – a <u>word</u> or SOUND is emphasized.
(17) *arrow (→)* – a feature of interest to the analyst.
(18) *empty parentheses (   )* – transcription doubt, uncertainty; words within parentheses are uncertain.
(19) *double parentheses ((   ))* – non-vocal action, details of scene.

References

Atkinson, J. M. and Heritage, J. (eds) (1984) *Structures of Social Action: Studies in Conversation Analysis*. Cambridge: Cambridge University Press.

Boxer, D. (2002) *Applying Sociolinguistics: Domains and Face-to-face Interaction*. Amsterdam: John Benjamins.

Braine, G. (ed.) (1999) *Non-native Educators in English Language Teaching*. Mahwah, NJ: Lawrence Erlbaum.

Canale, M. and Swain, M. (1980) Theoretical bases of communicative approaches to second language teaching and testing. *Applied Linguistics* 1 (1), 1–47.

Chaudron, C. (1988) *Second Language Classrooms*. Cambridge: Cambridge University Press.

Cook, V. (1999) Going beyond the native speaker in language teaching. *TESOL Quarterly* 33 (2), 185–209.

Cullen, R. (2001) The use of lesson transcripts for developing teachers' classroom language. *SYSTEM* 29 (1), 27–43.

Drew, P. and Heritage, J. (1992) Analysing talk at work: An introduction. In P. Drew and J. Heritage (eds) *Talk at Work: Interaction in Institutional Settings* (pp. 3–65). Cambridge: Cambridge University Press.

Freeman, D. and Johnson, K. E. (1998) Reconceptualizing the knowledge-base of language teacher education. *TESOL Quarterly* 32 (3), 397–417.

Jefferson, G. (1972) Side sequences. In D. Sudnow (ed.) *Studies in Social Interaction* (pp. 294–338). New York: Free Press.

Johnson, K. E. (1995) *Understanding Communication in Second Language Classrooms.* Cambridge: Cambridge University Press.

Johnson, K. E. (1999) *Understanding Language Teaching: Reasoning in Action.* Boston, MA: Heinle and Heinle.

Klingner, J. K. and Vaughn, S. (2000) The helping behaviors of fifth graders while using collaborative strategic reading during ESL content classes. *TESOL Quarterly* 34 (1), 69–98.

Lazaraton, A. (2002a) *A Qualitative Approach to the Validation of Oral Language Tests.* Cambridge: Cambridge University Press.

Lazaraton, A. (2002b) "But this is very Minnesotan": Incidental displays of cultural knowledge in the ESL classroom. Manuscript submitted for publication.

Lerner, G. H. (1995) Turn design and the organization of participation in instructional activities. *Discourse Processes* 19, 111–131.

Liu, J. (1999) Nonnative-English speaking professionals in TESOL. *TESOL Quarterly* 33 (1), 85–102.

McHoul, A. W. (1978) The organization of turns at formal talk in the classroom. *Language in Society* 7, 183–213.

McHoul, A. W. (1990) The organization of repair in classroom talk. *Language in Society* 19 (3), 349–377.

Markee, N. (1995) Teachers answers to students' questions: Problematizing the issue of meaning making. *Issues in Applied Linguistics* 6 (2), 63–92.

Markee, N. (2000) *Conversation Analysis.* Mahwah, NJ: Lawrence Erlbaum.

Medgyes, P. (1992) Native or nonnative: Who's worth more? *ELT Journal* 46, 340–349.

Mehan, H. (1985) The structure of classroom discourse. In T. A. van Dijk (ed.) *Handbook of Discourse Analysis Volume 3: Discourse and Dialogue* (pp. 119–131). London: Academic Press.

Milambiling, J. (2000) How nonnative speakers as teachers fit into the equation. *TESOL Quarterly* 34 (2), 324–328.

Pomerantz, A. (1984) Agreeing and disagreeing with assessments: Some features of preferred/dispreferred turn shape. In J. M. Atkinson and J. Heritage (eds) *Structures of Social Action: Studies in Conversation Analysis* (pp. 57–101). Cambridge: Cambridge University Press.

Pomerantz, A. and Fehr, B. J. (1997) Conversation analysis: An approach to the study of social action as sense making practices. In T. A. van Dijk (ed.) *Discourse as Social Interaction, Discourse Studies: A Multidisciplinary Introduction* (Vol. 2) (pp. 64–91). London: Sage Publications.

Riggenbach, H. (1999) *Discourse Analysis in the Language Classroom. Volume 1: The Spoken Language.* Ann Arbor: University of Michigan Press.

Sacks, H. (1984) Notes on methodology. In J. M. Atkinson and J. Heritage (eds) *Structures of Social Action: Studies in Conversation Analysis* (pp. 21–27). Cambridge: Cambridge University Press.

Sacks, H., Schegloff, E. A., and Jefferson, G. (1974) A simplest systematics for the organization of turntaking in conversation. *Language* 50, 696–735.

Samimy, K. K. and Brutt-Griffler, J. (1999) To be a native or nonnative speaker: Perceptions of "non-native" students in a graduate TESOL program. In G. Braine (ed.) *Non-native Educators in English Language Teaching* (pp. 127–144). Mahwah, NJ: Lawrence Erlbaum.

Saylor, K. J. (2000) "But this program is designed for native speakers . . .": The perceived needs of nonnative English speaking students in MA TESOL programs. Unpublished Plan B Paper, University of Minnesota, Minneapolis.

Schegloff, E. A. (1993) Reflections on quantification in the study of conversation. *Research on Language and Social Interaction* 26 (1), 99–128.

Schegloff, E. A., Jefferson, G., and Sacks, H. (1977) The preference for self-correction in the organization of repair in conversation. *Language* 53, 361–382.

Schegloff, E. A. and Sacks, H. (1973) Opening up closings. *Semiotica* 7, 289–327.

Ulichny, P. (1996) Performed conversations in an ESL classroom. *TESOL Quarterly* 30 (4), 739–764.

Wong, J. and Olsher, D. (2000). Reflections on conversation analysis and nonnative speaker talk: An interview with Emanuel A. Schegloff. *Issues in Applied Linguistics* 11 (1), 111–128.

Chapter 4

"Practicing Speaking" in Spanish: Lessons from a High School Foreign Language Classroom

JOAN KELLY HALL

The study reported in this chapter investigates the processes and outcomes of Spanish language learning as they were constructed in the communicative practices of a first year high school Spanish-as-a-foreign-language classroom. The study draws on recent research demonstrating the intrinsic link between learners' extended engagement in their classroom activities with other more expert participants and their development of particular constellations of communicative knowledge, skills, and abilities. Using transcriptions of classroom interactions occurring over a nine-month period, I identify the significant communicative routines by which this high school community defined and developed its understandings of and skills in "speaking Spanish-as-a-foreign language." It was found that over the academic year the level of intellectual, social, and linguistic content remained low, and the students became less actively involved. The findings make visible the consequentiality of high school foreign language study, since what the students learn in these first years of language learning, both in terms of what counts as language and as the process of learning, sets the foundation upon which their subsequent development is based. Such understandings can help in the creation of alternative learning contexts and practices that are more likely to develop students' skills and abilities in using the target language that we consider to be appropriate for meeting their academic, social, and communicative needs.

Introduction

A view of second and foreign language classrooms as communities of learners has gained much currency these last few years among researchers in the field of applied linguistics interested in the study of language learning (e.g. Boxer & Cortes-Conde, 2000; Duff, 1995, 1996; Duff & Early,

1999; Hall, 1998; Lin, 1999a, 1999b, 2000; Poole, 1992; Toohey, 1998; Willett, 1995; Zuengler & Cole, 1999). In such communities, learning and teaching are considered to be inseparable parts of a socially situated, collaborative process involving learners' extended engagement in their classroom activities with other more expert participants, such as their teachers. Through such participation, learners are socialized into particular communicative skills, abilities, and understandings of the target language. At the same time, they are socialized into particular identities as learners and users of the target language.

This process of socialization is realized to a large extent through the use of language and, more specifically, through the recurring language routines or communicative practices constructed in the face-to-face interactions between teachers and students (Schieffelin & Ochs, 1996). In these interactions, teachers play a crucial role in that they provide models of what they consider appropriate ways of using and interpreting the target language and, through various means of assistance, guide learners into particular understandings and ways of using these patterns of interaction. Moreover, in their allocations of turns in the interactions, teachers mediate the opportunities their students will have to participate in and learn from them (Shultz *et al.*, 1982). In so doing, teachers, and more specifically the interactional practices they construct in their interactions with the students, shape students' communicative abilities as both learners and users of the target language in fundamental ways. From this perspective of learning, a key to understanding fully both the processes and outcomes of learners' development lies in our close examination of the communicative practices into which they are socialized.

Background

The focus of much recent research on language classroom communities from this perspective has been on the socialization practices of *second* language contexts. Toohey (1998) and Willett (1995), for example, examined the socialization practices of elementary classrooms that included ESL learners. Their findings reveal how the children's participation in different instructional routines led their teachers to perceive the children's language abilities and prospects as good language learners differently. These perceptions, in turn, led to further differentiation in terms of the kinds learning opportunities the teachers made available to the children, and their subsequent language development. Additional research on second language contexts has focused on both secondary level classrooms and university settings that included ESL learners, as well as ESL classrooms (e.g. Duff & Early, 1999; Jacoby & Gonzalez, 1991; Poole, 1992; Zuengler & Cole, 1999).

Although considered important in their own right as language learning communities, the socialization practices of *foreign* language classrooms have been given far less research attention. Of those classrooms that have been examined, most of the focus has been on communities of English language learners. Lin (1999a, 1999b, 2000), for example, investigated the socialization practices of several junior form English language classrooms in Hong Kong, and Duff (1995, 1996) provided details of the socialization practices of English immersion classrooms in Hungary.

While the findings from such studies have been helpful in providing us with insights into the varied communicative practices by which individuals are socialized into communities of learners of English as a foreign language, they do not tell us anything about the classroom worlds of learners of languages other than English. Investigations of such classrooms are especially important given the languages' status relative to English as the world's lingua franca, and the limited opportunities that learners in the United States, particularly at the high school level, have to use the languages outside of the classroom. Such limited contact outside of the classroom context makes the environments created *in* foreign language classrooms of critical importance to learners' communicative development.

It was with the recognition of the need for such empirical evidence on which to build a more encompassing theory of language learning, and, in turn, provide for a more adequate conceptualization of language pedagogy that the study reported on here was undertaken.

The Study: A Primary Socialization Practice of a First Year Spanish-as-a-foreign-language Classroom

The data presented here come from a year-long investigation of a first year high school Spanish-as-a-foreign-language classroom. Since oral communication is both a primary medium of learning and an object of pedagogical attention in foreign language classrooms, and since for most foreign language learners, their classroom practices are a primary, if not sole, source of the target language, I considered the socialization practices of these classrooms to play an especially significant role in shaping learners' understanding of and ability to communicate in the target language.

As noted earlier, determining where learners' extended participation in their classroom practices leads in terms of the development of communicative skills and abilities in the target language, and whether these paths of development are appropriate to learners' social, academic, and other communicative needs requires minimally an examination of the practices themselves. Such examination includes analysis of their conventional purposes, rhetorical frameworks, and linguistic resources. Thus, the primary questions guiding the study were:

- What are the communicative practices into which students are being socialized into in this particular community of learners?
- Where do they lead the learners in terms of particular understandings of and communicative skills and abilities in Spanish?

In what follows, I first give a brief synopsis of the methods used to collect and analyze the data. I then present the findings on one particular communicative activity designed by the teacher to provide students with opportunities to "practice speaking Spanish." I discuss the communicative activity in terms of its conventional linguistic and interactional features and the particular uses and understandings of Spanish into which the students were being socialized through their extended involvement in it.

Setting and participants

The classroom community was located in a suburban public high school and was comprised of one teacher and 15 students who were studying Spanish for the first time. I should note that the composition of the student body varied slightly throughout the year. At the beginning of the academic year, the community was comprised of 16 students. Shortly after the year began, two students joined the original group, raising the total number of students to 18. By the end of the first semester, however, three had dropped the course, making a total of 15 students for the second semester. Of this group of 15, 10 were Anglo, one was Hispanic and four were African-American. Four of the students were male and 11 were female. Fourteen were ninth graders and one was in tenth grade. All were taking this course because it was part of their college preparatory. At the time of the study, the teacher had been teaching both Spanish and French for over 15 years and she was the chair of the foreign languages department at her school. While not a native speaker of Spanish, the teacher was considered by her peers to be fully proficient in the language.

Methodology

The approach to the collection and analysis of data taken here is best described as interactional sociolinguistic, or micro-ethnographic (Garcez, 1997; Watson-Gegeo, 1997). In comparison to ethnographies of communication, which entail a more encompassing analysis of the communicative habits of a community in their totality (Hymes, 1980: 13), micro-ethnographies entail a close focus on social interactions, and in particular on the particular means by which they are jointly constructed. As pointed out by Watson-Gegeo (1997: 138), micro-ethnographies "may offer a detailed analysis of only one type of event or even a single instance of an event, perhaps contrasted with a second type of instance found in another context."

The primary source of data for this study are video and audio tapes recorded during weekly visits to the classroom for one full academic year, beginning in August and ending in May. During each visit, I recorded the classroom activities, took notes on my observations of them, and collected all materials used in the activities, such as written exercises, transparencies and so on. Thirty video and audio tapes were collected over the academic year.

For this particular investigation, I was interested in examining the classroom interactions that were conducted solely or primarily in Spanish and whose instructional aim, according to the teacher, was to "practice speaking." I was interested in this particular instructional activity since, in conversations with the teacher at the beginning of the school year, she indicated that she considered it to be important to the students' communicative development in Spanish and so was a major component of her teaching. Thus, I considered the activity of "practicing speaking" to be a primary source for the development of the students' communicative abilities in and understandings of Spanish.

Initial analysis of the 30 tapes revealed that seven of the tapes were of classes conducted by the student teacher apprenticing with the regular classroom teacher, and contained little extended use of Spanish. It further revealed that the classroom talk of eight of the remaining 23 tapes was primarily in English. The focus of the interactions of these classes included the direct instruction of grammar, review of written work, the discussion of upcoming school events, and the management of classroom concerns. In a few cases, there was little to no talk because students were taking a quiz or test. The classroom interactions of remaining tapes of 15 50-minute class meetings were conducted primarily in Spanish, and thus were used for this analysis.[1]

The tapes were transcribed in four stages. Initially, a research assistant transcribed each audio tape. The video tapes were used primarily to clarify when it was difficult to comprehend the talk on the audio tapes, or when it was unclear who was speaking. The transcripts and tapes were then passed to the classroom teacher, who listened to the tapes and modified the transcripts accordingly. She also assisted in identifying speakers, interpreting the interactions and in other ways provided useful information and insights about the interactions from her "insider" viewpoint. The transcriptions were then passed back to the research assistant who recorded the modifications. As a final check, I listened to the tapes and confirmed the modifications. Where there were discrepancies, the teacher was the final judge. Those places where no one was able to understand the taped interaction were marked as unintelligible.

Once the tapes were transcribed, the teacher was asked to indicate on the transcripts those portions of the interactions where the official instructional aim was to provide the students with opportunities for practice in speaking Spanish, noting the points at which this particular instructional routine began and when it ended. Thus, it was the teacher who provided the initial framework for the activity of "practicing speaking" on which the more detailed examinations of the event in the second stage of analysis, explained below, are based. It was determined from the teacher's analysis that the average length of time spent on the instructional activity of "practicing speaking" over the 15 classes was approximately 25 minutes per class.

The second stage of analysis entailed identifying the recurring patterns of communicative actions used by the teacher and students in their interactions with each other in this particular activity. The function of each utterance was decided based on the role it played in moving the interaction along. Functional frameworks of the conventional or typical sequence of utterances were then developed and used as analytic grids in making systematic comparisons with subsequent interactions within and across the 15 class meetings.

Findings

Analysis of all instances of the routine of "practicing speaking" revealed the following characteristics. First, it was, not surprisingly, the teacher who took primary responsibility for beginning the activity, orchestrating its development and ending the activity. She provided most of the talk, decided what counted as a relevant topic and a relevant comment on the topic, and moved the interaction from student to student and contribution to contribution, deciding which communicative behaviors of the students were to count as part of the performance. Her questions and comments were usually directed to the whole group of students rather than to any particular individual student. That is, when she talked, she talked to the group at large, rarely singling out any individual student.

For their part, students contributed to the interaction by offering responses to teacher questions and comments at will. They could also ask their own questions, or in some other way comment on or add to the ongoing talk when they wanted to. That is, they did not have to bid for the floor with raised hands, but rather could decide for themselves when to take a turn, and so could make a contribution without having to wait to be called on by the teacher. In this respect, the interactions were more similar to conversations among acquaintances or friends rather than to typical teacher–student interaction, where students are usually selected for turns by the teacher or must bid for them by raising their hands (Cazden, 1988; Patthey-Chavez, 2002). Student contributions were sometimes acknowledged by the teacher and sometimes even by other students. Generally, however, the students were not required to pay strict attention to or extend the talk of the teacher or each other.

As the teacher talked to the large group, the students often interacted with their nearby seat mates. While there was occasional use of Spanish in these whispered side sequences, English was the predominant code. As long as the students interacted with each other quietly, and were not major distractions to the larger official instructional discourse, the teacher did not prevent them from doing so. Thus, there was usually a steady hum of background talk among the students throughout each class meeting. When the level of noise from the small group interactions became too loud, the teacher called for the attention of all the students, and once she had it, began again speaking to the large group. While there were a few instances during the year when the teacher needed to speak sternly in order to re-secure the large group attention, acts which were primarily conducted in Spanish, the students never became totally disruptive or unruly. They always allowed themselves to be called back to the task, and become involved with the teacher's steady stream of talk once again.

Excerpt 1, taped in early October, two months into the school year, is an example of the teacher–student interaction that typified this instructional practice.

Excerpt 1[2]

1	T:	A Wimpy le gustan las hamburguesas Popeye dice no Wimpy dice
		(*Wimpy likes hamburgers Popeye says no Wimpy says*)
2	S1:	Wimpy
3	T:	Wimpy Wimpy dice Popeye me prestas dinero para una hamburguesa y te lo devuelvo el lunes el martes el miércoles el jueves el viernes qué día
		(*Wimpy Wimpy says Popeye loan me some money for a hamburger and I'll return it to you on Monday on Tuesday on Wednesday on Thursday on Friday what day*)
4	S2:	El viernes
		(*on Friday*)
5	T:	Es el martes y te lo devuelvo el martes siempre es el martes ya el martes que hamburguesa hoy y te devuelvo el dinero. give you the money back el martes
		(*it's on Tuesday and I'll return it to you on Tuesday always it's on Tuesday already that hamburger today and I'll return your money on Tuesday*)
6	S2:	So he pays the money
7	T:	Sí es Wimpy verdad sí me gusta Wimpy sí te gusta Popeye
		(*yes it's Wimpy right yes I like Wimpy yes do you like Popeye*)
8	S2:	Sí me gusta Popeye
		(*yes I like Popeye*)
9	T:	Ah bueno pues a Wimpy les gusta uh le gustan las hamburguesas verdad a Wimpy hamburguesas bueno a Popeye hamburguesas
		(*ah good well Wimpy like uh Wimpy likes hamburgers right Wimpy hamburgers good Popeye hamburgers*)

As we can see here, the teacher does most of the talking and her talk is primarily in Spanish. Although she does not call on any specific student to answer the two questions she poses in turns 3 and 7 (*qué día* and *te gusta Popeye*) one student who apparently had been attending to the interaction answers them. The student's attempt to figure out what the teacher is talking about, as seen in his comment "So he pays the money" in turn 6 is further evidence of his active attention to this particular stretch of talk. Although it is difficult to tell whether the student understands the point the teacher is trying to make about Wimpy, he apparently understands the question the teacher asks about Popeye as he responds appropriately. Although it is not noted in the transcript, a steady hum of voices provides a background to this interaction. Evidently the teacher does not consider it disruptive, as she makes no attempt to stop it.

A closer examination of instances of the instructional routine as they were constructed by the teacher and students over the academic year revealed two slightly different versions. The first, which, for lack of a more original title I have termed *the listing and labeling of objects and concepts*, involved just that – the listing and labeling of such rudimentary items as, for example, food, articles of clothing, numbers, colors, days, months, seasons, dates, family relationships, and items found in the class-room. Excerpt 2, also taped in October, is a typical example of the direction taken by this particular rendition.

Excerpt 2

1	**T:**	Ok aquí tenemos Coca Cola tenemos Pepsi Cola tenemos Fresca cómo se llaman
		(*ok, here we have Coca Cola we have Pepsi Cola we have Fresca what are they called*)
2	**S1:**	Budweiser
3	**T:**	Refresco refresco sí se llaman refrescos sí y aquí hay refresco. Rápidamente qué es ésto
		(*soft drink soft drink yes they're called soft drinks yes and here there is a soft drink. Quickly what is this?*)
4	**S2:**	O::u
5	**S1:**	Uhum ice cream.
6	**T:**	Helado muy bien señor el helado
		(*ice cream very well sir ice cream*)
7	**S1:**	Helado
		(*ice cream*)
8	**T:**	Clase qué es ésto aquí
		(*class what is this here*)
9	**S3:**	Papas fritas
		(*french fries*)
10	**T:**	Papas fritas muy bien señorita aquí clase
		(*french fries very well miss here class*)
11	**S4:**	Kweso
12	**T:**	Muy bien queso queso hay queso aquí
		(*very well cheese cheese there is cheese here*)
13	**S3:**	Mantequila
		(*butter*)

14	**S2:**	Uh mantequilla
		(butter)
15	**T:**	Mantequilla mantequilla aquí
		(butter butter here)
16	**Ss:**	( )
17	**T:**	Limonada limonada muy bien limonada sí los refrescos son

17 **T:** Limonada limonada muy bien limonada sí los refrescos son
( ) la limonada yo no considero limonada refresco no sé sí no
yo no sé para mí no es para mí ( ) [ok limonada. por favor
(lemonade lemonade very well lemonade yes soft drinks are lemonade
I don't consider lemonade a soft drink I don't know yes I don't know
for me it isn't for me [ok lemonade please)

18 **Ss:** [( )

19 **T:** Clase qué es esto
(class what is this?)

20 **Ss:** Ensalada
(salad)

In this activity, the teacher points to a transparency on an overhead projector with a picture of food items displayed on a table. As she does, she asks the large group "Qué es ésto?" (What is this?), or simply points and asks "Aquí" (here), as we see in turns 3, 8, 10, and 12. There is no particular order to the turn-taking; those students who are following the interaction and feeling so inclined respond with the word or words of the item to which the teacher is pointing.

During the first part of the year, the specific subject of the listing and labeling routine was usually based on pictures or other visual cues displayed by the teacher on the overhead projector or in her hand. During the second semester, pictures and exercises found in the classroom textbook were a frequent source of items. As noted earlier, while the teacher was directing the large group of students through the interaction, individual students were allowed to talk quietly to each other, even if their talk had little to do with the official topic of the instructional activity. The listing and labeling usually ended when the level of noise from the small group interactions became too loud or the teacher decided to move on to something else.

The other version of the instructional routine was what I have termed *lexical chaining*. It typically began with a question that required a yes or no response such as "Te gusta la música?" (Do you like music?) or "Tienes sueño?" (Are you tired?). Only on a few occasions was a wh-question such as "What did you eat for Thanksgiving?" or "What did you get for Christmas?" used. This routine varied from *listing and labeling* primarily in that student responses, whether just a yes or no, or a listing of items, were usually not known to the teacher, and all were expected to be in complete sentences in Spanish.

There were two ways the routine proceeded. Sometimes the same question was asked of several students. At other times a word or two was changed making it a slightly different but syntactically related question. If a student's answer was not a complete sentence, or if part of the utterance was not in Spanish, the teacher usually repeated the student's response in Spanish, adding whatever was needed to make it a complete sentence. Sometimes the student repeated the teacher's utterance, but it was not demanded of him or her. As with the first version, this interactional routine usually ended when the small group talk became loud enough to disrupt the large group interaction, or when the teacher decided to move on to a different instructional activity. Excerpt 3, taken from a class conducted in May, at the end of the academic year, is an example of this version of the routine.

Excerpt 3

1	**T:**	Sueño tiene sueño tienes sueño señor
		(*sleepy he is sleepy are you sleepy sir*)
2	**S1:**	No I'm great feeling great
3	**T:**	[No tengo
		(*I'm not*)
4	**S2:**	[Tengo sueño
		(*I'm sleepy*)
5	**S1:**	No tengo es swal [swal
6	**T:**	[sueño
7	**S1:**	No tengo sueño
		(*I'm not sleepy*)
8	**T:**	No tengo sueño (to another student) tú tienes sueño señor la verdad sí
		(*I'm not sleepy are you sleepy sir the truth yes*)
9	**S2:**	( )
10	**T:**	Tengo sueño
		(*I'm sleepy*)
11	**S2:**	Sí tengo sueño
		(*I'm sleepy*)
12	**T:**	Sí tengo sueño sí tengo sueño
		(*yes I'm sleepy yes I'm sleepy*)
13	**S2:**	Sí tengo sueño
		(*yes I'm sleepy*)

14   **T:**   Sí tengo sueño
              (*yes I'm sleepy*)
15   **S3:** No tengo sueño
              (*no I'm not sleepy*)
16   **T:**   Yo tengo sueño pero no tengo   [mucho sueño
              (*I'm sleepy but I'm not very sleepy*)
17   **S4:**   [What's sueño
18   **S1:** Tired man
19   **T:**   Sueño tener sueño sí él tiene mucho sueño en la clase de
              español verdad
              (*sleepy to be sleepy yes he is very tired in Spanish class right*)
20   **S5:** Sí
              (*yes*)
21   **T:**   Pero tambien tiene sueño en la clase de álgebra tiene sueño en
              la clase de inglés es correcto
              (*but also he is sleepy in algebra class he's sleepy in English class is
              that right*)
22   **S5:** No
23   **T:**   No no es correcto solo en la clase de español
              (*no it's not right only in Spanish class*)
24   **S5:** No
25   **T:**   No no en la clase de español, okay, por favor tienes miedo de
              cucarachas
              (*no not in Spanish class ok please are you afraid of cockroaches*)
26   **S6:** Medo?
27   **T:**   Tienes miedo de cucarachas sabes cucarachas cucarachas Raid[3]
              (*are you afraid of cockroaches you know cockroaches cockroaches*)
28   **Ss:** [Oh oh, oh
29   **S6:** [Sí tengo miedo de cucarachas
              (*yes I'm afraid of cockroaches*)
30   **T:**   Sí tengo miedo de cucarachas yo no tengo sí tienes miedo de
              cucarachas
              (*yes I'm afraid of cockroaches I'm not yes you are afraid of cock-
              roaches*)
31   **S6:** Sí tengo la cucaracha
              (*yes I have a cockroach*)
32   **T:**   Tienes una cucaracha o tienes miedo de cucarachas
              (*do you have a cockroach or are you afraid of cockroaches*)
33   **S6:** Huh
34   **T:**   Miedo
              (*fear*)

35	**S6:**	[Do I like 'em
36	**T:**	[Are you scared of 'em
37	**S6:**	Yes I'm afraid of them
38	**T:**	Oh ok, tengo miedo
		(*oh ok I'm afraid*)
39	**S6:**	Tengo miedo
		(*I'm afraid*)
40	**T:**	De cucarachas
		(*of cockroaches*)
41	**S6:**	De cucarachas
		(*of cockroaches*)
42	**T:**	Tengo miedo de las cucarachas
		(*I'm afraid of cockroaches*)
43	**S6:**	Tengo miedo de cucarachas
		(*I'm afraid of cockroaches*)

As we see here, the teacher begins by asking a student a simple yes-or-no question. Because the student initially answers in English, the teacher leads him through the construction of an appropriate response in Spanish as seen in turns 3, 6, and 8. Once this is accomplished, she moves on, asking the same question of another student. The interaction continues in the same way up until turn 19 when the teacher qualifies the question by asking whether one of the students felt tired in the Spanish class. This leads to a slightly extended interaction with the student (turns 19–25), who appears to be confused about the topic of the teacher's comments. Rather than sorting through the student's misunderstandings, however, the teacher switches topic with her question "Are you afraid of cockroaches," in turn 25. This, as we see, also leads to some confusion. The student who engaged with the teacher in this part of the routine evidently thought that she was being asked if she *liked* cockroaches (turn 35). In an effort to clarify what she was asking, the teacher translated her question into English (turn 36), and after helping the student to produce a complete utterance in Spanish (turns 38–43), moves along with the lexical chaining.

To recap, the instructional routine "practice speaking" constructed by the teacher in her interactions with the students took place almost entirely in Spanish, with the teacher providing most of the talk. In addition, she chose the topics for discussion, and took full responsibility for moving the conversation from topic to topic and student to student. Teacher questions and comments were generally directed to the group at large rather than to specific students. Students who wished to contribute to the interaction did not usually have to bid for turns, but, instead, were able to contribute voluntarily.

Finally, two slightly different versions of the practice were realized over the year. In the first version the questions asked by the teacher were most often display questions, where the teacher was familiar with the names of the objects and concepts that the students were asked to list or label. In the second version, what I have termed lexical chaining, the questions posed by the teacher were usually about learner preferences and so student responses, while predictable, were not necessarily known by the teacher. What linked the utterances together was not a larger, topical focus, but rather chains of similar lexical items.

Over the course of the academic year, two changes to the instructional routine of "practicing speaking" were noted. At the beginning, the class engaged in it for short periods, about four or five minutes at a time, sometimes interspersing several renditions of it over the 50-minute class period. As the year progressed, the amount of time spent "practicing speaking" increased so that, by the end of the academic year, the routine lasted up to 30 minutes at a time.

In addition to the change in duration of the routine, there were some subtle changes to the quality of student involvement. At the beginning of the year, student interest in participating in the routines seemed high. They regularly attempted to figure out what the teacher was saying as she talked and seemed eager to contribute to the discourse. At any one time, several students would respond to the teacher's questions, and they usually did so animatedly, evidenced by the high number of simultaneous turns, the varied pitch of their utterances, the multiple repetitions of the teacher's and others' utterances and the fast pace of the talk. As the year progressed, however, the students seemed to lose interest. They took less responsibility for moving the interaction along, volunteering fewer responses, and paying less attention to their peers' contributions. Moreover, there were fewer simultaneous turns, less echoing of each other's words, and the teacher more frequently had to ask the same question several times to elicit a student response.

While there were slight changes to the duration of the routine and the student involvement in them, one aspect of the routine remained the same over the year: There was little to no variation in its linguistic, cognitive, and interactional substance and thus in the skills and abilities needed to participate in it. In the first part of the year, the activity of "practicing speaking" consisted of short, simple speech acts involving questions and comments on topics that were conceptually familiar and uncomplicated, making it easy for learners not only to guess the communicative intent of the teacher's talk, but to contribute to the interactions themselves. Moreover, they were able to participate voluntarily, and their participation rarely had to consist of more than a phrase or two. As a beginning practice for appropriating novices into using and interpreting general oral communicative skills in Spanish, these features seem reasonable, and even helpful.

However, if we compare Excerpts 1 and 2, which occurred in October, two months into the academic year, to Excerpt 3, which occurred in late May, two weeks before the school year ended, we can find few significant changes in these features. By and large, the content of the routines and the knowledge and skills needed to participate in them remained conceptually, linguistically, and interactionally simple. Teacher questions and comments, for example, remained at low cognitive and linguistic levels as they rarely asked students to do more than list familiar objects or respond to very simple yes-or-no questions. Likewise, student contributions remained at an equally low level. Their contributions rarely extended beyond short phrases and, in providing them, the learners rarely had to attend to each other's contributions, as there continued to be little attempt by the teacher to weave them into some larger topical or thematic discussion.

In summary, the particular understandings of and skills and abilities in Spanish into which this first year high school Spanish class of students was being socialized via their participation in the instructional routine of "practicing speaking" entailed little more than the listing and labeling of some common objects and concepts, and providing some personal information that, for the most part, centered on confirming one's likes and dislikes. Over the year, the duration of the routines increased, the level of intellectual, social, and linguistic content remained low, and the students became less actively involved.

Discussion

Several concerns about the communicative world of Spanish into which the students were being socialized in the routine of "practicing speaking" arise from these findings. Perhaps the most significant is its paucity of socially or intellectually challenging Spanish communicative skills, abilities, and understandings. As we saw in the excerpts, the use of Spanish into which the students were being socialized was lacking in almost anything that could be considered cognitively, linguistically or socially meaningful, or motivating. Rather, it was comprised of little more than lists of simple vocabulary words, simple grammatical structures, and simple communicative acts. In terms of learning to speak Spanish, the set of skills needed to be full participants was minimal at best, involving little more than listing, labeling, repeating after the teacher, or recalling. Rarely did the students' participation involve the use of abstract concepts or syntactically complex utterances. Nor were they given opportunities to discuss intellectually weighty matters, or even temporally displaced events. Instead, the focus remained on the concrete here-and-now world of the classroom, using only the most basic of personal expressions to do so.

Likewise, since from the beginning participation in the routine involved primarily having only to listen to the talk of the teacher, only the simplest conversational skills were required. Students could participate as much or as little as they wanted, and needed to do little more than shout out their utterances. On the positive side, these features gave the interactions more of a conversational or small talk, rather than instructional, feel to them, and so engendered little discomfort in participating on the part of the students.

On the negative side, however, the features did not make it necessary for students to have to monitor the unfolding talk to detect and correct possible sources of misunderstanding, and redirect the flow of interaction. Since there was no larger discussion topic or theme to which they were required to connect their utterances, the need for other equally complex skills such as inferring, anticipating, and building upon previous utterances in the joint creation of topically complex thought, was also absent. If, as argued by Vygotsky, we "grow into the intellectual world of those around us" (1978: 88), the world of Spanish into which these students were being socialized, at least as reflected in the routine of "practicing speaking," was linguistically and otherwise distressingly insufficient for nurturing the development of anything but the most feeble of Spanish language users.

Now one may argue that, because these were novice learners of Spanish, such a cognitively and communicatively limited environment was needed to help reduce the amount of complexity with which the students had to cope in the target language and thereby provide a "safe" learning environment. Such an argument might be justified in explaining the communicative environment created in the first few weeks or even months of language study. However, it does not explain its lack of development over the year.

It is worth noting that, as intellectually, socially, and linguistically lacking as the routine was, the students did not develop any overt signs of major dysfunction or dissatisfaction with it over the academic year. When not actively participating in the practice, individual students worked on homework from other classes, engaged quietly in small talk with their neighbors, occasionally rested their heads on their arms or fidgeted quietly in their seats. As the year progressed, these individual and small-group activities became more frequent, but they rarely turned into unruly behavior. It was not that the students did not have the power or agency to resist the kind of communicative environment that was being constructed for them in their interactions with teacher. There were numerous ways in which they could have been disruptive. However, they were not.

As I noted earlier, these students were in the college preparatory program and thus considered capable learners. Perhaps they felt that the consequences for resisting the boredom arising from the rather inane chatter would have negatively affected not only the grades they received in this class, but, more generally, their placement in the track. Alternatively, they might not have minded this world. After all, the teacher never demanded that they give their full and active attention to the routine at all times. As long as the students did not get out of hand and overtly threaten the teacher's authority, they were allowed to create fairly comfortable spaces in their neck of the classroom, talking to neighbors, catching up on work for other classes, daydreaming, and in other ways living quietly along the borders of the instructional practice. They may have considered it a welcome respite from other schooling demands, a time they could spend doing something else while "practicing Spanish." In any case, expectations of what counted as Spanish and how to speak it that the students were developing through their participation in this routine were, at best, minimal.

As much research on classroom discourse over the years has shown (e.g. Barnes, 1992; Cazden, 1988; Gutierrez, 1994, 1995; Nystrand, 1997), the discursive conditions of this interactional routine are not so very different from those found in classrooms of other subject matters. Without denying that negative consequences can result from extended involvement in such learning environments in any subject matter, I would like to suggest here that the consequences of being socialized into such practices are likely to be especially critical to foreign language learning. For many learners of foreign languages, at least in the US, their first, and sometimes their only exposure, to the other language is in the classroom. This makes the communicative conditions and the processes of learner socialization into these fairly self-contained worlds of critical importance in shaping both the form and content of the learners' development. The beginning years of language learning are especially significant in that the communicative conditions created in these classrooms are the birth place of what come to be known as "foreign language" and "foreign language learning." What the students learn here, both in terms of what counts as language and as the process of learning, sets the foundation upon which their subsequent development is based. And, as we saw here, providing cognitively, linguistically, and socially limited resources to first-year learners in a routine whose specific intent is to provide opportunities for them to "practice speaking" Spanish does not provide much groundwork upon which subsequent learning experiences in speaking Spanish can build.

Conclusion

To be sure, what I have presented is only a very partial glimpse of one world of foreign language learning into which novice learners are socialized. A more complete understanding of the link between the development of target language skills and abilities, including the skills and other resources needed to use the language to interact with others, and the pedagogical conditions we create in our classrooms requires close examination of the socialization practices of a wide variety of foreign language learning environments across multiple levels. It also entails close examination of the particular ways individual learners are appropriated into these communicative worlds, the varied ways in which they position themselves in relation to the varied modes of assistance and the developmental outcomes that result from these processes. Findings from such investigations will contribute to our understanding of the varied paths our learners' development in using the target language takes. They will also help us construct a more adequate theory of language learning and, concomitantly, alternative learning contexts and practices that help develop students' skills and abilities in using the target language that we consider to be appropriate for meeting their academic, social and communicative needs.

Notes

1. Of the 15 tapes, nine were from fall semester (one from August, four from September, three from October, one from November) and six were from spring semester (one from January, two from February, one each from March, April, and May).
2. The transcription conventions used in this and subsequent excerpts include a bracket [to indicate simultaneous talk, and empty parentheses ( ) to indicate unintelligible talk. The English translation appears in italics below each turn at talk.
3. Raid is the name of an insect spray.

References

Barnes, D. (1992) *From Communication to Curriculum*. Portsmouth, NH: Boynton/Cook.

Boxer, D. and Cortes-Conde, F. (2000) Identity and ideology: Culture and pragmatics in content-based ESL. In J. K. Hall and L. S. Verplaetse (eds) *Second and Foreign Language Learning Through Classroom Interaction* (pp. 203–220). Mahwah, NJ: Lawrence Erlbaum.

Cazden, C. (1988) *Classroom Discourse: The Language of Teaching and Learning*. Portsmouth, NH: Heinemann.

Duff, P. (1995) An ethnography of communication in immersion classrooms in Hungary. *TESOL Quarterly* 29 (3), 505–537.

Duff, P. (1996) Different languages, different practices: Socialization of discourse competence in dual-language school classrooms in Hungary. In K. Bailey and D. Nunan (eds) *Voices from the Language Classroom: Qualitative Research in Second Language Education* (pp. 407–433). New York: Cambridge University Press.

Duff, P. and Early, M. (1999) Language socialization in perspective: Classroom discourse in high school humanities courses. Paper presented as part of the AAAL 1999 Conference Colloquium, *Understanding Language Socialization in Educational Settings: Research on Youth*, Stamford, Connecticut.

Garcez, P. (1997) Microethnography. In N. Hornberger and D. Olson (eds) *Encyclopedia of Language and Education, Volume 8: Research Methods in Language and Education* (pp. 187–196). Dordrecht: Kluwer Academic Publishers.

Gutierrez, K. (1994) How talk, context, and script shape contexts for learning: A cross-case comparison of journal sharing. *Linguistics and Education* 5, 335–365.

Gutierrez, K. (1995) Unpackaging academic discourse. *Discourse Processes* 19, 21–37.

Hall, J. K. (1998) Differential teacher attention to student utterances: The construction of different opportunities for learning in the IRF. *Linguistics and Education* 9 (3), 287–311.

Hymes, D. (1980) *Language in Education: Ethnolinguistic Essays*. Washington DC: Center for Applied Linguistics.

Jacoby, S. and Gonzales, P. (1991) Creation of expert-novice in scientific discourse. *Issues in Applied Linguistics* 2 (2), 149–181.

Lin, A. (1999a) Resistance and creativity in English reading lessons in Hong Kong. *Language, Culture and Curriculum* 12 (3), 285–296.

Lin, A. (1999b) Doing-English-lessons in the reproduction or transformation of social worlds? *TESOL Quarterly* 33 (3), 393–412.

Lin, A. (2000) Lively children trapped in an island of disadvantage: Verbal play of Cantonese working-class schoolboys in Hong Kong. *International Journal of the Sociology of Language* 143, 63–83.

Nystrand, M. (1997) *Opening Dialogue: Understanding the Dynamics of Language and Learning in the English Classroom*. New York: Teacher's College Press.

Patthey-Chavez, G. G. (2002) Measuring participation. Paper presented at the 2002 AAAL conference, Salt Lake City, Utah.

Poole, D. (1992) Language socialization in the second language classroom. *Language Learning* 42 (3), 593–616.

Schieffelin, B. and Ochs, E. (1996) The microgenesis of competence: Methodology in language socialization. In D. Slobin, J. Gerhardt, A. Kyratzis, and J. Gao (eds) *Social Interaction, Social Context and Language: Essays in Honor of Susan Ervin-Tripp* (pp. 251–263). Hillsdale, NJ: Lawrence Erlbaum.

Shultz, J. J., Florio, S., and Erickson, F. (1982) Where's the floor? Aspects of the cultural organization of social relationships in communication at home and in school. In P. Gilmore and A. Glatthorn (eds) *Children In and Out of School: Ethnography and Education* (pp. 88–123). Washington, DC: Center for Applied Linguistics.

Toohey, K. (1998) "Breaking them up; taking them away": Constructing ESL students in grade one. *TESOL Quarterly* 32 (1), 61–84.

Vygotsky, L. S. (1978) *Mind in Society: The Development of Higher Psychological Processes*. Cambridge, MA: Harvard University Press.

Watson-Gegeo, K. A. (1997) Classroom ethnography. In N. Hornberger and D. Olson (eds) *Encyclopedia of Language and Education, Volume 8: Research Methods in Language and Education* (pp. 135–144). Dordrecht: Kluwer Academic Publishers.

Willett, J. (1995) Becoming first graders in an L2: An ethnographic study of language socialization. *TESOL Quarterly* 29 (4), 473–504.

Zuengler, J. and Cole, K. M. (1999) You're not in middle school anymore: Language socialization in freshman science classroom. Paper presented at the AAAL 1999 Conference Colloquium, *Understanding Language Socialization in Educational Settings: Research on Youth*, Stamford, Connecticut.

Chapter 5

Repair of Teenagers' Spoken German in a Summer Immersion Program[1]

HEIDI HAMILTON

This study examines the language repair practices (following Schegloff et al., 1977) of four different groups of American teenaged learners of German and their Swiss teacher during a four-week live-in summer immersion program. Analyses identify the trouble sources in spoken language produced by the learners that triggered either other-initiated repair sequences by the teacher or self-initiated repair sequences by the learners. Repair sequences are characterized within the following videotaped contexts-of-talk: (1) one beginner language class period (five learners); (2) one advanced intermediate language class period (eight learners); (3) one free-choice cultural activity period involving mixed-level learners (six learners); and (4) one conversation involving mixed-level learners cleaning their cabin (10 learners). In contrast to the majority of second language repair studies, this investigation focuses not on the relative success or failure of teacher feedback (e.g. error correction or identification), but on the influence of activity type and language ability on the interconnected repair practices of both teacher and learners.

Introduction

Fifteen-year-old Wilhelm stands in the middle of his cabin, looking somewhat confused. He and his friends are cleaning up their living space after breakfast before heading off to their first language class of the day. Holding up a pail, he says *Was machen wir mit die-se* . . . *diese* . . . *dieses Ding? Mit diesEM Ding?* ("What do we do with this . . . this . . . this thing? With this thing?"), first getting the gender of the noun wrong (*diese*), then coming up with the right gender but the wrong case ending (*dieses*). On the third try he gets it right (*diesem*).

Sixteen-year-old Karin looks up from the letter she is holding in her hand and reports on what her penpal from Switzerland has written. *Und dann . . . uhm . . . er hat über die USA gesprocht und er . . .* ("And then . . . uhm . . . he has spookt about the USA and he . . ."). Before she could finish her thought, her Swiss teacher, Moritz, said *Er hat über die . . .? Das hab' ich nicht verstanden* ("He did what? I didn't understand that."). She repeated the problematic part of her previous utterance, this time changing the form of the past participle of the verb "sprechen": *über die USA gesprachen* ("has spaken about the USA"). Unfortunately, the form is still wrong, but Moritz finally understands and offers the correct form: *gesprochen*. *Ja*. Karin repeats the form and continues her turn: *gesprochen. Ja, und er weisst es hat fünfzig Staaten und über Hollywood* ("spoken. Yes. And he knows it has fifty states and about Hollywood."), producing new "repairables" as she goes.

After describing himself as an *Ausländer* ("foreigner") in the United States, Moritz asks his advanced intermediate students: *Was glaubt ihr? Gibt es viele Ausländer in der Schweiz? Was denkt ihr?* ("What do you think? Are there many foreigners in Switzerland? What do you think?") Sixteen-year-old Peer says: *Ja*. The teacher asks again: *Glaubst du?* ("Do you think so?"). Peer takes the cue to expand upon his answer: *Ja. Für uhm business. Wie sagt man 'business'?* ("Yes. For uhm business. How do you say 'business'?"). Realizing he can't complete his thought in German, he asks his teacher for a specific word. The teacher complies with *Für die Wirtschaft* ("for the economy") and writes the errant word on the blackboard.

There is usually a great deal to be repaired in language produced by learners speaking their second language. Sometimes the wrong word is chosen. Other times the gender of a noun is incorrect. Still other times the verb conjugation is off. And, even if the individual lexical items are correct, the ordering of the words may be wrong – or they may be mispronounced. In cases such as these, there are choices to be made – choices by the speaker him- or herself (*Should I keep monitoring and changing my language as I go or should I just keep on trying to make my point clear, knowing that I'm making error after error?*) and choices to be made by the conversational partner (*Do I insert myself into the ongoing interaction by asking a clarification question or do I just let her keep talking? What if I really don't understand what she's saying anymore?*).

These choices made by the speaker or the conversational partner are not without consequences: The use of repair can get in the way of ideas; by the time the grammatically correct case ending has been identified and produced, the speaker's train of thought may be derailed. Repairs can be humiliating or even demoralizing for some learners who seem to think that the identification of such errors in their language use is an attack on their intelligence or character. On the other hand, the withholding of repairs may slow or even thwart a learner's language development. And some learners seem to be energized by the challenge of attempting to get "everything right" in whatever they say. The issues surrounding language repair are important in any interaction involving non-native speakers but become potentially monumental when they are played out within a residential immersion environment, where opportunities to speak the target language are available in a wide variety of contexts all day long.

In this chapter we explore the language repair practices of four different groups of teenagers and their teacher when they were confronted with issues such as those illustrated above – when trouble sources arose in the language produced by the learners – within a four-week-long high school credit session at *Waldsee*, the summer German program of Concordia Language Villages in northern Minnesota. Concordia Language Villages is the oldest and most extensive summer residential program for elementary and secondary students in the United States and offers language and cultural immersion programs with annual summer enroll-ments of over 6000 young people,[2] ages 7–18, in the following 12 languages: German, French, Spanish, Russian, Japanese, Chinese, Korean, Norwegian, Swedish, Finnish, Danish, and English as a Second Language (Italian will be added in summer 2003). These camp programs take place in retreat-style communities where counselors/instructors and learners live everyday life in the target language, typically engaging in a wide variety of activities including sports, arts and crafts, dancing, cooking, swimming, nature programs, singing, banking, and shopping. Several times a day, learners meet with a small group of peers (usually six to eight learners) at their language level and an instructor/counselor to focus specifically on language forms and functions that then can be practiced in the ongoing daily activities.

Concordia Language Villages staff training does not at present include any hard-and-fast rules about how instructors should respond through-out the day to non-native-like language use by the learners. Learners are strongly encouraged to use the target language as extensively and accu-rately as possible for their language level and are offered incentive programs involving "secret" counselors and daily language pledges to help provide external motivation, but there are no language contracts for villagers to sign nor any type of punitive measures for use of their first language.

Background

We will discuss these repair practices within the framework set out by sociologists Schegloff *et al.* (1977) in a seminal article 25 years ago to account for the organization of repair by adult native speakers of the English language. The notion "repair" refers specifically "to practices for dealing with problems or troubles in speaking, hearing, and understanding talk in conversation (and in other forms of talk-in-interaction, for that matter)" (Schegloff, 1997: 503). This definition allows us to see that a wide range of trouble sources can be identified either by the current speaker (for example, difficulties in pronouncing a word, coming up with a particular word, and monitoring the informational needs of the conversational partner) or by the current listener (for example, volume that is too low, a word that is not recognized, or a presupposition that is not shared).

Once a trouble source is identified, a repair can be initiated by either the speaker (called "self-initiated repair") or by the hearer (called "other-initiated repair"). These two types of repair initiation have different organizational consequences. Based on conversational interactions among adult native speakers of English, Schegloff *et al.* (1977) found that speakers of the talk containing the trouble source ordinarily initiate their own repairs and carry them out within the same turn (as we saw Wilhelm do in changing from *diese* to *dieses* to *diesem* in the example above). It is much less common for the conversational partner to step in and actually initiate a repair of the speaker's language (as we saw Moritz do in Karin's case above); if the interlocutor does initiate the repair, it is generally left to the original speaker to resolve the problem in the very next turn. That means, then, that an other-initiated repair usually takes several turns to unfold.

Despite this "preference" for self-initiation and resolution of trouble sources in speakers' language use, Schegloff *et al.* (1977) raised the possibility that repairs initiated by the conversational partner may be more common in interactions involving communicatively mismatched interlocutors, such as between parents and their children. Schegloff *et al.* (1977) speculated that such other-initiated repair may indeed be used as a resource to socialize the less-competent partner into the surrounding discourse community. Somewhat like training wheels on a bike, such repairs coax learners toward the use of the more "preferred" self-initiated repair over time.

It was this brief comment in the closing paragraphs of Schegloff *et al.* (1977) that sparked my interest in this topic. Having a long-standing research interest in the effects of Alzheimer's disease on conversational language use, I had already studied other-initiated repairs within the discourse-level communication breakdowns so typical of interactions involving Alzheimer's patients (Hamilton, 1994a, 1994b), arguing that these repairs were indicative of a patient's increasing difficulties with pragmatic comprehension. Following Schegloff, it was clear that conversations between healthy interlocutors and individuals with Alzheimer's disease could be characterized as "mismatched" in terms of communicative competence. This mismatch could then account for the relatively large amount of other-initiated repair in these interactions, although its relationship to socialization was unlikely.

In addition to the examples of other-initiated repair associated with Alzheimer's disease, my 20-plus years of experience working as a counselor and researcher with Concordia Language Villages had filled my head with even more examples of other-initiated repair. The source of these repairs – typically interactions between a second language learner and his or her teacher – could clearly be characterized as interactions between speakers who were mismatched in terms of communicative competence, but, in contrast to the Alzheimer's cases, it seemed quite plausible that the repairs *could* be functioning to socialize learners into the larger discourse community. I began to wonder what a more complete analysis of repair would tell us about learners, teachers, and what they thought about their own learning environments. Further I wondered about the possible role that repair might play in socializing learners into the immersion discourse community and the possible barometer it might be of learners' language development over time.

Of course, readers familiar with mainstream second language acquisition literature will be well-versed in the arguments – pro and con – regarding positive vs. negative evidence and how these relate to second language acquisition. In this literature, what we have here been calling "repair" is termed "negative evidence," which is further broken down into two types (Long, 1996): *explicit* negative evidence that refers to overt error correction and *implicit* negative evidence that refers to recasts of the problematic language, where the focus on the message is maintained at the same time the correct form is supplied. I will leave to those experts (see, for example, Doughty & Williams, 1998; Lightbown & Spada, 1990; Long, 1991, 1996; Lyster & Ranta, 1997; Pica *et al.*, 1989; Schmidt & Frota, 1986; and Swain, 1985) any discussions regarding how effective these types of feedback might be in helping learners reach higher levels of proficiency and accuracy.

Research Questions

As a discourse analyst with my particular background, I will pursue this general topic from the different perspectives outlined above; that is, (1) by examining the interrelationships between a teacher's other-initiated repairs and the learners' self-initiated repairs as being mutually influenced by the activity in which they are currently engaged; (2) by seeing these repair practices as windows on users' learning and teaching philosophies; and (3) by relating these practices to the maintenance of and socialization into the surrounding language-learning discourse community as described by Olshtain and Celce-Murcia (2001: 711). Within a live-in second language immersion environment such as *Waldsee*, where learners interact (formally or informally) on a daily basis with many different language users, mutual understanding of what counts as a "trouble source" or "repairable" in the learners' discourse is a crucial piece in building a discourse community where expectations are clear. For example, when does the use of the learners' first language (English) constitute a "repairable"? Does the notion of "repairable" shift according to the context-of-talk throughout the day (mealtime vs. art project vs. classroom instruction)? Can more advanced language learners expect to find more or less of their language use subject to repair than beginners?

To these ends, then, the present study examines both the use of other-initiated repairs by one Swiss teacher and the use of self-initiated repairs by his American teenaged students within four different videotaped contexts-of-talk at *Waldsee*. The contexts-of-talk include: (1) one beginner language class period (five learners); (2) one advanced intermediate language class period (eight learners); (3) one free-choice cultural activity period involving mixed-level learners (six learners); and (4) one mixed-level interaction with students cleaning at "home" in their cabin (10 learners). The primary research questions to be answered are:

- Were the four contexts-of-talk different from each other in terms of the relative proportion of repairs initiated by the teacher and his students?
- Were the four contexts-of-talk different from each other in terms of types of trouble sources that triggered repairs?

In order to provide a fuller understanding of these repair practices, we need to characterize the four contexts-of-talk more generally, both in terms of the relative proportion of conversational turns and in terms of the use of the learner's first language, English. To this end, the following secondary research questions will be answered:

- How are turns-at-talk distributed between the teacher and the learners in the four contexts-of-talk?
- What percentage of teacher's and learners' turns-at-talk in the four contexts-of-talk contain the learners' first language (English)?

In the next section of this chapter, we provide a description of the research site, the subjects, and the four contexts-of-talk examined, as well as outline procedures for the data collection and analysis. Then we present key findings related to the four research questions outlined above, focusing on the following four areas across the four contexts: (1) distribution of turns-at-talk; (2) use of English; (3) proportion of repair-initiation turns; and (4) trouble sources as triggers for repair initiation. In the following section, we place these findings within a more general discussion of *Waldsee*'s complex immersion environment with its range of activities over the course of the day. Within this environment, teachers' and learners' goals may shift and influence the types of trouble sources that may trigger a repair sequence in a particular context. We close by suggesting that a multifaceted understanding of situated, naturally occurring repair practices related to second language learners' spoken language may inform current classroom practices as well as future studies of second language learning and development.

Methodology

Description of the site and the subjects

The research reported on in this chapter (and the source of the above repair scenarios) is part of ongoing research at Concordia Language Villages (see Hamilton *et al.*, 2004; Hamilton & Cohen, forthcoming[3]). As mentioned above, the data for this particular study was collected during one four-week high school credit session in summer 1995 at *Waldsee*, the German program of the Concordia Language Villages. *Waldsee* is the oldest of all of the Concordia Language Villages, having been founded at the height of the cold war in 1961 by a professor in the German Department at Concordia College in Minnesota.

Mission and goals
As all of the village programs, *Waldsee* has as its mission "to prepare young people for responsible citizenship in our global community." Following from this mission, then, it is not surprising that Concordia Language Villages has several goals for its programs, only one of which

relates *exclusively* to the learning of the target language. These goals include: (1) safeguarding the personal health and safety of each and every participant; (2) building and maintaining a community that encourages tolerance of and respect for others; (3) providing varied opportunities for participants to learn and practice the target language; (4) providing varied opportunities for participants to learn about cultural norms and directly experience cultural practices related to the target language studied; (5) providing varied opportunities for participants to explore issues of relevance to the world at large (e.g. environment, war/peace, justice, literacy, health, and human rights); and (6) providing opportunities for participants to learn and practice skills *via the target language* from among the wide range represented by the staff (e.g. woodcarving, calligraphy, dancing, canoeing, sewing, fencing, soccer, and baking). Virtually all Concordia Language Villages programming strives to fulfill several of these goals simultaneously; that is, within a safe and respectful environment, participants use the target language to experience relevant cultural practices, explore global issues, and/or learn and practice new skills. This multiplicity of goals is important to keep in mind as a backdrop upon which repair practices are carried out.

Physical site

Waldsee is a real village that shares an 830-acre tract of land on Turtle River Lake northeast of Bemidji, Minnesota, with the French, Norwegian, Finnish, and Spanish villages. *Waldsee* is made up of many different kinds of buildings and spaces: a dining hall, a train station, activity buildings, immigrant cabins, stores, cafés, a bank, a health center, residential buildings, a library, a sauna, a soccer field, a marketplace, a beach on a large lake, a ropes course, a rustic theater hidden away in the woods, a wilderness campground, and several nature trails and campfire circles.

Time allocation

Waldsee has its learners 24-hours a day, seven days a week, for sessions of one week, two weeks, or four weeks. One-week programs are designed as an introduction to the language and culture for first-time (typically very young) participants. Two-week programs are offered for all age groups; language learning within these programs focuses on conversation with little or no written work. Four-week programs are intensive fully accredited high school credit programs offered only to high-school age participants; upon successful completion, Concordia Language Villages recommends the granting of credit for one year of high school foreign language.

The following sample daily schedule is meant to give the reader a sense of the rhythm of the *Waldsee* day.[4] Typically, learners wake up around 7:30 a.m. and are immersed in a variety of language and cultural activities until they go to bed around 10:00 p.m.

8.10	breakfast
9.00	cabin time (clean-up and preparation for the day)
9.45	first formal instruction period
10.30	song session
11.00	break
11.30	cultural activity period
12.30	lunch
13.15	rest time in the cabin
14.00	second formal instruction period
15.00	activity period
15.45	break
16.15	third formal instruction period
17.15	study hall (and mail distribution)
18.15	fourth formal instruction period
19.00	evening meal
20.30	evening program or study hall
22.00	Good night!

The interactions that provide the data for this study were taped during the cabin time after breakfast between 9:00 and 9:45, during the first formal instruction period from 9:45–10:30 (beginning and advanced intermediate classes), and during the cultural activity period from 11:30–12:30.

Participants

At any given time at *Waldsee*, there are approximately 180 learners and 60 counselors/instructors. Just under half of the staff members are native speakers of German; the vast majority of the non-native speakers on staff have excellent or nearly native command of the target language supported by significant amounts of experience living abroad. They range in age from 18 through 40, with most in their early to mid-20s. Some are trained as language teachers; others have skills and knowledge that are important in other ways to the community, including music, art, sports, environmental sciences, and drama. The learners come from across the United States as well as from several foreign countries. They range in age from 7 to 18 years. Approximately half learn German in school. Each summer more than half of the previous year's participants – staff and learners alike – return to *Waldsee*.

The participants in the present study included 18 high school students (eight girls and ten boys) ages 14–17. Three boys and two girls were learners in the beginners' course; the advanced intermediate course consisted of five boys and three girls; the mixed-level cultural activity period consisted of five girls and one boy (three participants were from the intermediate class and three from the advanced intermediate class); all 10 boys lived together in the same cabin (three boys were in the beginners' class; two boys were in the intermediate class; and five boys were in the advanced intermediate class). The teacher in the study, Moritz, was a Swiss citizen in his mid-20s who taught German at a secondary school in Aarau, Switzerland, and had additional experience as an exchange teacher of German in France. He was teaching in the *Waldsee* four-week credit program for his second summer.

Opportunities for language learning and practice

From the moment the learners arrive on the first day, they enter into a "playworld" with a wide variety of opportunities to learn and use the language in different times and places, with different people and for different purposes (see Hamilton & Cohen, forthcoming, for a more complete description of this "playworld"). Learners gather up the components of a new "identity": they arrive at the border of the "new" country, show their "passports," and go through customs. They choose a new name, find out what new "city" (cabin) they will be living in, open a bank account and change their US dollars into Euros; they are surrounded by German language, music, and signs. Within a few hours of arrival, they will be eating the types of food that German-speaking Europeans eat.

Learners interact with a whole range of different villagers and instructors throughout the day – from wake-up routines in their cabins through breakfast with a different group of friends, large group singing sessions, small language groups, soccer games, stained glass activities, nature hikes, working on the village newspaper, and in numerous other activities. Living groups are made up of learners who are of the same sex and approximately the same age; learning groups are made up of learners who are more or less at the same language level, with less consideration to age and sex; and activity groups are mixed in terms of age, language level, and sex, but homogeneous in terms of areas of interest.

Procedures for data collection

In order to obtain the videotapes that form the basis of this study, a research assistant from the *Waldsee* staff accompanied Moritz into two different language classes and the free-choice mixed-language-level cultural activity period. Since these tapings took place during the last week of the program, the students were all familiar and comfortable with Moritz and the research assistant, allowing for naturalistic interactions despite the presence of the camcorder. The research assistant did not tape the fourth interaction (the informal conversation among the boys in Moritz's cabin), as it was thought that the presence of an outsider to the cabin would alter the interaction substantially. Instead, Moritz himself was given the camcorder and asked to tape his interaction with the 10 boys in his cabin during clean-up time following breakfast one morning. Although the camcorder undoubtedly altered the interaction in the cabin somewhat, the shift was arguably much less than if a "non-resident" had come in to tape.

The decision was made to focus initially on these four interactions, because they all involved the same teacher. This factor allows us to surmise that differences in the teacher's repair use across situations were more likely to be attributable to the different language levels of learners or to the perceived activity at hand than to the teaching style of the instructor. Additionally, learner language use in two different situations as well as teacher reaction to the same learners in two different situations could be compared, since (1) all male learners from the language classes lived together in the same cabin with Moritz; and (2) three learners from the advanced intermediate class participated in Moritz's cultural activity session.

In order to help the reader envision the larger context of the repair practices and their illustrations below, a brief synopsis of the four contexts follows:

> *Beginners' Class (5 learners)*: At the beginning of the period, Moritz pretended that he had an imaginary fly "Bob" in his hands. Bob wanted to get to know *Waldsee* and Moritz invited the learners to design a tour of the village for him. During the first half of the class period, the students took turns coming up to the whiteboard to draw a picture of the location Bob should fly to next, starting with the dining hall, on to the cabins, the town square, the train station, the beach, the arts and crafts center, and finally going to the store for a snack. As Bob "reached" each geographic location, then, Moritz asked the learners questions about what Bob should see and do there: swim at the beach, make a name tag at the arts and crafts center, and so forth. About half-way through the class period, the tour came to an end and the students reviewed orally where the fly had flown and what he had seen and done.

Advanced Intermediate Class (eight learners): Moritz started the class off by taking a bundle of sticks out of a bag and saying: *Guckt mal, was ich gekriegt habe!* ("Look at what I got!"). As part of a cultural reenactment, the night before all the villagers had put their shoes out for *Sankt Nikolaus* to fill with candies and fruit. Instead of a nice surprise, Moritz woke up to find these sticks. He used this event as a classroom warm-up by having the learners discuss the holiday tradition and talk about what they each had received in their shoes. After approximately 15 minutes, he put the sticks away and announced that he had a puzzle for the learners, asking *Was bin ich?* ("Who am I?"). The students proceeded to describe Moritz and finally came up with the transition point into the rest of the lesson – that, as a Swiss citizen, he was a *foreigner* in the United States. A classroom discussion about issues of foreigners in Switzerland ensued.

Cultural Activity Period (6 learners): This session was part of a week-long cultural activity led by Moritz for a mixed-level group of learners. He had brought letters written in German by his high-school students in Aarau, Switzerland, specifically for the learners at *Waldsee*. The day before the taped session each learner had received a letter and had read it. The activity period on the day of taping was filled with oral reports from the learners on each student based on what the student had written in the letter. The next step in the process had the *Waldsee* learners write letters that Moritz carried with him back to Switzerland for his students to read.

Cabin (10 learners): In this informal interaction, the boys had just returned from eating breakfast in the dining hall and were cleaning their cabin before heading off to their first language instruction period of the day. Most of the language used during this interaction had to do with the boys carrying out specific tasks, such as picking their clothes up off of the floor, vacuuming the carpet, and placing any lost-and-found items onto a table in the corner of the room. Interspersed within this task-based talk was some light-hearted discussion about activities and some time-related concerns about finishing class projects.

Procedures for data analysis

In preparation for analysis, the tapes were transcribed based on Tannen (1989) and coded for: (1) turns-at-talk by teacher and learners; (2) turns containing English (and, within that set, those containing "gratuitous" uses of English; (3) repair initiations of learners' talk (other-initiated repair by the teacher as well as self-initiated repair by the learners);[5] and (4) troubles (or "repairables") that were the sources of these repair initiations. Trouble sources included: grammatical errors; lexical difficulties; misunderstanding of content; lack of expansion; use of English; low volume (too soft); and non-native pronunciation. Illustrations of both kinds of repair initiation (self and other) as well as of each type of trouble source follow.

Self-initiation by learner

Excerpts 1–4 illustrate repairs that were initiated by the learners themselves. In excerpt 1, the learner, Peer, responded to Moritz's question about where *Knecht Rupprecht* had put the bunch of sticks that Moritz was holding in his hand.

Excerpt 1: Grammar as trouble source

1	**Moritz:**	Knecht Rupprecht hat mir eine Rute . . . Ja, wohin hat er mir die Rute gelegt?
		(Knecht Rupprecht (put) a bunch of sticks in my . . . Yes, where did he put the bunch of sticks?)
2	**Peer:**	In <u>den</u> Schuhen
		(<u>In</u> the shoes)
3	**Moritz:**	Ja
		Yes
4	**Peer:**	In <u>die</u> Schuhe
		(<u>Into</u> the shoes)

(from the advanced intermediate class)

In line 2, Peer incorrectly used the dative case following the two-way preposition "in" (*in den Schuhen* "in the shoes"). This prepositional phrase indicates that the sticks were lying motionless inside the shoes, whereas Moritz's question had asked about *Knecht Rupprecht's* action in putting the sticks *into* the shoes. The answer to this type of question demands the accusative case (**in die** *Schuhe* "into the shoes"). Without any prompting by Moritz – in fact after Moritz responded *Ja* to the semantic content of Peer's first turn – Peer then noticed the problem in his language production, and initiated and resolved the repair in line 4.

In Excerpt 2, learner Wilhelm was offering a possible definition of the word *Niedergelassene* (an individual who takes up residence, but does not necessarily wish to remain, in a geographic location). He thought this term referred to a person who would like to become a Swiss citizen.

Excerpt 2: Lexicon as trouble source

Wilhelm: Er will ein Schweizer <u>bekommen</u> . . . uh . . . werden.
                (He wants to <u>receive</u> a Swiss person . . . uh . . . become.)

(from the advanced intermediate class)

In his answer he made a common error, using the German word *bekommen* to mean "become." He recognized this trouble source almost immediately and initiated the lexical repair, this time providing the correct verb, even though the definition itself was inaccurate.

In Excerpt 3, learner Peer had reached the conclusion that he was unsure of the exact meaning of *Rute*. He saw what Moritz was holding up in front of him, but was unsure whether the term itself referred to a stick or to a branch (see turn 3).

Excerpt 3: Content as trouble source

1	**Peer:**	Was genau ist eine Rute?
		(What exactly is a "Rute"?)
2	**Moritz:**	Das [points to branch] ist eine Rute.
		(This [points to bunch of sticks] is a "Rute.")
3	**Peer:**	sticks or branch?
4	**Moritz:**	Ja, eine Rute hat mehrere mehrere Zweige, weißt du?
		(Yes, a "Rute" has several several twigs, you know?)

(from the advanced intermediate class)

He initiated the repair in line 1 ("What exactly is a 'Rute' ") which Moritz attempted to resolve in turns 2 and 4 ("This is a 'Rute' " and "A 'Rute' has several several twigs, you know?").

In Excerpt 4, Moritz asked a question in turn 1 that had a possible one-word answer ("What else can one drink . . . in the dining hall?") Another learner had already answered the original question with *Milch* ("milk").

Excerpt 4: Lack of expansion as trouble source

1	**Moritz:**	Was kann man noch trinken . . . im Gasthof?
		(What else can one drink . . . in the dining hall?)
2	**Wolfi:**	Wasser . . . Man kann Wasser trinken.
		(Water . . . One can drink water.)

(from the beginners' class)

In turn 2, Wolfi answered with one word (*Wasser*), recognized the lack of expansion as a possible trouble source (Moritz often expanded brief answers or asked learners to expand on them), and provided a full sentence answer (*Man kann Wasser trinken*).

Other-initiation by teacher

Excerpts 5–7 illustrate repairs initiated by Moritz to trouble sources that he identified in learners' language use. In Excerpt 5, Moritz tried indirectly to get Lars to help the other boys clean up the cabin. In line 2 Lars answered in English. Moritz then responded to the trouble source in line 3 by acting as if he did not hear or understand Lars' utterance in English ("Excuse me, please?").

Excerpt 5: English as trouble source

1	**Moritz:**	Lars, wir räumen auf!
		(Lars, we're cleaning up!)
2	**Lars:**	All my stuff is clean.
3	**Moritz:**	Wie, bitte?
		(Excuse me, please?)
4	**Lars:**	Ich rohme . . . räume auf.
		(I'm cloning . . . cleaning up.)

(from the cabin)

In the next turn, Lars responded to the repair initiation by saying that he was cleaning up. Interestingly, his statement in turn 4 contained a successfully performed self-initiated self-repair on the pronunciation of the word *räume* (*Ich rohme . . . räume auf*).

In Excerpt 6, Hannelore started to answer Moritz's question about what one can do in the dining hall at *Waldsee*. Turn 1 was apparently not loud enough for Moritz to understand, and he initiated a repair based on this trouble source in turn 2.

Excerpt 6: Low volume as trouble source

1	**Hannelore:**	Man kann
		(One can)
2	**Moritz:**	Ja, ein bißchen lauter. Ich verstehe nichts.
		(Yes, a little louder. I can't understand anything.)
3	**Hannelore:**	Man kann essen. [said more loudly]
		(One can eat.)
4	**Moritz:**	Man kann essen. Ja.
		(One can eat. Yes.)

(from the beginners' class)

In the next turn (3), Hannelore corrected the identified problem and spoke loudly enough so that Moritz could hear and confirm her answer in turn 4.

In Excerpt 7, Lea was listing the courses that her pen pal had on his schedule for the next school year. When she came to the word *Musik*, she pronounced it as an English word with primary accent on the first syllable.

Excerpt 7: Non-native pronunciation as trouble source

1	**Lea:**	Biologie, Chemie, Turnen, Zeichnen, und music. uh.
		(Biology, chemistry, gymnastics, drawing, and music. Uh)
2	**Moritz:**	und MUSIK.
		(and MUSIC.)
3	**Lea:**	Musik uhm
		(Music uhm.)
4	**Moritz:**	Musik zum Frühstück.
		(Music at breakfast.)

(from the cultural activity period)

In turn 2, then, Moritz initiated a repair of this non-native pronunciation, providing Lea with the German pronunciation (including a different vowel sound and primary accent on the second syllable). In turn 3, Lea repeated the German pronunciation correctly. Before she could continue her utterance, Moritz jumped in to remind her that she had heard the word *Musik* pronounced correctly many times already that session as part of a breakfast routine called *Musik zum Frühstück*, where learners listened to the music of a range of European composers in the dining hall.

Findings

We now return to the four research questions posed in the introduction to this chapter. Findings in response to the two secondary research questions will be presented first – in the next two sections – in order to provide a richer understanding of the contexts within which teacher and learner repair practices were carried out. Findings regarding these repair practices in response to the two primary research questions are then presented in the following two sections.

How are turns-at-talk distributed between the teacher and the learners in the four contexts-of-talk?

As seen in Table 5.1, the percentage of turns-at-talk taken by Moritz during the four contexts indicates that he was having a lively back-and-forth discussion in the classroom instruction as well as in the cultural

Table 5.1 Distribution of turns-at-talk

Turns-at-talk	Beginning level	Intermediate advanced level	Cultural activity period	Cabin cleaning
Teacher	240 (53%)	238 (49%)	150 (53%)	69 (28%)
Learner	216 (47%)	244 (51%)	134 (47%)	175 (72%)
Totals	456	482	284	244

activity period. In those three settings, his turns-at-talk made up between 49% and 53% of all turns. This means that the learners were more-or-less trading turns-at-talk with their teacher (accounting for between 47% and 51% of all turns), rather than, for example, sitting and listening to a lecture, on the one hand, or doing group work, on the other. The one different context in terms of turn distribution was the cabin cleaning, where Moritz accounted for only 28% of the turns-at-talk, with the boys sharing the other 72%.

What percentage of teacher's and learners' turns-at-talk in the four contexts-of-talk contain the learners' first language (English)?

As seen in Table 5.2, the percentage of teacher turns containing English indicates no difference in perception regarding the appropriateness of target language use in the classroom as well as in the cabin. Moritz consistently spoke only German throughout all four interactions. The one exception involved Moritz giving the English equivalent of *mehrere* ("several") in the advanced intermediate class when learners thought it meant "more" (probably due to the fact that the closely related lexical item *mehr* means "more").

Table 5.2 Numbers of turns containing English (and percentages of total turns)

Turns containing English	Beginning level	Intermediate advanced level	Cultural activity period	Cabin cleaning
Teacher	0/240	1/238	0/150	0/69
Learners	26/216 (12%)	9/244 (4%)	15/134 (11%)	61/175 (35%)

In contrast, the percentage of student turns containing English shows a clear difference in perception about the appropriateness of target language use in the classroom and cultural activity period as compared with the cabin. The percentage of student turns containing English ranged from 4% to 12% in the classroom and in the cultural activity period compared with 35% in the cabin. When those utterances containing English that related to cognitive processes involved in learning a language are subtracted (such as "no, wait," "I don't know," "what's the word for X?"), the distinction becomes even greater. The percentage of learner turns that contain "gratuitous" English is reduced to 1% to 3% in the classroom as compared with 34% in the cabin.

Were the four contexts-of-talk different from each other in terms of the relative proportion of repairs initiated by the teacher and his students?

An examination of the percentage of teacher turns involved in an other-initiated repair of learner talk, as seen in Table 5.3, indicates that *quantitatively* the teacher did *not* distinguish between the language levels in classroom instruction when pointing to trouble sources in learners' language use.[6] Moritz initiated repair of the beginning learners' language in 26% of his turns; in the advanced intermediate class this percentage was 21%. In the cultural activity period, 15% of Moritz's turns were involved in the initiation of a repair. This slightly lower percentage may indicate that he was focused relatively less on eliminating language troubles in the learners' language and more on allowing exploration of the cultural content at hand.

Table 5.3 Repair initiations by learners and teacher (percentage of total turns-at-talk)

Type of repair	Beginning level	Intermediate advanced level	Cultural activity period	Cabin cleaning
Other-initiated repair by teacher	62/240 (26%)	51/238 (21%)	22/150 (15%)	6/69 (9%)
Self-initiated repair by learners	24/216 (11%)	29/244 (12%)	28/134 (21%)	15/175 (9%)

In contrast to these three contexts, however, Moritz's repair practices indicate that he perceived the conversation in the cabin to be a distinctly different sort of language learning activity than the more formal language instruction periods. As compared with the findings above, only 9% of his turns in the cabin conversation were used to initiate repair of a trouble source in the student talk.

In order to illustrate the distinction Moritz seemed to be making in these two contexts, it is instructive to examine the following two transcript excerpts. In Excerpt 8, taken from the warm-up phase of the advanced intermediate class period, Moritz initiated repairs of the language used by one of his learners, Gerd.

Excerpt 8

1	**Moritz:**	Was hast du gefunden . . . in deinem Schuh?
		(What did you find . . . in your shoe?)
2	**Gerd:**	Ich habe <u>nicht</u> meine__ Schuh gesehen.
		(I have not seen my shoe.)
3	**Moritz:**	Du hast deinen Schuh nicht gesehen? Warum nicht?
		(You have not seen your shoe? Why not?)
4	**Gerd:**	Ich habe <u>es</u> unter unser<u>em</u> Haus gelegt, und ich <u>habe</u> nicht dort____ gegangen.
		(I put it under our cabin, and I <u>have</u> [incorrect auxiliary verb] not gone there.)
5	**Moritz:**	Ich <u>habe</u> gegangen?
		(I <u>have</u> [incorrect auxiliary verb] gone?)
6	**Gerd:**	Ich bin gegangen.
		(I have [correct auxiliary verb] gone.)
7	**Moritz:**	Du bist nicht dorthin gegangen?
		(You have [correct auxiliary verb] not gone there?)
8	**Gerd:**	Nein.
		(No.)

In line 2, Gerd made two grammatical errors – gender on the possessive pronoun (*meine* instead of *meinen*) and word order placement of the negative (*nicht*). In line 3, Moritz recast with both errors corrected. Then in the next turn (line 4), Gerd made four new errors. This time, Moritz directed Gerd's attention to what is arguably the most basic error (the use of the auxiliary *haben* instead of *sein* with *gehen*). This time he posed the question to him containing the original mistake. Gerd picked up on this and rephrased in line 6. In line 7, then, Moritz asked a more expanded question (and one that was semantically correct as well, as it included the negation left out in the pedagogically asked question in line 5). Obviously, Moritz was very attuned to the language forms that Gerd was producing in the classroom setting and was willing to put the progress of the discourse topic temporarily on hold while these trouble sources were publicly worked out.

We now contrast this practice with that in the cabin. Moritz had just heard Gerd say that he was angry and asked why in line 1. In line 2, Gerd made two grammatical errors involving the auxiliary verb *haben* – the first related to number agreement (*hat* instead of *haben*) and the second related to word order within the clause (the inflected auxiliary verb needs to be in the clause-final position within the subordinate clause).

Excerpt 9

1	**Moritz:**	Warum bist du sauer?
		(Why are you mad?)
2	**Gerd:**	Oh, weil die Leute hier <u>hat</u> nicht aufgeräumt.
		(Oh, because the people here has not cleaned up.)
3	**Moritz:**	Oh, dann müßt du es ihnen sagen, sie sollen aufräumen.
		(Oh, then you have to tell them, they are supposed to clean up.)
4	**Gerd:**	AUFRÄUMEN!
		(CLEAN UP!)

In stark contrast to his actions in the classroom discourse (as seen in Excerpt 8), in his next turn (line 3) Moritz simply responded to Gerd's frustration as voiced in line 2 and drew no attention whatsoever to either of the two grammatical errors.

Turning now to an examination of the learners' repair practices in Table 5.3, we see that the percentage of learner turns containing self-initiated repair indicates no clear difference in the perceived language learning activity on the part of learners in three of the contexts: the two formal instruction periods and the cabin cleaning. In the formal instruction periods, 11% and 12% of learner turns contained self-initiated repairs as compared with 9% of the learner turns in the cabin. Like Moritz, the learners did not act differently with regard to repair initiation across the two language classes; unlike Moritz, however, the learners continued to be attentive to trouble sources in the language they used in the cabin and acted on these troubles sources by initiating their own repairs.

The one context that appeared to be treated differently by the learners was the cultural activity group, where they actually repaired more than in the other three contexts –a full 21% of their turns-at-talk contained self-initiated repairs. Two possible accounts come to mind: First, the activity that was being carried out in this period (reading and reporting on the content of letters from Moritz's students in Switzerland) contained a good deal of new information for the learners – new content, unfamiliar lexical items, and unusual Swiss dialect pronunciations. As the learners worked through their individual letters it is easy to imagine how their attention would have been directed to problems in understanding and pronunciation that would then have resulted in a repair initiation in order to remove obstacles to understanding what they were interested in reading and reporting on. Secondly, the division of labor regarding repair initiation appeared to have shifted from that of the classroom instruction periods. In this cultural period, Moritz initiated repair turns less frequently (15% of his total turns as contrasted with 26% and 21% in the classroom), possibly because he saw this cultural program as focused slightly more on the cultural content than on the language per se. As his proportion of repair turns decreased, the learners' proportions increased (from 11% and 12% to 21%), keeping the overall proportion of turns that contain repair initiation at 36% (as compared with 37% and 35% in the classrooms).

Were the four contexts-of-talk different from each other in terms of types of trouble sources that triggered repairs?

A number of initial observations can be made by looking at the findings displayed in Table 5.4. First of all, it is clear that some trouble sources were treated similarly by the learners and their teacher and others were treated differently. As an example of similar treatment, we notice that both Moritz and his learners attended to lack of utterance expansion by initiating repairs of this type in the language learning class and the cultural activity period, but not in the cabin. This indicates that they both perceived the practice of utterance expansion to be relevant to the more formal learning contexts but not to the informal conversation in the cabin. As examples of differential treatment, we notice that there are two types of trouble sources – content misunderstandings and volume – that were attended to by only the learners or by Moritz. Misunderstandings of content were addressed only by the learners and volume problems were addressed only by Moritz. When one looks at the crucial areas of pronunciation, grammar, and lexicon, however, one makes the following interesting observation: Moritz, although vigilant in the more formal learning contexts, was unresponsive to these trouble sources in the informal cabin setting; the learners, however, continued to

Table 5.4 Trouble sources as triggers for repair initiation (as percentages of total number of repair initiations per context by learners and teacher)

Trouble source	Beginners		Advanced intermediate		Cultural activity		Cabin	
	Moritz	Learners	Moritz	Learners	Moritz	Learners	Moritz	Learners
Grammar	24/62 (39%)	11/24 (46%)	17/51 (33%)	10/29 (34%)	10/22 (45%)	9/28 (32%)	0	8/15 (53%)
Lexicon	4/62 (6%)	6/24 (25%)	4/51 (8%)	12/29 (41%)	2/22 (9%)	4/28 (14%)	0	4/15 (27%)
Content	0	3/24 (12%)	0	1/29 (3%)	0	6/28 (21%)	0	1/15 (7%)
Expansion	21/62 (34%)	3/24 (12%)	11/51 (22%)	2/29 (7%)	3/22 (14%)	1/28 (4%)	0	0
English	9/62 (15%)	0	3/51 (6%)	1/29 (3%)	0	1/28 (4%)	5/6 (83%)	1/15 (7%)
Volume	3/62 (5%)	0	7/51 (14%)	0	2/22 (9%)	0	1/6 (17%)	0
Pronunciation	1/62 (2%)	1/24 (4%)	9/51 (18%)	3/29 (10%)	5/22 (23%)	7/28 (25%)	0	1/15 (7%)

monitor their language for these trouble sources in *all* four settings, including the cabin.

Focusing now specifically on grammatical trouble sources, we see that, for the beginner and advanced intermediate classes, respectively, 39% and 33% of Moritz's repair initiations within the formal classroom settings were triggered by these, as were 45% within the cultural activity period. These percentages are in stark contrast to 0% of Moritz's repair initiations in the cabin that had to do with grammatical trouble sources.

Turning to the learners, 46% (beginners) and 34% (advanced intermediate) of learner self-initiated repairs within language classes were triggered by initial grammatical difficulties. For learners in the cultural activity period, 32% of self-initiated repairs had to do with grammatical problems. Even within the cabin conversation, learners self-monitored for grammatical "repairables," with 53% of their self-initiated repairs occurring in response to grammatical trouble sources.

Discussion

Moritz's language use with his learners indicates that he thought he should speak the target language *exclusively* throughout the day with all learners, regardless of language level, relative formality of setting, or ongoing activity. It also suggests that he perceived a difference between the more formal language instruction periods and the cultural activity period, on the one hand, and the informal interactions with the boys in his cabin, on the other. Evidence for this difference in perception comes from his relative proportion of turns-at-talk across the contexts (49% to 51% on the one hand and 28% on the other), his relative lack of repair-initiation in the cabin (only 9% of his turns-at-talk were involved in this activity), and the fact that he pointed out no grammatical, lexical, or pronunciation problems in the learners' language use in the cabin when he did this extensively in the more formal contexts. These practices indicate that he viewed cabin interactions as opportunities for unimpeded use of the target language. Other aspects of his repair initiation practices indicate that Moritz focused during the cultural activity period slightly less on linguistic form and more on moving the content along than he did during the two language class periods. Evidence for this difference comes from the percentages of his overall turns-at-talk that were involved in initiating a repair of learners' language use (26% and 21% of all turns in the class periods and 15% in the cultural activity period).

An examination of the learners' language use, however, paints a different picture. When one looks solely at the relative use of English vs. German, it is clear to see that learners, like Moritz, perceived the cabin interaction to be a different kind of language learning context than the other three. The learners used a great deal more English in the cabin than they did either in the classroom or in the cultural activity period; through his reduced numbers of repair initiations in the cabin, Moritz seemed to put up with that usage, even though he himself continued to use German exclusively. What is particularly striking is the following finding: When the students *did* speak German in the cabin (65% of their turns-at-talk), they continued to self-monitor their utterances for native-like grammar, lexicon, and pronunciation. From this perspective, the learners' expectations of themselves did not match those that their teacher had for them, in that they clearly did *not* pay less attention to their grammar in the least formal contexts of use.

It is important, of course, to bear in mind the limitations of this study. To allow the in-depth analyses of teacher–learner interactions undertaken here, the decision was made to focus solely on one teacher with four different groups of learners. Extensions of this methodology to larger numbers of teachers and learners in a variety of target languages and language learning environments would help to clarify the interrelationships that have begun to be understood in this study; that is, how teacher and learner repair practices are related to each other and to the contexts-of-talk in which they are carried out. In addition, future studies could pay greater attention to the linguistic shape of repairs initiated by both teachers and learners and could make finer differentiations within trouble source categories; this finer level of detail would be expected to identify subtle differences in practice due either to teacher accommodation to different language levels or to learner socialization over time.

Conclusions

When speakers or their conversational partners are confronted with a trouble source, there are choices to be made. One can act on the trouble source or one can ignore it. If one decides to act, there are additional choices to be made. Does one simply point out the problem and look to the other to solve it? Does one identify the problem and present the solution in the same turn? What factors influence the choice that is ultimately made?

This study has indicated that a close examination of the repair practices of both teachers and learners can be a useful and appropriate tool – in tandem with an analysis of relative use of English and the target language – in understanding what teachers and learners think about language learning at different language levels and across activity types. Based on the findings of this study, I would like to sketch out one possible answer to the questions posed above regarding influences on choice – one that relates the overriding goals of a learner–teacher interaction to the range of trouble sources just discussed.

To illustrate this point, consider the following: Within a language learning approach that values using the target language as a vehicle for a variety of discussions, and aims to create an environment for fluent and courageous use of the target language, taking time out for (what may turn out to be) extended repair sequences may not be an appropriate use of time. If a teacher's primary goal in a particular context is to provide opportunities for free-flowing conversation where learners can build up their self-confidence to speak in the second language, then a grammatical trouble source is less likely to trigger a repair initiation than would the use of English.

Within a language learning approach that instead places its emphasis on accuracy and complexity at all levels – pronunciation, grammatical choices, lexical breadth – and values less the exchange of ideas and the building of interpersonal relationships, carrying out targeted repair sequences is a very highly valued practice. If a teacher's primary goal in a particular interaction with his or her learners is to focus on language structure, and a learner produces a spoken utterance containing a grammatical trouble source, then another less relevant goal at the moment (such as moving the discourse topic along) will be put on hold until the trouble source is resolved – even if the delay is quite lengthy, as we saw above in Excerpt 8.

These distinctions have not only to do with teaching philosophies, but also with learners' own preferences and with the activity at hand. As is well known, learners' goals vary – from an intense focus on accuracy to the detriment of fluency and complexity to a high value on communication and creativity with much less importance assigned to accuracy and complexity. (See Schulz, 1996, for an interesting discussion of learners' preferences regarding error correction.) Indeed, the first type of learner may well continue to self-monitor for grammatical trouble sources, as some of the boys did in their cabin conversations, even in the face of the teacher's own shifted focus away from grammatical accuracy towards opportunities for fluent conversation.

Within a complex immersion environment such as *Waldsee* – with its different kinds of activities over the course of every day – a teacher's goals will shift, ranging from a relatively heavy focus on language form in a particular language class period to a relatively heavier focus on cultural comparisons in an activity period to a focus on allowing free-flowing communication in the second language within the cabin or during break-time, for example. A natural tension develops as teachers try to balance these goals and to respond in a fluid and flexible way at the same time as their learners are attempting to discern and appropriate repair practices that are most useful and comfortable for them in different circumstances – whether they identify a problem and come to terms with it themselves, seek out help from conversational partners, or learn to respond to the initiation of repair by conversational others. It is by examining naturally occurring, situated learner and teacher practices in response to this tension that we can begin to learn about the full complexity of these practices, their interrelationships with each other, and the situational conditions that influence them.

In closing, I encourage classroom teachers to use the discussion and illustrations in this chapter as a springboard to reflect on their own discourse practices and those of their students as they interact with each other. Do present classroom interactions offer students a wide variety of opportunities to learn and practice the language? Do teachers' repair practices adjust and accommodate to the different goals that accompany these varied opportunities? Have students been given a chance to learn about repair practices and to reflect on their own preferences and use? Have students thought about how these practices impact the discourse that they hear and produce? Are students aware of how their own repair practices are interrelated with those of their teachers?

It is my hope that future projects investigating the connection between repair practices and second language learning and development may benefit from this multifaceted understanding of repair: that repair practices of teachers will be understood as working in concert with those practices of second language learners, and that the sensitivity of these interconnected practices to differences in ongoing contexts-of-talk will be appreciated. Examining the impact of the practices of only one interactional partner on their other is akin to listening to one hand clapping.

Notes

1. I gratefully acknowledge the fine work and enthusiastic support of my research assistant, Kristin Brobst, and the willingness of Moritz and his students to have their interactions taped. I also appreciate greatly the encouragement of *Waldsee* dean, Karl (Dan Hamilton), and the unwavering support of Christine Schulze, Executive Director of Concordia Language Villages.
2. With the addition of academic-year programming, the annual enrollment total rises to 9500.
3. Hamilton and Cohen (forthcoming) report on a research project entitled "Language Learning in a Non-school Environment," funded by the US Office of International Education through a grant to the National Language Resource Center housed at the Center for Advanced Research on Language Acquisition (CARLA), University of Minnesota, Minneapolis. Although the data analyzed in the present chapter were collected and analyzed before the start of the University of Minnesota research project, I do gratefully acknowledge the importance of this later project in helping to illuminate the contextual factors and broader implications of the repair practices discussed here. Special thanks to Andrew Cohen of the University of Minnesota for his ideas, encouragement, and support.
4. This was the daily schedule during the data collection in summer 1995; relatively minor changes in the schedule have been made since that time.
5. Because this investigation focuses only on repair of learners' language, I did not code the teacher's language use for self-initiations of repair of his own language nor for learners' other-initiations of the teacher's talk.
6. *Qualitative* differences in the shape of the repair are also likely to exist. This issue, however, is beyond the scope of this chapter.

References

Doughty, C. and Williams, J. (eds) (1998) *Focus on Form in Classroom Second Language Acquisition.* Cambridge: Cambridge University Press.

Hamilton, H. E. (1994a) *Conversations with an Alzheimer's Patient.* Cambridge: Cambridge University Press.

Hamilton, H.E. (1994b) Requests for clarification as evidence of pragmatic comprehension difficulty: The case of Alzheimer's disease. In R. L. Bloom, L. K. Obler, S. DeSanti, and J. S. Ehlich (eds) *Discourse Analysis and Applications: Studies in Adult Clinical Populations* (pp. 185–200). Mahwah, NJ: Lawrence Erlbaum Associates, Inc.

Hamilton, H. E. and Cohen, A. (forthcoming) Creating a playworld: Motivating learners to take chances in a second language. In J. M. Frodesen and C. A. Holten (eds) *At the Heart of It All: Discourse Studies and Language Teaching and Learning.*

Hamilton, H. E., Crane, C., and Bartoshesky, A. (2004) *Doing Foreign Language: Adapting the Best Practices of Concordia Language Villages to the Foreign Language Classroom.* Prentice Hall.

Lightbown, P. and Spada, N. (1990) Focus-on-form and corrective feedback in communicative language teaching: Effects on second language learning. *Studies in Second Language Acquisition* 12 (4), 429–448.

Long, M. (1991) Focus on form: A design feature in language teaching methodology. In K. de Bot, D. Coste, C. Kramsch, and R. Ginsberg (eds) *Foreign Language Research in Crosscultural Perspective* (pp. 39–52). Amsterdam: John Benjamins.

Long, M. (1996) The role of the linguistic environment in second language acquisition. In W. C. Ritchie and T. K. Bhatia (eds) *Handbook of Language Acquisition* (pp. 413–468). New York: Academic Press.

Lyster, R. and Ranta, L. (1997) Corrective feedback and learner uptake: Negotiation of form in communicative classrooms. *Studies in Second Language Acquisition* 19 (1), 37–66.

Olshtain, E. and Celce-Murcia, M. (2001). Discourse analysis and language teaching. In D. Schiffrin, D. Tannen, and H. E. Hamilton (eds) *The Handbook of Discourse Analysis* (pp. 707–724). Oxford: Blackwell.

Pica, T., Holliday, L., Lewis, N., and Morgenthaler, L. (1989) Comprehensible output as an outcome of linguistic demands on the learner. *Studies in Second Language Acquisition* 11 (1), 63–90.

Schegloff, E. (1997) Practices and actions: Boundary cases of other-initiated repair. *Discourse Practices* 23, 499–545.

Schegloff, E., Jefferson, G., and Sacks, H. (1977) The preference for self-correction in the organization of repair in conversation. *Language* 53 (2), 361–382.

Schmidt, R. and Frota, S. (1986) Developing basic conversational ability in a second language: A case study of an adult learner of Portuguese. In R. Day (ed.) *Talking to Learn* (pp. 237–326). Rowley, MA: Newbury House.

Schulz, R. A. (1996) Focus on form in the foreign language classroom: Students' and teachers' views on error correction and the role of grammar. *Foreign Language Annals* 29 (3), 343–364.

Swain, M. (1985) Communicative competence: Some roles of comprehensible input and comprehensible output in its development. In S. M. Gass and C. G. Madden (eds) *Input in Second Language Acquisition* (pp. 235–253). Rowley, MA: Newbury House.

Tannen, D. (1989) *Talking Voices.* Cambridge: Cambridge University Press.

Chapter 6

Codeswitching Patterns and Developing Discourse Competence in L2

HELENA HALMARI

Becoming bilingual does not only mean that an individual acquires discourse competence in more than one language; it also means that the speaker develops a competence to alternate between the two available languages to convey subtle pragmatic messages while in the company of other bilinguals. In this chapter, I investigate the codeswitching patterns in a set of longitudinal data collected from naturally occurring conversations by two young Finnish Americans during their 12 years in the United States, in order to show the following two processes: (1) how codeswitching patterns may be seen as a reflection of developing English discourse competence; and (2) how the two languages are alternated in naturally occurring discourse among bilingual family members as a means of conveying a vast array of subtle pragmatic messages. From very early on, the developing bilingualism allows the speaker to operate within the resources of two languages, and while register shifting among monolinguals is a comparable phenomenon, the use of two totally different languages allows the bilingual to accentuate the subtle pragmatic messages that he or she wants to send. The 12 years of exposure to both Finnish and English have allowed the development of relatively balanced bilingualism with a solid discourse competence not only in the L2 but also in the way the L1 and L2 can be combined as a powerful interactional means.

Introduction

Codeswitching and second language acquisition (SLA)

The study of codeswitching – the mixing of two or more languages within the same conversational episode – has by now acquired a legitimate status within the field of linguistics in general, and within bilingualism studies more specifically. The way that bilinguals mix their two languages while conversing with other members of their bilingual discourse community has proven to provide rich information for a number of areas within linguistics. Data from bilingual codeswitching have been investigated by syntacticians interested in gaining insight into the universal properties of language, by psycholinguists dedicated to learn more about the organization of the bilingual mind, by sociolinguists investigating how the choice of code reflects various societal constructs such as power and prestige, by discourse analysts interested in language switching as a discourse-organizational strategy, and by pragmaticians searching for evidence of interpersonal relations and conversational dynamics. Important pioneering research on codeswitching as part of developing or already acquired bilingual communicative competence was carried out on Spanish–English codeswitching (to mention a few see, e.g., Genishi, 1981; Huerta, 1978; Lance, 1975; Lindholm & Padilla, 1978; Lipski, 1978; McClure, 1981; Poplack, 1980, 1981; Valdés Fallis, 1976; Zentella, 1981).

Codeswitching is regarded largely as belonging to bilingualism research. In the areas of discourse analysis and pragmatics, the research question is often the following: What functions does codeswitching fill in discourse? Attempts to answer this question have produced interesting descriptive studies and taxonomies of the functions of codeswitching (e.g. Gumperz, 1982; Hatch, 1976). More recently, in the area of conversation analysis, Auer (1984, 1998) has focused on codeswitching as an interactional strategy. In second language acquisition research, however, codeswitching has not typically been a central area of interest; it has rarely been the focus per se. Most comprehensive accounts of SLA do mention codeswitching, but often it gets mentioned as a compensatory strategy – something that second language (L2) speakers may resort to when their competence in the L2 falls short, and codeswitching is not typically discussed as a part of the developing L2 competence.

While the study of interlanguages has become an established part of SLA research (Selinker, 1972), there have been few studies of bilingual discourse, specifically attempting to answer the question of the role of codeswitching as part of the second language acquisition process (see Boeschoten & Backus, 1997, for one of these). The purpose of this chapter is to contribute to the filling of this gap. Studying bilingual children's speech and their mixing of first language (L1) and L2 in a natural submersion setting informs us of those discourse-situational factors – topics, goals, participants – that are conducive to the use of the learner's second language. And, while the focus of this chapter is more on description than on classroom applications, the knowledge gained from studying bilingual speech patterns is potentially applicable for language teachers wishing to create speech situations in classrooms in which the use of the learners' L2 "comes more naturally."

Studying Bilingual Discourse to Inform Second Language Acquisition

Becoming bilingual does not only mean that an individual acquires discourse competence in more than one language; it also means that the speaker develops a competence to alternate between the two available languages to convey subtle pragmatic messages while in the company of other bilinguals (see, for example, Olshtain & Blum-Kulka, 1989; Scarcella *et al.*, 1990; Schiffrin, 1996; Zentella, 1997, 1998). In this chapter, I investigate the codeswitching patterns of two young Finnish Americans in two subsets of data collected from naturally occurring conversations in an English L2 naturalistic submersion setting. These data are a small portion of data collected in a longitudinal study since the subjects' arrival in the United States. The purpose is to look at these naturally occurring discourse data in order to inform second language learning by specifically investigating the following two processes: (1) how codeswitching patterns reflect developing English discourse competence; and (2) how the two languages are alternated among bilingual family members as a means of conveying a vast array of subtle pragmatic messages.

Along the lines of the general theme of this volume, I here look at bilingual speech in naturalistic language acquisition, not in order to provide supporting evidence for the question of the functions of codeswitching per se, but to underscore the role of codeswitching as an integral part of the naturalistic second language acquisition process (for the study of the use of codeswitching in a formal immersion program, see, for example, Vesterbacka, 1991). I show how, during the early stages of L2 acquisition, the young L2 acquirers practice the use of their L2 through play and through language play. I also show how this alternation between their L1 (Finnish) and L2 (English), with time, turns into a highly elaborate discourse competence. At earlier stages of developing bilingualism this alternation is more patterned and more predictably associated with certain discourse functions. At later stages of bilingualism when the L2 has been fully entrenched, the alternation patterns, while remaining explicable, become less predictable. Codeswitching can thus be seen not as an indication of a lack of knowledge of either language, but as an arsenal for intricate interpersonal interaction (see, for example, Backus,

1999; Backus & van der Heijden, 1998; Boeschoten & Backus, 1997; McClure, 1981; Moffatt & Milroy, 1992).

This chapter sees codeswitching as first providing an opportunity for L2 learners to practice their L2 in a safe environment with other members of their developing bilingual discourse community; when the L2 has been acquired, codeswitching continues to play an important, enriching role among the members of this speech community. A welcome side effect of continued codeswitching in an L2 environment is also its role as a means of heritage language maintenance – an important issue too often forgotten when the emphasis is on L2 learning. In immigrant families, home is often the only place where the L1 is heard and used, and when immigrant children enter school, the possibility of the loss of their heritage language becomes tangible. In the case of the children in this study, a shift to English in sibling-internal interactions – even at home – started to happen after only one semester in an American elementary school. Codeswitching, however, provided a needed outlet for continued – albeit partial – use of the L1 during the times when the subjects were cut off from practicing their heritage language skills in an L1 monolingual environment. In the early days of bilingualism, codeswitching allowed my subjects to practice their L2, English; after English had been acquired, it allowed them to maintain their heritage language, Finnish. This dual benefit of codeswitching is rarely acknowledged by purists and prescriptivists.

Data and Background

My data come from a longitudinal case study of child L2 acquisition in a naturalistic submersion setting. The subjects are two siblings, S2 and S1, whose L1 is Finnish and L2 English. The girls, daughters of the author, were 7.9 (S2) and 6.8 (S1) when the family moved from Finland to California. Neither of the subjects had any extensive exposure to English before leaving the L1 setting. Both entered a private elementary school in California (second and first grades) and they were provided with no formal ESL instruction.

Data collection started in the fall of 1990 and continued through the writing of this chapter, covering altogether 11 and a half years. The purpose of this longitudinal case study is to learn about the subjects' codeswitching patterns, their use of English versus Finnish, their temporary incipient L1 attrition, and their L2 acquisition of English. The data consist of transcripts of audio-recordings, written correspondence, field notes, interviews, and observations. For the purposes of this article, I will focus on (1) samples from the early data to indicate how codeswitching into English was used as a means to practice the developing L2; and (2) a data sample collected after English had been fully acquired. The latter sample (Example 7) is included to illustrate how code alternation reflects the developed bilingual competence. Based on the findings of this study, I claim that naturally occurring bilingual speech offers important data to inform second language learning. Looking at bilingual language-mixing, especially in children's speech, helps us to understand which situational factors naturally trigger a switch to L2.

Findings

Codeswitching in early bilingual development

During the early years of developing bilingualism, the young subjects (at that time, 8 and 9 years of age), practiced their use of English spontaneously while engaged in play. In order to see how the girls used codeswitching as a means to practice a developing L2 competence, let us look at the following excerpt (Example 1) from the year 1990 – a time when the girls had lived in California for 19 months. This set of data consists of a 53-minute audio-recorded segment, where the girls are playing with little toy dolls in their room. The excerpt starts with S2 speaking in the voice of two dolls. The hyphens in the transcript indicate different doll characters speaking. The characters that S2 is here playing are two "guys," who start with an argument: first, one is telling the other one to "shut up." Then the argument continues about who is going to marry a certain "babe doll," whose part S1 picks up playing. The dolls are speaking in the L2, English. It seems that by playing in the roles of these characters, the young L2 learners are practicing various L2 registers.

Andersen (1992) has reported similar findings in the practice and varied use of different registers in L1 English by kindergarteners during a puppet game. Clearly, the register S2 is practicing here is a "macho register" – probably something she has been exposed to at school, or while watching TV, and in which she is now trying out her skills. Note the frequent use of the word *man* (lines 1, 3, 11, 46); other vocatives like *stupid* (line 2), or *boy* (line 5); also formulaic spoken register expressions like *shut up* (16) or *shut up, man* (lines 8, 10, 13–15), *well excuse ME* (line 19), and *no way* (line 23). Note also the use and repetition of certain idiomatic formulaic expressions, such as *man will you shut up* (lines 13–15), *come on, man* (line 35); *I'll bet you, I bet you, bet ya* (lines 26–27, 59), *too bad* (line 43), and *She's so cool* (24). The dolls provide a perfect venue to try out different

spoken registers. (English translations of Finnish utterances are on the
extreme right.)

Example 1

1	**S2:**	-Yeah. Then we're all good friends, <u>man</u>.	
2		-We've gotta choose our pants <u>stupid</u>!	
3		-Oh <u>man</u> you don't have to shout!	
4		-These are too small for me.	
5		-<u>Boy</u> /? / guess what those are?	
6		-Oh I should /? / too small, too!	
7		-Opposite. . . . Uh uh uh uh.	
8		<u>Shut up maːn</u>! Will ya! [0. 10] Uh uh uh uh uh uh uh uh	
9	**S1:**	/? / [whispering]	
10	**S2:**	-<u>Will you shut up man</u>.	
11		-<u>Man</u> I hate when you SAY that.	
12		You always say	
13		<u>Man will you shut up</u>	
14		<u>Man will you shut up</u>	
15		<u>Man will you shut up</u>	
16		-Well yeah? <u>I'll bust you out</u>. . . . SHUT UP! . . .	
17		-See! Now you /scared/ children	
18		/? / get meː!	
19		-<u>Well excuse ME</u>.	
20		Could you just put on your pants.	
21		The babe's waiting out there.	
22		I think I'm gonna marry her you know.	
23		-<u>No way</u>! I get her.	
24		<u>She's so cool</u>. Huh?	
25		-I know. But I still will get her. . . .	
26		-Hey, <u>I'll bet you</u>.	
27		<u>I bet you</u>.	
28		I will get her.	
29		You know how come?	
30		We'll ask her <u>which one do you w- want when you grow up</u>.	
		Okay?	
31		-Okay!	
32	**S1:**	-**Tai.** <u>Would you like</u> the-	Or.
33		the girl heard all the stuff that they <u>spoked</u>?	
		[	
34	**S2:**		Uh-ah-uh-uh [sings]
35		-<u>Come on man</u>. [sings]	

36	**S1:**	-Hey! Hey!
		[
37	**S2:**	[sings]
38	**S1:**	-Hey! Hey hey hey hey guys.
39	**S2:**	/? /
40	**S1:**	-<u>I marry you</u>, both of you.
41	**S2:**	-You're not allowed to!
42	**S1:**	-I am not?
43		<u>Too bad- that's too bad</u>.
44		I heard <u>all that you talked</u>.
		[
45	**S2:**	-It's against the law.
46		A::hh! <u>Oh ma:n</u>! [Giggling]
47	**S1:**	/? / [giggles]
48	**S2:**	/? /
49		-[sings:] What did you /? / do in uh uh uh uh uh uh
50		Come on let's go by the river.
51	**S1:**	-Okay.
52	**S2:**	-Let's get on on our boat
		[
53	**S1:**	-Hey, hey ah- my sister <u>will marry one of you</u>
54		<u>and I will marry one of you</u>.
55	**S2:**	-[hums] Which one? [sings]
56	**S1:**	-I don't know.
		[
57	**S2:**	[sings]
58	**S1:**	-I guess Tom.
59	**S2:**	[sings] hh-hh-hh-hh see? <u>Bet ya</u>. a:rh!
60	**S1:**	-hh-hh. But my sis- my sister's better.
61		She's better . . . being a boy.
62	**S2:**	-Alright!
		[
63	**S1:**	-/? / she likes girls better.
64		But she likes the only thing there is, she likes girls better.
65		That's all
66		but she plays with boys more.
67	**S2:**	[hums, sings, hums]
68	**S1:**	Oh . . . **Jooko että nää ei ollu kertonu-**
		These had not told, okay?
69		<u>would you like</u> they haven't told their mom- parents?
70	**S2:**	**Joo.** [sighs] [sings] Yeah.

71   **S1:**   And the daddy <u>came</u>
72   <u>to worry</u> about them
73   because they were <u>susposed</u> to be <u>at six o'clock home</u>.

But how does codeswitching figure in? How can the codeswitching patterns inform us of the girls' acquisition of English? Note the switches to Finnish in line 32, where S1 says *tai*, "or" in Finnish, and in line 68 where she says *Jooko että nää ei ollu kertonu-*, "These had not told, okay," or, "Let's pretend they had not told." From the voices of the dolls, who speak in English, she is switching to Finnish, the L1, to set up the stage of the play. In line 70, S2 agrees, saying *Joo*, "Yeah" in Finnish. In earlier work (Halmari & Smith, 1994), we discussed how the girls in their doll-play showed a prevalent tendency to frame the negotiation of the play by a switch into their L1, Finnish. Out of the total of 61 language switches during the 53 minutes of the audio-recording, 38% (n=23) were switches to Finnish from English at the onset of negotiation – to frame that the speaker was stepping out of the doll character and starting to speak as herself.

As Example 1 indicates, the setting up of the stage for the continuing play was not necessarily all done in Finnish: In line 69, S1 switches back to English: *would you like they haven't told their mom- parents*, and this is a good reminder of codeswitching as a creative, rather than rigid and predictable phenomenon. However, codeswitching into Finnish – either at the onset of the negotiation segment or within the negotiation segment – was characteristic of all segments where the girls stepped out their in-character doll roles and spoke as themselves. Some use of Finnish tended to mark these "behind-the-scenes" stagings of the ongoing play. What is remarkable, however, is that there was no switching while the girls were speaking in character; in other words, the dolls spoke only English. This is an interesting observation, especially since some of the little dolls had been acquired already when the girls lived in Finland. Clearly, the girls used the in-character play to practice their developing L2.

In addition to lexical practice, Example 1 provides a wide array of different L2 speech acts that the learners practice using through the dolls. There are assertions (for example, line 1), questions (line 5), orders – both direct (line 8) and indirect (lines 10, 20), threats (line 16), apologies (line 19), denials (line 23), bets (lines 26–27), exclamations (line 46), suggestions (line 52), and even a reprimand (line 17). From the point of view of developmental pragmatics, it is clear that the young L2 learners are coping well with their newly acquired L2. Next, I will look at the syntactic development of English.

From the point of view of syntactic development, the L2 acquisition is progressing as well as within the area of pragmatic development. In fact, looking both at the pragmatic development and the syntactic development through the analysis of spoken data can, in important ways, inform second language acquisition. From the point of view of syntax, the language is fairly simple; there are only a few complex sentences: an embedded nominal clause as a direct object in line 22 (*I think I'm gonna marry her you know*), and a complex embedded question in line 30 (*We'll ask her which one do you w- want when you grow up*). Note that the embedded question in line 30 would call for the syntax of an indirect question but is in the form of a direct one. Lines 32–33 and 69 also include embedded structures: *Would you like the- the girl heard all the stuff that they spoked? would you like they haven't told their mom- parents?* Here the *would you like-* construction (meaning "Let's pretend that . . .") is part of the negotiation of the play (the setting of the scene), and it is not fully idiomatic from the point of view of the target language. Another embedded clause is found in line 44: *I heard all that you talked*. Thus, despite the overall simplicity of the spoken structures, embedded structures are starting to emerge, and the conversational tasks that the girls are handling are varied and appropriate. Through the dolls who assert, give orders, and ask questions, the young subjects are practicing their discourse skills in English, and all this takes place in the safe disguise of role-play.

Notwithstanding the advanced forms and functions that appear in the data at this stage, there are still reminders that while the girls are on their way to the mastery of their L2, they are not there yet. Example 1 includes a few clear indications of the subjects' interlanguage stage. There is interlanguage variation in S1's use of the auxiliary *will* to indicate the future: in line 40, the girl-doll's promise *I marry you*, iterated through S1, is lacking the auxiliary *will*; however, in lines 53–54, she uses that target language structure: *Hey, hey ah- my sister will marry one of you and I will marry one of you*. In line 33, instead of the irregular past tense form *spoke*, S1 uses the overgeneralized regular hybrid form *spoked* (with double marking for the past tense), and in line 44 the verb *talk* is used nonidiomatically and without the preposition *about* (*I heard all that you talked*). In lines 71–72, the clause *the daddy came to worry about them* is most likely meant to mean "the/their daddy started to worry about them." Line 73 shows S1's idiolectal form for the verb *supposed* (*susposed*), and the same line (*because they were susposed to be at six o'clock home*) also indicates that S1 has not yet acquired the L2 ordering of adverbials (place before time) – obvious transfer from the Finnish freer word order. It is interesting that most of the non-target-language-like forms are produced by S1, the younger sibling. This seems to support the findings of numerous studies on L2 acquisition in non-naturalistic, experimental, settings: the L2 acquisition rate for older subjects is higher (for an overview, see Long, 1990).[1]

All in all, however, the conversations produced at this early stage of developing bilingualism were fluent and showed surprisingly few deviations from target language norms. Long (1996: 416) reminds us of "the (usually) well-formed speech" of children acquiring their L1s; it may be that the age when the subjects of this study started their L2 acquisition (7 and 6) allowed for a process similar to L1 acquisition (see, for example, Long, 1990). Also, the cognitive development of a 9- and 8-year-old may additionally help in the L2 acquisition process (Lightbown, 1978). Long (1996: 447) suggests that conversation may "[nourish] emergent L2 syntax" (see also Sato, 1988). In my data, the spontaneous use of English, its simplicity and simultaneous relative fluency and grammaticality provide support for Swain's (1985) "comprehensible output hypothesis." Studying actual spoken data allows us to see the influences on acquisition processes.

While in Example 1, S2 is practicing the "macho" register in her developing L2, in Example 2, she is practicing the familial female vs. male registers: those of mother and father dolls. She starts as the mother doll, saying "Honey" and switches quickly to Finnish to direct the play, to explicate to S1 that the father doll had gone to look for the missing "boys." The short episode also ends in a codeswitch to Finnish, when S2 indicates to S1 in line 14 that the dolls need "another boat." Note that the word *boat* in itself is in English; it is the change to matrix Finnish that frames the sentence as a side-remark. S1, when providing the boat, also speaks Finnish (*Tässä! "*Here!"), since she is off-character.

The use of endearing terms such as *honey* and *dear* must have been acquired while in the L2 environment, since Finnish married couples do not typically use them. Gender-role socialization is hence evident in this sequence. The enactment is vivid: The mother doll speaks in a sweet, quiet tone of voice; the father doll sounds stern and quite masculine.

Example 2

1	**S2:**	-Honey.	
2		**Okei. Se oli menny katteleen.**	Okay. It had gone to look for (them).
3		-Honey.	
4		-What IS it dear?	
5		-Dear.	

6		-What IS it <u>honey</u>?	
7		-I got an idea.	
8		-What IS it?	
9		-Go see from the woods.	
10		Go first see	
11		if one of the boys /? /	
12		it means /? / the river . . .	
13		I wish you luck.	
14		**Nää tarvii jonkun toisen** boatin.	These (dolls) need another **boat**.
15		[sings]	
16	**S1:**	**Tässä!**	Here!

In the early months of developing bilingualism the girls frequently, and spontaneously, sought opportunities to informally practice English at home, where the default language was Finnish. One such practicing venue was what they called the "comedies." In the following "comedy" (which actually turned out to be a tragedy), the participants are the family cat Tahvo (the female protagonist) and a male doll, Alvin. The voice is S2's.

Example 3

1	**S2:**	Okay here's a comedy again.
2		-Oh Tahvo
3		-Okay.
4		-What are you doing?
5		-Can you just . . . stop doing those things
6		asking me "what are you doing, what are you doing, what are you doing"
7		-No. I want to know you very well and I shall marry you one of these days.
8		-Don't you get it. I don't wanna get married yet.
9		-Oh yes you do, hey, how about a- hey oh yes, I forgot to show you my shirt
10		-Oh the plain old shirt that always says the same thing.
11		Yee yee, always says the same thing,
12		-Watch this, come on you are supposed to look at my shirt.
13		so. watch this: I LOVE YOU
14		-yep, always

15		-you wanna do it?	
16		-No. I don't like you very much.	
17		-oo, come on, yes you do . . .	
18	[to **S1:**]	**Eikun tää puhuu sen aikana kun se on /? /**	No, this is talking while it's /? /
19		-Your hand is so soft	
20		I just love the way of it. Mm. My darling [sighs]	
21		-Come on . . . Alvin, would you never stop that	
22		same old thing that you are /? / talking to me	
23		/? / I love you /? /	
24		Why are you doing that always to me?	
25		Couldn't you find some other girls.	
26		-no no	
27		**[screams] Nysse purottaa sen kaivoon.**	Now she drops him into the well
28		-I love you	
29	**S1:**	**Huutaa kaivosta.**	Shouts from the well.
30	**Mom:**	**Tyttö purotti sen pojan kaivoon vai.**	The girl dropped the boy into the well, right?
31	**S1:**	**Aha.**	Aha.
32	**S2:**	**Joo.**	Yeah.
33	**Mom:**	**Ja poika huusi että "I love you."**	And the boy shouted that "I love you."
34	**Girls:**	[laugh]	
35	**Mom:**	**Voi mitä . . . rakkautta.**	Oh what . . . love.
36	**S2:**	**Se tyttö ei- tykkää lainkaan siittä pojasta.**	That girl doesn't-like that boy at all.
37		**Eiks se poika ookkin vähän ällöttävä?**	Isn't he a bit icky?
38	**Mom:**	**Vähän ylimakee.**	A bit overly sweet.
39	**S2:**	[laughs] **Vähän ällöttävä.**	A bit icky.

Note that in line 1, S2 introduces the comedy (off-character) in English. This is atypical, but it underscores the non-predictability of language choice. In line 18, the explanatory side-remark to S1 is in Finnish, and when S2 in line 27 explains why the boy, Alvin, screams (he is cruelly being dropped into the well by the girl he is courting), this explanation is again in Finnish. S1 joins the reporting in line 29 in Finnish, explaining that the boy is shouting "I love you" from the well. The evaluation and discussion of the comedy after it is finished is carried out in Finnish.

The use of the L2 during the doll-play and the enacted comedies was spontaneous and, I would even claim, subconscious. However, during the early months of developing bilingualism, there were also more conscious efforts to practice the use of English in the secure home setting. In Example 4, the girls are doing pretence interviews, and S2 asks mother to interview her. Mother starts the interview in the default home language, Finnish (lines 3–7), but, in line 8, S2 whispers to her, asking her to carry on the pretend interview in English. The mother questions this request, and S2's answer in lines 12 and 14, coupled with laughter, indicates that she has not really thought why English should be used. The younger sister's reasoning for this choice (*[Because] we are in America* (lines 13, 23–24)) gets accepted (lines 25–26), and the pretend interview unfolds – in English:

Example 4

1	S2:	**Äiti. Eikun äiti ensiks se haastattelee ny MUT.**	Mother. No, mother will interview ME now.
2	S1:	**Okei.**	Okay.
3	Mom:	**Okei. Hyvää huomenta.**	Okay. Good morning.
4		**Mikä on nimenne?**	What is your name?
5	S2:	**[S2's name] [laughs]**	
6	Mom:	**Aa saanko kysyä**	E:r may I ask
7		**mikä on [. . .**	what is [. . .
8	S2:	**[[whispers]**	[(whispers)
9	Mom:	**Englanniks?** E:r what is your favorite sport?	In English?
10	S2:	Basketball.	
11	Mom:	Why do I have to speak English?	
12	S2:	[laughter] because er-	
		[[	
13	S1:	[laughter] we are in America. [0. 4]	
14	S2:	because I say so [laughter]	
15	Mom:	Well, that's not a good reason.	

16	**S2:**	Just-
17	**Mom:**	You understand er Finnish Ms Halmari don't you?
18	**S2:**	Yeah, yeah. Er- Let's just speak English now.
19		Just-
		[
20	**S1:**	Because this-
21	**Mom:**	If you tell ME the reason.
22	**S2:**	[Sighs, laughs]
23	**S1:**	Because we're in America.
24		because we're in America, say that.
25	**S2:**	Because we're in America.
26	**Mom:**	Okay, that'll do.

Another venue for the subjects to practice their use of L2 was in English children's chants. In Example 5, the girls are complaining about a neighbor girl; their obvious bonding language is the heritage language, Finnish, which marks them as separate from the little American girl under criticism. Yet, even in this exchange, the girls' language play, the repetition of an English children's chant, provides a means to practice English, while they are simultaneously bonding in Finnish:

Example 5

1	**S2:**	**Hm Hm Kerran se aina sano että**	Er er Once she always said that
2		"See you later alligator	
3		hanging from the refrigerator-	
		[	
4	**S1:**	refrigerator	
5	**S2:**	no backs!"	
6		**Aina s-** "no backs, no backs, no backs"	Always sh-
7	**S1:**	**Nii:n se on niin TYHmä.**	Ye:s she is so STUpid.
8	**S2:**	[coughs]	
9		**Sitten se aina**	Then she always
10		**sanoo sillon sano et**	says then said that
11		"Who cares	
12		carebear I'll pull down your underwear-	
		[	
13	**S1:**	bear I'll pull down your underwear	

14	S2:	no backs!"	
15	S1:	Niin tota, niille jos sanoo /jos/	Well, if you tell them /if/
		[	[
16	S2:	Jos se	If she
17		sanoo sillain	says like that
18		niin mä sanon että	so I will say that
19		"Well I: AM not a bear."	
20	S1:	Niin. Ja sitten niin tota	Yes. And then if well
21		jos se sanoo sillein niin	if she says like that so
22		ja jos sille sanoo jotain TOLlasta	and if one says something like THAT to her
23		niin sillon se sa- se sanoo	so then she sa- she says
24		heti että että että "Who car-"	immediately that that that
25		sitten jos sanoo sitä että	then if (one) says it that
26		s- sille että "Who cares carebear	h- to her that
27		I'll pull down your underwear"	
28		niin sitten se sanoo	so then she says
29		että että että että	that that that that
30		"back to you scoopydoo, no backs!"	
31	S2:	Mm. Se on tyhmä.	Mm. She is stupid.
32		Se on pönttöpää.	She is a meathead.
33	S1:	Ni:i.	Ye:ah.

The above examples provide strong support to Hatch's claim of "language learning evolv[ing] *out of* learning how to carry conversations" (1978: 404). Since it was unnatural for the girls to speak English to each other at home, where the default language was Finnish, doll-play and enacted comedies and interviews provided a more "natural" opportunity for the practice in the L2 at home.

Codeswitching: A means to L2 acquisition and bilingual competence

During the early years of the subjects' bilingualism, the role of English was limited; it was reserved for certain topics (e.g. school-related discussions) and for certain, fairly well-defined, pragmatic purposes (e.g. dissociation from other Finnish interlocutors) (Halmari, 2000). From very early on, the developing bilingualism allows the speaker to operate within the resources of two languages, and while register shifting among monolinguals is a comparable phenomenon, the use of two totally different languages allows the bilingual to accentuate the subtle pragmatic messages that he or she wants to send.

It is a well-known fact that the length of residence in an L2 environment is most likely to lead to an increased use of the L2 by the immigrant population (e.g. Schumann, 1978). During the 11 and a half years of accumulated data from the same Finnish–American bilinguals, I have, to a degree, been able to witness what Myers-Scotton (1998) refers to as "matrix language turnover." While during the initial years of data gathering, Finnish tended to be the base language for most utterances spoken at home, after several years in the L2 environment, English had become the base language for most bilingual interactions. The following two sentences are nine years apart and illustrate this change. In Example 6(a), the base language is Finnish; in (b), it is English.

Example 6
(a)   Nää tarvii jonkun toisen **boat**in. (1990)   These (dolls) need
                                                            another **boat**.

(b)   This **pannu** is too small. (1999)   This **pan** is too
                                                            small.

Nonetheless, Finnish was still used among the bilingual family members, and the discourse domains, where either English or Finnish dominated, did not completely overlap. Certain discourse domains seemed to be better suited for Finnish, while English dominated others. The 12 years of exposure to both Finnish and English have allowed the development of relatively balanced bilingualism with a solid discourse competence not only in the L2 but also in the way the L1 and L2 can be combined as a powerful interactional means.

My final example (7) illustrates several instances of code alternation by the girls. The example is lengthy and is presented below in sections. This example comes from the year 1999, after the girls had lived 10 years in the L2 environment. In this exchange, S1 and Dad are the main protagonists. S2 and Mom are also present. The topic is the curfew, the time when the girls should come home each night. The discussion so far has been a jovial one and, as a joke, S1 brings up the curfew issue, without remembering that this is not a good topic since Dad wants the girls home earlier than the time of the current agreement, negotiated with the mother. The girls know very well that they cannot push the time any further, but, as a joke, in English, S1 suggests in lines 5–6 that their curfew could be changed to 3 a.m. Dad reacts immediately, starting from line 9, expressing his disapproval of the current 2 a.m. curfew. He speaks in Finnish, the only English word in his turn being the word *curfew* itself – the Finnish equivalent would be the tedious "home-coming-time" *kotiintuloaika*.

Example 7

1	**S1:**	**Määkin voin ahristaa teitä kaikkia.**	I could also distress you all.
2	**Dad:**	**Millä te meitä ahristatte.**	How are you gonna distress us?
3	**S1:**	I don't know.	
4	**S2:**	[laughs] It was funny though.	
5	**S1:**	How about change the curfew to like-	
6		three o'clock or something [laughs]	
7		**Ahdistetaan teitä vähän!**	Distress you a bit!
8	**Girls:**	[laugh]	
9	**Dad:**	**Jos mulle puhutte siitä** curfew**sta**	If you talk to me about the **curfew**
10		**niin mää oon ollu koko aika**	I have all the time been
11		**sitä mieltä että**	of the opinion that
12		**teirän on kaheltatoista viimeistään**	by twelve at the latest you
13		**oltava kotona.**	have to be home.
14	**Girls:**	[laugh]	
15	**S1:**	[laughs] Oh boy,	
16		I shouldn't have brought THAT up.	
17	**S2:**	[laughs] You're a BUTTnugget!	

In lines 14–17 (above), the girls both try to continue the conversation as a light, friendly one: they laugh, S1 says in English that she shouldn't have brought THAT subject up, and S2 confirms this in English: *You're a BUTTnugget!* Of course, by talking to each other in English, the girls are aligning with each other, against the to-be-expected Finnish "sermon" by the father. Since it is obvious that joking about the topic will not help, S1 quickly changes the tactics to a serious argument, which involves a change of her language from English into Finnish – the only possible choice that might lead into a positive outcome with Dad, who, after all, has the power to change the curfew to a much earlier time, should he not be properly convinced. In lines 18–20 (below), S1 addresses Dad, in almost monolingual Finnish. She is about to revert back to English in line 19 with the personal pronoun *I*, but repairs herself quickly and produces a full Finnish sentence *Mää oon NIIN TYYTYVÄINEN tohon kahteen* "I'm so happy/content with the two o'clock [curfew]." Dad continues to state his argument expressing his disapproval about the current curfew in lines 21–39.

Example 7 (continued)

18	S1:	Kato ny mitenkä hyvin meillä on menny	Look now how good we've been
19		mää oon, I- mää oon	I am, I- I am
20		NIIN TYYTYVÄINEN tohon kahteen.	SO HAPPY with that two o'clock
		[	[
21	Dad:	Mää oon niinkun sanonu-	I have said like-
22		mää oon sanonu äitillenne että	I've told your mother that
23		että jos jotakin tapahtuu	if something happens
24		niin se on sitten,	then it is,
25		mua ei syytetä mistään	I won't be blamed for anything
26		mitä tapahtuu niin että	that happens so that
		[	[
27	S2:	Ei niin!	You won't!
28	Dad:	mulla /ei oo osuutta/ asiaan	I have nothing to do with it
29		että mää oon sanonu mielipiteeni	and I've told my opinion
30		että mää oon JYRKÄSTI sitä vastaan	that I am STRONGLY against it
31		mää oon TÄYSIN eri mieltä	I COMPLETELY disagree
32		mää en oo siihen ikinä suostunu	I haven't ever agreed to it
33		siihen kahteen.	to two o'clock.

34	Mom:	(Otaksää isä kupin kahvia /viä/?)	(Will you take a cup of coffee still, dad?)
35	Dad:	Mun mielestä se on	In my opinion it is
36		AIVAN liian myöhänen aika	TOTALLY too late
37		ja- sillon	and- then
38		kahentoista jälkeen	after twelve
39		ei tierä mitä sillon tapahtuu.	no-one knows what then happens.

Now, the two sisters pick up completely different roles in the ensuing verbal battle with Dad. While S1 takes the responsibility of providing a counter-argument against Dad in Finnish, defending the current curfew, the elder sister, S2, picks up the role of a conversational cheerleader to S1: most of her turns are repetitions and backchannels in English to S1's Finnish turns. S2's use of English shows strong alignment with S1 and simultaneously against the Finnish-speaking father. In line 41 (below), she repeats in English what S1 has just said in Finnish: *I'm almost an adult*; in line 57, she starts repeating in English what her sister just said in Finnish; in line 63, she completes S1's Finnish sentence in English: it would be "no life," if the curfew were changed to be earlier; in line 95 she starts to repeat in English what S1 has just said in Finnish: *They become-*; in line 102 by *They are buttmonkeys!* and by laughing, she applauds S1's argument in line 94, where S1 says that kids whose parents restrict their lives too much will themselves become irritating and selfish; in line 119, S2 offers an English word to support S1's Finnish argument, and in line 127, she repeats S1's concluding words: *I rest my case.*

The only times that S2 speaks Finnish, is when she is not providing alignment messages to S1, but speaking directly to the father: in line 27 (above), where she strongly asserts to Dad that should something bad happen to the girls because of the late curfew, the father is not responsible; in line 75 (below), where she directly confronts the father about the definition of "decent people"; and in line 106, where, overlapping with S1, she joins her to provide further evidence of the detrimental consequences of an early curfew.

Example 7 (continued)

| 39 | | ei tierä mitä sillon tapahtuu. | no-one knows what then happens. |
| | | [| [|

40 S1:   [S2's name] on kohta aikuinen.   [S2's name] is almost an adult.

41 S2:   I'm almost an adult.
42 Dad: Sitten kun [S2] on kahreksantoista   When [S2] is eighteen
43   niin sitten mää antasin [S2's name]lle, I would then let [S2]
44   kahteen, mutta ei enempää   (stay out) till two, but not more.

          [[
45 Girls: hh!?
46 Dad: Siihen asti mää pitäsin sitä   Until then I would keep it
47   kahreksaa- kahtatoista.   at eight- twelve.
48 S1:   [laughs] KAHREKSAA!   EIGHT!
49 Dad: Arki- Arki-iltoina niin kymmeneltä   Week- weeknights at twelve and
          ja-
50 S1:   [Laughs]
51 Mom: [Laughs] Let's make it 8 a.m.
52 Dad: ja perjantaina ja lauantaina   and on Fridays and Saturdays
53   niin kahreltatoista.   well at twelve.
54 S1:   But. Sää et tiedä kuinka e:r   But. You don't know how e:r
55   masentunu mää olisin   depressed I would be
56   jos mun täytyis kaheltatoista tulla   if I had to come home at twelve.
          kotiin.
57 S2:   I'd be like-
58 Dad: Ei ois mitään syytä olla masentunu.   There'd be no reason to be depressed.
59   Saisit olla tyytyväinen että   You should be happy that
60   että vanhemmat välittää   (your) parents care.

          [[
61 S1:   Mää olisin ihan kauhistunu   I'd be completely horrified
62   Ei niin kun minkäännäköstä niin kun   It would be no kind of like

63	**S2:**	No life.	
64	**S1:**	No life, I know.	
65	**Dad:**	**Kyllä, siinä sitä** lifeia **oliskin**	Yes, that would be **life**
66		**kun sais olla-**	when you could be-
67		**ihmisten aikana kotona.**	home at a decent time.
68	**S2:**	Yi-huu! [laughs mockingly]	
69	**Dad:**	**Se olis niinkun oikeus ja kohtuus**	It would be fair and just
70		**Kohtuullista. Ikään nähden ja muuten.**	Just. Taking your age and all into consideration.
71	**S1:**	/? /	
72	**Dad:**	**Sillain täällä on muilla-**	That's how things are with other-
73		**muilla tota- niin**	other like-
74		**fiksujen ihmisten lapsilla on niin.**	decent people's children.
75	**S2:**	**Mitä ne fiksut ihmiset on?**	What are those decent people?
		[	[
76	**S1:**	**Fiksut ihmiset.**	Decent people.
77		**Mikä on fiksu ihminen?**	What is a decent person?
78	**Dad:**	**Kouluja käyneet**	Educated
79		**ja oppineet ja älykkäät.**	and learned and intelligent.
		[	[
80	**S1:**	**Fiksu ihminen-** it's like- /? /	A decent person- it's like- /? /
81	**S2:**	[/? / Heh.	
82	**Dad:**	**et- ne jok- ihmiset joista ei välitetä,**	that those who are not cared about
83		**vanhemmat ei välitä, niin** /? /	the parents don't care about, so /?/
		[	[
84	**S1:**	**Semmoset ihmiset**	Such people
85		**joilla on kauheen aikaset** curfew:t	who have really early **curfew**s

86		niin ne- ne lapset on screwed-up.	so they- those kids are **screwed-up**.
87		They- get to do nothing. [	[
88	**Dad:**	**Ei.**	No.
89	**S1:**	**Ihan tosi, sää et tiedä**	Really, you don't know
90		**miten** screwed-up **ne on.**	how **screwed-up** they are.
91		**Sää et tiedä mimmosia**	You don't know what
92		**kauheita ihmisiä niistä tulee.** [	horrible people they become. [
93	**Dad:**	**Ei.**	No.
94	**S1:**	**Niistä tulee ärsyttäviä, itsekkäitä, perse- munia**	They become irritating, selfish, dumb- asses.
95	**S2:**	[They become-	
96	**S1:**	**jonka kanssa kukaan ei halua olla.**	with whom no- one wants to be.
97		**Koska mää tunnen /? /** [	Because I know /?/ [
98	**Dad:**	**Niille tulee-**	They will get-
99		**Niille tulee vahva itsetunto**	they will get good self-esteem
100		**sen takia että niistä on vanhemmat välittäny.**	because their parents have cared about them.
101		**Ja huolehtinu** [	And worried (about them) [
102	**S2:**	They are buttmonkeys! [laughs]	
103	**S1:**	**EI, koska ne vihaa niitten vanhempiansa**	NO, because they hate their parents
104		**koko elämänsä**	all their lives
105		**mää tierän /ne/-** [	I know / they /- [

106	S2:	Sitten ne tekee /? / juttuja /? /	Then they do /? / things /? /
		[	[
107	S1:	Mää tiedän ihmisiä	I know people
108		jokka vihaa vanhempiansa	who hate their parents
109		koska ne ei anna niitten tehrä mitään.	because they won't let them do anything.
110		Ja ne on ihan hulluja and-	And they are totally crazy **and-**
111	S2:	[laughs]	
112	Dad:	Miten sää voit sitä tietää	How can you know
113		kun ettehän te seurustele	since you don't socialize
114		NIITTEN kanssa	with THEM
115		kun te ootte kaiken sen-	because you are with all-
116		muitten kanssa /? /	with all others /?/
		[	[
117	S1:	No mulla on paljon	Well I have
118		kavereja joitten vanhemmat on /? /	many friends whose parents are /?/
		[	[
119	S2:	Acquaintances	
120	S1:	Mulla, ei, mulla ei oo acquaintance**ja,**	I've got, no, not **acquaintances,**
121		Mulla on hyviä kavereita	I've got good friends
122		jokka on semmosissa tilanteissa,	who are in those situations,
123		and it's not fair.	
124		ja ne on ihan fucked up in my opinion.	and they are quite **fucked up in my opinion.**
125		heh.	
126		I rest my case.	
127	S2:	I rest my /?/ case.	

While S2's job is to provide alignment messages to S1 in English and occasionally join S1 to address Dad in Finnish, S1, through most of the exchange, struggles to stick to Finnish – the language that Dad will listen to. And this is the strongest indication of the fact that English has indeed become the stronger language for her during the 10 years. Every now and then, in the middle of her turn, she slips back to English for a little while: I already mentioned line 19 (above), where she quickly self-repairs; other examples are in line 54 (above), where the argumentative conjunction *but* comes from English, while the rest of the turn is in Finnish. Line 64 (above), *No life, I know*, is in English, but this is addressed to her sister and the language there sends a message of alignment with her. Other "slips" into English can be seen above in lines 80 (*it's like*), 85 (*curfew*), 86 and 90 (*screwed-up*), 110 (the conjunction *and*), and line 120 (*acquaintance+j+a*, which is a word repeated from S2's earlier turn, but now with Finnish number and case marking).

We need to remember that Finnish for S1 is by now the weaker language, and it is because the stakes are so high in this conversation that she is able to produce most of her turns in monolingual Finnish. What, however, is interesting is that evaluative comments, such as the one above in line 87, *They- get to do nothing*, and 123–124, *and it's not fair. ja ne on ihan* ("and they are quite") *fucked up in my opinion*, are in English. (Evaluation was one of the prominent functions of codeswitching already back in 1990 (see Halmari, 1993).) Particularly interesting is that when S1 has laid out her whole argument, she, in English, wraps it up in line 126: *I rest my case*. The father, however, is not quite finished yet, and, again, S1 picks up the argument in monolingual Finnish in lines 130–134 (below). As long as S1 sees that there is some hope about persuading Dad to be happy with their current curfew, she sticks to Finnish. When, however, in lines 138–139 the father implies a correlation between late curfews and smoking marijuana, S1, in lines 140–142, switches to English. This switch is meaningful; it can be seen as a symbol of protest and an indication of giving up the verbal battle. Seeing her attempt to persuade the father in Finnish as hopeless and feeling that the father's remark is unreasonable, S1 thus, quite emphatically, switches to HER language of authority, English: *Uh-uh, I'm sorry, I have to correct you there. I don't smoke marijuana*. This is a language she by now has fully acquired and is able to use for the purpose of pragmatic messages.

Example 7 (continued)
126   I rest my case.
127 **S2:**   I rest my /? / case.
            [

128	Dad:	Ne- niitten vanhemmat	The- their parents
129		osottaa että ne välittää.	show that they care.
130	S1:	Ei. Ei ei ei. Jos ne välittäis	No. No no no. If they cared
131		niin ne antais niitten pitää ees	they would allow them to have
132		vähän enemmän hauskaa.	at least a little bit more fun.
133		Ne ei saa-	They can't
134		niillei oo minkään näköstä	they have no kind of
		[	[
135	Dad:	/?/	/?/
		[	[
136	Mom:	(Anna mulle-	(Give me-
137		Antakaa mulle vähän vettä.)	Give me some water.)
138	Dad:	Poltetaan marijuanaa tua porukoissa	Smoking mari- juana in groups
139		ja muuta.	and stuff.
140	S1:	Uh-uh, I'm sorry,	
141		I have to correct you there.	
142		I don't smoke marijuana.	

Discussion: Studying Bilingual Speech to Inform L2 Acquisition

The rationale of studying bilingual conversation – conversation where the speakers' L1 and L2 both appear, intertwined in a blissful combination – in order to learn more about L2 acquisition, is not apparent at first sight. In fact, language purists have doomed codeswitching as a sign of a poorly learned L2, or an L1 on its way to oblivion. It is true that classroom-based research on L2 learning provides exact, quick, and quantifiable answers to questions of L2 learning. Experimental studies, while not attempting to portray naturally occurring discourse data, allow the researcher to focus on specific and well-defined questions of the L2 learning process. It is no wonder that longitudinal studies that draw their data from naturally occurring discourse, looking into the language learning process across speech situations and over years, have not been commonly employed to inform second language learning. The data for longitudinal studies, such as the present one, are tedious to collect. The data do not lend themselves to immediate and clear-cut interpretation. A short transcript will not necessarily tell us anything about the L2 learning process, since sometimes the research participants can carry on a conversation for a long period in their L1, or they may be engaged in mixing that, at the surface, looks quite random. What is needed is a lot of data in order to see a trend; otherwise, there is a danger of focusing on details and not seeing what the bigger picture is, what the generalizable trends are.

My claim is that longitudinal data such as exemplified above provide important keys to inform second language learning. What we have seen in the present study is a long-term tendency for the naturally occurring use of English, the L2, in certain speech situations. By looking at the early data, when the girls were still in the process of acquiring English, they themselves, with no prompting, created situations in which L2 use appeared natural. The doll-play allowed them to practice the L2 "in-character" – the same principle that is employed with adults for instance in the suggestopedic method of second language teaching. Doll-play also allowed the girls to practice a number of different registers to which they had been exposed – an important aspect of L2 pragmatic development. The repetition of formulaic expressions and children's chants was proba-bly a sign of subconscious practice in the L2. And while it was somewhat unnatural for the girls to speak English to each other and especially to their mother in their roles as children of a Finnish-speaking household, role-playing games (doll-play, "comedies," and pretend skits and interviews) provided an acceptable use of the L2, the marked language, in interactions between family members. Play provided venues to practice the L2.

When the L2 had been fully acquired, however, the motivations for codeswitching changed. During early bilingualism, when the girls were still acquiring English, they used their English output for language acquisition purposes – albeit subconsciously. It is to be noted that had the family's conscious goal not been the maintenance of Finnish, as well as the full acquisition of English, the girls would, by the end of the data-gathering period (after more than 10 years in the United States), probably have switched over to monolingual English even in most family-internal interactions. Yet, because of their annual visits to a mono-lingual Finnish environment, the girls were still able to use their L1 for most pragmatic purposes even after all the years in the United States, and so codeswitching in family-internal interactions continued to take place. Nonetheless, towards the end of the data-gathering period, this codeswitching had acquired a different pattern: No longer were the two languages mixed so that one or the other could be practiced; the research participants used codeswitching now to send intricate pragmatic messages to each other and to their interlocutors. These messages had to do with alignment and bonding, disalignment, persuasion, and overall organization of discourse – the framing of what was being done within the interaction.

Since the early days of codeswitching studies, several functions have been assigned to codeswitching. However, these functions have rarely been looked at in longitudinal data from the same bilinguals in order to see the trends and tendencies of how codeswitching is first used to practice the L2 and later on to communicate pragmatic messages. A better and more in-depth understanding of what intricate goals are being obtained by a switch from L1 to L2 and vice versa can, I argue, be achieved by investigating a long period of bilingualism and by drawing data from lengthy stretches of discourse. Strong motivation for switching codes has prevailed, emerged, and strengthened over the decade of developing bilingualism, and learning about the patterns of language switching allows us to learn about the L2 acquisition process. In addition, the strong pragmatic motivation to alternate between the use of L1 and L2 has, in part, prevented the complete shift to monolingual English during the years in the United States. The data reconfirm the power of codeswitching as an interactional strategy that bilinguals can resort to in order to achieve an extremely rich range of communicative goals.

Using bilingual data to inform second language learning is, however, not unproblematic. The functions of codeswitching are often difficult to interpret, and, without an intimate understanding of the speech situations under scrutiny, as well as the interpersonal relationships between speakers engaging in codeswitching, it is difficult to see why one language is reserved for one discourse task and the other language for another. Unlike in L2 classroom-based research and in experimental laboratory studies of L2 learning, the factors entering into the picture cannot be neatly controlled. However, as a source of data complementing the more controllable studies, it is possible to understand the L2 learning process more deeply. In the attempt to understand L2 learning in a naturalistic submersion setting, bilingual discourse data provide a valuable window to the minds of bilingual speakers and their subconscious, natural means of coping with a life situation where a command of more than one language is critical.

Furthermore, I would like to suggest that, by looking at naturally occurring bilingual data, a more general level of knowledge than merely new knowledge of the L2 acquisition process can be obtained. A source of distress among discourse analysts is that we are lacking a well-defined theory, a model of discourse. We are looking for patterns of the organization of discourse and generalizable tendencies of register variation, but sometimes the task seems overwhelming and all that we seem to be left with are endless taxonomies of how the various features of a given speech situation seem to coincide with certain linguistic forms, codes, or registers. Framing of certain speech episodes by a switch to L1 or L2 in bilingual discourse will help us understand discourse-organizational issues better. Study of bilingual codeswitching provides an excellent window to these types of investigations, since switching from one language to another is often the most salient marker of the speaker's shifting from one conversational task to another.

Pedagogical Implications

If theories of discourse in general and L2 learning in particular can benefit from the language alternation patterns found in naturally occurring bilingual data, what is the message of this investigation to the classroom teacher of a second language? How, if at all, can L2 instruction benefit from these findings? The answer is not simple. While the study does suggest and support the superiority of certain already widely used methods and techniques (such as suggestopedia and the use of games and play, other meaningful activities, songs, and rhymes), the classroom L2 learning situation is fundamentally different from the situations in which my research participants, intuitively and voluntarily, employed these "techniques" and "activities." In other words, my two participants had the advantage over most foreign language learners throughout the world: they were continuously submerged in the L2 setting. For them, learning English was not an option.

L2 classroom teachers may hand their young students dolls to play with, together with directions that the dolls do not know the students' L1; they may teach their students English children's rhymes and songs; they may ask them to carry on pretend plays and pretend interviews – and while teaching elementary school English in Finland, I certainly did all of this. Yet, as long as the students when they leave the classroom find little use for their newly acquired language patterns, those patterns are not likely to be reinforced. All the same, this study is far from implying that teaching communicative competence to young learners – in settings with plenty of role-play and other activities that the students' L2 monolingual peers engage themselves in – should not be the preferred method, as compared to less communicatively oriented teaching methods. Even if classroom activities that promote the use of students' L2 do not, in a foreign language setting, lead to such swift language learning as in a submersion setting, this does not mean that foreign language students should not be provided with these foreign language learning experiences. If codeswitching studies show that certain speech situations are likely to prompt the spontaneous use of the L2, these situations should be abundant in any L2 and foreign language classroom.

What this study also shows is that the use of the L1 during the L2 learning process is not detrimental to the outcome. If bilingual children in a bilingual setting are able to employ their two languages for their appropriate purposes and can become skillful users of the two codes for a number of pragmatic and rhetorical goals, there is little reason to insist that only the L2 be used in language classrooms. On the other hand, should language teachers not manage to create more natural motivations for their students' L2 use, this mandatory – albeit unnatural – use of the L2 throughout all class sessions might be what they need to resort to. The mandatory use of the L2, however, is not more likely to create fluent L2 speakers than the more motivated, voluntary use that arises from genuinely meaningful communication tasks.

One issue that this study makes clear is the role of practice in L2 use. In child L2 acquisition, the role of output is essential. In order to achieve a competence that allows the speaker to draw most effectively from both language resources, the learner needs to practice. In naturalistic L2 acquisition, this practice takes place so spontaneously that one is left wondering if this is a universal discourse pattern – a discourse pattern prompted by naturalistic submersion, a pattern leading to full bilingual competence.

The examples in this study indicate that codeswitching may provide the language learner, in the early stages of language learning, an opportunity to practice the language in a non-stressful, non-arbitrary setting. In advanced learners, codeswitching becomes a way to enrich interaction with other bilinguals and to stay connected to the L1. The task remaining for the L2 and foreign language teacher is the simulation of the naturalistic environment where acquisition may take place. The task remaining for all teachers of immigrant children is to make sure that by the time the L2 is fully acquired, L2 acquisition has not happened at the expense of the student's heritage language.

Note

1. The flipside of language acquisition is language attrition. Cohen (1989) has suggested a connection between literacy and attrition: preliterate children might be more susceptible to attrition than literate children. This suggestion

is also verified in my data from the early years: The younger subject's codeswitching patterns showed signs of L1 attrition (Halmari 1992). The younger subject was preliterate at the time of initial exposure to English, and it is interesting to speculate whether this had something to do with the fact that her English also showed more errors than the English of her older sister, who was literate at the time of initial exposure to L2, and whose codeswitching patterns did not show as strong signs of incipient loss of Finnish. Investigating the connections between interlanguage errors and literacy vs. preliteracy would, however, require data from more subjects than this case study can offer.

References

Andersen, E. S. (1992) *Speaking With Style: The Sociolinguistic Skills of Children*. London: Routledge.

Auer, P. (1984) *Bilingual Conversation*. Amsterdam: John Benjamins.

Auer, P. (ed.) (1998) *Code-switching in Conversation: Language, Interaction and Identity*. London: Routledge.

Backus, A. (1999) Mixed native languages: A challenge to the monolithic view of language. *Topics in Language Disorders* 19 (4), 11–22.

Backus, A. and van der Heijden, H. (1998) Life and birth of a bilingual: The mixed code of bilingual children and adults in the Turkish community in the Netherlands. In L. Johanson (ed.) *The Mainz Meeting: Proceedings of the Seventh International Conference on Turkish Linguistics, August 3–6, 1994* (pp. 527–551). Wiesbaden: Harrassowitz Verlag.

Boeschoten, H. and Backus, A. (1997) Code-switching and ongoing linguistic change. In L. Johanson (ed.) *Turkic Languages* (pp. 41–62). Wiesbaden: Harrassowitz Verlag.

Cohen, A. D. (1989) Attrition in the productive lexicon of two Portuguese third language speakers. *Studies in Second Language Acquisition* 11 (2), 135–149.

Genishi, C. (1981) Codeswitching in Chicano six-year-olds. In R. P. Durán (ed.) *Latino Language and Communicative Behavior* (pp. 133–152). Norwood, NJ: Ablex.

Gumperz, J. J. (1982) *Discourse Strategies*. Cambridge: Cambridge University Press.

Halmari, H. (1992) Code-switching strategies as a mirror of language loss: A case study of two child bilinguals. In D. Staub and C. Delk (eds) *The Proceedings of the Twelfth Second Language Research Forum* (pp. 200–215). East Lansing, MI: Michigan State University, Papers in Applied Linguistics-Michigan.

Halmari, H. (1993) Code-switching as an evaluative device in bilingual discourse. *Issues in Applied Linguistics* 4 (1), 91–118.

Halmari, H. (2000) On pragmatic motivations for code choice in Finnish–English codeswitching: Evidence from a longitudinal study. Paper presented in the panel "From intentionality to variability: Pragmatic motivations for code-switching," at the Seventh International Pragmatics Conference, Budapest, Hungary, July 9–14, 2000.

Halmari, H. and Smith, W. (1994) Code-switching and register shift: Evidence from Finnish-English child bilingual conversation. *Journal of Pragmatics* 21, 427–445.

Hatch, E. M. (1976) Studies in language switching and mixing. In W. C. McCormack and S. A. Wurm (eds) *Language and Man: Anthropological Issues* (pp. 201–214). The Hague: Mouton.

Hatch, E. M. (1978) Discourse analysis and second language acquisition. In E. Hatch (ed.) *Second Language Acquisition: A Book of Readings* (pp. 401–435). Rowley, MA: Newbury House.

Huerta, A. (1978) Code switching among Spanish–English bilinguals: A sociolinguistic perspective. Unpublished doctoral dissertation, University of Texas, Austin.

Lance, D. M. (1975) Spanish–English code switching. In E. Hernández-Chávez, A. D. Cohen, and A. F. Beltramo (eds) *El Lenguaje de los Chicanos: Regional and Social Characteristics of the Language Used by Mexican Americans* (pp. 138–153). Arlington, VA: Center for Applied Linguistics.

Lightbown, P. (1978) Question form and question function in the speech of young French L2 learners. In M. Paradise (ed.) *Aspects of Bilingualism* (pp. 21–43). Columbia, SC: Hornbeam.

Lindholm, K. J. and Padilla, A. M. (1978) Language mixing in bilingual children. *Journal of Child Language* 5, 327–335.

Lipski, J. M. (1978) Code-switching and the problem of bilingual competence. In M. Paradis (ed.) *Aspects of Bilingualism* (pp. 250–264). Columbia, SC: Hornbeam.

Long, M. H. (1990) Maturational constraints on language development. *Studies in Second Language Acquisition* 12 (3), 251–285.

Long, M. H. (1996) The role of the linguistic environment in second language acquisition. In W. C. Ritchie and T. K. Bhatia (eds) *Handbook of Second Language Acquisition* (pp. 413–468). San Diego, CA: Academic Press.

McClure, E. (1981) Formal and functional aspects of the codeswitched discourse of bilingual children. In R. P. Durán (ed.) *Latino Language and Communicative Behavior* (pp. 69–94). Norwood, NJ: Ablex.

Moffatt, S. and Milroy, L. (1992) Panjabi/English language alternation in the early school years. *Multilingua* 11 (4), 355–385.

Myers-Scotton, C. (1998) A way to dusty death: The matrix language turnover hypothesis. In L. Grenoble and L. Whaley (eds) *Endangered Languages: Language Loss and Community Response* (pp. 289–316). Cambridge: Cambridge University Press.

Olshtain, E. and Blum-Kulka, S. (1989) Happy Hebrish: Mixing and switching in American–Israeli family interactions. In S. Gass, C. Madden, D. Preston, and L. Selinker (eds) *Variation in Second Language Acquisition: Discourse and Pragmatics* (pp. 59–83). Clevedon: Multilingual Matters.

Poplack, S. (1980) "Sometimes I'll start a sentence in Spanish *y termino en español*": Toward a typology of code-switching. *Linguistics* 18 (7–8), 581–618.

Poplack, S. (1981) Syntactic structure and social function of codeswitching. In R. P. Durán (ed.) *Latino Language and Communicative Behavior* (pp. 169–184). Norwood, NJ: Ablex.

Sato, C. J. (1988) Origins of complex syntax in interlanguage development. *Studies in Second Language Acquisition* 10 (3), 371–395.

Scarcella, R. C., Andersen, E. S., and Krashen, S. D. (eds) (1990) *Developing Communicative Competence in a Second Language* (Issues in Second Language Research). New York: Newbury House.

Schiffrin, D. (1996) Interactional sociolinguistics. In S. L. McKay and N. Hornberger (eds) *Sociolinguistics and Language Teaching* (pp. 307–328). Cambridge: Cambridge University Press.

Schumann, J. (1978) The acculturation model for second language acquisition. In R. Gingras (ed.) *Second Language Acquisition and Foreign Language Teaching* (pp. 27–50). Arlington, VA: Center for Applied Linguistics.

Selinker, L. (1972) Interlanguage. *International Review of Applied Linguistics* 10, 209–231.

Swain, M. (1985) Communicative competence: Some roles of comprehensive input and comprehensible output in its development. In S. M. Gass and C. Madden (eds) *Input in Second Language Acquisition* (pp. 235–253). Rowley, MA: Newbury House.

Valdés Fallis, G. (1976) Social interaction and code-switching patterns: A case study of Spanish/English alternation. In G. D. Keller, R. V. Teschner, and S. Viera (eds) *Bilingualism in the Bicentennial and Beyond* (pp. 53–85). Jamaica, NY: Bilingual Press.

Vesterbacka, S. (1991) Ritualised routines and L2 acquisition: Acquisition strategies in an immersion program. *Journal of Multilingual and Multicultural Development* 12 (1), 35–43.

Zentella, A. C. (1981) *Hablamos los dos.* We speak both: Growing up bilingual *in el Barrio.* Unpublished doctoral dissertation, University of Pennsylvania, Philadelphia.

Zentella, A. C. (1997) *Growing up Bilingual.* Malden, MA: Blackwell.

Zentella, A. C. (1998) Multiple codes, multiple identities: Puerto Rican children in New York City. In S. M. Hoyle and C. T. Adger (eds) *Kids Talk: Strategic Language Use in Later Childhood* (pp. 95–112). New York: Oxford University Press.

Part III: Studying Elicited Spoken Discourse to Inform Second Language Learning

Overview

This section of the volume offers examples of studies that clearly make the connection between linguistic and pragmatic competence. The four chapters herein illustrate how taking on an additional language necessarily entails knowing how to present oneself as one would wish – one of the most difficult tasks in a language other than one's L1.

The chapters make use of data derived from various types of role-plays, interviews and discourse completion tasks. Carrie Taylor-Hamilton's chapter, "Giving Directions as a Speech Behavior: A Cross-cultural Comparison of L1 and L2 Strategies," is an example of a combination of ethnographic methods and interview data. Taylor-Hamilton studies speaking as it occurs in an EFL setting, Arabic-speaking Abu Dhabi, focusing specifically on the problematic speech behavior of giving directions. Issues of identity are important in this data, as who the direction-asker is in relation to the direction-giver in this context directly affects the strategies chosen for the speech behavior. In order to compare L1 and L2 strategies, the author collected L1 Arabic baseline data and L1 British English data. For the L2 EFL data, she elicited directions through interviews in which she asked EFL students to tell her how to get to various places in and around Abu Dhabi. In addition, she used ethnographic interviews to tap into an *emic* perspective on direction-giving from members of the Abu Dhabi speech community in which the study took place. Through this combination of methodologies, using both qualitative and quantitative analysis, the chapter offers insights into one aspect of speaking that is difficult, not only for L2 learners, but for L1 speakers as well.

A second chapter in this section reports on a study carried out by Koji Konishi and Elaine Tarone: "English Constructions Used in Compensatory Strategies: Baseline Data for Communicative EFL Instruction." The chapter focuses on L1 speakers interacting with L2 learners in an EFL environment, with implications for communication skills. Konishi and Tarone specifically focus on Communication Strategies (CS) based on L1 syntactic patterns that emerge from the native speakers to show that practice using these patterns aids language learning in the FL setting. The study clearly demonstrates that CS use benefits from instruction, especially when instruction goes beyond vocabulary to build syntactic structures. The methodology of the study, that of analyzing speaking through role-plays, demonstrates the correlation between attributes of objects and the development of syntactic patterns.

The third chapter of this second section is by Kathleen Bardovi-Harlig and Tom Salsbury: "The Organization of Turns in the Disagreements of L2 Learners: A Longitudinal Perspective." The authors examine turn structure in disagreement exchanges to reveal what it means to be competent in oppositional talk contexts. The data consist of conversational interviews between adult students in intensive ESL study, and graduate students specializing in SLA. Based on studies of disagreements from a CA perspective, the authors demonstrate how opting out of disagreements and delaying disagreements can only be seen through the lens of the turns of a complete conversation. Methodologically, the study incorporates conversation elicitation tasks and CA. Moreover, the authors study oppositional talk over a period of time, thus offering a longitudinal advantage in the insights gleaned from the analysis. This research illustrates an important link between linguistic and pragmatic development.

The final study reported in this section is by Leslie M. Beebe and Hansun Zhang Waring: "The Linguistic Encoding of Pragmatic Tone: Adverbials as Words that Work." The authors employ a DCT instrument in which lower and higher proficiency ESL students are asked to respond to rude remarks. The DCT here was designed after large-scale collection of spontaneous instances of rude exchanges. Beebe and Waring are thus able to study the connection between grammatical and pragmatic proficiency, demonstrating how the ability to use adverbials appropriately contributes to pragmatic tone. The authors show the importance of learning how to express assertiveness and the dangers of being perceived as taking a hostile or rigid tone. These dangers are inherent in becoming socialized into a community of practice, since taking on the identity of ingroup membership entails knowing what counts as acceptable or rude.

Chapter 7

Giving Directions as a Speech Behavior: A Cross-cultural Comparison of L1 and L2 Strategies

CARRIE TAYLOR-HAMILTON

This chapter addresses research done on direction-giving in L2 English and compares it to baseline data in L1 English and L1 Arabic. The research, conducted in the United Arab Emirates, reveals that L2 English speakers are using a combination of strategies that differs from the combination of strategies used in the baseline data. I conclude that these differences may arise from issues in social identity or from transfer of training.

Introduction

Direction-giving is a commonly taught speech behavior in second language classrooms, one that is familiar to every language teacher. It is most often taught as part of the first year or beginner's curriculum, and is usually perceived to be one of the "easier" speech behaviors for language learners in their acquisition of pragmatic competence. Curriculum developers and textbook writers often assume that the speech act of giving directions only requires learners to be able to use the imperative and to learn a few simple vocabulary items, such as "right," "left," and "straight ahead." A perusal of introductory textbooks in commonly used ESL/EFL series reveals that many of the models of direction-giving are based upon the writer's intuition about how directions are given, but not on how authentic directions are given by first language speakers. These models often tend to ignore or minimalize very important aspects of direction-giving, such as use of landmarks, reference to street names, and, most significantly, the mixing of various direction-giving strategies to form a coherent sequence. In addition, in their search for low-level functions of language that can be put in an introductory text, writers

149

sometimes gloss over both the grammatical and the cultural complexity of direction-giving.

Researchers have rarely examined the speech behavior of direction-giving among second-language (L2) learners. As Kasper and Rose (1999) have noted, most interlanguage pragmatics research has been done on speech acts that involve the cross-cultural perception of politeness, such as requests and apologies. Most of the speech acts that have been addressed in interlanguage pragmatics research have social consequences for the second language learner; when Thomas (1983) referred to socio-pragmatic and pragmalinguistic failure, she was referring to the kind of failure in speech acts that would lead to social breakdown. Studying direction-giving looks at speech behavior failure of another kind, a more practical kind of failure that results not necessarily in social misunderstanding but in getting lost.

One of the reasons that there has been a noticeable lack of direction-giving studies, whether among first-language (L1) or second-language (L2) speakers or in comparison, is that there has been an assumption that most cultures view, think, and talk about space in similar ways. Foley (1997: 215) states that it has long been assumed that "we are predisposed to conceive of space in relativistic and egocentric terms, projecting out from the anatomical patterns of our bodies." In other words, researchers have assumed that different cultures talk about space in relational terms – that is, left, right, straight ahead – because of a universal perception of space being in relation to our own bodies. However, studies such as that conducted by Levinson (1997) among the Guugu Yimithirr of Australia show that some cultures may conceive of and talk about space entirely in cardinal terms such as north, south, east, and west. Brown and Levinson (1993) drew on the example of spatial description in Tzeltal to show that space can be talked about in terms that are non-relational. In the case of Tzeltal, local topography defines spatial description: an uphill/downhill axis forms the basis of all formulation of location in the language. Thus, the assumption that all languages rely primarily on relational directions and to a lesser degree on cardinal directions or landmarks is a false one.

The case of Tzeltal underscores the point that we cannot assume that there will be a one-to-one correspondence in the form that direction-giving takes between any two languages, any more than we can assume that there is a one-to-one correspondence in the form of apologies or requests, for example. It is therefore crucial that we study the baseline data of a speaker's L1 and the L2 so that we may better understand the nature of L2 direction-giving.

Background

In order to understand how a teacher might wish to teach direction-giving in a classroom, it is important to study exactly how direction-giving is done in first language contexts. Although countless studies have been conducted in cognitive science and cognitive psychology on the nature of spatial description, surprisingly few have been done on spatial description within the giving of directions. There are a number of studies on how humans find their way in urban environments ("wayfinding") and only a very small number of studies on how humans describe the route to a particular destination ("route description").

A British study on giving directions over the phone (Psathas & Kozloff, 1976) provided an analysis of how directions in English are structured. The study was mostly based on tape-recorded conversations in which directions were given over the telephone, but the data also included some face-to-face direction-giving encounters, which were written down but not tape-recorded. The analysis revealed that the direction-giving encounter is typically divided into three parts: an introductory section that defined the context of giving directions; an intermediate section in which the actual directions were given; and a final section which restated some directions and ended the encounter.

Similar to the Psathas and Kozloff study, other studies have attempted to establish a common pattern in the direction-giving sequence. For example, Wunderlich and Reinelt (1982), which was based on German data and attempted to categorize route descriptions into three parts, ending by establishing "a minimal standard model of route description" (pp. 195–196). In the same volume, Klein (1982: 168) looked at local deixis in route directions, or what was referred to as "route communication."[1] The study was based on 40 direction-giving sequences collected in a natural context in the main downtown shopping district of Frankfurt, Germany. This study showed a difference between those who gave directions in a step-by-step fashion and those who gave them in one long monologue, and also pointed out that most direction givers planned their route according to a mental "skeleton" of fixed points.

Another study (Denis, 1997) attempted to describe the underlying pattern used in describing a route, using data from 20 French-speaking undergraduates describing a university campus route. The researcher found landmarks to be a crucial component in the direction-giving sequences that he collected, and as such he constructed a recursive model of direction-giving that was based upon the establishment of fixed points and the description of the paths between those points.

Mark and Gould (1995) took a different tactic from the previous studies. In a cross-linguistic study of wayfinding directions in verbal discourse, the researchers collected 31 sequences of driving directions from white[2] English-speaking American participants in three North American cities and 22 sequences of driving directions from Spanish-speaking participants in Valencia, Spain. The results in both languages were compared for deictic references, reference frames, use of language concerning distance and direction (including use of repetition to indicate distance), description of turns, style of presentation (tense, voice, etc.), and conventional metaphors used in direction-giving. Although much of the article stemmed from the study of vehicle navigations systems, the authors also compare their findings to concepts such as narrative understanding, and models of spatial cognition.

Historical and situational background

The research presented in this chapter is based on a study conducted at the Abu Dhabi Men's College in the Higher Colleges of Technology, in the United Arab Emirates. All courses in the college were taught in English, and therefore semi-intensive courses that prepare students to study and function in English were essential. The present study is based on questions about direction-giving that arose within such semi-intensive EFL classes.

Research questions can arise from small issues in the classroom context. In the case of this study, the primary research question arose while I was teaching intensive English to these first-year technical college students. All the teachers in this program expressed dread at having to teach the unit on giving directions because it was so difficult for the students, and the students seemed to dread the unit as well. The consensus was that the students were "hopeless" at giving directions, and teachers were perplexed as to why such a simple, straightforward English function could prove to be so very difficult for these young Arab men. The male students were giving long, extremely detailed sequences of directions that the teachers found almost impossible to process. This raised the question of why accurate direction-giving in English seemed to be such a challenge for these students, and if direction-giving was equally difficult for them in their own language.

There are a number of unique practical and historical factors that affect the giving of directions in Abu Dhabi and throughout the UAE, and these factors have arisen in response to the unusual course of development that this country has taken over the past three decades. The need for giving directions in an urban context has probably only existed for about 30 years in Abu Dhabi. Before that time, only a few small towns existed, and within those towns there were usually only a very small number of permanent structures. There was typically a fort, a lookout tower, one or more mosques, and perhaps a few stone houses. Most of the houses were *barasti* or "palm-reed" huts, which were small structures built from reeds and not intended to last very long. In other words, historically there has been little need for giving directions within a town, since the towns were small enough for most people to know where everything was, and since few permanent structures existed anyway.

Since the oil boom of the 1960s, huge modern cities have sprung up. The phenomenal growth of these cities in the last 30 years has created a need for giving directions, but oftentimes the elements critical to giving directions (from a Western perspective) are missing. Street names are not common in cities in the UAE and are non-existent in towns and villages. Because of the desert landscape and the rapid development of modern, featureless cities, there are few landmarks by which to navigate. Furthermore, the UAE has an enormous expatriate population from India, Pakistan, the Philippines, Indonesia, and many Western countries. These groups often live separately and thus develop very different sets of important landmarks. Obviously, both the rapid development of the country and the multi-ethnic character of its society are contributing factors to the complexity of direction-giving in this particular place.

Research Questions

Recall that the research questions in this study arose from a classroom context. The primary research questions involved investigation of direction-giving strategies:

- How do speakers of L2 English give directions in English?
- What strategies do they use to give directions?
  How do L2 English speakers' norms in giving directions compare to the norms for L1 English and the speakers' own L1?
- What role does language transfer or transfer of training (including textbook modeling) have to play in the acquisition of English L2 direction-giving?

Research Design

As indicated above, this study was conducted at the Abu Dhabi Men's College, in the Higher Colleges of Technology, and the sample consisted of native Arabic-speaking students and native Arabic- and English-speaking faculty. The tape-recorded data include 46 direction-giving sequences of L1 Arabic speakers giving directions in L1 Arabic (hereinafter referred to as the L1 Arabic data), 50 direction-giving sequences of L1 English speakers from the United Kingdom giving directions in L1 UK English (hereinafter referred to as the L1 UK English data), and 118 direction-giving sequences of L1 Arabic speakers giving directions in L2 English (hereinafter referred to as the L2 English data).

Sample

The L1 Arabic data were collected from 46 male native speakers of Emirati Arabic, studying in Term 2 of the Certificate and Diploma (CD) course (a low-level technical training course for students who made less than 60% on their final high school exams), offered at the Higher Colleges of Technology. Two of the participants for the Arabic L1 data collection in the L1 Arabic data were also participants in the L2 English data.

The L2 English data similarly were collected entirely from male native speakers of Arabic, studying in Term 2 of the Higher Colleges CD Program. All 118 participants had studied English in high school and had had two terms (approximately four months) of preparatory "bridge year" English at the college. However, they had not been streamed for English ability prior to placement in the program, and there was a great deal of variation in L2 English ability within the group. Their CD English classes had included a unit on giving directions, which had been covered by all participants prior to this task.

The L1 UK English data were collected from English, Welsh, Scottish, or Irish adult male and female speakers of English, all of whom were faculty or supervisors at Abu Dhabi Men's College or Abu Dhabi Women's College. Since the English curriculum in the Higher Colleges is based on a UK standard of English, it was decided to collect directions only from those who were native speakers of a UK/British Isles variety.

Instruments

The aim of the study was to answer the research questions by collecting direction-giving sequences from Emirati L2 English speakers and comparing the strategies used in those sequences to direction-giving sequences in baseline data (L1 English speakers and L1 Arabic speakers). The possibility of using a discourse completion task was not considered, since the direction-giving needed to be done under authentic time pressure and cognitive demands. Since direction-giving is a speech behavior that usually takes place on the street between a person who is unfamiliar with a place and another person who is familiar with the place, the best procedure to follow would have been to ask directions on the street and tape-record the interactions. However, since a woman stopping a strange man on the streets to ask for directions is not common in Emirati culture, another procedure had to be devised. Instead, I decided to ask male university participants to answer a direct question (as would be posed on the street) and audiotape their responses.

These audiotaped interviews were planned as one-on-one sessions that would last five to ten minutes each. The data collection consisted of short, one-on-one interviews with the respondent being asked a direct wayfinding question – "How do I get to x" – with the response being tape-recorded. It was felt that this type of elicitation procedure, although a kind of role-play, would produce responses that were as close to authentic as possible.

Data collection procedures

The interviews for the L2 data were conducted in a small room adjacent to the faculty offices in the college. Participants were sent down from their English classes to do the interview as a "practice speaking test." They were told that they would be recorded, and the recorder and the microphone were in full view of the participants as they were being interviewed. As a warm up, participants were asked six general information questions and the answers were written down on a form. This practice was in keeping with the kinds of practical English tasks they were learning in the classroom. The questions, however, were specifically designed to elicit information that would be useful to this study. They included name, address (area of the city), date of birth, place of birth, occupation, years of English study, other countries visited and length of stay, and whether or not the speaker could drive and owned a car. The interviews took between five and ten minutes each, depending on factors such as proficiency or desire to elaborate.

I then asked the participants to do a description task that was unrelated to the study at hand in order to "warm them up" for speaking. After this task was completed, I asked the participants for directions to one well-known location, assuming the interlocutor was driving a car and starting from the college. I chose the destination from a prepared list and the choice was based on where the student was from, where the student currently resided, whether or not he had a driver's license, and whether or not he had a car. Thus, for example, a student from Abu Dhabi who lived in Abu Dhabi and drove his own car would be asked directions to the telephone company or the *souq* (market) or a local hospital. I would therefore ask a student from the outlying areas who did not drive and did not have a car to give directions to his home area from the college, assuming that he came that way every day and would be familiar with it. The destinations used were abundantly familiar to the student and easy enough to describe while at the same time eliciting a good deal of language production. The respondents were allowed to speak freely, with appropriate back-channeling. I also asked occasional questions to clarify a response, without prompting or helping the direction-giver in any way.

The Arabic baseline data were gathered about two months later in a similar fashion. The majority of the participants were different from the L2 group: only two of the participants had taken part in the L2 data gathering procedure. Participants came to the same room at Abu Dhabi Men's College to do a similar "practice speaking" with me under the same conditions. However, this time at the end of each interview, I asked the participants if they would mind answering some questions in Arabic in the next room. They were given the opportunity to refuse if they felt uncomfortable with the task. They were also offered candy as a small token of thanks for helping with this project.

Participants went to a nearby office, where a native speaker of Arabic was waiting with a tape recorder. Three Arabic-speaking teachers (two males from Palestine and Algeria and one female from Syria) at the college helped with this task. When the participants came into the room, the teachers asked them three questions each in Arabic. The teachers asked for their names, where they lived, and whether or not they were drivers. They then chose one destination from a list that I had prepared, and the choice was again based on maximizing success for the speaker. All questions and all responses were in Arabic.

The collection of L1 English data proceeded in a different manner since a speaking-test format was not feasible in this case. The interviews were conducted over a period of weeks, and about six months after the L1 Arabic data was collected. I identified native speakers of UK/British Isles English who were working in the college system and asked them to participate. These interviews usually took place either at the participant's desk or in the teacher resource room. I asked the UK participants directly to give directions to either a well-known supermarket or other common destinations for expatriates in Abu Dhabi. Their answers were recorded on a hand-held tape-recorder that was in full view.

After all the data were collected, I conducted ethnographic interviews with two pairs of Emirati students in the form of a "ride" around Abu Dhabi. These two two-hour interviews provided rich information on perception of space and place in Abu Dhabi, as well as very valuable information regarding Emirati perspectives on direction-giving.

Procedure for data analysis

To reiterate, three sets of data were collected: primary data in L2 English from 118 male native speakers of Emirati Gulf Arabic, baseline data in Arabic from 46 male speakers of Emirati Gulf Arabic, and baseline data in L1 English from 50 male and female speakers of UK/British Isles English. Each set of data was coded and analyzed for direction-giving strategies, and a statistical analysis was carried out using SPSS.

The study of direction-giving strategies in any language would most likely involve data on the following strategies: relative directions (right, left, in front of, behind), absolute (north, south, east, west), or landmarks/place names (the Co-op supermarket, the falcon statue). The data in this study were found to include these three kinds of strategies, following Levinson's (1992) model of "three distinctive kinds of location conception" (p. 20). In addition, following L. Brown (1998), the use of road names as a "navigational strategy" (p. 2) was included, since this type of strategy is commonly present in data describing an urban area. Therefore, the types of strategy use counted in this data consisted of relative directions, cardinal directions, landmarks, and street names. Of these, relative directions, landmarks, and street names proved to be the most commonly used strategies in all three types of data. Use of cardinal directions was extremely rare, but since this counts as a major strategy in most languages, it was necessary to include it and verify the low incidence of use.

The results were analyzed using a one-way ANOVA to compare the incidence of strategy use across all groups and a Tukey test to analyze the significance of the differences among the three groups. Both of these procedures were done using the Statistical Package for Social Sciences (SPSS).

Findings

The study revealed a number of differences in the strategies selected by L1 English speakers, L2 English speakers, and L1 Arabic speakers. The result of the frequency count for strategy use can be seen in Table 7.1. According to the ANOVA analysis for this data (included in Appendix 2), comparing percentage of strategy use across all three groups, the

Table 7.1 Average number of strategy uses per sequence

Data source	Average number of landmarks/ sequence	Average number of street names/ sequence	Average number of relational directions/ sequence
UK L1 English (50 sequences)	2.04	2.26	5.26
Emirati L2 English (118 sequences)	0.96	0.80	5.58
Emirati L1 Arabic (46 sequences)	2.59	1.09	4.41

difference among the three types of strategies is highly significant ($p < 0.000$) across all three language types.

The Tukey test (also in Appendix 2) shows that, in the results for landmarks, the difference between L2 English and L1 English is highly significant, as is the difference between L2 English and L1 Arabic. There is no statistically significant difference in the use of landmarks in L1 English and L1 Arabic. For street names, the Tukey test reveals that there is a statistically significant difference only between L2 English and L1 English. In the third area, there is a significant difference in the use of relational directions between L1 English and L2 English, and there is also a difference between L2 English and L1 Arabic. However, there is no significant difference between L1 English and L1 Arabic in the use of relational directions.

This statistical procedure shows us that, in the case of landmarks, the L2 speakers are using significantly fewer landmarks in their directions than do L1 Arabic speakers and L1 English speakers. L1 English speakers and L1 Arabic speakers do not have a significant difference in their use of landmarks, so it is notable that L2 speakers are choosing to leave the landmarks out. The analysis of the use of street names reveals that the L2 speakers are using significantly fewer street names in L2 English than do native speakers of English, but not significantly more than speakers of L1 Arabic. In other words, for the street names, the L2 behavior is more like L1 Arabic. For the analysis of relational directions, the Tukey procedure shows that the L2 speakers are using more relational directions than speakers of L1 English and L1 Arabic, although L1 English and L1 Arabic use relational directions with similar frequency.

In other words, in two cases out of three, the L2 speakers are using direction-giving strategies in frequencies that are not like L1 English and not like the L1 Arabic. In every case, the use of strategies is significantly different from L1 English, and only in one case (street names) is the frequency of a strategy similar to that in L1 Arabic.

The average number of landmarks per direction-giving sequence reveals that Emirati participants speaking L2 English used half as many landmarks as L1 UK English speakers. Interestingly, however, Emirati speakers using L1 Arabic to Arabic-speaking interlocutors actually had a higher (0.55 higher) average use of landmarks per sequence than did native speakers of L1 English. However, this slight difference does not have statistical significance.

A similar result is shown for use of street name strategies. Emirati participants giving directions in L2 English used far fewer street names than did native speakers of L1 UK English, and these results do show a statistically significant difference. Native speakers of UK L1 English used almost three times as many street names when giving directions. The average number of street names used per sequence did not rise a great deal when Emirati participants were giving directions in Arabic to an Arabic interlocutor; the number rose only from an average of 0.80 per sequence to an average of 1.09 per sequence.

Relational directions were clearly used more than either landmarks or street names among all three groups of respondents. The table shows a very similar use of relational directions in L1 UK English and L2 English. Native speakers of L1 UK English used an average of 5.26 relational directions per sequence, whereas Emirati speakers of L2 English used a slightly higher average of 5.58 relational directions per sequence. The slight difference between these two is statistically significant, according to the results of the Tukey test. Surprisingly, the use of relational directions appeared lower among L1 Emirati Arabic speakers. When speaking in Arabic to an Arabic interlocutor, participants used an average of only 4.41 relational directions per sequence, the lowest average of the three groups. It is therefore possible to say that native speakers of Emirati Arabic used the most relational directions of all groups when speaking in L2 English (although only slightly more than L1 English), and the fewest relational directions of all groups when speaking in Arabic.

The occurrence of cardinal directions was so rare that it was not included in the strategies chart. There were two uses of cardinal directions in the L2 English data, two uses in the L1 Arabic data, and three uses in the L1 UK English data.

Discussion

The findings show that Emirati L2 English speakers were using significantly fewer landmarks and street names than in L1 English, yet using a similar and slightly higher number of relational directions. Thus, it appears that the frequency with which L2 learners used these three strategies differed from the baseline data. The L2 speakers were not using more relational directions, but they were using more in proportion to the number of landmarks and street names used than did L1 English and L1 Arabic speakers.

It appears that the Emirati L2 English learners were following neither Arabic norms nor English norms for the balance of strategy use in direction-giving. Emirati L2 English speakers were using street names and landmarks only half as much as they were used in the baseline English data, but they were using relational directions with almost the same frequency as the baseline L1 English data. However, in baseline Emirati Arabic L1 data, the use of relational directions was less frequent and the use of landmarks was more frequent than in the L2 data or the English baseline data.

The outcome of the frequency count for strategy use in this study raises many questions. When we compare the average numbers for strategy use among the three language groups as presented in Table 7.1, it becomes obvious that of the three strategies most commonly used, landmarks and relational directions are the two that are being used in proportionately different ways.

Relational directions

As stated previously, the strategy that was used the most frequently in all groups and in the most consistent way in all groups was relational directions. In UK L1 English and Emirati L2 English, relational directions were used an average of almost 5.3 times per sequence and almost 5.6 times per sequence respectively, which presented a high frequency of use for these two groups. Only in Arabic did we find a somewhat lower (4.4) average use per sequence. It seems possible just from the overall frequency of occurrence of this strategy to claim that relational directions probably represent the canonical direction-giving strategy in both English and Emirati Arabic. However, their use as the premier strategy was more clearly defined in English, both in the L1 and L2 data. In other words, the difference between the frequency of relational directions compared to the frequency of other strategies was clearer and more striking in English than in Arabic. Since the Arabic data had a lower frequency average of relational directions and a higher frequency average of landmarks, the supremacy of relational directions did not appear so clear-cut. It may be that, in Emirati Arabic, the use of relational directions as a primary direction-giving strategy is less well defined or less agreed-upon than in English.

All of the participants had prior exposure to direction-giving strategies in English textbooks, portrayed primarily in relational terms, before being asked to give directions in Arabic. Also, the Arabic direction-giving data were collected at the college, where English was the language of instruction and where the English L2 direction-giving data were collected. Both of these facts could have influenced the frequency of relational strategies in the Emirati Arabic data. Unfortunately, it was not possible to determine the extent of the influence from English.

It is also evident within the data that many of the participants found the use of relational directions in English a difficult and challenging task. There were numerous instances of confusion regarding the words for right and left and even the concepts of right and left. Although this was probably due to lack of knowledge of the terms in English, it is possible to speculate that some lack of familiarity with this strategy in Arabic caused difficulty for some participants. However, it is interesting to note that, in spite of this difficulty, the L2 participants used this strategy more than any other.

Street names

The use of street names was twice as common in the L1 English data as it was in the L2 English data. This difference was highly statistically significant, according to the Tukey test. However, the use of street names in L2 English is only slightly more frequent than the use in L1 Arabic. The ethnographic data collected for this study also points out that Emiratis consider street naming to be an uncommon strategy in direction-giving, one that is perceived to be "Western."

The infrequent use of street names among L2 participants and L1 Arabic participants may have to do with general problems of street naming in Abu Dhabi. Street signs have only recently been put up in the city, and most streets are known by several names. Streets have numbered names (Fourth Street), map names (Hazaa bin Zayed Street), and what are known as "taxi driver" names (Passport Road). The "taxi driver" names usually refer to the most prominent destination on the road, but often have historical reference to a destination or landmark that was once there but is no longer in existence. Therefore, the naming of streets is a very complex matter in which participants must judge by which name the interlocutor might know the street. It is not surprising that Emirati L2 speakers would choose to use street names less with a foreign interlocutor, due only to confusion about which name to use.

Landmarks

Perhaps the most salient finding of the data is that there were clear-cut differences between the L1 data sets and the L2 data set in the use of the strategy of landmarks. The use of landmarks (such as "the Maqta Bridge" or "the Etisalat building") in Emirati L2 English was surprisingly infrequent, given that the strategy of landmark use is common in both L1 English and L1 Arabic. The L2 English data showed an average use of just slightly less than one landmark per sequence. However, even in a cursory look at the data (see data samples in Appendix 1), the absence of landmarks was a striking feature of the L2 sequences compared to the more frequent use of landmarks in L1 English and L1 Arabic. The L1 English data revealed a use of slightly more than two landmarks per sequence, and the L1 Arabic data had an even higher average of more than two and a half landmarks per sequence. Clearly, Arabic speakers in this study commonly used landmarks when giving directions in their L1,[3] and English speakers frequently used the landmark strategy in their own L1. This brings us to question of why Arabic speakers using L2 English would employ only half the number of landmarks normally occurring in the native language and the L2.

In this case, L2 speakers were neither transferring a strategy commonly used in the speech behavior in their own L1, nor were they aiming for the L2 norms for the same speech behavior. One possible explanation for this could be that they were "opting out" (Bonikowska, 1988: 169) of one particular part of the speech act of referring within the speech behavior of giving directions. Bonikowska states that, "the opting out choice is as much a pragmatic choice as any strategic choice employed in speech act performance, made through activating the same components of pragmatic knowledge." In other words, it is the social or practical motivation behind the choice not to perform the speech act that needs to be studied.

In the case of Arabic-speaking participants opting out of using the speech act of reference by using landmarks, there could have been two (possibly related) motivating factors. One explanation could be lack of vocabulary knowledge in L2. The participants in this study were for the most part low-proficiency students of English who could have either lacked the necessary vocabulary for referring to landmarks or who could have lacked confidence in their ability to refer to local landmarks in English. It is necessary to take both of these reasons into consideration, for lack of vocabulary alone cannot explain the choice to opt out. This is because the vocabulary needed to refer to landmarks is, in the majority of the cases, the same in both Arabic and English. However, the students who participated in this study were not necessarily aware of this fact. As young people who were for the most part very unfamiliar with English-speaking people, they may have assumed that English-speaking people had *different* proper names for things like Etisalat. They may have even assumed that a word like "Sheraton" could be an Arabic word, and felt that, since they did not know the English name, they would simply opt out of referring to it.

This brings us to the second explanation for lack of landmarks in the L2 data: the act of choosing a proper noun to refer to a place is a *social* choice that takes place within a *social* context. The choice to use landmarks or not may be related less to knowledge of the language than it was to knowledge of the kind of language to use with a particular interlocutor. In other words, the decision not to use landmarks when giving directions may have been based on the fact that the participants were not just giving directions to a disembodied, neutral, hypothetical figure (as they would in an EFL textbook-based task, for example) but rather to a real, living foreign female interlocutor. The choices that they were required to make had to be based not only on their own knowledge of Abu Dhabi, but also on what they could assume that this foreign female interlocutor knew about Abu Dhabi.

Furthermore, their choices of landmarks could have reflected their choice of displaying their language identity. Participants in this study had the option of choosing strategies that were more like their L1 or more like the L2. They also had the option of choosing landmarks that would be relevant in their own society or landmarks that they think might be relevant to L1 English speakers. In both cases, they were making a sociolinguistic/pragmatic choice to reflect a particular identity, which could be expressed along a continuum of identity between their own L1 culture and the L2 culture. In choosing a landmark, they chose a place for themselves along that continuum.

The problems of formulating place and the social complexity of choosing a way to refer to a particular location are discussed in Schegloff (1972). There was much in his discussion of how we formulate place that can help explain why the L2 participants in this study used so few landmarks. One of the three factors that Schegloff listed as necessary for formulation of place was membership analysis. In discussion of membership analysis, he maintained that certain forms of place formulation would automatically mark someone who asks for directions as a stranger. He gave the example of asking for the "Long Island Train Terminal" instead of "Penn Station" in New York, and claimed that formulating a place in such a way automatically excluded the person who was asking from the co-membership category of the New Yorker who was being asked. In the case of this L2 direction-giving study, it seems possible that something similar may have occurred. The fact that I asked for directions to a particular place *using English* may have marked me immediately as a non-member of the membership group "those who live in and know Abu Dhabi." Furthermore, since Abu Dhabi is a fairly small place, the fact that I had to ask for directions at all probably emphasized the lack of co-membership and marked my identity even further as an outsider.

In the same section on membership analysis, Schegloff goes on to talk about "expectable recognizability": how the choice of a particular place name places a requirement on the part of the speaker that the hearer perform an analysis of the relevance of the name to both speaker and hearer (Schegloff, 1972: 116). In other words, if a participant in this study used a landmark name, he was both assuming that his interlocutor would have the ability to recognize its relevance within the context of Abu Dhabi and imposing a requirement upon the interlocutor to analyze its relevance. This would constitute an assumption of knowledge that many participants probably felt they could not be certain of as well as an imposition on someone of higher status (a teacher, a researcher, an older female) that they may have felt was too strong.

Furthermore, the participants may have had yet another motive in not using landmarks. The use of a particular place name is somewhat risky, especially to an L2 learner, because it is an opening for possible negotiation. Many of these participants may have been trying to avoid the possibility that I would not recognize the place name and thus ask them about it, opening up unfamiliar territory that they would have to negotiate in their limited English.

There are many considerations that a speaker must take into account when using a noun phrase to refer to a specific entity, and thus the speech act of referring can be a "collaborative process" (Clark & Wilkes-Gibbs, 1986: 1). Much of the information about the collaborative nature of referring is relevant to the use or non-use of landmarks by L2 speakers in this study. Clark and Wilkes-Gibbs propose that, when a speaker uses a specific noun phrase, such as a landmark name, the speaker intends and believes that the noun phrase will become a part of the "common ground" of the speaker and the hearer. They go on to say that "if at any moment in making the reference, he [the speaker] thinks that it [the noun phrase] won't [become part of the common ground], he should change or expand on what he has done so far" (Clark & Wilkes-Gibbs, 1986: 7; brackets mine). They further propose the idea that both speaker and hearer must be able to accept one another's references in order for conversation to proceed. They state that, "conversations proceed in an orderly way only if the common ground of the participants accumulates in an orderly way" (Clark & Wilkes-Gibbs, 1986: 9).

However, unfortunately, the choice of opting out of using a landmark as a specific reference often backfired on the participants, producing more complication in the direction-giving sequence at a later stage. To understand how the complications arise, it is important to understand a principle put forth by Clark and Wilkes-Gibbs. At the end of their 1986 article, they proposed that selection of a specific noun phrase within a conversation is governed by a guiding principle, which is the need to "minimize collaborative effort." The principle of least collaborative effort predicts that there will be trade-offs between making the first attempt at referral as specific as possible and making the effort to re-state or elaborate on the reference at a later point in the conversation.

The participants in this study who opted out of using landmarks may have been doing so in what they perceived as an effort to reduce collaborative effort in the direction-giving sequence, but they failed to notice that reducing the initial effort of formulation of reference could result in trade-offs later in the sequence. They had to be explicit either in using landmarks or in using relational directions, and the fact that they failed to specify a landmark often meant that they had to produce a more complex set of relational directions at some point in the sequence. Since relational directions may be in some sense more difficult to keep track of, this resulted in confused direction-giving on the part of the speaker and less understanding on the part of the hearer.

In summary, it is important to point out that the difference in the use of landmarks in L1 Arabic and L2 English may represent a social choice on the part of the participants. The task of giving directions to a foreign female interlocutor may have presented a context in which the participants felt they lacked not only linguistic knowledge but a certain kind of social knowledge as well. To use a landmark, speakers have to be able to make predictions about what kind of knowledge they share with their interlocutors about a place, and to do this they must be able to assume that the knowledge that they and their interlocutors have does indeed intersect at some point. It is noteworthy that the participants failed to use landmarks because it may indicate that they failed to conceive of any kind of shared membership with the researcher. They were students; the researcher was a teacher. They were locals; the researcher was a foreigner. The list could go on, but from this short list alone, it is easy to see why they might come to the conclusion that no "common ground" could accumulate in these sequences.

Limitations

The present study was limited by two major factors. Gender was an issue, and many of the decisions made in this study were forced by reasons of social segregation. A gender-balanced study was not really a practicality, since most of the female students in the UAE are extremely limited in their ability to move around the town freely. Thus, comparison of the two groups would have been confounded by a serious lack of direction-giving experience on the part of the females. The choice to include female participants in the UK L1 data was also made for practical reasons, since there were only a limited number of UK male teachers who were accessible.

The second limitation was that the interlocutors who collected the L1 Arabic data were not all male and none of them were native speakers of Emirati Arabic. It would have been better to have native speakers of the same variety of Arabic as the participants in the study (as Arabic has a wide variety of dialects). However, it would have been culturally inappropriate to ask Emirati females for help with these interviews, and, due to sexual segregation, I had little opportunity to interact with male Emiratis who could have helped. Thus, the interviews had to be conducted by non-Emiratis who were familiar with Emirati Arabic.

Pedagogical Implications

There are several findings from this study of direction-giving that are important for the study of L1 speaking data for second language acquisition research in general and interlanguage pragmatics research in particular. The first and most significant finding concerns the differences in the use of strategies in L1 baseline data and L2 data. Not only were there some differences in baseline L1 and L2 production in direction-giving, but the data also revealed that the direction-giving units in many ESL/EFL textbooks may be based on a misleading assumption about how directions are actually given in L1 English.

Second language teaching should be informed through studies of speaking in L1, and the results of this study can be useful in discussing some ways in which the teaching of giving directions in English could be transformed and enhanced. The data also reflect the fact that, at least for some L2 learner groups, the approach to teaching directions in many current ESL/EFL texts could be a source of confusion. Many ESL/EFL texts approach direction-giving in a simplified way, relying almost entirely on imperatives and relational directions, that do not reflect the true complex nature of the speech behavior in English. If beginning texts rely too much on the strategy of relational directions, this could lead to overgeneralization of patterns that, while common in English, do not represent direction-giving in its entirety.

If textbook writers examine authentic direction-giving in English, rather than relying on intuition for dialogue development, this could lead to textbook direction-giving dialogues that have an appropriate balance of native-like direction-giving strategies. This research project provides a clear example of how the study of baseline L1 English norms can inform both textbook writing and L2 teaching. Although it is neither practical nor feasible for teachers to gather this information themselves, researchers can provide this kind of insight that might lead to improvements in teaching.

Another part of a new approach should be to take into account that there is an intercultural aspect to giving directions in a second language. ESL/EFL texts may need to acknowledge that different cultural groups who are learning English may view space and place differently. In other words, students from different countries who are studying English in London, for example, may all have a slightly different view of which places in London are significant for direction-giving. It would therefore be beneficial for a textbook unit on direction-giving to start out with activities that require L2 learners to discuss their view of a particular place and discuss which landmarks, streets, and areas held significance for them. This would also provide the teacher with an opportunity to present the students with a "local" picture of place by identifying landmarks of special importance to native residents of the city. These kinds of activities would increase students' awareness that the cultural context of L2 English learning may view a place differently from the way that their own cultural groups view it, and would have the additional effect of improving intercultural awareness in general.

Conclusion

One of the reasons that direction-giving is a speech behavior worthy of study is that it has for so long been considered a kind of "universal" act, one that would vary little from language to language and culture to culture. Teachers, textbook writers, researchers, and indeed people in general make false assumptions about this speech behavior, assuming simplicity when in fact there is great complexity. In summarizing research done on space and direction-giving, Foley (1997) states, "Basically, the view [within linguistics and cognitive psychology] is the following. Spatial conception is informed by innate, presumably biologically based universals, so that it is essentially the same in all languages and cultures" (1997: 215; brackets mine). If the assumption in linguistics and cognitive psychology has been that we all talk about space in essentially the same way, the naive and untutored assumptions among second language teachers and second language textbooks have been at least equally universalist. In second language teaching, direction-giving has been thought of as something that does not vary from language to language, a speech behavior that carries little cultural baggage and can be taught as having a one-to-one correlation between native language and L2. Furthermore, it has been taught as a speech behavior that has little to do with social context. It has been considered both socially and linguistically neutral for teaching purposes. The findings of the present study are useful in that they have pointed out that there are patterns and strategies in direction-giving that may differ from one language to another, and that direction-giving, far from being a socially neutral speech behavior, is thoroughly situated in and sensitive to social context.

Furthermore, the findings of this study point out that we cannot assume that our intuitions about a speech behavior in our native language are correct and we also cannot assume that there will be straightforward transfer of even the most seemingly neutral speech behaviors in second language learning. What we know about language, and especially what we teach about language, needs to be based upon study of authentic production. However, even knowledge about the norms of an event for a speech community will not necessarily override the perceived social needs of a second language speaker. In her discussion of cross-cultural pragmatics, Boxer (2002: 162) states, "Vestiges of communication styles persist. . . . Because of this, we cannot merely hope to 'educate' the newcomer into a new set of norms." Instead, as language teachers we can hope to study and expose learners to the most authentic set of norms, and then allow them to use those norms as they see fit in meeting their own social needs.

Notes

1. Interestingly, Klein remarks that there is no agreed-upon name for this kind of communication in English, an insight which had also occurred to me while

trying to research this subject. He states that German has one term for this activity, "Wegauskunft."

2. Mark and Gould explicitly state that they excluded non-white participants in order to avoid "complicating factors" in their study (1995: 388–389).

3. Indeed, the ethnographic interviews revealed that participants considered use of landmarks to be the primary direction-giving strategy commonly used among Emirati nationals. Use of relational directions and especially street names was considered to be a bit odd or foreign.

Appendix 1: Data samples

Examples from L1 UK/British Isles data

I: B39, tell me, can you tell me how to get from here to Spinney's?

B39: Ok, you come out the front of the college and you go on to 11th Street. Go straight along 11th Street, over Airport Road, over 24th Street, over 26th Street, and when you come to 30th Street [unint] 30th Street, you take a right.

I: Ok

B39: You take that right turn, you go straight down until you get to Lamcy Plaza, there's a junction there at Lamcy Plaza. At Lamcy Plaza, the junction at Lamcy Plaza, you turn left, and go through one set of lights and at the second set of lights you take a right turn, and you'll find Spinney's on your left.

I: Ok, thank you very much.

I: Can you tell me how to get from here to Spinney's? Big Spinney's?

B22: The big Spinney's, right, ok, Carrie. From here to Spinney's. Not very good from here to Spinney's. Uhmmm, first of all you come out of the Corniche, so you come out . . . out from the college . . . and . . . from here from the college? The actual college itself?

I: Yeah. Yeah.

B22: Ok, so you come out of the college, go out of the main gate we come in through, take a right, and then just continue until you hit . . . well, I only know the roads by numbers, so number six. No, it's not number six, number four (laughs). I don't know! Anyway, you go down there and continue all the way down to the end to the Corniche. And you'll know when you hit the Corniche because you've got the sea in front of you. And then take a left and go all the way along until you come to the end of the buildings, and you can see a little island over to your right. At the end of the buildings there's the old Women's College on your left, but . . . you need to go up beyond that to the traffic lights where you can take a right to the junction. I don't know this is maybe a few kilometers along. And then you would do in fact a u-turn to the left, and then go back on yourself, take the first right and Spinney's should be there, and if it's not there it will be somewhere in the near vicinity.

I: Ok (laughing)

Examples from L2 English data

I: Do you know where the women's college is in Khalidiya?

A59:   (long pause) . . . women's college?

I: Abu Dhabi Women's College?

A59:   College?   Yes, yes

I: If I'm here at this college and I must go to the women's college, can you tell me how to go there?

A59:   Ahhh . . . (cough) . . . go st . . . here the street, go straight on and one signal uhhh go straight on, next signal go straight g-g-go straight on and turn right, turn right, yes, see the signal, go straight on, another signal, go straight on (whispers to himself) another signal go straight on and gooo . . . go left, and the signal not go [unintelligible] and go right . . . go straight on. Ana one signal, the next sig-signal, go right. It's behind, behind Corniche

I: Ok

A59:   . . . opposite, opposite Corniche.

I: You said that you work in Mussafah at Adnoc?

A65:   Yes.

I: Can you tell me how to go from this college to Adnoc in Mussafah?

A65:   Ok, uhhh you enter . . . yeah, yeah . . . you enter in Higher College, ok? Go to street Muroor, Muroor street, go to . . . street? Ok, after two, two, what?

I: Uh, lights?

A65:   L-l-l-lights, t-two lights, turn right [interruption from faculty member] ok, after t-turn right, go to the uh, go to street, street, street, yeah, yeah you see maybe four light, after turn left and go to street. Go to street uh maybe uh, uh 12 k- kilometers, after the . . . right, you see l-light, ok, and go right, you see three what this?

I: Roundabout?

A65:   R-r-roundabout, three roundabout, and you can see Adnoc.

I: Ok, thank you very much, ok.

Appendix 2: ANOVA and Tukey analysis charts

Table A.1 ANOVA: Landmarks

	Sum of squares	df	Mean square	F	Sig.
Between groups	1.243	2	0.621	28.566	0.000
Within groups	4.589	211	0.022		
Total	5.831	213			

Table A.2 ANOVA: Relational directions

	Sum of squares	df	Mean square	F	Sig.
Between groups	2.466	2	1.233	32.824	0.000
Within groups	7.927	211	0.038		
Total	10.394	213			

Table A.3 ANOVA: Street names

	Sum of squares	df	Mean square	F	Sig.
Between groups	0.374	2	0.187	8.543	0.000
Within groups	4.617	211	0.022		
Total	4.990	213			

Table A.4 Tukey test results

Dependent variable		(I) Code	(J) Code	Mean difference (I–J)	Std. error	Sig.
LM_P	Tukey HSD	1	2	0.1186	0.02489	0.000
			3	−0.0606	0.03013	0.112
		2	1	−0.1186	0.02489	0.000
			3	−0.1793	0.02563	0.000
		3	1	0.0606	0.03013	0.112
			2	0.1793	0.02563	0.000
SN_P	Tukey HSD	1	2	0.1029	0.02496	0.000
			3	0.0649	0.03022	0.083
		2	1	−0.1029	0.02496	0.000
			3	−0.0380	0.02571	0.304
		3	1	−0.0649	0.03022	0.083
			2	0.0380	0.02571	0.304
RD_P	Tukey HSD	1	2	−0.2185	0.03271	0.000
			3	−0.0056	0.03960	0.989
		2	1	0.2185	0.03271	0.000
			3	0.2129	0.03369	0.000
		3	1	0.0056	0.03960	0.989
			2	−0.2129	0.03369	0.000

Note

I am grateful for the help of Ms Teresa Kerr at the University of the Incarnate Word for her invaluable help with the statistical analysis for this chapter.

References

Bonikowska, M. (1988) The choice of opting out. *Applied Linguistics* 9 (2), 169–181.

Boxer, D. (2002) Discourse issues in cross-cultural pragmatics. *Annual Review of Applied Linguistics* 22, 150–167.

Brown, L. (1998) Age and gender-related differences in strategy use for route information: A "map-present" direction-giving paradigm. On WWW at http://iac.fcla.edu/cgi-bin/cgiwrap/-fcliach/cgi2iac/UF?20515916.

Brown, P. and Levinson, S. C. (1993) "Uphill" and "downhill" in Tzeltal. *Journal of Linguistic Anthropology* 3 (1), 46–74.

Clark, H. and Wilkes-Gibbs, D. (1986) Referring as a collaborative process. *Cognition* 22 (1), 1–39.

Denis, M. (1997) The description of routes: A cognitive approach to the production of spatial discourse. *Cahiers de Psychologie Cognitive/Current Psychology of Cognition* 16 (4), 409–458.

Foley, W. A. (1997) *Anthropological Linguistics: An Introduction.* Oxford: Blackwell.

Kasper, G. and Rose, K. (1999) Pragmatics and SLA. *Annual Review of Applied Linguistics* 19, 81–104.

Klein, W. (1982) Local deixis in route directions. In R. J. Jarvella and W. Klein (eds) *Speech, Place, & Action: Studies in Deixis and Related Topics.* Chichester: John Wiley and Sons.

Levinson, S. (1992) Primer for the field investigation of spatial description and conception. *Pragmatics* 2 (1), 5–47.

Levinson, S. (1997) Language and cognition: The cognitive consequences of spatialdescription in Guugu Yimithirr. *Journal of Linguistic Anthropology* 7 (1), 98–131.

Mark, D. M. and Gould, M. D. (1995) Wayfinding directions as discourse: Verbal directions in English and Spanish. In J. Duchan, G. Bruder, and L. Hewitt (eds) *Deixis in Narrative: A Cognitive Science Perspective.* Hillsdale, NJ: Lawrence Erlbaum.

Psathas, G. and Kozloff, M. (1976) The structure of directions. *Semiotica* 17 (2), 111–130.

Schegloff, E. A. (1972) Notes on a conversational practice: Formulating place. In P. P. Giglioli (ed.) *Language and Social Context* (pp. 95–135). New York: Penguin.

Thomas, J. (1983) Cross-cultural pragmatic failure. *Applied Linguistics* 4 (2), 91–112.

Wunderlich, D. and Reinelt, R. (1982) How to get there from here. In R. J. Jarvella and W. Klein (eds) *Speech, Place, & Action: Studies in Deixis and Related Topics* (pp. 183–202). Chichester: John Wiley and Sons.

Chapter 8

English Constructions Used in Compensatory Strategies: Baseline Data for Communicative EFL Instruction[1]

KOJI KONISHI AND ELAINE TARONE

This chapter offers baseline data on the frequency of specific linguistic constructions used by native speakers of North American English in communication strategies referring to specified attributes of targeted items. The study analyzes the communication strategy use of 30 native speakers of English as they described 17 unfamiliar items to a listener with limited English language proficiency. For any given item, these speakers tended to select the same attributes for description. When a particular type of attribute was chosen for description, specific linguistic constructions were often preferred. For example, some items were usually described in terms of their function rather than their appearance; in referring to the function of an item, speakers frequently used the construction: Subject + Verb + Superordinate Term + Postmodifier (such as a relative clause, adverbial clause or prepositional phrase). Attributes of appearance were preferred in reference to other items; in referring to the appearance of an item, native speakers more frequently used the construction: Subject + Verb + Premodifier + Superordinate Term. These findings have implications for SLA theory and for the teaching of both strategic communication skills and grammar in EFL contexts.

Introduction

In English as a foreign language (EFL) settings such as Japan, it is often extremely difficult to provide students with classroom activities that give them opportunities to use English communicatively. An added factor is that students may be highly motivated to learn the grammatical system of the English language in order to pass benchmark proficiency exams, and their teachers, who may not be native speakers of English, may not be able to rely on their intuitions to the extent their native speaker counterparts can, relying instead upon explicit study of English grammar. In such cases, both EFL teachers and students may believe that classroom communicative activities are a waste of time. They need to understand, in relatively specific ways, how classroom communicative activities might actually help students to master linguistic structures in English.

A primary purpose of this chapter is to examine the discourse of native speakers in order to establish a baseline for instruction. Scholarship in discourse analysis has focused primarily on the production of two kinds of oral discourse: *interactional discourse* and *transactional discourse* (cf. Yule, 1997). Interactional discourse establishes or maintains social relationships, whereas transactional discourse conveys information. Speakers use *communication strategies* (CSs) to resolve difficulties they encounter in expressing an intended meaning. In the field of applied linguistics, CSs have been studied primarily in the context of transactional discourse.[2] Perhaps one reason for this is that, in transactional discourse, it is possible for research purposes to more clearly identify an intended message and the CSs used to convey that message. It is less straightforward to identify intended meanings and consequent CSs in naturalistic interactional discourse.

In this chapter, we will take the position that communication strategy training is a practical and effective pedagogical tool for overseas communicative language teaching, one that can provide authentic communicative practice, as well as opportunities to learn and practice a core set of English linguistic expressions. What may be needed in EFL settings is a kind of baseline data not commonly available: models of fluent English speakers'[3] use of communication strategies, including core vocabulary and other linguistic expressions that they select. Following the recommendations and procedures set out in Tarone and Yule (1989), we provide native-speaker baseline data in this chapter. Keeping in mind the strong orientation EFL students have toward the goal of mastery of English linguistic forms, we will identify English syntactic patterns that were produced by native speakers of English in the use of communication strategies, and will suggest that one rationale for conducting communicative activities which elicit communication strategies in EFL classrooms is that such activities provide students with opportunities to acquire and practice those syntactic patterns. Teaching students to use communication strategies can meet twin goals that are often viewed as contradictory in teaching EFL: improving students' ability to use the second language (L2) communicatively and improving their mastery of a core set of English syntactic patterns.

Background

We have stated above that speakers use communication strategies (CSs) to resolve difficulties that they encounter in expressing intended meanings; these may be either *reduction strategies* or *compensatory strategies*. Reduction strategies are used more or less to avoid referring to the problematic referent, and compensatory strategies are used to enable the speaker to refer to it in spite of the difficulties:

> Imagine, for example, that a learner in an ESL class is doing a task that requires that he refer to a balloon, but realizes that he doesn't know how to say "balloon." When this happens the learner may either choose not to refer to the object at all (an avoidance or reduction strategy) or try to find some other linguistic expression that will allow them to refer to it (a compensatory strategy). . . . For example, the learner might use an holistic approximation, referring to a related object (e.g. "something like a ball"); or be more analytic, describing the properties of the referent, as with circumlocution focused on either its physical properties ("a spherical shape, filled with air or gas and tied with a string") or its function ("we use them to decorate at birthday parties"). Code-related strategies may also work, as with code-switching ("globo"), foreignizing ("globe"), or word coinage ("airball"). The speaker may use nonverbal gestures or sound imitation, or appeal for assistance ("How do you say *globo* in English?"). (Tarone, in press)

It is important to note that, in natural communication situations, communication strategies are used both by learners (students) and by native speakers (e.g. teachers) for the purpose of collaboratively coping with mismatches in their linguistic systems (cf. Yule & Tarone, 1991). Tarone has defined communication strategies as "mutual attempts of two interlocutors to agree on a meaning in situations where requisite meaning structures do not seem to be shared" (1980: 420). From the perspective of collaborative theory (Wilkes-Gibbs, 1997) this "agreeing on a meaning" is viewed as a "grounding process," the interactive process of presenting and accepting ideas in "establishing common ground": building common knowledge through communication. In attempting to establish common ground with a listener, so that both can agree on the meaning being communicated, a speaker's selection of one or another of the strategies named above depends on her assessment of its likelihood of success with her particular interlocutor. This is true whether the speaker is a native speaker or a learner of the second language, a teacher or a student.

Both reduction and compensatory strategies are used by speakers in the process of interacting with others, and are inherently interactive in their very nature. Because CSs are inherently interactive in this way, tasks and activities promoting interactive communication strategy use (e.g. Yule, 1997) are often a good choice for EFL teachers looking for ways to encourage their students to use communication strategies in the classroom.

There are two broad approaches to research on communication strategies (Kasper & Kellerman, 1997; Yule & Tarone, 1997). One popular research approach focuses on the cognitive processes involved in selecting one or another strategy. Researchers favoring this approach use a smaller number of categories in classifying types of communication strategy and believe that learners' cognitive processes are unaffected by instruction. For this reason, proponents of this approach argue that communication strategy use in a second language cannot be taught. Though observable linguistic differences exist between communication strategies in using the L1 and in using the L2, these researchers maintain that the underlying cognitive processes are the same, and so do not need to be taught. Examples of researchers working within this perspective are: Bialystok (1990), Bongaerts and Poulisse (1989), Kellerman (1991), and Poulisse (1990).

Proponents of the other popular research approach emphasize the linguistic expressions used in communication strategies, which are extensive and varied. These researchers focus on the core linguistic expressions in the L2 that are used in communication strategies. Researchers adopting this second approach argue that L2 learners can be taught the linguistic expressions needed for effective communication strategy use and given practice to improve their performance in using these L2 forms in communication strategies (Yule & Tarone, 1997). Examples of researchers taking this approach are: Dörnyei (1995), Faerch and Kasper (1983), Iwai (2000, 2001, 2002), Konishi (1995, 2001), Paribakht (1985), Tarone (1978), and Yule and Tarone (1991).

We take the approach espoused by the second group – that communication strategy use and the developing interlanguage itself benefit from instruction. We feel that it is helpful to teach students the L2 linguistic expressions they will need in communication strategies (CSs) and to provide them with opportunities to practice using them in communicative drills. Through instruction and communicative practice, they are likely to acquire key aspects of the interlanguage. But in EFL settings, where teachers are often not native speakers of English themselves and may feel insecure about their own mastery of the linguistic structure of English, how are those teachers to know what linguistic expressions they should teach for use in communication strategies? While there has been some work devoted to identifying core vocabulary useful for communication strategy use (e.g. Iwai, 2002; Tarone & Yule, 1989; Yule & Tarone, 1997), there has been little devoted to identifying the syntactic constructions used in those strategies.

We see a need for research that will identify the *syntactic constructions* that fluent speakers of the target language use when they employ compensatory strategies: that is, communication strategies that attempt to resolve communication difficulties. These syntactic patterns constitute oral baseline data that EFL teachers can use in providing their students with communication strategy training and in targeting goals for inter-language development. As Yule and Tarone (1997: 22) have stated: "it is useful to compare the linguistic forms used by L2 learners and those used by native speakers (NS) of the TL," adding that "the relevant L1 is not that of the learner, but that of the TL speakers."

Statement of Purpose

The purpose of this study is to elicit and analyze the syntactic patterns used by fluent English speakers in the compensatory strategies (CpSs) that they use in order to refer to items for which either they or their NNS interlocutor do not know the names. These syntactic patterns can be used to construct norms for usage by fluent English speakers, which can in turn be useful for classroom instruction both in CpS use and in English grammar. We believe that knowledge of these norms can help EFL teachers teach English more communicatively even as they teach English grammar to their learners.

In order to achieve these purposes, the following research questions were addressed:

(1) What types of syntactic patterns are used in CpSs produced by fluent speakers of English?
(2) What attributes do fluent speakers refer to in using CpSs for different types of items?
(3) Is there a relationship between the syntactic patterns used in particular CpSs and the attributes of the items being referred to?

Methodology

Participants

A total of 30 native speakers of North American English participated in the study, all undergraduate and graduate students at the University of Minnesota. The participants were evenly divided by gender (i.e. 15 males and 15 females), and ranged in age from 18 to 56 (mean age = 22.6 years). These students had a variety of majors at the university, most in the liberal arts, with a few science majors.[4]

Data collection

Data were elicited in oral role-plays with the first author. Participants were given 15 short descriptions of social situations, which included 17 items that the participants would need to refer to in their responses. These items were chosen to include a range of types of referents, and are listed below:

Referent types	*Words*
human beings:	bursar, caretaker
animals:	rhinoceros, ostrich, sea urchin
plants:	oak, lavender
instruments:	pliers, thermostat
food:	pasta, punch, nectarines
clothes:	coveralls
machines:	furnace, carburetor
vehicles:	ambulance
buildings:	laboratory

The participants were told to role-play a series of 15 situations in which they were interacting with a Japanese man whose English vocabulary was limited (see Appendix on pp. 195–196). In each situation, they needed to refer to the above items, but would have to use alternative expressions because the Japanese man did not know the right words. They were told not to use mime or body language. An example of a situation follows:

(1) You hear on the news that a rhinoceros has run away from the Minnesota Zoo. You try to tell Koji the news. However, he does not know the word, "rhinoceros" in English. Please explain it to him.

The researcher was present during the interview and played the role of interlocutor for the speaker by saying "uh huh" or "yeah" with a nod or smile in order to make this interview somewhat more natural.

Given the emphasis of this volume on research methodology, we would like to comment briefly on our choice of role-play as a way of gathering data for this study. Ideally, we would use a referential communication task with actual exchange of information to elicit data (Yule, 1997) rather than a role-play. However, we wanted at least 30 speakers, and the likelihood that we would be able to find 30 Japanese listeners, all of whom were unfamiliar with the same 17 English words, seemed slim. We opted for a less natural role-play task with the same role-playing Japanese listener, so that the task would at least be the same for all 30 native speakers.

The data were collected and audio-taped on seven different days in November 1999 in a room at the campus of the University of Minnesota. A compact cassette tape recorder was in plain view. Each role-play was 20–30 minutes in length.

Data Analysis

The responses in each role-play were transcribed and entered into a database using Microsoft Excel 2000. The syntactic patterns each subject used when s/he referred to each item, seemed to fall into four main types, with four patterns composed of the very general categories Subject (S), Verb (V), Superordinate Term (ST), Premodifier (PrM), Postmodifier (PoM) predominating, and a fifth category composed of other elements less commonly present in definitions:

(2) Subject (S) + Verb (V) + Premodifier (PrM) + Superordinate Term (ST)

    (e.g. An ostrich is a very large bird.)

S + V + ST + Postmodifier (PoM)

    (e.g. Bursar is a person who works with accounts.)

S+ V + PrM + ST + PoM

    (e.g. A rhinoceros is a big animal with a horn on its nose.)

S + V + ST

    (e.g. Punch is a drink.)

Other structures

    (e.g. If somebody encounters an emergency, you should call an ambulance for him/her.)

These categories were chosen for analysis because they are helpful for pedagogy in Japan, and also straightforward in terms of data analysis. "Postmodifier," for example, is a very general category that can be realized using a range of syntactic structures, from relative clauses to adverbial clauses to prepositional phrases. All of these structures contribute to end-weight, for which the English language has a strong preference (Yule, 1998: 257), in marked contrast to Japanese, which has a preference for beginning-weight in message organization (Konishi, 1994). The syntactic patterns identified above that use postmodifiers are known to be especially difficult for Japanese learners of English, and important targets for pedagogy.[5] If the types of compensatory strategies that naturally require the use of linguistic constructions with a good deal of postmodification can be identified, then it can be argued that practice in the use of these compensatory strategies will provide valuable communicative opportunities for Japanese students who want to acquire and practice English constructions with end-weight and postmodification (using relative clauses, adverbial clauses, or prepositional phrases).

In addition to identifying syntactic patterns, the analysis recorded the attributes each speaker mentioned when referring to each of the 17 items. These fell into seven categories: *function*; *appearance* (including *touch* such as *its skin is rough* or *the surface is smooth*); *location / habitat / origin / occasion*; *growth / nature*; *recipe*; *taste / smell*; and *other attributes* (e.g. physical actions) (see Konishi, 2001, for a detailed discussion of these). In this chapter, we will focus primarily on the categories of *function* and *appearance*, and to a lesser degree, on *taste/smell* and the syntactic patterns used in CpSs that refer to referents with those attributes.

In tabulating the five types of linguistic structures, the description of each item referred to by each subject was treated as one unit. If a subject used two linguistic structures such as S + V + PrM + ST and S + V + ST + PoM to refer to an item, one count each was tabulated. However, repetition was excluded. That is, if a subject used the same kind of linguistic structure twice in referring to the same item, we did not count this twice. In tabulating the seven attribute categories, if a subject used one kind of category twice or more to refer to an item, we gave two or more counts to this category. However, we excluded the repetition of the same word or phrase. The following examples illustrate the method of analysis:

(3) Description of *Pliers* by subject 7 (Pliers / S7)
    Pliers are a tool. They are a tool *that you use to grab things* [Function].

(4) Description of *Rhinoceros* by subject 27 (Rhinoceros / S27)
    A rhinoceros is *a large animal* [Appearance]. It's *a mean animal* [Nature].

In Example (3) above, two linguistic structures occur – S + V + ST and S + V + ST + PoM – and one attribute: function. In Example (4), there is one instance of S + PrM + ST even though in fact this linguistic structure appeared twice. Two attributes are referred to: appearance and nature.

Using Microsoft Excel 2000, the frequencies for the five syntactic patterns and for the seven types of attributes were calculated in response to research questions #1 and #2. In the analysis for research question #3, a Kendall's tau correlation[6] was calculated (using SPSS 1999) in order to discover the relationship between the five syntactic patterns and the seven attribute categories.

Results

Research question 1: What types of syntactic patterns are used in the compensatory strategies used by fluent English speakers?

Table 8.1 shows the kinds of syntactic patterns that native English speakers used in communication strategies referring to the different items in this study. Note that the native speakers as a group seemed to have definite preferences for using particular syntactic patterns for particular referents. In other words, these different patterns were not used equally across all items. For example, S + V + ST + PoM was used most frequently in referring to *bursar, caretaker, carburetor, laboratory, pliers, furnace, thermostat,* and *ambulance,* but hardly at all for *ostrich, oak,* and *nectarine.*

Research question 2: What attributes do fluent speakers refer to in using CpSs for different types of items?

The attributes mentioned when the informants referred to each of the 17 items in the study are listed in Table 8.2. The findings showed that in using compensatory strategies, the native English speakers in the study tended to prefer mentioning particular attributes for particular items. Table 8.2 shows us the kinds of attributes that the informants referred to for each of the 17 items. For example, in referring to *caretaker* and *laboratory,* the speakers mentioned function 98% and 80% of the time respectively, while function was never mentioned in referring to such items as *oak, pasta,* and *nectarine.* Items that seemingly elicited a preference for mention of the attribute of function were *caretaker, bursar, laboratory, ambulance, thermostat, pliers,* and *furnace.* Items eliciting a preference for mention of the attribute of appearance were *oak, nectarine, rhinoceros,* and *coveralls.* Other attributes were mentioned to a lesser extent, some more with some items than others, but space does not permit much analysis in detail here. For more detailed analysis of these, and a cluster analysis of these items, see Konishi (2001).

Table 8.1 The frequency of syntactic patterns used in referring to each item[7]

Linguistic structures/ items	S+V+ST+ PoM n (%)	S+V+PrM +ST+PoM n (%)	S+V+ PrM+ST n (%)	S+V+ ST n (%)	Other structures n (%)	Total n n (%)
Bursar	23 (77)	3 (10)	1 (3)	0 (0)	3 (10)	30 (100)
Caretaker	25 (83)	0 (0)	0 (0)	0 (0)	5 (17)	30 (100)
Pliers	17 (52)	5 (15)	5 (15)	6 (18)	0 (0)	33 (100)
Carburetor	26 (87)	3 (10)	0 (0)	0 (0)	1 (3)	30 (100)
Furnace	18 (55)	3 (9)	6 (18)	1 (3)	5 (15)	33 (100)
Thermostat	15 (50)	6 (20)	1 (3)	2 (7)	6 (20)	30 (100)
Ambulance	14 (45)	11 (35)	4 (13)	1 (3)	1 (3)	31 (100)
Laboratory	24 (73)	5 (15)	1 (3)	1 (3)	2 (6)	33 (100)
Rhinoceros	3 (10)	14 (47)	11 (37)	2 (7)	0 (0)	30 (100)
Ostrich	1 (3)	10 (33)	13 (43)	6 (20)	0 (0)	30 (100)
Sea urchin	7 (23)	13 (43)	3 (10)	2 (7)	5 (17)	30 (100)
Oak	1 (3)	9 (30)	19 (63)	0 (0)	1 (3)	30 (100)
Lavender	9 (26)	3 (9)	13 (38)	9 (26)	0 (0)	34 (100)
Pasta	7 (23)	4 (13)	13 (43)	5 (17)	1 (3)	30 (100)
Punch	6 (20)	3 (10)	13 (43)	8 (27)	0 (0)	30 (100)
Nectarine	1 (3)	2 (6)	23 (66)	8 (23)	1 (3)	35 (100)
Coveralls	11 (35)	4 (13)	12 (39)	3 (10)	1 (3)	31 (100)
Total	208 (39)	98 (18)	138 (26)	54 (10)	32 (6)	530 (100)

Notes: Percentage in each cell = frequency of each linguistic structure used in referring to each item/ frequency of all linguistic structures used in referring to each item (*n*). Percentages in each cell are rounded off to the nearest whole number; this means the sum of percentages may add up to one more or less than 100% in some rows. S = Subject, V = Verb, ST = Superordinate term, PrM = Premodifier, PoM = Postmodifier.

Research question 3: Is there a relationship between the syntactic constructions used in CpSs and the attributes of items being referred to?

Table 8.3 shows that there were some strong correlations between reference to particular types of attributes, and the type of syntactic pattern used. In this section we discuss the strongest such correlations.

Table 8.2 The frequency of attributes used in referring to each item

Attributes/ items	Function	Appearance including Touch	Location/ Habit/ Origin/ Occasion	Recipe	Growth/ Nature	Taste/ Smell	Other attributes	Total n
	n (%)	n (%)	n (%)	n (%)	n (%)	n (%)	n (%)	n (%)
Bursar	71 (77)	0 (0)	20 (22)	0 (0)	0 (0)	0 (0)	1 (1)	92 (100)
Caretaker	58 (98)	0 (0)	0 (0)	0 (0)	0 (0)	0 (0)	1 (2)	59 (100)
Rhinoceros	0 (0)	48 (64)	24 (32)	0 (0)	0 (0)	0 (0)	3 (4)	75 (100)
Ostrich	0 (0)	43 (47)	9 (10)	0 (0)	0 (0)	0 (0)	40 (43)	92 (100)
Sea urchin	0 (0)	42 (48)	24 (27)	0 (0)	0 (0)	0 (0)	22 (25)	88 (100)
Lavender	7 (9)	28 (35)	1 (1)	0 (0)	13 (16)	0 (0)	10 (13)	79 (100)
Oak	0 (0)	83 (73)	5 (4)	0 (0)	16 (14)	0 (0)	10 (9)	114 (100)
Pasta	0 (0)	13 (22)	9 (15)	26 (44)	0 (0)	0 (0)	11 (19)	59 (100)
Punch	0 (0)	8 (12)	7 (11)	22 (34)	0 (0)	26 (40)	2 (3)	65 (100)
Nectarine	0 (0)	69 (73)	2 (2)	0 (0)	0 (0)	12 (13)	12 (13)	95 (100)
Coveralls	23 (22)	64 (62)	0 (0)	0 (0)	0 (0)	0 (0)	17 (16)	104 (100)
Pliers	58 (64)	28 (31)	0 (0)	0 (0)	0 (0)	0 (0)	5 (5)	91 (100)
Furnace	51 (62)	5 (6)	11 (13)	0 (0)	0 (0)	0 (0)	15 (18)	82 (100)
Thermostat	53 (72)	12 (16)	7 (9)	0 (0)	0 (0)	0 (0)	2 (3)	74 (100)
Carburetor	35 (46)	1 (1)	34 (45)	0 (0)	0 (0)	0 (0)	6 (8)	76 (100)
Ambulance	77 (69)	20 (18)	0 (0)	0 (0)	0 (0)	0 (0)	14 (13)	111 (100)
Laboratory	67 (80)	5 (6)	2 (2)	0 (0)	0 (0)	0 (0)	10 (12)	84 (100)
Total	500 (35)	469 (33)	155 (11)	48 (3)	29 (2)	58 (4)	181 (13)	1440 (100)

Notes: Percentage in each cell = frequency of each attribute used in referring to each item by the 30 subjects/frequency of all the attributes used in referring to each item (n). Percentages in each cell are rounded off to the nearest whole number; this means the sum of percentages may add up to one more or less than 100% in some rows.

Table 8.3 Kendall's tau correlation between linguistic structures and attributes

Attributes/ Linguistic structures	Function	Appearance including Touch	Location/ Habitat/ Origin/ Occasion	Growth/ Nature	Recipe	Taste/ Smell	Other attributes
S + V + ST + PoM	0.72**	-0.69**	-0.02	-0.22	-0.19	-0.32	-0.33
S + V + PrM + ST	-0.69**	0.57***	-0.07	0.27	0.31	0.38	0.31
S + V + PrM + ST + PoM	-0.19	0.32	0.18	-0.08	-0.08	-0.38	0.15
S + V + ST	-0.42*	0.37*	-0.14	0.03	0.34	0.60**	0.28
Other structures	0.39*	-0.31	0.13	-0.18	-0.15	-0.43*	-0.07

Notes: ** $p < 0.01$, * $p < 0.05$, $-1 \leqq \tau \leqq 1$
S = Subject, V = Verb, ST = Superordinate term, PrM = Premodifier, PoM = Postmodifier.

There was a significantly positive correlation between S + V + ST + PoM in CpSs referring to attributes of function ($\tau = 0.72$, $p < 0.01$), and a significantly positive correlation between S + V + PrM + ST in CpSs referring to attributes of appearance (including touch) ($\tau = 0.57$, $p < 0.01$). There was also a significantly positive correlation between S + V + ST in expressions referring to attributes of taste and smell ($\tau = 0.6$, $p < 0.01$), and a modestly positive correlation between S + V + ST in CpSs referencing attributes of appearance (including touch) ($\tau = 0.37$, $p < 0.05$).

Summary of results

The findings of the study provide a baseline description of the performance of fluent English speakers in using compensatory strategies to refer to a number of classes of items. First, it was found that items seemed to elicit mention of some attributes and not others. For example, *caretaker* was mentioned almost entirely in terms of function (98%), while *oak* favored mention of the attribute of appearance (73%):

(5) *Caretaker*/S14:   A caretaker is someone *who takes care of the property and the business* [Function].

(6) *Oak*/S22:   An oak is *a big* tree *with, er, big leaves* [Appearance].

In very general terms (though the relationship between class of item and attribute is analyzed in more detail in Konishi, 2001), we might say that professional occupations, machines, and instruments tended to be described in terms of their functions, while plants and animals tended to be described in terms of their appearance. Similarly, the attributes of taste and smell seemed to be used only for food / drink items and the aromatic herb item in the study. Of course, these were tendencies, not categorical rules; there were exceptions. For example, in referring to a seeing-eye dog, even though a seeing-eye dog is an animal, we would expect its main attribute not to be appearance but rather function. Therefore, instead of describing appearance, we might say *"This is a dog that helps a blind person"* or *"This dog guides blind people."*

Although any referent has its fundamental attributes, this does not mean that the referent itself necessarily determines what linguistic structures will be used to refer to it. Rather it seems that the attributes of the referent selected for attention by the speaker play a key role. Once certain attributes have been selected, it appears that certain linguistic structures are preferred. Thus, a second finding of this study is that, when speakers referred to particular attributes in describing these items, they gravitated toward use of certain types of syntactic constructions. In referring to the function of an item, speakers frequently used the construction: Subject + Verb + Superordinate Term + Postmodifier (such as a relative clause, adverbial clause or prepositional phrase). In referring to the appearance of an item, native speaker more frequently used the construction: Subject + Verb + Premodifier + Superordinate Term.

For example, in referring to *caretaker* in (5) above, S14 considered function to be the most important attribute of this item and chose S + ST + PoM as a construction. It would seem to be rather difficult to refer to function without using a postmodifier (PoM). Furthermore, the PoM used in such cases tended to be long. The subjects used relative clauses in PoM frequently: 83% of the 30 subjects used relative clauses in referring to *bursar* and *caretaker*; 76% used them in referring to *laboratory*; 57% used them in referring to *thermostat*; 52% used them in referring to *ambulance*; 55% used them in referring to *pliers*; 58% used them in referring to *furnace*; and 41% used them in referring to *carburetor*. (Other postmodifiers were adverbial clauses, as well as prepositional phrases, still providing end-weight, but usually shorter than relative clause options.)

In contrast, in referring to appearance, the subjects tended not to use long postmodifiers but rather short post- or premodifiers, as in (6) above, and (7) and (8) below. For example, when S26 and S22 referred to *oak*, both of them regarded appearance as the most crucial attribute. S26 used the PrM, *large*. S22 began with the same structure using *big* – but then added *with big leaves* as a PoM. By the same token, S3 began with unmodified *bird* as a ST, but then chose appearance as the most notable attribute in referring to *ostrich*, adding *It has very long legs*. S26, S22, and S3 chose S + PrM + ST, S + PrM + ST + PoM, and S + V + ST respectively. All three subjects touched on appearance but their CpSs were linguistically different from each other.

(7) *Oak*/S26:   An oak is a, is a large, very large tree [Appearance].

(8) *Ostrich*/S3:   An ostrich is a bird. It has very long legs [Appearance].

(9) *Punch*/S9:   Punch is a drink. It *tastes very good* [Taste].

(10) *Lavender*/S26: Lavender is a plant. It *smells good* [Smell].

Examples (9) and (10) show that S9 and S26 just said *good* or *nice* in referring to the attributes of taste and smell. Instead of using complicated structures, the subjects tended to choose S + V + ST in their CpS in referring to taste and smell. As a result, there was a significant positive correlation between S + V + ST and the attributes of taste and smell.

Other structures had a modestly positive correlation with the use of the attributes of function. Consider examples (11), (12), (13), and (14):

(11) *Furnace* / S15:   A furnace is run by electricity and keeps the house warm [Function / Other structures].

(12) *Thermostat* / S13: If you want house at certain temperature, you set the thermostat to whatever the temperature you want the house to be [Function / Other Structures].

(13) *Furnace* / S2:   A furnace is something that keeps the room warm [Function / S + V + ST + PoM].

(14) *Thermostat* / S8:   The thermostat is what controls the temperature of the furnace [Function / S + V + (ST) + PoM].

In referring to *furnace* and *thermostat*, the subjects mainly focused on function. Consequently, instead of referring to the target items, S13 and S15 encoded *furnace* and *thermostat* indirectly, that is, using what has been referred to as *"detouring strategies"* (Iwai, 2000: 137). In our study, these are classified as *other structures*. Detouring strategies deserve more attention from a pedagogical perspective. To use these strategies in examples (13) and (14) above, S2 and S8 chose to use *something* or *what* as a ST, and not a concrete ST such as *machine, device,* and *container*. Nevertheless, their utterances were clear. Overstreet and Yule (1997) might refer to this strategy as "locally contingent categorization."

A last interesting item is *coveralls*. Generally speaking, clothes have both attributes of appearance and function. As shown in Example (15) below, in referring to appearance, S24 used S + V + PrM + ST, while s/he used S + V + ST + PoM in referring to function. In describing appearance *in detail*, the subjects also tended to use S + V + ST + PoM as much, as shown in Example (16). These examples show us why S + V + PrM + ST and S + V + ST + PoM prevailed almost equally in referring to *coveralls* in our study as shown in Table 8.1:

(15) *Coveralls* / S24: Coveralls are like a pair of jeans [Appearance / S + V + PrM + ST]. They are something people wear when they're working outside [Function / S + V + ST + PoM].

(16) *Coveralls* / S4:   Coveralls are pants that have a bib attached, er, a front piece with straps that go over your shoulders [Appearance / S + V + ST + PoM].

Discussion

Arguments about the teachability of communication strategies have a tendency to be separated from discussions about the real world of the English as a foreign language classroom, in which grammatical and structural syllabi are commonplace, and are used in preparing students to pass benchmark examinations. We would like to suggest not only that communication strategies *can* be taught in such contexts, but that they *should* be taught there, for twin purposes. First, of course, embedding practice with communication strategies in daily EFL lessons is a good way to provide communicative practice in the use of English in a context in which it is very difficult to find opportunities to use English in authentic communication. But secondly, and more importantly, such activities enable the teacher to provide natural contexts that require the use of targeted English sentence structures, and so encourage the development of those structures in the learners' interlanguage.

A particularly important finding of the present study is that communication strategies referring to function naturally favor the use of sentence structures with extensive end-weight, or postmodification, while communication strategies referring to appearance seem to favor structures with premodification. Recall the position taken by researchers such as Bialystok, Dörnyei, Kellerman, and Poulisse, summarized at the beginning of this chapter, that communication strategies are unteachable because the cognitive processes of learners, which really matter in L2 CS use, are unaffected by instruction. We wonder if this is true. If communication strategies referring to certain attributes require the use of particular linguistic expressions, and if the word order of those linguistic expressions happens to be difficult for L2 learners to master, we suspect that learners' cognitive processing may indeed be affected by instruction and practice focused on mastery of those expressions. There is good reason to believe that mastery of L2 linguistic expressions requiring a substantial shift away from native language word order preferences does indeed require important changes in learners' cognitive processing of language. Processability Theory (Hyltenstam & Pienemann, 1985; Meisel *et al.*, 1981; Pienemann, 1998a, 1998b) outlines in very clear terms the way in which cognitive processing demands relate to the mastery of word order requirements in the L2. It certainly seems likely to be a major shift in cognitive processing to move from producing Japanese, with a strong preference for premodification, to producing English, with its strong preference for postmodification – and vice versa, of course.

The editors of the present volume state: "Once we have knowledge of what members of discourse communities successfully do in spontaneous spoken discourse, we can then apply these findings to situations in which novice language users are acquiring and employing an L2 in any domain and in variously configured communities and interactions" (p. 22). The results of the present study should be particularly helpful to EFL learners like those in Japan, who rarely interact with English-speakers outside the classroom. Because of their preference for beginning-weight in sentence organization, Japanese EFL learners need to be challenged with communicative activities encouraging them to use end-weight, with sentence structures such as S + V + ST + PoM rather than S + V + PrM + ST (for example). We have seen that, in using CpSs, there is a strongly positive correlation between S + V + ST + PoM and reference to attributes of function. In EFL classrooms in Japan, instead of asking EFL learners to learn end-weight solely by reciting drills that require them to combine sentences mechanically with relative pronouns, EFL teachers can teach end-weight by teaching students to use CS that focus on *function*. Students might be taught to refer to *function* using postmodification, where PoM requires a relative pronoun, an antecedent, and a relative clause, and then given ample practice with referential communication tasks such as those in Yule (1997), targetting items in which *function* is the dominant attribute.

Yule (1997) describes useful referential communication tasks that teachers can assign to students in the second language classroom to encourage the development of strategic competence (i.e. communication strategy use) in the second language. Plentiful illustrations of already developed tasks are provided, as well as principles to follow in devising new tasks and task formats to use for that purpose as well. Clearly, in light of the findings outlined above, teachers interested in eliciting reference to functions with related postmodification might want to try out these tasks with fluent speakers first to determine the kinds of prompts that elicit reference to function rather than appearance.

In addition, Takatsuka (1996) offers the following communication strategy exercises used in junior high schools in the Japanese context. In his first activity, which initially involves students in comprehension of compensation strategies, the teacher has an animal in mind, and the students have the task of guessing what animal it is. They listen to a series of hints that the teacher provides in English, using increasingly complex CpSs. Note that, in this kind of drill, where both interlocutors actually know the name of the animal, there is no real gap in their linguistic systems and no real negotiation of common ground. Rather the drill is done for pedagogical purposes, to provide practice in the comprehension of different CpS forms:

(17) Guess what it is (Takatsuka, 1996: 181)
    (a) First hint: A very large animal.

(b) Second hint: A very large animal that has a very long nose.
(c) Third hint: A very large animal that has a very long nose and
big ears.
[elephant]

Brown and Yule (1983) show that, in this sort of transactional communication task, once participants have been in a listening role, as receivers of information, they will be better speakers, or information transmitters in the same kinds of tasks. So, when Takatsuka's students have had experience with comprehension of CpSs in this exercise, guessing successfully, they may be given opportunities to change roles, working with partners in pair-work. The teacher may provide each student with a picture, and the students can take turns giving hints (to practice producing and processing different kinds of CpSs) and guessing. (The students should be told to begin their utterances with "It's a . . ." to encourage them to produce the kinds of structures shown in (17), rather than the probably more natural "It has/It's got a . . . .")

Of course, the baseline established by the present study suggests that references to animals in this kind of activity ought to elicit CpSs referring to the attribute of appearance, with relatively short pre- and postmodification. A later variation on this activity might provide speakers with photos of people in various vocational roles that the speaker must describe to a listener to enable her to identify those roles. This task would more naturally elicit CpSs focusing on the attribute of function, requiring more end-weight and longer postmodifiers than photos of animals.

A similar kind of guessing game is provided by Takatsuka in (18) below. Again, the teacher begins by using CpSs to describe an instrument or machine he has but does not know the name for, and encourages the students to use CpSs to do the same. As above, the baseline provided in our study predicts that postmodifying syntactic constructions will be most useful in CpSs referring to these objects. (Note in Takatsuka's example below that, consistent with the findings of the study reported here, the teacher's CpS referencing function contains a long postmodifier, while the student's guess has a CpS referencing appearance with a premodifier; both CpSs are italicized below.)

(18) Conversation drill (Takatsuka, 1996: 180; emphasis added)
A: I went shopping last Sunday.
B: Did you buy something?
A: Yes, I bought *a tool that is used for seeing very small things*.
B: Did you buy *a small round thing*?
A: Yes.

B: Well, is it a "mushimegane" ("magnifying glass" in Japanese)?
A: Yes, they call it a magnifying glass in English.

Teachers can experiment with variations on tasks such as this one, following the principles outlined in Yule (1997), and drawing on the baseline provided in this study, to provide their students with real opportunities for communication and communication strategy use, as well as chances to acquire and practice a range of useful English syntactic constructions.

Following the theme of the present volume, we have outlined ways in which EFL teachers can use the baseline data we have established on English speakers' use of compensatory strategies in referring to the attributes of function and appearance. In doing this, we have assumed that CSs and the linguistic expressions that realize them are indeed teachable. However, we would also argue that the position that CSs are either teachable or unteachable should be empirically tested. Accordingly, the first author and Chiaki Iwai are currently engaged in conducting a controlled experiment with Japanese EFL college students to determine the effects of beginning and mid-level EFL teaching materials focused on use of communication strategies requiring extensive postmodification. In a controlled longitudinal study with a pre-, post-, post-post test design, 73 Japanese learners in experimental groups and a control group are in the process of studying self-learning CALL material (titled ENGEL: English Generative Learning) that focuses on communication strategies requiring postmodification (Iwai & Konishi, in progress). We would hypothesize that explicit instruction and practice in the use of CSs requiring linguistic expressions with extensive postmodification will improve the performance of these learners in both the use of CSs, and the mastery of postmodification patterns in English. The latter, we would argue, will be made possible by using communicative practice as a vehicle for altering the learners' cognitive processes related to word order requirements for English.

The results of the present study should, of course, be interpreted with caution. The number of subjects was small – there were only 30 native speakers of English, all of them Americans. In addition, the number of items they were asked to respond to was small: only 17 items were used, and these were primarily concrete, observable entities. We are sure that use of other items, such as the abstract concepts used by Paribakht (1985), could entail the need for speakers to refer to other sorts of attributes, these requiring their own distinctive syntactic patterns. Other items may favor the use of word coinage or terms such as "thingamajig" or "whatchamacallit."

It would also be useful to replicate this study, asking native speakers to refer to items they themselves do not know the terms for in speaking to interlocutors who are also fluent speakers of English. Such items could be representative of domains that may be unfamiliar to the majority of speakers of the language, such as the items related to horse care depicted in Tarone and Yule (1989) and Yule (1997). It is possible that native speakers' choice of attributes and linguistic structures might be affected when they are using compensation strategies with an interlocutor who is also a fluent speaker of English.

There are many possibilities for replication of this study. However, we feel that the work reported here provides a good starting place for those interested in building a more comprehensive baseline of fluent English-speaker performance of communication strategies and the linguistic expressions commonly used to realize them.

Conclusions

Communication strategy training is a practical and effective pedagogical tool for overseas communicative language teaching, one that can provide both authentic communicative practice, and opportunities to learn and practice a core set of English linguistic expressions. To provide such training in EFL settings, we need models of fluent English speakers' use of communication strategies, including core vocabulary and other linguistic expressions they use. This study has identified such English syntactic patterns, patterns that were produced by fluent speakers of English in the use of communication strategies. We suggest that, in EFL settings, communicative classroom activities eliciting communication strategies should be used to provide students with opportunities to acquire and practice these patterns, with particular focus on those patterns that are problematic for the learners in question. We have argued that teaching students to use communication strategies can meet twin goals that are often viewed as contradictory in teaching English as a foreign language: improving students' ability to use the L2 communicatively, and improving their mastery of a core set of English syntactic patterns. In particular, we have recommended instruction focused on the use of English postmodification patterns, patterns our study established as predominant in CSs referring to the attribute of function.

Although our study is limited, involving only 30 informants and investigating only 17 items involving a limited set of attributes, it provides a model for other researchers to use in building an empirical baseline to answer the question of how fluent speakers of English realize their communication strategies linguistically. Our study could be expanded and built upon in many ways: for example, by using more informants, including fluent and highly proficient non-native speakers of English as well as native speakers; by expanding the range of items referred to; by using more interactive two-way referential communication tasks; by exploring the relationships between syntactic constructions used and attributes of the items referred to; by finding relationships between constructions used and the interactive context in which the task was provided. In the meantime, we hope that our study provides EFL teachers and learners with a useful initial baseline on the norms of fluent speakers of the English language in the use of communication strategies, and the syntactic patterns that instantiate them. We also hope that we have persuaded these teachers and learners that the use of communication strategy activities in the EFL classroom can both improve students' ability to use the L2 communicatively, and improve their mastery of some important and difficult English syntactic patterns.

Notes

1. The study reported in this chapter is described in more detail, using a communicative framework derived from Yule and Tarone (1997), in Konishi (2001).
2. Lazaraton (personal communication) suggests that CSs may also occur in interactional discourse. While this seems intuitively to be true, it is also true that, at the present time, all the CS research of which we are aware has been done in the context of transactional discourse.
3. In view of the increasing use of English as an international language, and the need for international norms of usage, we feel that what is essential for establishment of baseline English language data is that the baseline speakers be fluent and highly proficient, but not necessarily native speakers. In the case of the present study, the speakers *were* native speakers of North American English. But we believe that highly proficient non-native speakers of English could also be used to establish baseline data in similar studies to this one.
4. These majors were advertising ($N = 1$), aerospace engineering ($N = 1$), anthropology ($N = 1$), art ($N = 3$), computer and information sciences ($N = 1$), education ($N = 2$), ESL ($N = 5$), French ($N = 1$), genetics ($N = 1$), geophysics ($N = 1$), German ($N = 1$), Japanese ($N = 5$), linguistics ($N = 1$), nursing ($N = 1$), political science ($N = 1$), psychology ($N = 1$), public relations ($N = 1$), scientific and technical communication ($N = 1$), and sociology ($N = 1$).
5. In the experience of the first author in teaching EFL in Japanese high schools for nearly 20 years, post-modification in English constitutes one of the most discouraging features of the language for Japanese learners.
6. Kendall's tau is a nonparametric statistic for determining the probability of a relationship between two sets of data, regardless of whether the observed data being compared are in the same or different orders for the two variables. Kendall's tau seems suitable in this case since the two variables are clearly of different orders.

7. While the N for this study was 30 subjects, some subjects used more than one syntactic pattern to refer to an item; this is reflected in the last column, where the total *n* (# of syntactic patterns used by the group to refer to a particular item) ranged from 30 to 35.

Appendix: Data elicitation situations

Please read the directions and speak to the tape recorder in front of you.

(A) Directions

Please read each of the following situations and then respond to it as if you are in an actual conversation. We are not testing the uniqueness of your responses. All of the names used there are pseudonyms (Dick, Jim, Kana, Koji, Lincoln, and Sally). In each situation, please assume that:

> (a) You are talking with your Japanese friend, Koji; (b) Because of his limited English vocabulary, he could not understand what you would say if you used the normal words; (c) You cannot use mime and body language because they are useless to him; (d) Therefore, you have no choice but to use alternative expressions.

(B) Recording from here

(1) Koji asks you what your father does. You try to answer this by using the word "bursar," but Koji cannot understand the word. Please explain it to him.

(2) You are working at a big company as a caretaker. Koji says to you, "By the way, Jim/Sally, what are you doing now?" You try to answer this by saying "caretaker," but Koji cannot understand the word. Please explain it to him.

(3) You hear on the news that a rhinoceros has run away from the Minnesota Zoo. You try to tell Koji the news. However, he does not know the word "rhinoceros" in English. Please explain it to him.

(4) Your friend, Dick, runs a ranch and is a highly amusing man. He keeps an ostrich there. You try to tell this Koji. However, he does not know the word "ostrich" in English. Please explain it to him.

(5) You go swimming at the seashore in California with Koji. When you swim, you happen to step on a sea urchin. It hurts and you feel a sharp ache in the foot. You ask for Koji's help saying "sea urchin." It makes no sense. Please explain it.

(6) Koji wants to send something nice to his wife. You recommend sending a potted plant, lavender. As usual, he does not know this in English. He says to you, "Food or something?" Please explain it.

(7) You go to one of the Minnesota State Parks with Koji. There, you would like to take his picture; hence, you say to Koji, "Please stand up under an oak." In response, he says, "I don't know where. Near to the big pond?" Around the oak tree, there are many kinds of trees and flowers. Please explain it.

(8) You go to the Mall of America in Minnesota with Koji. There are all kinds of different shops there. You go to a restaurant to eat pasta and drink punch. You say to Koji, "I would like pasta and punch there." Koji is totally

confused and says to you, "Did you punch somebody in the past?" Please explain what pasta and punch are respectively to him. First, pasta, and then punch, please.

(9) You ask Koji to go to a grocery store to buy nectarines. At this store, there are many kinds of fruits and vegetables. Please explain to Koji what kind of thing a nectarine is.

(10) You say to Koji, "I am going to buy coveralls at Tanger Outlet Center. As usual, it makes no sense to Koji. He says to you, "What are c . . . rals?" Please explain it.

(11) At Koji's house, you help him to patch up the roof of his house and need a pair of pliers. You shout at Koji on the roof, "Please bring me a pair of pliers?" Koji replies to you from the ground, "You need a pair of pants?" Oh, dear. Please explain it.

(12) At Koji's house, the furnace does not work well. After checking it, you find out that the thermostat in the living room is out of order. You have to explain these items to him. Koji comes from the warmest place in Japan. He has no ideas about them at all. Please explain these items. First, furnace, and then thermostat, please.

(13) Koji's car is out of order. You find out that its carburetor does not work. At the living room, you say to Koji, "You need to replace a carburetor." Koji is too poor at mechanics to understand it. He replies to you, "I have to have my car washed?" Please explain it.

(14) Koji's daughter, Kana has been sick for four days. You think it is very serious; hence, you say to Koji, "Please call an ambulance." He is at a complete loss as to what he should do. He says, "Call the police?" Please explain to him what an ambulance is.

(15) You are working at a laboratory. You talk to him on the telephone. You say to Koji, "Let's meet at Lincoln laboratory." As usual, he does not know the word. He says to you, "Where? At a park?" Please explain to him what a laboratory is.

References

Bialystok, E. (1990) *Communication Strategies: A Psychological Analysis of Second-language Use.* Oxford: Basil Blackwell.

Bongaerts, T. and Poulisse, N. (1989) Communication strategies in L1 and L2: Same or different? *Applied Linguistics* 10 (3), 253–268.

Brown, G. and Yule, G. (1983) *Teaching the Spoken Language.* Cambridge: Cambridge University Press.

Dörnyei, Z. (1995) On the teachability of communication strategies. *TESOL Quarterly* 29 (1), 55–84.

Faerch, C. and Kasper, G. (1983) *Strategies in Interlanguage Communication.* London: Longman.

Hyltenstam, K. and Pienemann, M. (eds) (1985) *Modeling and Assessing Second Language Acquisition.* Clevedon: Multilingual Matters.

Iwai, C. (2000) *Communication Strategies in the Use of Second Languages.* Hiroshima: Keisui-sha.

Iwai, C. (2001) Analysis of high school English textbooks from the perspective of communicative competence. *Annual Review of English Language Education in Japan* 13, 31–40.

Iwai, C. (2002) Designing a teaching syllabus for communication strategies. Paper presented at the Triennial Congress of AILA (International Association of Applied Linguistics), Singapore, December.

Iwai, C. and Konishi, K. (in progress) An empirical study on instructional effects using communication strategy teaching materials. Research funded by the Japan Society for the Promotion of Science.

Kasper, G. and Kellerman, E. (eds) (1997) *Communication Strategies: Psycholinguistic and Sociolinguistic Perspectives*. Harlow: Longman.

Kellerman, E. (1991) Compensatory strategies in second language research: A critique, a revision, and some (non-)implications for the classroom. In R. Phillipson, E. Kellerman, L. Selinker, M. Sharwood-Smith, and M. Swain (eds) *Foreign/Second Language Pedagogy Research* (pp. 142–160). Clevedon: Multilingual Matters.

Konishi, K. (1994) Communication strategies and English language teaching. Paper presented at the tenth annual conference of the Shikoku English Language Education Society, Tokushima, Japan.

Konishi, K. (1995) Teaching compensatory strategies in the Japanese ESL classroom: A core vocabulary and its pre-/postmodification – with special reference to a strategic syllabus. *Matsuyama University Academic Research Association: Studies in Language and Literature* 15 (1), 81–112.

Konishi, K. (2001) Native English speakers' use of communication strategies as EFL teaching norms. *Matsuyama University Academic Research Society: Studies in Language and Literature* 20 (1), 1–28.

Meisel, J., Clahsen, H. and Pienemann, M. (1981) On determining developmental stages in natural second language acquisition. *Studies in Second Language Acquisition*, 3 (2), 109–135.

Overstreet, M. and Yule, G. (1997). Locally contingent categorization in discourse. *Discourse Processes* 23, 83–97.

Paribakht, T. (1985) Strategic competence and language proficiency. *Applied Linguistics* 6 (2), 132–146.

Pienemann, M. (1998a) *Language Processing and Second Language Development*. Philadelphia, PA: John Benjamins.

Pienemann, M. (1998b) Second language acquisition: The procedural skill hypothesis. *Studia Anglica Posnaniensia* 33, 317–331.

Poulisse, N. (1990) *The Use of Compensatory Strategies by Dutch Learners of English*. Dordrecht: Foris.

SPSS (1999) *SPSS Base 10.0 Application Guide*. Chicago, IL: SPSS Inc.

Takatsuka, S. (1996) Teaching communication strategies: A lesson aimed at teaching postmodifying structures for paraphrase. *The Bulletin of Faculty of Education Okayama University* 102, 165–184.

Tarone, E. (1978) Conscious communication strategies in interlanguage: A progress report. In H. D. Brown, C. Yorio, and R. Crymes (eds) *On TESOL '77: Teaching and Learning English as a Second Language* (pp. 194–203). Washington, DC: TESOL.

Tarone, E. (1980) Communication strategies, foreigner talk, and repair in interlanguage. *Language Learning* 30 (2), 417–431.

Tarone, E. and Yule, G. (1989) *Focus on the Language Learner*. Oxford: Oxford University Press.

Tarone, E. (in press) Speaking in a second language. In E. Hinkel (ed.) *Handbook of Research in Second Language Teaching and Learning*. Hillsdale, NJ: Lawrence Erlbaum.

Wilkes-Gibbs, D. (1997) Studying language use as collaboration. In G. Kasper and E. Kellerman (eds) *Communication Strategies: Psycholinguistic and Sociolinguistic Perspectives* (pp. 238–274). New York: Longman.

Yule, G. (1997) *Referential Communication Tasks*. Mahwah, NJ: Lawrence Erlbaum.

Yule, G. (1998) *Explaining English Grammar*. Oxford: Oxford University Press.

Yule, G. and Tarone, E. (1991) The other side of the page: Integrating the study of communication strategies and negotiated input in SLA. In R. Phillipson, E. Kellerman, L. Selinker, M. Sharwood-Smith, and M. Swain (eds) *Foreign Language Pedagogy: A Commemorative Volume for Claus Faerch* (pp. 162–171). Clevedon: Multilingual Matters.

Yule, G. and Tarone, E. (1997) Investigating L2 reference: Pros and cons. In G. Kasper and E. Kellerman (eds) *Advances in Communication Strategy Research* (pp. 17–30). New York: Longman.

Chapter 9

The Organization of Turns in the Disagreements of L2 Learners: A Longitudinal Perspective

KATHLEEN BARDOVI-HARLIG AND TOM SALSBURY

This chapter reports on the development of oppositional talk in L2 English conversation. In oppositional talk, speakers express opposing views. Oppositional talk in American English includes disagreements, challenges, denials, accusations, threats, and insults. In this chapter, we analyze the sequence and structure of turns in disagreements, following Pomerantz's (1984) analysis. The disagreements were collected during a one-year longitudinal study of 12 learners of English as a second language as they interacted with native speakers during conversational interviews. Whereas most learners started the study with direct disagreements, all of the learners elaborated their disagreements as time passed. Learners elaborated disagreements in at least four ways: they increased the amount of talk, included agreement as well as disagreement components, postponed the disagreement to later positions in their initial turns, and used multiple turn structure to potentially avoid disagreement. Only through the studying of speaking can the development of turns be understood.

Introduction

The purpose of this chapter is twofold: to report on the development of disagreements in interlanguage and to demonstrate the value of studying speaking in interlanguage pragmatics research. The two are intertwined: the essential development of oppositional talk, to which disagreements belong, lies in its turn structure, and turn structure is only available through talk.

In our longitudinal corpus of conversational interviews we not only see disagreements that are more complex than anything we could have orchestrated through elicitation tasks, but we also see a wider range of controversial and mundane topics than we would have attempted to introduce. In addition, we have been able to observe humor, friendship, and play through language as well as variation among and within learners. Because the conversations are complete, they contain the resolution of the disagreements as well as their initiation, providing a built-in evaluation of the communicative success of the turns. The participation of native speakers in the conversations provides a simultaneous profile of on-line native speaker disagreements, important in keeping us from idealizing the target as we observe native speaker variation alongside learner variation. We hope that these benefits to studying speaking will be illustrated as we report on the development of turn organization in our longitudinal study of oppositional talk. We will return to discuss these points at the close of the chapter.

Background

In oppositional talk, speakers express opposing views. American English provides a number of different illocutionary structures for accomplishing oppositional turns at talk including disagreements, challenges, denials, accusations, threats, and insults (Vuchinich, 1990). Oppositional talk is widely researched in the sociolinguistic and the conversational analysis literature dealing with native speakers (see, e.g., Georgakopoulou, 2001; Golato, 2002; Grimshaw, 1990; Gruber, 2001; Kotthoff, 1993; Muntigl & Turnbull, 1998; Pomerantz, 1984; Rees-Miller, 2000), although relatively less research on agreements and disagreements has been conducted on the speech of learners and nonnative speakers (Beebe & Takahashi, 1989; Pearson, 1986).

Disagreements occur as responses. Typically they counter an interlocutor's proposition P with an utterance that asserts the opposite, *not P* (Rees-Miller, 2000), in (1) from Pomerantz (1984):

(1) Native speakers (Pomerantz, 1984)
    Well, never mind. It isn't important.
    Well, it is important.

In her seminal article, Pomerantz (1984) divides disagreements into strong disagreements and disagreements that are not strong. Strong disagreements consist only of disagreement components as in (1) and (2), from our corpus. In the following examples from our corpus, the learner is identified by a culturally and linguistically appropriate pseudonym, and the language sample is identified by the date and month of stay. (The year is not indicated to increase the anonymity of the learners.)

(2) Marta, 1-22, Month 5
Marta: I live with the American family
Donna: oh, good!
Marta: no good because all day the family only work, work, never I see home, never

In contrast, disagreements that are not strong include agreement components. They are formed as partial agreements and partial disagreements and may include qualifications, exceptions, and additions. Pomerantz argues that the agreement components of disagreements themselves are weak agreements. The fact that the agreement components are weak allows nominal agreement tokens such as *yeah* to stand in for an agreement when speakers agree before they disagree, as the learner does in (3), line 3, taken from our corpus:

(3) Takako, 3-10, Month 7
Takako: You know cows smells so bad!
Kristen: Not as bad as pigs though
Takako: Yeah, but sometimes cows like more than pigs

Disagreements tend to be both delayed and mitigated. They are delayed both within a single turn and over multiple turns, occurring late in a single turn and later in a series of turns as speakers attempt to minimize the effect of the disagreement. Pomerantz argues that the structure of disagreement turns stems from the fact that they are typically dispreferred responses; when speakers offer an assessment, they typically invite agreement. An exception to this, according to Pomerantz, is the self-deprecating assessment after which a disagreement is the preferred turn. In such a case, the disagreement is unlikely to be delayed or hedged. There is one such example that occurs in our corpus in the speech of a native speaker when a learner, Marta, says that her speaking is no longer improving:

(4) Marta, 3-31, Month 7
1 **Marta:** it's very good when you enjoy, eh, you do, because,
2 eh, I think when you enjoy, you are better, and better,
3 and better, and better, when you don't, don't like your
4 work or something, you are so so so so. For example,
5 in level 1, I think I learn so much, I improve ??? speak-
6 ing, but now is no, but now is stop
7 **Donna:** no, no, no, no
8 **Marta:** *yes, yes, yes, yes*

Donna's strong disagreement *no, no, no, no* is what is required in this context. Most disagreements are not invited, however, and it is that fact that they are dispreferred responses that leads speakers to soften them through agreement components and delay. Pomerantz summarizes the character of disagreements (generally, dispreferred responses) in contrast to agreements (generally preferred responses) as follows:

a.   Agreements have agreement components occupying the entire agreement turns; disagreements are often prefaced.
b.   Agreements are accomplished with stated agreement components; disagreements may be accomplished with a variety of forms, ranging from unstated to stated disagreements. Frequently disagreements, when stated, are formed as partial agreements/ partial disagreements; they are weak forms of disagreement.
c.   In general, agreements are performed with a minimization of gap between the prior turn's completion and the agreement turn's initiation; disagreement components are frequently delayed within a turn or over a series of turns.
d.   Absences of forthcoming agreements or disagreements by recipients with gaps, requests for clarification, and the like are interpretable as instances of unstated, or as-yet-unstated, disagreements. (1984: 65)

It is possible to employ Pomerantz's analysis of turn organization to interpret the available reports of L2 disagreements. Both naturalistic interaction (Beebe & Takahashi, 1989; Pearson, 1984) and DCT responses (Beebe & Takahashi, 1989) have been observed, although we review only the reports of interactional data here. Investigations of nonnative speaker production of disagreements show that nonnative speakers may opt out of producing a disagreement, or, if the disagreement is performed, it may vary in level of directness. Pearson (1984) found that half of the students in an EFL setting at a Japanese university were "either not expressing agreement/disagreement when they could/should have done so, or they were expressing it explicitly" with such forms as *I agree* or *I disagree* (Pearson, 1986: 51). Pearson's (1986) analysis of 900 minutes of "normal everyday chat type conversation" (51) revealed that, in that setting, native speakers of English disagreed with each other much less often than they agreed (48 disagreement tokens to 137 agreement tokens). When the native speakers in her corpus did disagree, "attempts are made linguistically to reduce its challenge or threat" (52). In fact, 40 of the 48 documented disagreements were mitigated, 21 with agreement components, and only 8 were not mitigated.

Pearson points out that ESL/EFL textbooks often give equal emphasis to agreement and disagreement, suggesting that English L2 learners are erroneously led to believe that native English speakers express disagreement as frequently as they express agreement. In light of Pomerantz's description, the learners who express direct disagreement may not only be too direct as observed by Pearson, but they may also disagree too soon in cases where *I disagree* occurs at the beginning of an oppositional turn.

Beebe and Takahashi (1989) report on an incident between a male Japanese student speaking in English with his female professor. The Japanese student never explicitly disagreed with his professor, choosing instead to ask seemingly factual questions in an attempt to get his professor to go over her arguments repeatedly until she eventually saw the flaws in her own reasoning. The professor reported that it was more embarrassing to repeat her own flawed argument than it would have been if the student had simply disagreed with her. They report that Japanese L2 speakers of English often use questions "as an expression of disagreement or a statement of opinion" (203), and this strategy is often a source of confusion for Americans. The use of questions was also reported by Bardovi-Harlig and Hartford (1991) as a strategy used by international graduate students to avoid overt rejections of their advisers' advice. Whereas the overt disagreements reported by Pearson flout the practice of delaying of the disagreement, the questioning reported by Beebe and Takahashi and confirmed in a second academic setting by Bardovi-Harlig and Hartford goes beyond delaying the disagreement, to avoiding it. In the academic setting where questions to faculty are typical, professors may miss the intended illocutionary force of questions as non-agreement and take them at face value as requests for information. As Pomerantz shows, questions are typical in prefacing dispreferred turns such as disagreement. However, it seems that American interlocutors do not expect questions to stand in for disagreements and in the absence of overt disagreement components, they fail to interpret the questions as such.

The Present Study

The longitudinal corpus on which we base the present study was collected as part of a study of grammatical development in second language acquisition. Modeled on an earlier longitudinal study by Bardovi-Harlig (2000), the study collected oral data from learners every two weeks and written journals on a daily basis. At the end of the one-year observational period, we identified 12 participants who had the greatest longevity and the most consistent participation in the study and included their language samples in the corpus. We have used the oral data from the corpus to study the development of conditionals (Salsbury, 2000) and modality as related to pragmatics (Bardovi-Harlig, 2003; Salsbury & Bardovi-Harlig, 2000, 2001).

Method

It is uncontroversial to say that the dominant means of data collection in the study of interlanguage pragmatics up to this point has been the discourse completion task or DCT. Written production questionnaires differ from talk in a number of ways: they are written, they allow time for planning, and they are non-interactional. Written production questionnaires are well studied (e.g. Bardovi-Harlig & Hartford, 1993b; Johnston *et al.*, 1998; Kasper & Dahl, 1991; Rose, 1992; Rose & Ono, 1995) and their limitations are widely known. Instead of elaborating further on disadvantages of production questionnaires, we will demonstrate the unique contributions to our understanding of second-language pragmatics that studying speaking affords.

The setting

The ESL learners were students in the Intensive English Program at Indiana University. The learners met with graduate students in the masters-level second language acquisition classes in the fall and spring semesters. Graduate students were assigned to a learner as part of a dual program. The graduate students served as conversational partners for the ESL students and the ESL students served as informants for the graduate students' SLA class assignments. At the outset of the study the learners were enrolled in the lowest two levels of the seven-level program. First- and second-session ESL students were not typically eligible to participate in the conversational partner program regularly sponsored by the IEP, so the exchange was met with enthusiasm. When graduate students were not available, the second author met with the learners. The graduate courses met for a full semester which covered two seven-week sessions of the Intensive English Program. Graduate students and ESL learners met for an hour every week at their mutual convenience for a minimum of six meetings per semester. Graduate students met with informants for the first 12 elicitation sessions (September–May) and the second author of this chapter met with the informants in the final six elicitation sessions (May–August).

Data collection

Every other week the graduate students were given a picture-based conversation elicitation task or varying selections of emotion cards from which the learners were asked to select a topic (following Rintell, 1989). In later elicitation sessions, the emotion cards were replaced with open-ended questions to promote conversations (see Salsbury, 2000). Our tasks were designed to take no more than half of the conversation time. The remainder of the meetings was completely open. This arrangement led to friendly and comfortable exchanges between the graduate students and the ESL students. Partners got to know each other rather well, as the following exchanges show. In (5) the learner comments on the graduate student's prior learning of German (Jill was a Ph.D. student of German). In (6), the NS interlocutor assesses the learner's personality:

(5) Bashir, 10-28, Month 2
  Jill:　　　See Arabic is hard
  Bashir:　No, not hard, not hard, you learn Germany, it will be easy for you

(6) Marta, 7-23, Month 11
  Marta:　Now, mm, now, sometimes, yes, sometimes, I feel now, even now I am very shy, the people say I am not shy, but
  Donna:　You're shy! Oh, honey, you're not shy!
  Marta:　Yes, yes, sometimes, I am very very shy, yes, and I say, Marta, go ahead, go! Talk! Oh! Yes
  Donna:　If I were to describe you, to somebody, shy would not come up, I would not say shy

The learners who continued in the study met new conversation partners in the second semester. The partners in (2) and (6), Marta and Donna, became such good friends that they continued meeting for the rest of the academic year.

Due to a greater number of ESL students than graduate students, some graduate students were occasionally assigned two learners. The graduate student met with both of the learners at the same time. The dyads and triads differed only in the number of learners participating, and came about only out of necessity. Although we worried at first that this would decrease the amount of time each learner had to talk, this actually increased the talk between learners and decreased the talk of the graduate students, resulting in many rich and spontaneous learner-to-learner conversations.

A total of 166 taped conversational interviews lasting from 30 minutes to an hour were collected from the 12 primary learners and transcribed. For the present study we selected all but two of the 12 participants. The two participants who were excluded from the present study provided little or no spontaneous oppositional talk during the elicitation sessions. The ten learners selected represented eight first-language backgrounds with native speakers of Arabic, Korean, Spanish, Japanese, and Russian, a Catalan/Spanish bilingual speaker, and a Bambara/French bilingual speaker. Table 9.1 shows the learners and their native-speaker and learner interlocutors.

The conversations covered a broad range of topics, including politics, polygamy, TOEFL, present and future school concerns, language learning, religion, culture, and marriage. The dynamic between learners and their native speaker interlocutors in the elicitation sessions often resulted in enthusiastic participation of all involved. All oppositional talk was spontaneous. None was intentionally elicited as part of the study.

Table 9.1 ESL learners and native-speaker and learner interlocutors

	ESL learner	L1	NS interlocutors	ESL interlocutors
Male	Faisal	Arabic	Melinda, Tom	Mousa
	Jalil	Arabic	Jack, Tom	Sergei
	Bashir	Arabic	Tom, Jill, Allen	Sergei
	Mousa	Bambara/ French	Alejandra, Bob, Tom	Faisal, Takako
	Sergei	Russian	Jack, Allen	Jalil, Bashir
	Jordi	Catalan/ Spanish	Jack	Jalil
Female	Marta	Spanish	Ashley, Donna, Susan, Tom	Takako
	Eun Hui	Korean	Dana, Samantha, Tom	None
	Takako	Japanese	Aubrey, Kristen, Tom	Mousa, Marta
	Natasha	Russian	Donna	None

Analysis

All exchanges in which disagreement was expressed in response to another speaker's statement were included in the corpus for this study. As discussed earlier, disagreements simply express an opinion contrary to that of the interlocutor. They may be grammatically negative as in (5) or (6) or grammatically positive as in (1) and (4), line 8. We do not divide agreements according to their grammatical polarity, but only point this out to complete the description. Some of the disagreements are playful, as can be seen in Marta's echoing of Donna's turn in (4), line 7.

The learner may have the first or second disagreement depending on who offers the assessment. If the interlocutor offers the first assessment, the learner may disagree in the second turn as in (7), line 2. If the learner offers the assessment and the NS interlocutor disagrees in the second turn, the learner may disagree in the third turn, reasserting his or her original assessment as in (8), line 4, and (4), line 8. The disagreement may, of course, be negotiated over the course of many more following turns:

(7) Takako, 6-22, Month 10
1 **Tom:**   . . . I think that drivers here are rude
2 **Takako:**   not always, like very often, but you know

(8) Eun Hui, 6-19, Month 10
1 **Tom:**   . . . have you thought about getting a part time job?
2 **Eun Hui:** no, because my speaking is bad
3 **Tom:**   no, I think you could do very well
4 **Eun Hui:** no, but I mean, when I speak with native speaker, they
5   didn't understand, ah, so, another my Korean friend,
6   she is a graduate student now, but she, when I, when
7   I, [ ] she have to interview with [ ] but, she, drop,
8   drop out, three times, because her speaking

There were three major types of statements that met with oppositional turns in our data: assessments, suggestions (assessments of a situation resulting in a stated course of action), and facts. In (9) two learners, Faisal and Mousa, disagree about Mousa's assessment of one year as a long time (line 2). Faisal disagrees in line 3, and Mousa counters in line 7, reasserting that it is a long time, but adding a qualifier, *for me*, thus limiting the scope of his claim:

(9) Mousa and Faisal, 8-6, Month 12
1 **Mousa:**   yeah, sure, I know that, because, I know that I didn't
2   know any English, so, I know that I will take, I have
3   to take long time
4 **Faisal:** but it's not long time, a year
5 **Mousa:**   huh?
6 **Faisal:** it's not long time, like one year
7 **Mousa:**   one year? yeah, it's long time for me, yeah
8 **Faisal:** it's long time, you think, one year?

In (10), Takako rejects the assessment of the situation being resolvable by riding her bicycle as Kristen suggests in line 1:

(10) Takako, 3-10, Month 7
1 **Kristen:** well, you can take a bicycle, that's what I do
2 **Takako:**   I don't want to ride bicycle during the winter, it's too
3   cold! You, usually you use bicycle in the winter, really!
4   Oh!
5 **Kristen:** but I'm from Indiana, no problem

In (11) Jalil counters Sergei's presupposition that Gorbachov would stay in a hotel, suggesting instead that he would stay in "the building of your country," possibly an embassy. Other disagreements over facts include dates and ages:

(11) Jalil with Sergei, 9-25, Month 1
1 **Jack:**   would go to see Michael Gorbachov?
2 **Sergei:**   maybe, what hotel he stay?
3 **Jalil:**   no, maybe not stay in the hotel, . . . the building of your
              country?

Longitudinal development of turn organization

All of the learners elaborated their disagreements as time passed. The earliest examples of oppositional talk were strong, that is, they were disagreements with no agreement elements. Note that strong disagreements may include downgraders, such as *maybe* or *well*. For example in the first month, in Example (11), Jalil says *No, maybe not stay in the hotel*. Learners move on from such short and direct disagreements to elaborated disagreements. Learners may elaborate disagreements in at least four ways: increase the amount of talk in the disagreement portion; include agreement as well as disagreement components; postpone the disagreement to later positions in their initial turns; and use multiple turn structure to potentially avoid disagreement. Learners moved at their own pace, not only grammatically as we have documented for these learners earlier (Bardovi-Harlig, 2003; Salsbury & Bardovi-Harlig, 2000, 2001), but also in terms of their turn organization. Because the learners differ in rate of development and in terms of self expression, they are best compared to themselves rather than to others or in aggregate group descriptions. In the sections that follow, we examine the disagreements of three learners to illustrate the acquisitional stages of turn organization. We have selected samples from two women and one man who represent four language backgrounds, Korean, Spanish, and Bambara-French. We have selected a conservative learner, a risk taker, and a balanced learner.

A conservative learner: Eun Hui. In our previous analysis of these learners' grammatical development, we examined their acquisition of modality (Salsbury, 2000; Salsbury & Bardovi-Harlig, 2001). Modality includes not only modals, but all expressions which convey speakers' (un)certainty toward the proposition that they express. We analyzed all the learners modal expressions and the means that they used to realize them. In comparison to other learners in the study, Eun Hui is a conservative learner who uses few modalized utterances and few types of expression. The first illustration of the development in turn structure is taken from Eun Hui's corpus. The three disagreements in (12)–(14) address the same topic: assessments of her developing ability in English. Three of the women in our study (Eun Hui, Marta, and Takako) were very concerned with their progress in English. Although an analysis of their grammar and their pragmatics shows objective development, the learners characteristically countered their NS interlocutor's assessments of progress. In (12) Eun Hui is direct in her disagreement, beginning her response with "Really!" followed by "no" in line 2. She offers that her interlocutor's listening is good, although her speaking is bad. She further attributes being understood to her teachers' abilities to understand her (lines 2–5) rather than to her success at making herself understood:

(12) Eun Hui, 1-22, Month 5

1	**Samantha:**	Your English is good [reconstructed turn] . . .
2	**Eun Hui:**	really! No, my speaking is very bad! Your listening
3		is good. My class teachers, some teachers under-
4		stand me, understand my speaking, some people's
5		don't understand my speaking

(13) Eun Hui, 2-6, Month 6
1   **Samantha:**   well, I think you speak very well now!
2   **Eun Hui:**   English is very difficult

(14) Eun Hui, 3-13, Month 7
1   **Samantha:**   but think of right now you are already studying
2   hard, and I think you're an excellent student . . .
3   **Eun Hui:**   but, ah, IEP course, course and ah, actually univer-
4   sity lecture's different, right, so maybe, maybe
5   university, this lecture is, I can't understand some-
6   times
7   **Samantha:**   I can't either, so you're not alone

Two weeks later, in (13) Eun Hui is much more subtle in her response. She does not accept the assessment of her interlocutor, offering instead an observation as to the difficulty of English. A month later in (14), there is an implied agreement indicated by *but* (line 3) as though she were saying "I am a good student *in the IEP* but. . . ."[1] She then goes on to say under what conditions that assessment would not hold true, namely in other university classes which are different from IEP courses.

Eun Hui shows the use of the partial agreement/partial disagreement (Pomerantz, 1984) in mid-June and early July, 10–11 months after arrival. We call this the agree-before-disagree strategy for its transparency. Eun Hui's first example of the agree-before-disagree strategy in (15), the agreement, *I know your mean*, is unconventional. The conciliatory *I know your mean* serves two purposes: to provide partial agreement and to establish her competence so that her subsequent *I don't think so* is understood as true disagreement rather than a noncommittal response indicating comprehension difficulty:

(15) Eun Hui, 6-19, Month 10
1   **Tom:**   but if you don't take any IEP classes, then you have
2   no connection to the university, cause IU has to accept
3   you first as a student, do you see what I mean?
4   **Eun Hui:**   *I know your mean, but I don't think so*
5   **Tom:**   no? ok

In the following month, Eun Hui uses a conventional marker of agreement before disagreement when she uses *yeah but* in (16) (LoCastro, 1986). The use of *yeah but* gives a nominal nod to agreement without elaborating it, allowing the disagreement to be the focus of the contribution:

(16) Eun Hui, 7–10, Month 11

```
1  Tom:      it's a cultural difference, do you think ... but I know
2            in Asia, you can agree or disagree, it's more of a
3            written culture ...
4  Eun Hui:  yeah, but, in Korea, in Korea culture, during our class, we
5            don't say many things, but even though I know about
6            that, just we have to polite attitude during class, but
7            that is not, not helpful for us, but we have many class-
8            mate, may, ah, about 60 student, so
```

Eun Hui's corpus of disagreements shows longitudinal development from elaborated strong disagreements to unconventional agreements with disagreements, to the conventional agreement-before-disagreement signaled by *yeah but*. These represent the middle range of the acquisitional sequence, as Marta's corpus shows.

A risk-taker: Marta. Marta is a risk taker who will tackle any topic of interest to her. Our previous analysis of her interlanguage development (Salsbury, 2000; Salsbury & Bardovi-Harlig, 2001) shows that her linguistic development is slower than many of the learners in the study. Her expression of modality is dominated by the lexical stage, resulting in the use of *maybe* and *I think*. The modals *can* and *will* eventually emerge in her grammar. This rate of development, a long period of lexical expression, followed much later by grammatical development, coupled with her desire to express herself, lead to a high token count of modal expressions (with many different occurrences) with a low type count (she uses the same expressions over and over, and her pragmatics outstrips her grammar). Marta's disagreements show development of turn organization during the 12 months of observation, but at the same time, she shows relatively slower linguistic development than many of the other learners in the study. Like others, Marta's first disagreements are strong, and relatively unelaborated as in (17), line 3. In (18), lines 3–4 Marta shows an elaboration of a strong disagreement:

(17) Marta, 1-22, Month 5

```
1  Marta:  I don't know, eh, what is, I don't know
2  Donna:  ... maybe Gina
3  Marta:  no, Gina, no, Gina no, she is tall, for me
4  Donna:  oh, so shorter than Gina
```

(18) Marta, 1-22, Month 5
1   **Marta:**   . . . I live with the American family
2   **Donna:**   oh, good!
3   **Marta:**   *no good because all day the family only work, work, never*
4   *I see home, never . . . I can no . . .*

Later in the same conversation, Marta uses an agreement-before-disagreement strategy in the excerpt in (19). Marta begins the agreement with a marker of *yes, but, but, yes* (line 6) and continues to state her agreement *the people believe in the Mary*, thus agreeing with Donna's assessment in lines 3–5. Marta has trouble articulating her disagreement to the second conjunct, *all Christians believe the Virgin Mary is very special*. Her turn structure sets up a slot for the disagreement, however, first by using the marker *yes, but*, which summarizes the organization of the turn, and second by following the full agreement with the marker *but* in line 7:

(19) Marta, 1-22, Month 5
1   **Marta:**   . . . maybe the people don't believe in the Virgin, the
2   Maria, maybe, but I believe
3   **Donna:**   well, I think even, I think all Christians believe like the
4   Virgin Mary is the mother of Jesus and she's very
5   special
6   **Marta:**   *yes, but, but, yes, the people believe in the Mary, because*
7   *when when ehm, born, no "tuvo" when have baby,* but
8   after, she say me, say you
9   **Donna:**   ahhhh, I don't know
10 **Marta:**   is different, yes, only this is different
11 **Donna:**   I think, the Catholic – I'm not very religious, but I
12   think the Catholic religion thinks that Mary is more
13   important –
14 **Marta:**   important, yes
15 **Donna:**   also the other Christians think she is important
16 **Marta:**   yeah, she's only for the when she born baby, but after
17   is no important, yes for me is important, ah, I don't
18   have, I have other – Mary (shows a pendant of the
19   Virgin Mary)
20 **Donna:**   oh, that's pretty, you wear it everyday?

Donna's back channel response *ahhhh, I don't know* leads to Marta's articulation of her disagreement, *is different*. Donna then helps her articulate her actual claim which is that the Virgin Mary is more important in the Catholic church than in other Christian religions (lines 11–13) which forms the disagreement portion of her contribution. She voices her agreement to Donna's framing of her position in line 14. Although Marta receives Donna's linguistic help in this and other episodes (see Salsbury & Bardovi-Harlig, 2001), she succeeds in establishing the turn organization herself, using the agreement-before-disagreement structure. In this case, Marta's effective use of turn structure outstrips her linguistic expression.

Throughout the corpus, Marta continues to evolve as a speaker, balancing agreement and disagreement in her oppositional talk. She often comes to her agreement components later in the disagreement, using the reverse order of the preferred *yeah but* strategy. In (20) she employs a *no, but yeah* strategy, asserting her position *even now I am very shy* in lines 3–4, and only later in line 12 agreeing, with qualification, that she is not shy when she knows someone well. Pomerantz's analysis suggests that the inclusion of agreement components is different from the postponing of the disagreement (by placing agreement first), and that is borne out acquisitionally as well:

(20) Marta, 7-23, Month 11

1	**Donna:**	so, how does that affect your life now?
2	**Marta:**	now, mm, now, sometimes, yes, sometimes, I feel now,
3		even now I am very shy, the people say I am not shy,
4		but
5	**Donna:**	*you're shy! Oh, honey, you're not shy!*
6	**Marta:**	*yes, yes, sometimes, I am very very shy, yes, and I say,*
7		*Marta, go ahead, go! Talk! Oh! Yes*
8	**Donna:**	*if I were to describe you, to somebody, shy would not come*
9		*up, I would not say shy*
10	**Marta:**	really, I am very very shy. No, ok, how can I say,
11		maybe when I had good relationship with somebody,
12		for example, you, Tom, I'm very open, but when I
13		don't know somebody, and I feel no comfortable, I
14		very very shy
15	**Donna:**	. . . that's natural . . .

Marta's corpus shows that a learner's competence can progress at different rates in different areas. Although the literature has illustrated many cases of grammatically proficient learners whose pragmatics lags behind, we have seen fewer cases like Marta's: learners who struggle linguistically to keep up with their own development in L2 pragmatics. Marta's corpus also shows that the preferred order of agree-before-disagree has to be learned. This is revealed when Marta undertakes fully articulated agreement components.

A fast learner–high type/high token: Mousa. In contrast to Marta, Mousa shows the most advanced grammatical development with respect to the expression of modality among the learners in our present corpus. He exhibits many uses of modalized utterances and a wide variety of modal expression in direct contrast to Marta who also uses many utterances, but sticks with the same linguistic expressions. Mousa uses lexical modals as well as grammatical ones, showing the highest use of would and could among the 12 learners in the longitudinal study. Mousa's use of modalized utterances show that his grammatical development continues at the same brisk pace as his pragmatic development, giving his conversations a different character than that of some learners.

In addition to his gains in grammar, Mousa shows the full range of turn organization identified by Pomerantz, going farther than any other learner in the corpus. He shows the lengthening of turns, the use of partial agreements with disagreements, and the postponement of the disagreement within a turn as in (21). In addition, he exhibits the postponement of disagreement across turns, employing a skillful questioning of his interlocutor's intent to disagree, a turn that signals many dispreferred turns, and that allows a speaker to back down from an oppositional stance, if desired.

(21) Mousa, 1-21, Month 5

1	**Bob:**	so your intention is to go back to Mali to study . . .
2	**Mousa:**	*no, no, here, yeah* . . . is depend on university, they need
3		some TOEFL score, like some university need 525,
4		some university, 550, something like that is different,
5		but the university that you, you plan to apply, if you
6		know their TOEFL score, so if you can get, if you get
7		this TOEFL score, here, so you can apply, and go for
8		begin to study for enter graduate, I think it is not, yeah,
9		if you, I know if you stay for study all IEP, you can,
10		you have to learn ??? so,

(22) Mousa with Ibrahim, 1-21, Month 5

1	**Ibrahim:**	I think, what wise??? for you, Mousa, if you want to
2		prove, or if you want to practice, it's better to, to find
3		your roommate
4	**Mousa:**	yeah, to, to . . . roommate, yeah, but now, I already, I
5		would not like to change again, my place, I would like
6		to stay

(23) Mousa with Bob, 2-4, Month 6a

1	**Bob:**	he'll have two wives too
2	**Mousa:**	no, he won't have two wives

Mousa's disagreement in (23) is strong with no agreement elements. In (22) Mousa employs the previously discussed nominal agreement strategy marked by *yeah but*. His grammatical development, namely the use of *would*, allows him to soften his disagreement. This is in noticeable contrast to Eun Hui and Marta in whose oral corpus *would* emerges only at the end of the year. Mousa continues to benefit from the flexibility that his grammatical development affords him when he provides the strong response in (23) which is indistinguishable from the strong responses of a native speaker.

In Month 10 Mousa continues his pragmatic and grammatical development, as he hedges his disagreement with *quite*. Like Marta, he still begins his turn with a statement of the disagreement (line 2), later adding the agreement, in the *but yeah* order (lines 20–22):

(24) Mousa, 6-17, Month 10

1	**Tom:**	. . . it's called test anxiety . . .
2	**Mousa:**	*I don't have quite like this, but I have a little, but not quite*
3		*like this,* always, in, I think, in, every exam, we, don't,
4		the most thing, the most important thing for me is
5		time, like I'm not someone who can work like very fast,
6		yeah, always, like ah, for example when I was in high
7		school, and they give like ah, my, my, my study like
8		the section of, ah, ??? or mathematics, like very strong,
9		it was like four hours ??? yeah, only mathematic, so,
10		but I take my time, but is very, is very precise, like,
11		sometimes I can do like little bit more than half, but
12		everything, I, I, I, did like is right
13	**Tom:**	perfect
14	**Mousa:**	right, right, so I can get like ??? like good score, so
15		some people they finish, but almost everything wrong,
16		yeah, most of time, sometime like almost I finish, but
17		I don't finish quite, but I always get good score,
18		because I go by reason, reasoning, yes, don't go by ???,
19		so this is sometime that I didn't have this ability, like
20		to work very fast, this is difficult for me, *but I don't*
21		*have really the anxiety of taking test, it's not quite like this,*
22		*but I think the time is the most problem for me* . . . not too
23		much time, I you don't finish also, you don't have too
24		much chance to get good score, no

The agree-before-disagree order is seen the following month in another exchange between Tom and Mousa. In (25), line 7, Tom sympathizes with the fact that Mousa has not decided on what type of wife he will choose, stating that he is too young to have to do so, but he misstates Mousa's age in so doing, saying, *well, you're only 18.* In line 8 Mousa first agrees with the proposition that he has time to decide, and later disagrees with Tom's facts by clarifying his age as 21 not 18, conforming to the preferred agree-before-disagree order:

(25) Mousa, 7–10, Month 11

1	**Tom:**	and so you think your wife, do you think she'll be a
2		woman that who works at home, or will she work in
3		the office, what would you rather, who would you
4		rather marry?
5	**Mousa:**	ah, I don't know exactly which woman I will get
6		married, that's why I cannot decide
7	**Tom:**	well, you're only 18
8	**Mousa:**	yeah, I cannot decide, *no, no, I'm not 18, I'm 21 . . .*

Later in July (Month 11), Mousa negotiates a lengthy disagreement with Takako. He postpones his disagreement not only within a single turn, but across several turns as he gives Takako the opportunity to withdraw her opinion and avoid his impending disagreement. Before the excerpt begins, Mousa had introduced the topic of polygamy as practiced in his country. At the opening of the excerpt in (26) the interviewer asks whether he would marry more than one woman:

(26) Mousa with Takako, 7-24, Month 11

1	**Tom:**	would you marry more than one woman?
2	**Mousa:**	ah, I don't think, I don't know, I haven't decide yet
3	**Tom:**	I think he'd be more honest with me if you weren't
4		here!
5	**Takako:**	yea! Because I don't know, like, first, I, first I heard
6		about like more than one wife, like I thought, why is
7		that, but now, like, I mean, I don't want to my husband
8		to have more than one wife, but, honestly, I mean, I
9		don't care . . .
10	(two turns)	
11	**Mousa:**	*you said like, if your, you don't care if your, your, your*
12		*husband has other wife?*
13	**Takako:**	I don't know
14	**Mousa:**	*you don't care about that?*
15	**Takako:**	like, now, I'm a little bit thinking, before I didn't like
16		it, but now

17	**Mousa:**	if you say that, I will say no, no
18	**Takako:**	*I don't care*
19	**Mousa:**	*no, no, no, you care!*
20	**Takako:**	because I, I mean, if I like the, the other wife, if I can
21		be a friend or something, then, probably I don't care
22	**Tom:**	really!
23	**Mousa:**	no, no, if you really love someone, no, no, if, we have
24		?? they have trouble, how like you can love your
25		husband, and you can see your husband like take
26		another wife, you cannot ??? we have a lot of trouble,
27		but, we still have, but I think this is not true, you say
28		that, if you really love someone, no, you cannot accept

In this exchange, Mousa demonstrates the full extent of his organizational structure of oppositional talk. When he says that he is undecided on the matter of having more than one wife in line 2, Takako replies that at first she didn't like the idea of a man having more than one wife, but says, *honestly, I mean, I don't care* in lines 8–9. Mousa requests clarification in two consecutive turns in lines 11–12 and 14. Clarification is a turn that is associated with dispreferred turns such as disagreement (Pomerantz, 1984), as in Mousa's turn *you said like, if your, you don't care if your, your, your, husband has other wife?* And later *you don't care about that?* After the second clarification in line 13 Takako says, *like, now, I'm a little bit thinking, before I didn't like it, but now* in line 15. Mousa responds in line 17, warning Takako that potential disagreement is imminent: *if you say that, I will say no, no.* At this point, it is still possible for the disagreement to be withheld (Pomerantz, 1984), but Takako continues with *I don't care* in line 18 and finally Mousa responds in strong disagreement, *No, no, no, you care!* in line 19. This multi-tiered disagreement shows that Mousa's interlanguage sustains a native-like turn structure when negotiating oppositional talk.

Mousa's relatively rapid development and his robust corpus reveal the major stages of development of turn organization in disagreements within a single learner. His is a grammatical path and his development seems almost effortless. The stages that can be identified in Mousa's corpus are supported and augmented by the corpora of the other learners. Their production data show the interim stages and the smaller steps that some learners take.

Acquisitional stages

Based on the longitudinal data from this corpus, the acquisitional stages can be described as follows:

(1) Strong disagreements, characterized chiefly by the occurrence of "no."
(2) Inclusion of agreement components with disagreement components.
(3) The postponement of disagreement components within a turn.
(4) The postponement of disagreement turns within a sequence of turns.

As the examples show, these main stages themselves may have stages. The use of strong disagreements divides into the early use of strong unelaborated disagreements followed by strong elaborated disagreements. As research in interlanguage pragmatics has shown earlier, length alone is not necessarily desirable (Bardovi-Harlig & Hartford, 1993a; Blum-Kulka & Olshtain, 1986). As learners are able to sustain more talk generally, agreement components begin to occur with the disagreement components. These are originally not ordered with respect to the disagreement components and later settle into the preferred order of agreement-after-disagreement. In the last stage, exhibited in this corpus only by Mousa, learners are able to postpone the disagreement not only within a single turn, but across many turns, possibly even avoiding the disagreement itself.

It is important to note that the strategies that result from these acquisitional stages are cumulative and form the learner's disagreement repertoire. Learners who can skillfully negotiate a disagreement with properly placed agreement components also show variation and employ direct disagreements. Thus, learners begin to show the same range of disagreements as native speakers. After all, the strong disagreement with which this chapter began is from a native speaker. Because native speakers also use unmitigated direct disagreements in our corpus – and these serve as input to the particular learners involved – we expect such direct disagreements will persist in interlanguage. What starts as an early stage remains as part of the variation – for both native speakers and second-language learners. There are cases of oppositional talk where short and sweet (and to the point) works best (cf. Bardovi-Harlig & Hartford, 1993a).

A closer look at the introduction of agreement elements across learners. There are at least two parts to the introduction of agreement elements in a disagreement: first, appearance, and second, the ordering of the agreement before the disagreement. These stages seem to apply to the full articulation of agreement elements as seen in examples (19) and (20), but not in the case of the *yeah but* formula. The use of *yeah but* may obviate the need for the speaker to articulate the agreement by providing the nominal agreement marker *yeah*. As the examples in the previous section show, through the use of *yeah but*, which superficially orders the elements of agreement before disagreement, learners may appear to use the preferred order sooner than they actually do. The true test case, then, is the use of fully articulated agreements and their position within the turn vis-à-vis the disagreement components.

Not surprising to the study of acquisition, but possibly less expected in pragmatics, is the fact that even the string *yeah but* emerges in stages. The learners in this study show widespread use of *but* alone to mark the disagreement. Due to the creativity that learners exhibit, we do not see much use of *yeah but* as an uninterrupted string. Only 14 instances of *yeah but* occur in the corpus, as in Takako's *yeah but sometimes cows like more than pigs* in (3), or Eun-Hui's *yeah, but, in Korea, in Korea culture, during our class, we don't say many things* in (16). The 14 instances are used by six of the ten learners and are distributed across first languages and speakers: Jalil and Bashir (Arabic L1), Mousa (L1s Bambara/French), Takako (L1 Japanese), Eun-Hui (L1 Korean), Natasha (L1 Russian), and Marta (L1 Spanish). What we see instead is a full agreement rather than a nominal one suggested by *yeah* that precedes the disagreement, but only in the third stage of acquisition of oppositional turn organization. These turns are creative and sometimes marked by a discontinuous *yeah . . . but*, but sometimes the markers themselves show development as in Takako's innovative, but nontargetlike use of *yeah, so* in (27), and Faisal's use of *yeah, no*:

(27) Takako, 5-28, Month 9
1 **Tom:**   yeah, you're easily influenced
2 **Takako:**   *yeah*, influence, *so*, I'm getting stronger too . . .

In (28) Faisal marks his agreement to the interviewer's *oh, man, you're lucky that you didn't die!* in line 8 with *yeah*, but continues his disagreement with *no* in *no, I'm not drive speed* in line 9. There are no agreement components, however minimal, in line 13 where Faisal maintains that 60 kilometers is not fast. The interviewer, however, does not let go of his position that anything fast enough to total the car is pretty fast as he gets Faisal to admit that he did in fact total the car in lines 14–15, bringing the disagreement to an end:

(28) Faisal, 7-28, Month 11
1 **Tom:**   wow! How did you crash the car and not hurt yourself?
2 **Faisal:**   ??? it's a tree
3 **Tom:**   oh, God! How did you crash into a tree, and not hurt
4   yourself
5 **Faisal:**   I put ah, the, the

6	**Tom:**	seatbelt?
7	**Faisal:**	yeah, in the ??? before I close my eyes, and boom
8	**Tom:**	oh, man, you're lucky that you didn't die!
9	**Faisal:**	yeah, no, I'm not drive speed, like just maybe, like say,
10		not miles, we didn't have miles in Saudi Arabia, 60
11		[kilometers?]
12	**Tom:**	wow, that's still pretty fast
13	**Faisal:**	no, but it's not fast
14	**Tom:**	so, did you total the car?
15	**Faisal:**	yeah

Very often, the agreement portion of the disagreement is not marked explicitly as in Example (29). Jalil and Jordi discuss the cultural problem of having a male doctor examine one's wife. The male native-speaker interlocutor, Jack, interjects three turns, but is largely ignored by the other men who continue to talk to each other until his third turn in line 21. In line 21 Jack gives a personal and cultural interpretation of the situation, *we try not to think of it*. At that point Jalil directly counters with *you tried, but, but that's the true*. The agreement component is not explicitly announced by a marker such as *yeah*, but it is unmistakable because Jalil echoes Jack's turn *we try not to think of it* with his own, *you tried*, which then leads into the disagreement, explicitly introduced by *but*:

(29) Jalil with Jordi, 1-21, Month 5

1	**Jalil:**	ah but wait, like ah, your wife, and she's go alone to
2		the doctor, and he make a check for her, what do you
3		think? What do you feel?
4	**Jordi:**	he's a doctor
5	**Jack:**	it's a different culture
6	**Jalil:**	yeah, different culture, but I think, but he didn't feel
7		anything, hurt, like oh, it's my blood, it's mine!
8		Nobody touch!
9	**Jack:**	. . . you could examined by a woman, I mean it's
10		happened to me
11	**Jordi:**	if you go to doctor and is a woman, what do you feel?
12	**Jalil:**	if I go to the doctor, she's a woman, nothing, here,
13		yeah, I didn't say anything, because I came here what
14		can I do, I can't change anything, because if I want, if
15		I didn't, I didn't like, go to my country, like, that's
16		right, but in my country, no. I cannot find it
17	**Jordi:**	but is different, in my country, for example, all the

18		doctor, gynecologist? Is woman or man
19	**Jalil:**	but what do you think when the doctor or the man
20		touch your wife body?
21	**Jack:**	we try not to think of it, Jalil
22	**Jalil:**	you tried, but, but that's the true. You didn't think
23		about the true, you didn't care about the true, but we
24		care
25	**Jordi:**	no, no, I don't change, you don't change, is not neces-
26		sary, but is, is the culture
27	**Jalil:**	yeah, difference of our culture, yeah, that's right

Jalil goes on to include Jordi and others in his assessment of Jack's stance, *You didn't think about the true, you didn't care about the true, but we care.* Jordi and Jalil close down the topic and the disagreement, again excluding their native-speaker interlocutor, agreeing that there is a difference in culture. The successful negotiation of the disagreement in this and many other exchanges shows that the use of an agreement marker is not necessary in the presence of an explicit agreement.

Thus, these additional examples show that the appearance of *yeah but* (and the *yes but* variant used by Marta) aids the learners in structuring their turns, but does not guarantee agree-before-disagree order when fully articulated agreement components appear. We also see that even *yeah but* has some acquisitional stages of its own as learner master the second conjunct.

Discussion and Conclusion

In this section we reflect on the design of the study and the importance of studying speaking to interlanguage pragmatics research. The longitudinal component of the design facilitated the acquisitional research; but the longitudinal design of the study is also a separate design issue because most research in interlanguage pragmatics is comparative rather than acquisitional (Bardovi-Harlig, 1999, 2001; Kasper, 1992; Kasper & Schmidt, 1996). Focusing instead on the conversational data alone, we see that it offers a wealth of information about the pragmatics of learners that far exceeds the time required for transcription, an objection that is often raised (Kasper & Dahl, 1991). Much can also be learned with smaller corpora than we used, following the lead of conversational analysts (see Lazaraton, Chapter 3, this volume). We will comment briefly on three areas: turn organization, general oral expression, and topic selection.

The chief concern for this chapter is that studying speaking allows us to understand turn organization, a goal that cannot be realized by written tasks. Disagreements evolve over a number of turns, as the examples in this chapter have shown. Although relatively simple strategies such as the use of *yeah but* plus an articulated disagreement could be elicited by a written production questionnaire, the strategy of postponing a disagreement across multiple turns could not. Moreover, disagreements require interaction, and the heartfelt energy to pursue them, as the examples have shown. In these conversations, all participants – native speakers and learners alike – pursued disagreements according to their own interests and opinions as the opportunity presented itself.

The use of spoken language to study what is essentially a feature of conversation is obvious. The study of conversation reveals the characteristics of learner speech, not only in the aspects of direct interest to interlanguage pragmatics, such as the organization of disagreement turns or particular speech acts, but also in the general area of expression and grammatical development which influence the learners' overall production. Oral expression and grammatical development are often masked when learners have the planning time that written tasks afford. As the examples show, all of the learner's oral–aural skills come into play: Even strong disagreements that assert "not P" in response to an interlocutor's assertion of "P" require that the learner be able to repeat the assertion and change its grammatical polarity (from positive to negative or negative to positive). Such oral ability speaks to Kasper and Blum-Kulka's (1993) claim that learners must not only have pragmatic knowledge, they must be able to access it smoothly. As all speakers know, accessing the right thing to say, on-line, when it counts, as in the case of an ongoing conversation, is crucial.

The recurrence of topics suggests that tasks may not need to be as tightly controlled as elicitation practices in interlanguage pragmatics have suggested. The issue of comparability of topics is naturally addressed by the fact that learners share certain concerns by virtue of their status as students and their age, for example, and as a consequence certain topics are repeated across learners. In our corpus of disagreements we saw numerous discussions of language ability and language learning, marriage, having children, and, among the men, polygamy. At the same time that we saw recurrent topics, we also observed a range and depth of topics that we would not have thought of addressing or would not have thought the learners wanted to address, including religion, presidential sex scandals, racism, and international relations, as well as marriage and children.

In studying speaking, the humor and language play of learners and their interlocutors is also evident, as when Donna's disagreement *no, no, no, no* triggered Marta's counter disagreement *yes, yes, yes, yes*. The study of talk as unplanned discourse also impresses an analyst with both learner and native speaker variation, within and across speakers. Authentic language samples from native speakers cut through the idealizations of native-speaker contributions and show that in ongoing casual conversation, the performance of learners and native speakers is often not far apart.

Finally, although our study was not designed to compare learners who participated as conversational partners with those who did not, we believe that our data suggest the pedagogical value of conversation to learners as a tool for growth not only in pragmatics, but in oral expression. This is not at all surprising given the claims of both the interactionist hypothesis (Long, 1996) and the output hypothesis (Swain, 1995, 1998). The opportunity to talk to both native-speaker interlocutors and other learners at length provides learners with the opportunity to tackle topics of interest to them and others and to stretch themselves as speakers. Nowhere was this more evident than in the conversations of Marta and her native-speaker interlocutor, Donna. Some learners with more outgoing personalities may be able seek out conversational opportunities for themselves, but all the learners in this study seem to have benefited from regular, sustained interaction with their graduate-student conversation partners.

Based on the conversational corpus we have collected, we would recommend the addition of a conversational component to enhance classroom instruction. These learners did not receive direct instruction in pragmatics during the course of the study; yet they showed progress in their disagreements. The occurrence of native-speaker and learner-interlocutor disagreements addressed to the learners to which they had to respond and the responses of the native-speaker and learner interlocutors to the learners' own disagreements serve as potential input to learners, potentially facilitating the learning experience. Explicit teaching of pragmatics in the classroom setting has also been shown to be beneficial (e.g. Rose & Kasper, 2001) and could enhance the progress of learners such as these. Recommendations for pedagogical activities related to disagreements can be found in Barsony (2003), Malamed (2003), and Wennerstrom (2003). We would recommend pairing such activities with regular opportunities for sustained conversation.

In closing, we turn our attention back to research design in interlanguage pragmatics: It is time to make the study of speaking a major source of data. Communicating with someone – especially speaking to someone – is such a basic function of language that it is remarkable that it is not better represented in the interlanguage pragmatics literature.

Acknowledgments

The authors wish to thank the Center for English Language Training at Indiana University for its support of this project. We would also like to thank the Applied Linguistics graduate students and ESL learners who participated in this project.

Note

1. We have identified disagreements strictly by their surface form, namely the turn asserting *P* by the first speaker and *not P* by the second speaker. It is possible that the turns of disagreements may serve additional functions in the conversation. As the editors have pointed out, the learner's disagreement in (13) may additionally be an example of a downgraded compliment response (Wolfson, 1989). Learner responses may not only reflect degree of pragmatic development, but other factors as well. Boxer's (1993) work has shown a gender bias in the tendency for self-complaints in American English. Eun Hui's response in (14) may reflect this tendency in the target language or among women more generally. Gender was not investigated systematically in this chapter.

References

Bardovi-Harlig, K. (1999) The interlanguage of interlanguage pragmatics: A research agenda for acquisitional pragmatics. *Language Learning* 49 (4), 677–713.

Bardovi-Harlig, K. (2000) *Tense and Aspect in Second Language Acquisition: Form, Meaning, and Use*. Oxford: Blackwell.

Bardovi-Harlig, K. (2001) Pragmatics and second language acquisition. In R. Kaplan (ed.) *The Handbook of Applied Linguistics* (pp. 182–192). Oxford: Oxford University Press.

Bardovi-Harlig, K. (2003) Understanding the role of grammar in the acquisition of L2 pragmatics. In A. Fernández, A. Martínez, and E. Uso (eds) *Pragmatic Competence and Foreign Language Teaching* (pp. 21–44). Castellon, Spain: Servei de Publicacions de la Universitat Jaume I.

Bardovi-Harlig, K. and Hartford, B. S. (1991) Saying "No": Native and nonnative rejections in English. In L. F. Bouton and Y. Kachru (eds) *Pragmatics and Language Learning* (Vol. 2) (pp. 41–57). Urbana-Champaign: University of Illinois, Division of English as an International Language.

Bardovi-Harlig, K. and Hartford, B. S. (1993a) Learning the rules of academic talk: A longitudinal study of pragmatic development. *Studies in Second Language Acquisition* 15 (3), 279–304.

Bardovi-Harlig, K. and Hartford, B. S. (1993b) Refining the DCT: Comparing open questionnaires and dialogue completion tasks. In L. F. Bouton and Y. Kachru (eds) *Pragmatics and Language Learning* (Vol. 4) (pp. 143–165). Urbana-Champaign: University of Illinois, Division of English as an International Language.

Barsony, O. (2003) "Actually, Steve, the deadline was Friday of last week, not this week . . ." Polite ways of correcting or contradicting our conversation partner's assumptions. In K. Bardovi-Harlig and R. Mahan-Taylor (eds) *Teaching Pragmatics*. Washington, DC: United States Department of State. Available at: http://exchanges.state.gov/education/engteaching/pragmatics.htm.

Beebe, L. M. and Takahashi, T. (1989) Sociolinguistic variation in face-threatening speech acts: Chastisement and disagreement. In M. R. Eisenstein (ed.) *The Dynamic Interlanguage: Empirical Studies in Second Language Variation* (pp. 199–218). New York: Plenum Press.

Blum-Kulka, S. and Olshtain, E. (1986) Too many words: Length of utterance and pragmatic failure. *Studies in Second Language Acquisition* 8 (2), 165–180.

Boxer, D. (1993) Complaining and commiserating: Exploring gender issues. *Text* 13, 371–395.

Georgakopoulou, A. (2001) Arguing about the future: On indirect disagreements in conversations. *Journal of Pragmatics* 33, 1881–1900.

Golato, A. (2002) German compliment responses. *Journal of Pragmatics* 34, 547–571.

Grimshaw, A. D. (ed.) (1990) *Conflict Talk: Sociolinguistic Investigations of Arguments in Conversations*. Cambridge: Cambridge University Press.

Gruber, H. (2001) Questions and strategic orientation in verbal conflict sequences. *Journal of Pragmatics* 33, 1815–1857.

Johnston, B., Kasper, G., and Ross, S. (1998) Effect of rejoinders in production questionnaires. *Applied Linguistics* 19 (2), 157–182.

Kasper, G. (1992) Pragmatic transfer. *Second Language Research* 8, 203–231.

Kasper, G. and Blum-Kulka, S. (1993) *Interlanguage Pragmatics*. Oxford: Oxford University Press.

Kasper, G. and Dahl, M. (1991) Research methods in interlanguage pragmatics. *Studies in Second Language Acquisition* 13 (2), 215–247.

Kasper, G. and Schmidt, R. (1996) Developmental issues in interlanguage pragmatics. *Studies in Second Language Acquisition* 18 (2), 149–169.

Kotthoff, H. (1993) Disagreement and concession in disputes: On the context sensitivity of preference structures. *Language in Society* 22, 193–216.

LoCastro, V. (1986) Yes, I agree with you, but . . .: Agreement and disagreement in Japanese and American English. Paper presented at JALT '86 Conference, Hamamatsu, Japan, November.

Long, M. H. (1996) The role of linguistic environment in second language acquisition. In W. C. Ritchie and T. K. Bhatia (eds) *Handbook of Second Language Acquisition* (pp. 413–478). San Diego, CA: Academic Press.

Malamed, L. (2003) "That's wrong!" – Improving the friendly discussion of controversial issues. In K. Bardovi-Harlig and R. Mahan-Taylor (eds) *Teaching Pragmatics*. Washington, DC: United States Department of State. Available at: http://exchanges.state.gov/education/engteaching/pragmatics.htm.

Muntigl, P. and Turnbull, W. (1998) Conversational structure and facework in arguing. *Journal of Pragmatics* 29, 225–256.

Pearson, E. (1984) Oral interactive testing at a Japanese university. *Cross Currents* 11 (2), 1–12.

Pearson, E. (1986) Agreement/disagreement: An example of results of discourse analysis applied to the oral English classroom. *I.T.L. Review of Applied Linguistics* 74, 47–61.

Pomerantz, A. (1984) Agreeing and disagreeing with assessments: Some features of preferred/dispreferred turn shapes. In J. M. Atkinson and J. Heritage (eds) *Structures of Social Action: Studies in Conversation Analysis* (pp. 57–101). Cambridge: Cambridge University Press.

Rees-Miller, J. (2000) Power, severity, and context in disagreement. *Journal of Pragmatics* 32, 1087–1111.

Rintell, E. M. (1989) "That reminds me of a story": The use of language to express emotion by second-language learners and native speakers. In M. R. Eisenstein (ed.) *The Dynamic Interlanguage: Empirical Studies in Second Language Variation* (pp. 237–257). New York: Plenum.

Rose, K. (1992) Speech acts and questionnaires: The effect of hearer response. *Journal of Pragmatics* 17, 49–62.

Rose, K. and Kasper, G. (eds) (2001) *Pragmatics in Language Teaching*. Cambridge: Cambridge University Press.

Rose, K. and Ono, R. (1995) Eliciting speech act data in Japanese: The effect of questionnaire type. *Language Learning* 45 (2), 191–223.

Salsbury, T. (2000) The acquisitional grammaticalization of unreal conditionals and modality in L2 English: A longitudinal perspective. Unpublished doctoral dissertation, Indiana University, Bloomington.

Salsbury, T. and Bardovi-Harlig, K. (2000) Oppositional talk and the acquisition of modality in L2 English. In B. Swierzbin, F. Morris, M. E. Anderson, C. A. Klee, and E. Tarone (eds) *Social and Cognitive Factors in Second Language Acquisition: Selected Proceedings of the 1999 Second Language Research Forum* (pp. 57–76). Somerville, MA: Cascadilla Press.

Salsbury, T. and Bardovi-Harlig, K. (2001) "I know your mean, but I don't think so": Disagreements in L2 English. In L. Bouton (ed.) *Pragmatics and Language Learning* (Vol. 10) (pp. 131–151). Urbana-Champaign: University of Illinois, Division of English as an International Language.

Swain, M. (1995) Three functions of output in second language learning. In G. Cook and B. Seidlhofer (eds) *Principle and Practice in Applied Linguistics* (pp. 107–124). Oxford: Oxford University Press.

Swain, M. (1998) The output hypothesis, focus on form, and second language learning. In V. Berry, V. B. Adamson, and W. Littlewood (eds) *Applying Linguistics: Insights into Language Education* (pp. 1–21). Hong Kong: English Centre, University of Hong Kong.

Vuchinich, S. (1990) The sequential organization of closing in verbal family conflict. In A. D. Grimshaw (ed.) *Conflict Talk: Sociolinguistic Investigations of Arguments in Conversations* (pp. 118–138). Cambridge: Cambridge University Press.

Wolfson, N. (1989) The social dynamics of native and non-native variation in complimenting behavior. In M. R. Eisenstein (ed.) *The Dynamic Interlanguage: Empirical Studies in Second Language Variation* (pp. 219–236). New York: Plenum.

Wennerstrom, A. (2003) Making contrasts in English. In K. Bardovi-Harlig and R. Mahan-Taylor (eds) *Teaching Pragmatics*. Washington, DC: United States Department of State. Available at: http://exchanges.state.gov/education/engteaching/pragmatics.htm.

Chapter 10

The Linguistic Encoding of Pragmatic Tone: Adverbials[1] as Words that Work[2]

LESLIE M. BEEBE AND HANSUN ZHANG WARING

The purpose of this chapter is to investigate the relationship between grammatical and pragmatic proficiency by studying how adverbials contribute to pragmatic tone. In our view, adverbials are "words that work" – little words that contribute significantly to pragmatic tone. A discourse completion test was administered to 20 lower- and 20 higher-proficiency ESL learners enrolled in an intensive English program in a major northeastern American university. The results of the study show that both the range and frequency of adverbials used were very similar between the lower- and higher-proficiency groups. However, the two groups differed in their use of adverbials to convey pragmatic tone. The lower-proficiency group tended to rely more upon sarcasm and intensifiers by repeatedly using a limited number of adverbs. The higher-proficiency learners, on the other hand, used a much wider range of adverbials to convey a much wider range of tones. They were able to use a little word like "just" to make a whole unspoken "off-record" claim. They sounded assertive, but not necessarily rigid or hostile. Based on these results, we speculate that there is an order of difficulty involved in pragmatic tone: intense and sarcastic tones may be easier to acquire and thus emerge earlier than subtle tones of assertiveness or aggression. We argue that grammatical proficiency does contribute to pragmatic proficiency, and that pragmatic proficiency should be looked for not only in the range and frequency of pragmatic strategies, but also in the skillful use of adverbials to convey off-record messages and to regulate the intensity or quality of tone. Teachers of pragmatics might benefit from the notion that adverbs are pragmatically rich items. Important work on a learner's pragmatic system can be done by either expanding the learner's repertoire of adverbs or exploring the full pragmatic potential of those adverbs already acquired.

Introduction

Kasper and Schmidt (1996) have challenged researchers in interlanguage pragmatics to tie their research questions to issues in second language acquisition (SLA). That is to say, interlanguage pragmatics must include research on developmental issues, not just usage. Bardovi-Harlig (1999) proposes an extension of Kasper and Schmidt's (1996) research agenda for acquisitional pragmatics, namely, exploring the relationship between the development of the grammatical and pragmatic systems. She argues that "research has not established that pragmatic competence is independent of grammatical competence," and that "although grammatical competence may not be a sufficient condition for pragmatic development, it may be a necessary condition" (Bardovi-Harlig, 1999: 677). In a similar vein, Kasper and Rose (1999) call for a detailed analysis of "form-function and function-form" in order to accurately ascertain, in the case of increased proficiency, "whether the greater variety of linguistic material is simply a reflection of expanded vocabulary and syntactic structures, or whether the more advanced learners have developed a better command of the pragmalinguistic potential of lexical and syntactic devices" (p. 88). In this chapter, we aim to investigate the relationship between grammatical and pragmatic proficiency by studying how adverbials contribute to pragmatic tone (not to be confused with tone as syllable pitch in tone languages). In our view, adverbials are "words that work" – little words that contribute significantly to pragmatic tone.

Background: Tone

In an attempt to create a theoretically coherent agenda to investigate tone, we proposed the following definition of tone:

> Tone is the affect indirectly conveyed by the Speaker or perceived by the Hearer. It may be conveyed by linguistic and/or nonlinguistic means (e.g. facial expression, body language, visual aids). Metaphorically, tone is the "color" of emotion and attitude on language. (Beebe & Waring, 2002)

We also proposed a taxonomy of linguistic devices that are invoked to create tone. These devices fall into four broad categories: phonetics/phonology, grammar, lexical choices, and discourse features. Although there is no academic study of tone per se to our knowledge that precedes our investigation, the concept of tone is widespread. Explicit references to the "tone" of someone's language are common in popular literature by journalists and academics and in everyday conversation. For instance, a search of Lexus / Nexus turned up 83 references to the "tone" of someone's language in the space of one week, the week ending March 5, 2002. Explicit references to the "tone" of language as well as to "tone of voice" appear in the popular nonfiction writing of sociolinguist Deborah Tannen, as well. Tannen (1986) refers to "tone of voice" as one of the "subtle signals" which, along with other signals such as intonation, pitch, and facial expression, work to "frame each utterance as serious, joking, teasing, angry, polite, rude, ironic, and so on" (p. 83). She cites an argument in which one spouse objects to the "tone" of the other's words, saying, "I'm talking about your *tone*" since the offensive part of the other's language was not in the actual words that were said, but, according to Tannen, "in the metamessage level of talk" (Tannen, 2001: 18).

Most of what has been written in academia, however, is not directly part of the pragmatics – let alone interlanguage pragmatics – literature, but rather comes from two other groups of sources. There is literature on theoretical / analytical frameworks for analyzing language (verbal or nonverbal) from related fields, such as Communication, Anthropology, and Sociolinguistics, which often explicates related theoretical constructs. There is also literature on empirical findings from studies of closely related constructs – affect and emotion. There are some notable references to tone in the second language acquisition (SLA) and interlanguage pragmatics (ILP) literature as well.

The first group of academic literature that deals with tone is found in the discussion of theoretical / analytical frameworks from various disciplines. Anthropologist Bateson (1972) coined the notion of "framing" by which we understand how we are to take stretches of talk – that is, as joking, teasing, ironic, or official. "Frame" is different from, but related to, the notion of tone since we might speak of an "official tone," a "polite tone," a "rude tone," or a "joking tone," just as we might speak of an "official frame" or a "joking frame." Later, sociologist Erving Goffman (1974, 1981) expanded upon the notion of frame, and elaborated on other constructs that are related to tone (e.g. footing, alignment, and stance). These notions are all part of what the discourse analyst explicitly, or the lay conversationalist inexplicitly, takes into consideration, we would argue, when concluding that there are differences in the "tone" of a stretch of talk.

Anthropological linguist Gumperz's (1982) notion of "contextualization cues" is also connected, although not explicitly by Gumperz, to the assessment of the tone of an utterance. Gumperz contends that "constellations of surface features of message form are the means by which speakers signal and listeners interpret what the activity is, how semantic content is to be understood, and how each sentence relates to what precedes or follows," and he identifies these features as contextualization cues (p. 131). What makes Gumperz's contextualization cues relevant to tone is that the cues may carry information, but these meanings are implicit and only become apparent from the constellation of cues and the interactive process of talk.

Communication Studies specialists look at the social, moral, and cultural processes involved in communicating emotion (e.g. Planalp, 1999), exploring literature from diverse fields, such as psychology, sociology, management, and philosophy. Planalp investigates the "cues" to emotion, such as facial, physiological, gestural, action, and verbal cues, as well as the absence of such cues. This research is relevant to the study of tone in that tone and tone of voice convey emotions or affect.

Sociolinguist Janet Holmes (2001) discusses analytical frameworks from sociolinguistic research that are related to the study of tone, although her discussion of the affective function/meaning of linguistic forms or strategies is not explicitly connected to tone. She refers to "formality" as one of the four basic dimensions of sociolinguistic analysis, along with power, solidarity, and function (Holmes, 2001).

Lastly, but most importantly, anthropological linguist Dell Hymes makes explicit reference to "tone" in his now famous SPEAKING acronym that appeared in his programmatic paper on the ethnography of speaking. Hymes's paper (1972) refers to Key for the K of SPEAKING, which he defines as the "tone, manner, or spirit in which an act is done" (p. 62). Hymes wrote:

> The signaling of key may be nonverbal, as with a wink, gesture, posture, style of dress, musical accompaniment, but it also commonly involves conventional units of speech too often disregarded in ordinary linguistic analysis, such as English aspiration and vowel length to signal emphasis. (1972: 62)

This point of view is close to the previously mentioned approaches, including the one taken in this chapter that linguistic (and nonverbal) devices, either individually or collectively, contribute to the "tone" of an utterance. Douglas (2000) has updated Hymes's SPEAKING categories for application to assessment for specific purposes, including "tone" as a category in his framework.

The second group of academic literature that is relevant to the study of tone is the empirical work of anthropological linguists who investigate language socialization along with other linguists and applied linguists who investigate emotion, affect, tone, or the neurobiological basis of affect in native language or interlanguage. By far the most valuable of these efforts for our purposes is the empirical research on language socialization, particularly the work of Ochs and Schieffelin.

Ochs (1986b) explores the linguistic conventions associated with affect in Samoan and how young children acquire knowledge of these conventions over developmental time. By "affect" she intends to cover the semantic domain that encompasses "emotional processes, structures, and concepts," such as "feelings, moods, dispositions, attitudes, character, personality, masking, double binds, undercutting, and the like" (p. 254). The most useful part of Ochs' study for our purposes is the discussion of the linguistic encoding of affect. Ochs finds (with reliance on earlier research of others as well) special affect particles, pronouns, and determiners, as well as interjections, terms of address, descriptors, prosodic features (e.g. loudness, intonation), and even front vs. back articulation in the oral cavity, to encode affect. She distinguishes between the "nature of the affect being conveyed" and the "intensity of the affect being conveyed" (p. 259), with forms called affect specifiers and affect intensifiers respectively.

Ochs and Schieffelin (1989) cite examples of a wide range of linguistic resources from various languages that express affect. In their edited volume, Schieffelin and Ochs (1986) bring together a group of articles (e.g. Clancy, 1986; Eisenberg, 1986; Miller, 1986; Ochs, 1986b; Schieffelin, 1986) that study the acquisition and socialization of affective language (see Ochs, 1986a, for an overview; also see Clancy, 1999; Ohta, 1994). Research by Goodwin and Goodwin (2001) on emotion as situated activity looks at how "displays of emotion emerge within interaction" (p. 254). This research is related to the acquisition of tone, as much as was the research of Ochs (1986b). The authors write that "what is called for is an *embodied performance* of affect through intonation, gesture, body posture and timing. An explicit emotion vocabulary is not necessary for powerful displays of emotion with language in its full pragmatic environment" (p. 254).

Other research on affect or emotion stems from the field of applied linguistics. Some of it deals with emotion vocabulary (e.g. Dewaele & Pavlenko, 2002). The lexicon related to emotion/affect is one group of linguistic devices that speakers use to convey tone (see Dewaele & Pavlenko (2002) for a valuable review of the literature in applied linguistics on emotion and language, as well as sources from the field of psychology).

Additional applied linguistic research on emotion/affect which relates to tone includes Rintell's (1984) work on the perception of emotion by second language learners, in which she argues that the expression of emotion is an illocutionary act, and her (1990) work in which she investigates, by extension, the varied strategies that native and nonnative speakers use to express their emotions. On another plane altogether, Schumann's (1997) research on the neurobiology of affect is related to tone.

Although the study of tone has not yet attracted major attention in interlanguage pragmatics, its role as an integral part of interlanguage pragmatics research has been made evident at various points since the late 1980s. Beebe *et al.*, (1990) and Takahashi and Beebe (1987) used qualitative analysis to discuss the "tone/content" of refusals when the frequency and order of pragmatic strategies (formerly "semantic formulas") failed to fully capture differences in pragmatic performance. For instance, in their research, a vague excuse was not pragmatically equivalent to a specific excuse (Beebe *et al.*, 1990). And the formality of expression deeply affected the pragmatic appropriateness of the language used even though it was not reflected in the choice of pragmatic strategies (Takahashi & Beebe, 1987). The importance of tone is also underscored in Raffaldini's (1988) situation test in which she makes a point of eliciting functions that "convey other than neutral tone" (p. 200).

Bisshop (1996) showed that Australian EFL learners' apologies were distinguishable from native speaker apologies largely on the basis of "tone," a factor that was obscured, in part, by the coding scheme of the widely known CCSARP study. In Beebe and Waring's (1997, in press) cross-sectional study on pragmatic development in responding to rudeness, higher-proficiency learners were found to use more "asserting strategies" as a group (including Insult, Threat, Challenge, Criticize, Sarcastic Compliment/Greet, Argue, Justify, Request), and lower-proficiency learners used more "acquiescing strategies" as a group (including Apologize, Thank, Acquiesce, Opt out). That is, higher-proficiency learners defended themselves more successfully against rudeness, indicating that the pragmatic "tone" of utterances was a crucial part of their acquired pragmatic competence.

Research Questions

While Beebe and Waring (1997, in press) found that the differences in tone shown in the responses to rudeness produced by ESL learners of different proficiency levels can be partially explained by the different clusters of pragmatic strategies employed, there were clearly some additional factors – some linguistic (i.e. structural) factors – that contributed to the differences in tone and content by higher- vs. lower-proficiency learners.

The higher-level learners used more words, but, more importantly, they used words more effectively and more subtly. This led us to ask what factors contributed to the differences in tone that clearly existed in the responses of the higher- vs. lower-proficiency learners.

Our initial hypothesis was that higher-proficiency learners were using off-record messages – conversational implicatures (Grice, 1975) – more than lower-proficiency learners. That is, they conveyed meaning (i.e. messages) beyond what they said with actual words. We also hypothesized that the higher-level learners were addressing the negative off-record messages in rude utterances said to them more than lower-level learners. Although we gathered some evidence to support these hypotheses, we ultimately decided that quantifying off-record messages was risky and unreliable, as the exact number of messages varied with the wording chosen to convey the messages. Consequently, we decided to look for linguistic structures that contributed to pragmatic tone. This would allow us to quantify more reliably, while continuing to use interpretive analysis on the pragmatic tone of the responses. And, secondly, this would allow us to address the very question that Bardovi-Harlig (1999) is suggesting we add to our research agenda in the field of interlanguage pragmatics – namely, what the relationship between grammatical and pragmatic proficiency is.

Therefore, in this study, we attempted to answer the following two research questions:

(1) How do lower- and higher-proficiency learners differ in the range, frequency of use, and grammaticality of adverbials?
(2) How does the use of adverbials contribute to pragmatic tone in responding to rudeness?

Method

Subjects

The subjects were enrolled in an Intensive English Language Program in a large English language institute in a major northeastern American university. They represented the 20 lowest-proficiency students and the 20 highest-proficiency students in levels 4 to 8. The levels of proficiency were determined by a grammar-based written placement test upon the student's admission into the Intensive Language Program. The 40 subjects include 16 males and 24 females from the following countries: Korea, Japan, Brazil, Argentina, China, Italy, and Turkey.

Instrumentation

A Discourse Completion Test (DCT) was designed as a data collection instrument. The DCT consisted of six situations where someone was rude and the subject had to respond to the rudeness. The six situations were selected from 750 naturally occurring examples of spontaneous rudeness (see Beebe, 1995). The DCT had two conditions: "You Would Say," and "You Would Feel Like Saying." The first condition gives the learners an opportunity to respond to rudeness in a way that reflects the social constraints against being rude to another person, even if only reacting to that person's rudeness. The second condition gives the respondent an opportunity to respond to rudeness in the way they might do if there were no social constraints holding them back.

Beebe and Cummings (1985, 1995), in a study on natural speech act data vs. written questionnaire data, found that, although the responses elicited through DCTs failed to reflect the amount of negotiation and depth of emotion in actual talk, DCTs were powerful in gathering a large amount of data quickly and systematically and in capturing the canonical shape of speech acts. In a cross-sectional study that compares performances between different proficiency groups such as ours, systematicity tends to take precedence. The DCT allows us to effectively control for the proficiency factor while looking at 20 learners at a time rather than only a few. It also offers us insights into what learners at a certain proficiency level think they would typically say in a certain situation. To partially compensate for the weaknesses of DCTs in eliciting extended negotiations and emotional depth, we ask for two types of responses, "Would Say" and "Would Feel Like Saying," hoping that what gets lost in the "Would Say" response would find its way into the "Would Feel Like Saying" response.

Data collection procedures

Data were gathered from classes in the Intensive English Language Program at a major university on the northeastern coast of the United States in the month-long winter session in January, 1997. A research assistant (as well as the language instructor in each class) was present at the DCT administration. The research assistant explained the instructions to the students before they began responding to the DCT, and she did not intervene once they started. All DCTs were completed within one hour.

Data analysis procedures

All adverbials in the data were identified and grouped by proficiency level of the ESL learner and by the "Would Say" vs. the "Would Feel Like Saying" conditions. Range was defined as the number of types of adverbials used. Frequency was determined by counting the number of adverbials used per group, per learner, and the average use of adverbials per learner within each group. The adverbials were also coded in terms of:

(1) grammaticality;
(2) pragmatic tone.

Pragmatic tone was in turn coded into the following three types:

(1) assertive tone (via going off-record) ("I just wanted to know when the professor is free.");
(2) intense tone ("You're so rude." "I'll never come here again.");
(3) sarcastic tone ("You're really kind.").

To clarify the first option, a speaker is going "off record" when what the speaker says is subject to more than one interpretation, and the additional interpretations are deniable. For instance, when someone says your hat is "interesting" to mean it is "terrible," the person can always deny that s/he meant "terrible" because that was never said "on record" (see Brown & Levinson, 1987; Grice, 1975).

Findings

Range and frequency of use of adverbials

Both the range and frequency of adverbials used were very similar between the lower- and higher-proficiency groups. Table 10.1 shows very similar ranges, modes, and mediums of adverbial use by the two groups. In addition, both groups used 21 different adverbials. In other words, the total range of adverbials was identical. Fourteen out of the 20 subjects in the lower-proficiency group used adverbials, and the number of adverbials used was 38. The average use of adverbials per learner in the lower-proficiency group was 1.9. Thirteen out of the 20 subjects in the higher-proficiency group used adverbials, and the number of adverbials used was 37. The average use of adverbials per learner in the higher-proficiency group was 1.85. Thus, the frequency of the adverbial usage was almost identical. The frequency of adverbial use by learners in

Table 10.1 Range, mode, and median of adverbial use among higher-
and lower-proficiency learners

	Higher	*Lower*
Range	0–7	0–5
Mode	3	2
Median	1	2

lower- and higher-proficiency groups is shown in Figure 10.1. Both
groups show a general tendency toward a decreasing number of users as
the number of adverbials increases. For instance, six lower-proficiency
learners and seven higher-proficiency learners used no adverbials,
whereas no lower-proficiency learner and only one higher-proficiency
learner used seven adverbials.

Examining more closely the distribution of adverbials used in the
"Would Say" condition vs. the "Would Feel Like Saying" condition, we
found that the lower-proficiency learners used adverbials more than five
times as often in the "Would Feel Like Saying" condition than they did
in the "Would Say" condition (i.e. 32 vs. 6). On the other hand, the higher-
proficiency group used adverbials almost an equal number of times in
both the "Would Say" and the "Would Feel Like Saying" conditions (i.e.
19 vs. 18). This shows that the "condition" variable was much more relevant to the lower-proficiency learners than the higher-proficiency learners

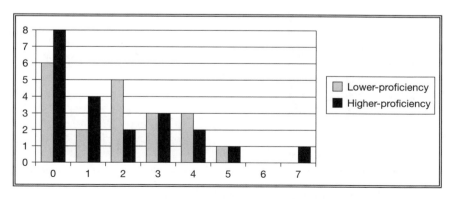

Figure 10.1 Frequency of adverbial use by lower- and higher-
proficiency learners

in the use of adverbials. It also suggests that, while the higher-proficiency learners may have been able to say basically what they felt like saying, the lower-proficiency learners held back in the "Would Say" condition.

Grammaticality

Examining the grammaticality of the adverbials used, we found that the lower-proficiency learners had an ungrammaticality rate of 32% on adverbials, whereas the higher-proficiency group had an ungrammaticality rate of only 16%. In other words, of all the adverbials used by the lower-proficiency group, approximately one-third were ungrammatical. This is not surprising as lower-proficiency learners were categorized as lower-proficiency partially on the basis of a grammar test.

What is interesting, however, is the distribution of ungrammaticality between the "Would Say" condition and the "Would Feel Like Saying" condition for the two groups. (See Figure 10.2.) For the lower-proficiency group, ungrammaticality went up in the "Would Feel Like Saying" condition as opposed to the "Would Say" condition (34% vs. 17%). The higher-proficiency group had an ungrammaticality rate of 11% in the "Would Feel Like Saying" condition and 21% in the "Would Say" condition. This suggests that, when the lower-proficiency learners tried to express their emotions and say what they really wanted to say, they did not have the linguistic means to do so correctly. For the higher-proficiency learners,

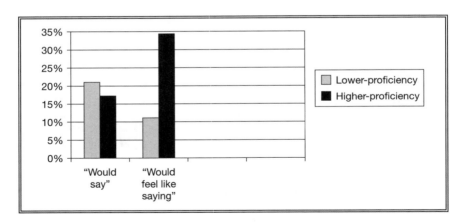

Figure 10.2 Ungrammaticality rate of higher- vs. lower-proficiency groups under "Would Say" and "Would Feel Like Saying" conditions

four out of the six instances of ungrammatical use occurred in the "Would Say" condition. In other words, ungrammaticality tended to surface in the "Would Say" condition more for the higher-proficiency group than in the "Would Feel Like Saying" condition. Due to the small numbers of tokens and the small difference between the groups, strong claims are not merited. We might speculate, however, that these findings suggest that the higher-proficiency learners, as opposed to the lower-proficiency learners, were not constrained by having insufficient linguistic means to express themselves as they wanted to.

Pragmatic tone

Besides the overall grammaticality level and the distribution of grammaticality between the "Would Say" and "Would Feel Like Saying" conditions, what truly differentiates the higher- from the lower-proficiency learners is the pragmatic tone conveyed by the adverbials they used. The two groups differed greatly in the way they used adverbials to convey assertiveness by going off record, to intensify and to show sarcasm. The groups differed both in the manner in which they achieved pragmatic tone and in the extent to which they relied on each type of tone (assertive tone, intense tone, and sarcastic tone) to respond to rudeness.

Assertive tone

The pragmatic proficiency of the higher-proficiency learners was most evident in their ability to convey assertiveness by going off record in responding to rudeness. The higher-proficiency group used adverbials to go off record much more frequently than the lower-proficiency group (see Figure 10.3), and 43% (16 out of 37 instances) of all adverbials used by the higher-proficiency group sent or addressed off-record messages, thereby creating an assertive tone. Only 3% (1 out of 38) of all adverbials used by the lower-proficiency group used an off-record message at all. In fact, the only utterance in which a lower-proficiency learner attempted to send an off-record message with an adverb was an incomplete one: "I'm just asking you how to get." The higher-proficiency learners, on the other hand, used a variety of adverbials to go off record on multiple occasions. The adverbials they used included "just," "not exactly," "properly," "always," "now," "also," "anyway," "not even," and "ever."

For example, in the situation where the bookstore clerk said to the customer, "If you want to browse, go to the library," one higher-proficiency Portuguese woman responded, "I just would like to take a look and see if

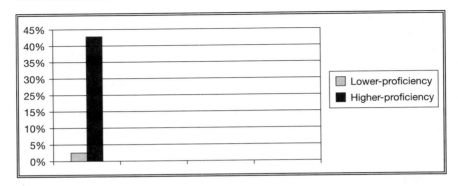

Figure 10.3 Percentage of adverbials used to send and/or address off-record messages

this is what I'm looking for. I don't want to damage your book." By using the adverb, "just," the respondent suggested off record that, contrary to the clerk's implied accusation, she was not acting inappropriately by looking at the books. This made her sound more assertive, but in a subtle way. In the situation where the receptionist said to a student seeking an appointment with a professor, "YOU'RE an adult. YOU pick a time," another higher-proficiency learner, a Turkish woman, responded, "Are you trying to be difficult or what? Please, do your job properly." Again, by using the adverb "properly" in the context of "please," the respondent was able to accuse the secretary, off record, of acting improperly.

Intense tone

If we merely look at the numbers, the lower-proficiency learners used adverbials to convey intensity more often than the higher-proficiency learners (29 vs. 23 instances). However, a closer analysis suggests that not only were some of the adverbials used by the lower-proficiency learners nonfunctional, they were also limited in range to "really," "very," "too," "never," "so," and "so much." For instance, one Korean woman said, "You are very rude to customers." Another Korean woman said, "You are too unkind." Still another responded, "He is so rude." All these adverbials (except "never") seemed to enact one pragmatic strategy, namely, to "chastise," and even "never" indirectly chastises when used to make a threat in response to rudeness. Sometimes, these adverbials intensify the sarcastic tone in the chastisement as in the response of a Spanish woman, "You are really kind. . . ."

By contrast, there was a greater range of intensifying adverbials used by the higher-proficiency learners. In addition to the "really," "very," "too," "never," "so," and "so much" used by the lower-proficiency learners, the higher-proficiency learners also used "now," "just," "always," "extremely," "completely," "also," "very much," and "not even" as well as "ever" in intensifying ways. For instance, when asked if the store carried a new mystery, and the bookstore clerk said, "I have NOOOO idea," a higher-proficiency Korean female responded, "I never see one clerk like you in any other bookstore. I really have to see your boss here." In the same situation, a higher-proficiency Japanese female said, "I see. But I would like to see it now. . . ."

In a different bookstore situation, a clerk refused a customer's request to see a book on display, saying, "If you want to browse, go to the library." A higher-proficiency Portuguese man responded: "I'm sorry, but I always want to take a look at the book before I make up my mind. . . ." In the elevator situation where a passenger said, "Have you ever heard the word 'excuse me'?" to someone who reached in front of the other passengers to push the "down" button, a higher-proficiency Spanish woman responded, "There's a lot of people and I didn't even touch you, stupid." And another higher-proficiency Portuguese male said: "Have you ever heard the word 'Fuck you'?"

Not only did the higher-proficiency learners use a much wider variety of adverbials to indicate intensity, these adverbials intensify six different pragmatic strategies, not just one, including not only "chastise," used by the lower-proficiency learners, but also "threaten" (e.g. "I really have to see your boss here"), "request" (e.g. "but I would like to see it now"), "justify" (e.g. "but I always want to take a look at the book before I make up my mind"), "argue" (e.g. "I didn't even touch you"), and "challenge" (e.g. "Have you ever heard the word 'Fuck you'?").

Among the adverbials used to convey intensity, the use of "never" seems particularly interesting. The specific utterances sounded very similar in the lower and the higher groups. In the bookstore situation where the clerk said, "If you want to browse, go to the library," a lower-proficiency Korean woman responded, "I'll never buy any book in this bookstore." A lower-proficiency Korean male said, "I never go to this store again." And, a higher-proficiency Japanese female said, "I will never buy books at this bookstore." In the situation where the bookstore clerk responded to a customer's inquiry with "I have NOOOO idea," a higher-proficiency Japanese female said, "I'll never come here (son of the bitch!)." In these utterances, both lower- and higher-proficiency learners used the adverb "never" to make threats, but the lower-proficiency learners used it more often. This finding suggests that, compared to the higher-proficiency learners, the lower-proficiency learners may have relied more on intensifying adverbials to increase the pragmatic force of their threats when responding to rudeness. Beebe and Waring (1997, in press) showed, however, that these same higher-proficiency learners were pragmatically more aggressive. But they accomplished this by choosing various aggressive pragmatic strategies more frequently (e.g. insult, threat, criticize, challenge), not so much by using one single intensifying adverb, "never." "Never" is quite possibly just an easier way to express a threat. It relies on one lexical item to do all the syntactic work, so it is not surprising that lower-proficiency learners favored it.

In sum, although the lower-proficiency learners used intensifying adverbials more frequently than the higher-proficiency learners, many of the adverbials they used were functionally ineffective due to their ungrammaticality. More importantly, the lower-proficiency learners used a more limited range of adverbials to express intensity compared to the higher-proficiency learners. The intense tone these adverbials conveyed was limited to the pragmatic strategy of chastising and threatening. The higher-proficiency learners, on the other hand, used adverbials to intensify the tone of a wider range of pragmatic strategies. To a certain extent, our finding supports Kasper and Rose's (1999) hypothesis that "more advanced learners have developed a better command of the pragmalinguistic potential of lexical and syntactic devices" (p. 88).

Sarcastic tone

Contrary to expectations, lower-proficiency learners seemed to rely upon a sarcastic tone more frequently than the higher-proficiency learners. They used adverbials to show sarcasm four times, whereas the higher-proficiency learners only resorted to sarcasm once. The lower-proficiency group typically used "really," "so," and "so much" to show sarcasm, saying the opposite of what they meant. For instance, when told in the bookstore, "If you want to browse, go to the library," one lower-proficiency Spanish woman said, "You're really kind, I'm impressioned. Thank you." The use of "kind" and "thank you" created the sarcastic tone. The learner is clearly not grateful, nor is she impressed with the clerk's kindness. However, the use of the intensifier, "really," also contributed to the sarcasm as it intensifies the sarcastic use of "kind."

The adverbials used to enhance a sarcastic tone by the lower-proficiency learners were almost identical to the limited adverbials they used for intensity without sarcasm. In fact, for the lower-proficiency group, sarcasm was consistently intense. The only example of sarcasm found in the higher-proficiency group shows that sarcasm was used along with chastising and sending an off-record message. When the bookstore clerk said he had "NOOOO idea" if they had a new mystery, a higher-proficiency Turkish woman said, "You also have NOOOO manners. Thank you very much for your help anyway." In this response, the higher-proficiency learner not only sarcastically thanked the clerk, but also chastised her partially with an off-record message that the clerk was being rude (having "NOOOO manners"). By using the adverb, "also," she suggested, in addition, that the clerk was incompetent (i.e. having "NOOOO idea") as well as being rude. Besides using intense tones to chastise and make threats, then, the lower-proficiency learners relied on sarcasm more often than the higher-proficiency learners. But qualitatively, when the higher-proficiency learners used sarcasm, the response had more "layers" to the tone and meaning. The sarcasm was only part of the overall tone conveyed by the higher-proficiency learners' use of multiple strategies.

Conclusion

Although this study is based on a small sample, we have found, at least for this group of learners, that the lower- and higher-proficiency ESL learners used adverbials to convey pragmatic tone in very different ways. The lower-proficiency group tended to rely more upon sarcasm and intensifiers by repeatedly using a limited number of adverbs. Their means of indicating intensity was also confined to a small number of adverbs, such as "too," "very," and "really." Chastising and threatening were the only two pragmatic strategies for which they used these intensifying adverbials. The higher-proficiency learners, on the other hand, used a much wider range of adverbials to express intensity. The adverbials were used to intensify a wider range of pragmatic strategies.

Overall, it seems that the lower-proficiency group had a tendency to resort to extreme measures in responding to rudeness. They used strong words such as "never," as in "I'll never come to this store," or "so," as in "You're SO kind." They tended to sound rigid and rather hostile. The higher-proficiency learners, on the other hand, were able to use a little word like "just" to make a whole unspoken "off-record" claim. Without sounding hostile or desperate, they often managed to address the off-record message in the rude person's utterance, and send an off-record message to chastise that person's inappropriateness. At the same time, they asserted their own rights. In the end, they sounded assertive, but not necessarily rigid or hostile.

The lower-proficiency learners' tendency to rely on intensifiers for threats and sarcasm might be due to the fact that the linguistic realization of these pragmatic tones is relatively uncomplicated. Stating the opposite of what happened with the intensifier "so" or making a threat with "never" is not as difficult as achieving multiple functions or messages with a little word like "just," "only," or "ever." In the case of "so" and "never," the form and function relation is simple, clear, and unidimensional. The function of "just," by contrast, is more complex and harder to account for. Depending on the context, its meaning and degree of off-recordness vary.

Based on these findings, we speculate that there is an order of difficulty involved in pragmatic tone, not unlike the order of difficulty established by Dulay and Burt's (1974) research on the grammar for second language acquisition. We are suggesting that intense and sarcastic tones may be easier to acquire than subtle tones of assertiveness or aggression achieved through using adverbials like "just," "only," and "ever" to go off record. Consequently, adverbials that intensify or convey sarcasm might emerge earlier in a learner's pragmatic performance than pragmatically complex utterances.

Therefore, we would argue that pragmatic development should be looked for not only in the pragmatic strategies (e.g. semantic formulas and speech acts) that make up the speech act set. It should be studied in the linguistic (i.e. "grammatical," including lexical) structures that are used to enact a pragmatic strategy. This means that grammatical proficiency does contribute to pragmatic proficiency, and pragmatic proficiency is accomplished not just by frequency of pragmatic strategies like insult, threaten, chastise, argue, or apologize, but also by skillful use of lexical choices, in our case adverbials, to convey off-record messages and regulate the intensity or quality of tone.

In light of our continuing effort to incorporate pragmatics into language teaching (e.g. Rose & Kasper, 2001), the above findings might be pedagogically valuable in a number of ways. For example, teachers of pragmatics might benefit from the notion that unlike *-ed* or *-s* endings, adverbs are pragmatically rich items, and that they are particularly handy in furbishing the tone of utterances. In teaching adverbs, important work on a learner's pragmatic system can be done by teaching the range of tones the adverbs might convey to a native ear. To expedite the pragmatic development of lower-level learners in particular, one can expand their repertoire of adverbs (without taxing their syntactic abilities), thereby equipping them with more resources to express tones. Alternatively, one can also teach them to make the best of the limited number of adverbs already acquired by fully exploring the pragmatic potential of these adverbs.

Notes

1. We have chosen to use the more general term, adverbials, in this chapter, instead of the narrower term, adverbs. Although our examples involve primarily adverbs, the generalizations in this chapter about using adverbials are applicable to other adverbials, such as "so much," which does occur in the data, and to other adverbials, such as prepositional phrases, which did not happen to occur in the data for this study.
2. An earlier version of this chapter was presented at the 2000 NYSTESOL Applied Linguistics Winter Conference. The authors would like to thank Linda Wine for assistance in data collection, as well as the administrators, teachers, and ESL students of the English language program where the data was collected. In addition, we would like to acknowledge the assistance of Wendy Gavis in the collection of some of the data used in the DCT.

Appendix: Discourse completion test on responding to rudeness

Directions: In the blank marked "You would say," please write the words you think you would actually say in order to handle the situation in a socially appropriate way. If you would say nothing, write "say nothing" in the blank. In the blank marked "You would feel like saying," please write the actual words you would feel like saying if you were not held back by social pressure.

1. You are a student calling to make an appointment to see your professor. You ask when the professor is free. The receptionist says, "YOU'RE an adult. YOU pick a time."

You would say: _____

_____

_____.

You would feel like saying: _____

_____

_____.

2. You go to a tourist bookstore where books are kept behind a counter. You ask to see a book on display. The lady behind the counter says, "If you want to browse, go to the library."

You would say: _____

_____

_____.

You would feel like saying: _____

_____

_____.

3. You are at a garage. You ask the garage attendant for directions for getting out of the city. All his reference points are unfamiliar to you, so you keep asking questions. He says, "Lady, what do you want me to do, draw you a map?"

You would say: _____

_____.

You would feel like saying: _____

_____.

4. You go to a bookstore and ask an employee if they have a new mystery called *Dead Reckoning*. The employee says, "I have NOOOO idea!" You ask if it's published yet. And again, the employee makes no attempt to help you, saying "I have NOOOO idea," sounding annoyed that you would ask.

You would say: _____

_____.

You would feel like saying: _____

_____.

5. You are in an elevator. You reach carefully in front of the other passengers to push the "down" button without bumping them. One of the passengers says, "Have you ever heard the word, 'excuse me'?"

You would say: _____

_____.

You would feel like saying: _____

_____.

6. You are an overweight man parking your car near a crosswalk. A woman with a child is afraid you'll run over her. You get into an argument, and she yells, "OH SHUT UP, you fat pig!"

You would say: _____

_____.

You would feel like saying: _____

_____.

Personal background information

Native language: _____.
Country of citizenship: _____.
Place of birth (city/state/province/country): _____.
Sex: Male/Female (circle one)
Age (optional): _____.
Highest educational level: High school/College/Graduate School (circle one).

References

Bardovi-Harlig, K. (1999) Exploring the interlanguage of interlanguage pragmatics: A research agenda for acquisitional pragmatics. *Language Learning* 49 (4), 677–713.

Bateson, G. (1972) *Steps to an Ecology of Mind*. New York: Ballantine.

Beebe, L. M. (1995) Polite fictions: Instrumental rudeness as pragmatic competence. In J. Alatis, C. A. Straehle, B. Gallenberger, and M. Ronkin (eds) *Linguistics and the Education of Teachers: Ethnolinguistics, Psycholinguistic and Sociolinguistics Aspects* (pp. 154–168). Washington, DC: Georgetown University Press.

Beebe, L. M. and Cummings, M. C. (1985) Speech act performance: A function of the data collection procedure? Paper presented at the TESOL Convention, New York, March.

Beebe, L. M. and Cummings, M. C. (1995) Natural speech act data versus written questionnaire data: How data collection method affects speech act performance. In S. Gass and J. Neu (eds) *Speech Acts Across Cultures: Challenges to Communication in a Second Language* (pp. 65–86). New York: Mouton de Gruyter.

Beebe, L. M. and Waring, H. Z. (1997) Pragmatic development: An oxymoron? Paper presented at the International TESOL Convention, Orlando, Florida, March.

Beebe, L. M. and Waring, H. Z. (2000) Pragmatic literacy: Words that work. Paper presented at the NYSTESOL Applied Linguistics Winter Conference, Borough of Manhattan Community College, February.

Beebe, L. M. and Waring, H. Z. (in press) Pragmatic development in responding to rudeness. In C. Holten and J. Frodesen (eds) *At the Heart of It All: Discourse Studies and Language Teaching and Learning*. Festschrift in Honor of Marianne Celce-Murcia. Boston: Heinle and Heinle/Thomson Learning.

Beebe, L. M., Takahashi, T., and Uliss-Weltz, R. (1990) Pragmatic transfer in ESL refusals. In R. C. Scarcella, E. S. Andersen, and S. D. Krashen (eds) *Developing Communicative Competence in a Second Language* (pp. 55–73). New York: Newbury House.

Bisshop, C. (1996) "I am apologize . . .": Asian speakers of English saying sorry in the Australian context. Unpublished manuscript, University of Melbourne.

Blum-Kulka, S., House-Edmondson, J., and Kasper, G. (eds) (1989) *Cross-cultural Pragmatics: Requests and Apologies*. Norwood, NJ: Ablex.

Brown, P. and Levinson, S. C. (1987) *Politeness: Some Universals in Language Usage*. Cambridge: Cambridge University Press.

Clancy, P. M. (1986) The acquisition of communicative style in Japanese. In B. Schieffelin and E. Ochs (eds) *Language Socialization across Cultures* (pp. 213–250). Cambridge: Cambridge University Press.

Clancy, P. M. (1999) The socialization of affect in Japanese mother–child conversation. *Journal of Pragmatics* 31, 1397–1421.

Dewaele, J. M. and Pavlenko, A. (2002) Emotion vocabulary in interlanguage. *Language Learning* 52 (2), 263–322.

Douglas, D. (2000) *Assessing Languages for Specific Purposes*. Cambridge: Cambridge University Press.

Dulay, H. and Burt, M. (1974) Natural sequences in child second language acquisition. *Language Learning* 24, 37–53.

Eisenberg, A. R. (1986) Teasing: Verbal play in two Mexicano homes. In B. Schieffelin and E. Ochs (eds) *Language Socialization across Cultures* (pp. 182–198). Cambridge: Cambridge University Press.

Goffman, E. (1974) *Frame Analysis: An Essay on the Organization of Experience.* Boston, MA: Northeastern University Press.

Goffman, E. (1981) *Forms of Talk.* Philadelphia, PA: University of Pennsylvania Press.

Goodwin, M. H. and Goodwin, C. (2001) Emotion within situated activity. In A. Duranti (ed.) *Linguistic Anthropology: A Reader* (pp. 239–257). Cambridge: Blackwell.

Grice, H. P. (1975) Logic and conversation. In P. Cole and J. Morgan (eds) *Speech Acts (Syntax and Semantics, Volume 3)* (pp. 41–58). New York: Academic Press.

Gumperz, J. (1982) *Discourse Strategies.* Cambridge: Cambridge University Press.

Holmes, J. (2001) *An Introduction to Sociolinguistics.* Harlow: Longman.

Hymes, D. (1972) Models of the interaction of language and social life. In J. Gumperz and D. Hymes (eds) *Directions in Sociolinguistics* (pp. 35–71). New York: Holt, Rinehart and Winston.

Kasper, G. and Rose, K. (1999) Pragmatics and SLA. *Annual Review of Applied Linguistics* 19, 81–104.

Kasper, G. and Schmidt, R. (1996) Developmental issues in interlanguage pragmatics. *Studies in Second Language Acquisition* 18, 149–169.

Miller, P. (1986) Teasing as language socialization and verbal play in a white working class community. In B. Schieffelin and E. Ochs (eds) *Language Socialization across Cultures* (pp. 199–212). Cambridge: Cambridge University Press.

Ochs, E. (1986a) Introduction. In B. Schieffelin and E. Ochs (eds) *Language Socialization across Cultures* (pp. 1–16). Cambridge: Cambridge University Press.

Ochs, E. (1986b) From feelings to grammar: A Samoan case study. In B. Schieffelin and E. Ochs (eds) *Language Socialization across Cultures* (pp. 251–272). Cambridge: Cambridge University Press.

Ochs, E. and Schieffelin, B. (1989) Language has a heart. *Text* 9, 7–25.

Ohta, A. S. (1994) Socializing the expression of affect: An overview of affective particle use in the Japanese as a foreign language classroom. *Issues in Applied Linguistics* 2, 303–325.

Planalp, S. (1999) *Communicating Emotion: Social, Moral, and Cultural Processes.* Cambridge: Cambridge University Press.

Raffaldini, T. (1988) The use of situation tests as measures of communicative ability. *Studies in Second Language Acquisition* 10 (2), 197–216.

Rintell, E. (1984) But how did you feel about that? The learner's perception of emotion in speech. *Applied Linguistics* 5 (3), 255–264.

Rintell, E. (1990) That's incredible: Stories of emotion told by second language learners and native speakers. In R. Scarcella, E. Anderson, and S. Krashen (eds) *Developing Communicative Competence in a Second Language* (pp. 75–94). Boston, MA: Heinle and Heinle.

Rose, K. and Kasper, G. (2001) *Pragmatics in Language Teaching.* Cambridge: Cambridge University Press.

Schieffelin, B. (1986) Teasing and shaming in Kaluli children's interaction. In B. Schieffelin and E. Ochs (eds) *Language Socialization across Cultures* (pp. 165–181). Cambridge: Cambridge University Press.

Schumann, J. (1997) *The Neurobiology of Affect in Language*. Boston, MA: Blackwell.

Takahashi, T. and Beebe, L. M. (1987) The development of pragmatic competence by Japanese learners of English. *JALT Journal 8*, 131–155.

Tannen, D. (1986) *That's Not What I Meant! How Conversational Style Makes or Breaks Your Relations with Others*. New York: William Morrow.

Tannen, D. (2001) *I Only Say This Because I Love You: How the Way We Talk Can Make or Break Family Relationships Throughout Our Lives*. New York: Random House.

Part IV: Studying Spoken Discourse to Inform Second Language Assessment

Overview

Part IV of the volume consists of three studies focusing specifically on assessment of L2 spoken discourse. Evaluation instruments currently in use are problematic, as are the options for devising new instruments and techniques for assessment of oral speaking abilities in an L2. What is to be judged and how it is to be judged become a looming issue in contexts where "proficiency" is perceived to be an ultimate goal. The elusive nature of "proficiency," the difficulty of ascertaining what ought to be the "norm" in the present-day world, and the near impossibility of achieving agreement on these issues, is the focus of the following chapters in this series of studies.

The section opens with Annie Brown's chapter: "Discourse Analysis and the Oral Interview: Competence or Performance?" Here, the author focuses on the problematic issue of the differential rating of candidate performance as judged by two different interviewers. While the issue has come up before in the literature, it is perhaps more timely now than ever. Brown's study constitutes one of the few examples of how CA techniques can be employed for analyzing assessment in oral interviews. Through close CA analysis of the two interviews, she demonstrates how oral assessment instruments can be dramatically different from ordinary conversation and how the way the individual interviewer conducts the session can sway the subsequent ratings made by outside raters. Implications for the future use of such instruments are drawn.

Carsten Roever then provides a second chapter on assessing spoken language: "Difficulty and Practicality in Tests of Interlanguage Pragmatics." As the title of the chapter indicates, the author focuses his attention on the issue of how to best assess *pragmatic* ability in spoken interaction. The issues are multiple, and continue to perplex those of us involved in applied linguistics. Roever's chapter carefully delineates the difficulties in testing sociopragmatic and pragmalinguistic skills, considers both receptive and productive assessment tasks in both online and offline formats, makes suggestions for research, and provides recommendations for the design and implementation of instruments for assessing pragmatic L2 ability.

Co-editor of this volume, Andrew Cohen, provides the final chapter of this section and of the volume: "Assessing Speech Acts in a Second Language." Cohen's chapter provides an historical view of efforts to assess oral language, specifically speech act performance. Drawing on the work of Dell Hymes as reinterpreted by Dan Douglas, the author describes in detail the importance of contextual parameters in designing speech act assessment instruments, especially with regard to the setting of the interaction. Cohen also examines the critical dimension of authenticity in speech act data, with specific attention to both task requirements and respondents' characteristics. Finally, as a pioneer in the use of verbal reports as insightful data in applied linguistics research, Cohen culminates his chapter with a discussion of the potential value of verbal report data as a means for validating performance in speech act assessment.

Chapter 11

Discourse Analysis and the Oral Interview: Competence or Performance?

ANNIE BROWN

Discourse analysis is an increasingly-used methodology in the service of language test validation. Empirical analyses of test discourse have provided insights into the construct of oral proficiency as operationalized in various types of speaking test, including monologic, tape-based tests as well as interviews and other types of face-to-face dialogic or group tests. They have also shown how factors such as the type of task or candidate background and can affect the quality of candidates' linguistic performance.

This study is concerned with the nature of oral interview discourse. The particular question addressed here is the effect that the choice of interviewer has on candidate performance and, hence, on ratings awarded to that performance. Through the detailed analysis of two interviews involving the same candidate with two different interviewers, we see how the quality of the candidate's linguistic behavior is to a large extent shaped by the interviewers' interactional and interview management style. These differences led to the candidate being awarded different ratings by a set of trained raters. A subsequent analysis of verbal reports produced by the raters reveals that, while the raters showed some awareness of the role of the interviewer in constructing the candidate's performance, the different ratings in the two interviews were ultimately a direct reflection of the rater's perceptions of candidate ability, based on the candidate's performance alone.

The study has implications for the assessment of oral ability in both formal and classroom settings. By showing how inextricably the interviewer is implicated in learners' test performance, it reminds us that care must be taken to ensure that all learners are treated fairly and equitably when assessments are being made. Further, it raises the question of whether it is possible at all to derive a measure of a single person's second language-speaking competence through dialogic interaction.

Introduction

Although language test validation and research tend to rely heavily on quantitative methods, in particular the analysis of score data, recent years have seen a steady increase in the use of qualitative research methodologies. This increase has been attributed to cross-fertilization of research in language testing and other areas of applied linguistics and to the challenge to the positivist epistemology of applied linguistics generally (McNamara *et al.*, 2002). It has also been attributed (Banerjee & Luoma, 1997; Kunnan, 1998) to the expanded conceptualization of validity which owes much to the work of Messick (e.g. 1989). As in other areas of educational measurement, validity is no longer viewed as a set of "measurable" phenomena but as an integrated and holistic judgment which is based on the collection of evidence from a number of different areas. In this revised conceptualization the main concern is the validity of the inferences made about test takers on the basis of their scores, that is, the *meaning* of scores, and what this requires, as Banerjee and Luoma (1997) point out, is a thorough understanding of tests, both process and product. It is in this area where qualitative approaches are of particular value.

One type of qualitative research methodology which has become increasingly prevalent in language testing research in recent years is discourse analysis (see, for example, Lazaraton, 2002). In their state-of-the-art article on "discourse and assessment," McNamara *et al.* point to the central role afforded assessments of oral proficiency within a communicative approach to language teaching and testing as the cause, and comment: "If structural linguistics was the source of the views on language of the formative period of post-war language testing, best represented in the work of Lado, then discourse analysis has taken its place for the assessment of oral language" (2002: 221).

Background: Discourse Analysis and the Validation of Second Language Speaking Tests

Until the 1990s it would be fair to say (with one or two notable exceptions) that there was very little research examining the "product" of oral tests in terms of the *discourse* produced rather than the *scores* awarded. Perhaps the main impetus for the growth of interest in the discourse of oral tests was the seminal article by van Lier (1989), which challenged the orthodox belief that the interaction in an oral interview reflected non-test conversational interaction and that it therefore allowed learners' second language conversational skills to be validly assessed. Since the publication of van Lier's article, the question of the nature of oral inter-view discourse and, hence, what skills are elicited from learners has been a major focus of research. Discourse analysis has, in addition, allowed a number of other important research questions to be addressed. These include how increasing levels proficiency can be characterized (e.g. Young, 1995; Brown *et al.*, 2002), the roles of participants (both candidate and interviewer) in terms of their linguistic actions (e.g. Lazaraton, 1992; Ross & Berwick, 1992), the effect on test performance of participants' characteristics, such as personality, acquaintanceship, or ethnicity (e.g. Berwick & Ross, 1996; Berry, 1997), and the effect of variables such as task type and performance conditions on test performance (e.g. Wigglesworth, 1997; O'Loughlin, 2001, 2002).

One particularly fertile area of validation research, as noted above, is concerned with the question of the relationship between test and non-test interaction, in particular the extent to which interview interaction is 'conversational.' Van Lier (1989) criticized the influential ACTFL oral interview (OPI) for its lack of authenticity as a 'conversational' event, commenting in particular on the hitherto lack of empirical analyses of test discourse. In the decade following the publication of van Lier's article, analyses of oral interview data began to appear with increasing frequency, culminating most recently in a collection of articles (Young & He, 1998) involving a range of oral interview tests in a range of languages. A general consensus has emerged from these and other analyses that, while oral interview interaction shares some features with non-test conversational interaction such as accommodation (Ross & Berwick, 1992; Cafarella, 1994; Lazaraton, 1996a) and repair (Lazaraton, 1996a: Egbert, 1998; Kim & Suh, 1998), it is essentially a distinct and institutional form of interaction, characterized primarily by a lack of symmetry in roles. Interviewers have been shown to control the choice, and opening and closing, of topics, whereas candidate speech has been found to be rela-tively reactive, with little evidence of conversational control or initiative (e.g. Perrett, 1990; Lazaraton, 1992; Ross & Berwick, 1992; Young & Milanovic, 1992; He & Young, 1998). The interviewer essentially asks questions while the candidate, in contrast, mainly supplies responses (e.g. Perrett, 1990; Lazaraton, 1992; Ross & Berwick, 1992; Young, 1995), and candidates' attempts to introduce topics are rarely ratified by the inter-viewer (Young & Milanovic, 1992; Young, 1995).

Most of the studies referred to above were concerned with character-izing differences in interviewer and candidate talk. For that reason they tended to focus on similarities amongst interviewers rather than differ-ences between them. However, theoretical perspectives on interaction such as sociocultural theory, based on the work of Vygotsky (Vygotsky, 1978; Lantolf & Appel, 1998), interactional competence theory (Hall, 1993; Jacoby & Ochs, 1995; Young, 1999), and conversation analysis (Sacks *et al.*, 1974; Psathas, 1995) all take as a basic premise the co-constructed nature of talk. As such they problematize the question of whose performance it really is, as McNamara (1997) so aptly points out. As a consequence, the question of comparability across interviewers arises: if the interviewer is indeed implicated in the candidate's performance, to what extent does the choice of interviewer affect (i.e. inhibit or enhance) candidates' opportunities to demonstrate their ability?

There is, in fact, growing evidence that interviewers do differ, at times quite considerably, in the ways they conduct their interviews, and that they have styles which are stable over time (see, for example, Ross, 1996; Lazaraton, 1996b; Brown & Lumley, 1997; Reed & Halleck, 1997; Brown, 2003). Ross (1996) argues that interviewers employ *procedural scripts*, that is, consistent approaches to the organization of the interview and presentation of prompts in order to allow them to release their attention to monitoring the candidate. He claims that any differences are the result of interviewers' individual self-monitoring and interactional styles.

The evidence suggests that interviewers differ along a number of dimensions in the way they conduct interviews. In a detailed discourse analysis of interviews from the Cambridge Assessment of Spoken English (CASE), Lazaraton (1996a) identified eight types of linguistic and interactional support offered to candidates by examiners. She also found (1996b) that interviewers differed in the extent to which they covered all the topics prescribed in the interview frame. Other studies found differences in the degree of rapport established with the candidate (Brown & Lumley, 1997; Morton *et al.*, 1997), and in the level of functional challenge set by the interviewer (Ross & Berwick, 1992; Reed & Halleck, 1997). Ross (1996) found differences in the way interviewers constructed their interview "prompts," and that these differences affected the quality of the speech produced by the candidates. The differences found in these studies have been claimed to be the result of interviewers' cultural background (Ross, 1996) or level of experience or expertise (Morton *et al.*, 1997). Brown and Lumley (1997) describe examiners who display a high level of support as having a general orientation towards "teacherliness."

The fact that the interaction is largely controlled by the interviewer, in terms of the selection, introduction, development, and closure of topical talk, together with the fact that interviewers have been found to differ in technique, at times substantially, gives rise to concerns about the fairness of oral interviews. If it the case that different interviewers elicit different quality performances from candidates and this affects the scores they are awarded, then this means the choice of interviewer is a potential source of unfairness and unreliability. In several of the studies referred to above which identified differences in interviewer behavior, questions were raised about the likely effect of these different behaviors on candidate performance, and hence the ratings awarded.

However, while a number of these studies speculate on the likely impact of interviewer behavior on ratings, few of the studies mentioned above have directly linked interviewer behavior to outcomes for candidates. While Brown and Lumley (1997), for example, identified a number of behaviors which they considered would make the test easier or more difficult, they also point out that the behaviors they identified "are perceived as *potential* threats to the fairness of the test and require verification through an analysis of the effect they may have on the scores awarded to candidates" (1996: 122; italics in original). Notable exceptions, however, are those by Morton *et al.* (1997) and Reed and Halleck (1997). Reed and Halleck's study showed a strong relationship between the level of functional challenge posed by the interviewer and ratings, in that the higher the level of functional challenge, the higher the rating was. Morton *et al.* found that candidates tended to receive higher scores when there were fewer indicators of rapport in the interaction. They explain this as raters compensating for what they perceived as a lack of interviewer competence. Both studies conclude that more emphasis needs to be placed on interviewer training in order to ensure comparability across interviews and fairness to candidates.

This chapter is concerned with the question of interviewer behavior and the impact this might have on candidate performance and on scores. The study addresses the following research question:

> How do interviewers differ and what impact does this have on candidate performance and on ratings?

Methodology

Research design

The question is examined in relation to a semi-structured conversational interview which until recently formed part of the International English Language Testing System (IELTS), a test used as part of the selection procedures for international students from non-English-speaking backgrounds applying to universities in the UK and other English-speaking countries.[1]

The test instrument

The IELTS Speaking Module consists of five phases of which the first and last, the opening and closing, are very short (Figure 11.1). Other than in the middle phase, which consists of a role-play, the Speaking Module is basically a conversational interview in which candidates are invited to talk on a range of topics covering a range of functional and discoursal skills (such as description, argument, narration, speculation). For the purposes of this study the role-play was excluded in order to focus more specifically on the conversational part of the interview.

Phases 2 and 4 of the IELTS interview, the "conversational" phases, are structured around a series of topics on which the interviewer attempts to engage the candidate in conversation. In Phase 2, "Extended Discourse," candidates are expected to speak at length about some very familiar topic either of general interest or of relevance to their culture, place of living, or country of origin. This involves explanation, description, or

---

Phase 1 – Introduction (1–2 minutes)
The candidate is encouraged to talk briefly about his/her life, home, work, and interests.

Phase 2 – Extended Discourse (3–4 minutes)
The candidate is encouraged to speak at length about some very familiar topic either of general interest or of relevance to their [*sic*] culture, place of living, or country of origin. This will involve explanation, description, or narration.

Phase 3 – Elicitation (3–4 minutes)
The candidate is given a task card with some information on it and is encouraged to take the initiative and ask questions either to elicit information or to solve a problem. Tasks are based on "information gap" type activities.

Phase 4 – Speculation and Attitudes (3–4 minutes)
The candidate is encouraged to talk about their [*sic*] future plans and proposed course of study. Alternatively the examiner may choose to return to a topic raised earlier.

Phase 5 – Conclusion (1 minute)
The interview is concluded.

Figure 11.1 The IELTS interview (from UCLES, 1997a: 14)

narration. In Phase 4, "Speculation and Attitudes," they are expected to talk about future plans, such as their proposed course of study. The aim in this phase is to elicit a demonstration of candidates' ability "to speculate, to express ideas, attitudes and plans with some precision, and to use language relevant to their particular academic, vocational, or other interests" (UCLES, 1997a: 11). Interviewers are provided with a list of suggested topics from which to select, along with guidance on the ways the topics might be developed.

The sample

Two interviews involving the same candidate, Lim, but conducted by two different interviewers, Jean and Cath, form the basis of the study. Jean and Cath are both trained and accredited IELTS examiners. The candidate, Lim, is a male Malaysian student, at the time of the study undertaking foundation studies prior to entering an Australian university.

Multiple ratings were elicited from accredited IELTS examiners for each interview using the IELTS band descriptors, which form a scale from 0 to 9. Each interview was rated by a different set of examiners in order to ensure that ratings for the respective interviews were independent. Eight ratings were elicited in order to ensure that the leniency or severity of individual raters did not unduly affect the picture of the candidates' proficiency. It transpired that Lim was perceived generally as being more proficient in the interview with Cath: the median rating was a six; with Jean he was perceived as less proficient: the median rating was a five (Table 11.1). This difference is not trivial; it can make the difference between acceptance into or rejection from the course of one's choice.

Analytic procedure

The choice of methodology for the analysis was driven by the question under consideration, that of the ways in which interviewers differ and the impact that these differences have on candidate performance and on ratings. There were a number of issues to consider.

Table 11.1 Ratings

Candidate	Interviewer	Ratings	Mean score	Median score
Lim	Jean	4 5 5 5 5 5 6 6	5.1	5
Lim	Cath	5 5 6 6 6 7 7 –	6.0	6

Firstly, as was noted above, interviewers have been found to differ along a number of behavioral dimensions. These include the rapport they are able to establish with test candidates, the extent to which they accommodate their speech to the level of the candidate, their questioning and feedback styles, and the degree of functional or topical challenge. However, different studies have operationalized these dimensions differently and, where claims were made about the possible impact, they were merely speculative. What is not known is whether or to what extent any specific variable actually has an impact on the quality of candidates' performance or the scores awarded. To privilege any of them in the analysis here by nominating them a priori would be to make assumptions about which behavioral features are likely to be the most influential.

However, while it is neither possible nor appropriate to document all differences in interviewer behavior, it can be assumed that those which directly affect aspects of candidate performance as described within the band descriptors (that is, the criteria by which the performance is judged) are likely to be particularly relevant. In other words, the analysis was guided both by the findings of the literature on interviewer variation and by the contents of the band descriptors.

In the case of the IELTS interview, the criteria are linguistic, task-based, and interactional. Raters are asked to focus on the extent to which the candidate has the "necessary knowledge and skills to communicate effectively with native speakers of English" (UCLES, 1997b: 24). This interactional orientation is captured within the IELTS band descriptors through the term *communicative effectiveness*, which refers to test takers' ability to *talk at length* on a *range of topics* and to display a range of *functional and discoursal skills* (description, argument, narration, speculation, for example).

Given the specific focus in the present study on the interplay of communication between interviewer and candidate, the approach taken in most earlier studies of interviewer variation of simply identifying and counting instances of behavior considered to be representative of the feature under investigation (such as accommodation, rapport or control) was held to be inappropriate here. As these earlier studies have shown, although specific interviewer behaviors may be identified, their effect on candidate performance remains purely at the level of speculation unless their interactional import is taken into account. What was needed, then, is an approach to analysis which took into account both interviewer behavior *and* subsequent candidate performance, that is, one which focused on the sequential ("real-time") development of the talk as a whole. This would allow us to ascertain not only the ways in which interviewer behavior differs, but also how these differences affect the quality of the candidate's talk and allow different pictures of his proficiency to be constructed by the raters.

An approach to the analysis of spoken interaction which takes this perspective, the turn-by-turn construction of interaction, is Conversation Analysis (Atkinson & Heritage, 1984; Sacks, 1992a, 1992b; Psathas, 1995). While Conversation Analysis (CA) was originally applied to the analysis of "natural" (i.e. non-test) conversational interaction, it is now also widely used in the analysis of institutional interaction, providing useful perspectives on the ways in which participants understand and carry out their roles within closely associated specific contexts (see, particularly, Drew & Heritage, 1992). In the context of the oral interview, CA can help us to describe and understand the nature of the interaction between interviewers and candidates.

The analysis itself followed the conventions of conversation analytic studies in that the transcription stage was an important part of the analysis, not a preliminary step. A CA transcription is necessarily detailed in order to ensure that no feature which might be of relevance to the participants themselves is omitted. Undertaking the detailed transcription entails close and repeated listening to the interviews, and forms the initial analysis in which patterns within the interaction begin to emerge. In terms of the overall organizational structure of the interviews, one of the initial findings was that the interviews consisted of a series of topical sequences, sequences of talk focusing on a particular topic. Because of this structure, the analysis took these topical sequences as relevant structural units within the interviews, and focused on the ways in which the two interviewers implemented their topical choices in order to elicit a performance from the candidate.

Repeated close listening to the interviews allowed the researcher to build up a picture of each interviewer's style of topic development and conversational management, as well as its impact on the candidate's speech. It emerged that the interviewers differed along a number of dimensions, and that they did indeed, as Ross (1996) claimed, exhibit stable styles. For the sake of brevity, the ways in which the two interviewers managed the interviews and elicited talk from the candidate will be described here through a selection of extracts drawn from each interview which reflect the general style of each interviewer.

Finally, in order to make explicit the link between interviewer conduct, candidate performance, and ratings, the discourse analysis is complemented by an analysis of verbal protocols produced by four of the raters for each of the two interviews. Immediately after rating the interviews these raters were asked to describe their perceptions of the candidate in

Table 11.2 Verbal reports

	Jean/Lim				*Cath/Lim*			
Rater	A	B	C	D	E	F	G	H
Score	4	5	5	5	5	6	6	6

order to justify the scores they awarded (Table 11.2). Through this triangulation of data types, ratings, verbal reports, and discourse, the study aimed to make explicit the relationship that exists between interviewer conduct and outcomes for candidates.

Findings

The analysis will be presented through a detailed inspection of segments of the two interviews. In particular, contrasts will be drawn between the behaviors of the two interviewers and the different effects these behaviors have on the performance of the candidate, Lim. As in other studies of interviewer behavior, inferences will be drawn regarding the likely impact of behavioral differences on ratings. Here, however, unlike in previous studies, these will be backed up by quotes from the verbal reports produced by the raters in which they justify their scores on the basis of the different candidate behaviors. This triangulation of data sources – test discourse and verbal reports – will, we believe, show convincingly how a single interviewee produces a performance that is rated higher or lower by not just one, but a set of raters, *expressly* because of the interviewer's style.

Jean

Jean's speaking style can be characterized as relatively informal in that it contains features found to be typical of conversational interaction such as latching, overlap, and interruption, which provide both a sense of engagement with the candidate and an interest in the topic under discussion (Tannen, 1984), as well as features such as reformulations and repair which are indicative of on-line planning. She speaks rapidly, and with a breathy voice. The pitch is highly modulated, a feature of speech which is also indicative of involvement.

While this style of speaking gives an impression of casualness, the overwhelming impression was nevertheless that Jean dominated the interaction with Lim. Her turns were often fairly lengthy, and she produced a lot of speech relative to the candidate. Jean introduced a number

of topics in her interview with Lim. Her topic-introductory turns tended
to follow a consistent pattern, exhibiting any of a range of moves. The
following is an example of one such questioning turn:

Extract 1: Jean and Lim

```
J: aha .HHH ^okay .hh ^can you tell me a little bit abou:t erm
   (0.5) perhaps wo:rk; work I kn- I know you probably don't work
   (.)in [yeah hh.] Malaysia you look (.) probably a bit too- .hh
   @you're obviously a student still@ .hh [yeah] erm (0.8) but you
   probably know about work in Malaysia, .hh generally_ (1.0)          5
   what's- what are the conditions like are people (.) you know do
   they work long hours, (.) is the pay good¿
L: (0.4) *er:* yeah *e:r* (.) in Malaysia or is (.) work I think
   (0.9) takes up ten hours per day. around ten- [ten hours¿]
   eight to ten hours per day.                                         10
J: so what time would they normally start.
L: *er:* eight, xxxx [ri:ght,] eight or until six; is normal.
J: right so it's quite a- quite a long day [for most isn't it .hh
L:                                          [yeah quite a long
   day.yeah                                                            15
H: .hh A:ND um .hh what sort of (.5) you know; (.) er >what I was
   just gonna say is there< (.) what sort of industries a:re (.) big
   industries in Malaysia. (.) are you aware of (.) what industries
   are important?
```

Jean's question sought to elicit an extended response, a description of
the work conditions in Malaysia. She set out her expectations through an
explicit request for information: "Can you tell me about work, work?"
She did not, however, stop here and wait for Lim to respond, but moved
immediately into a comment on the difficulty of the question for Lim as
a result of his likely lack of experience of work, in effect pre-empting and
excusing any difficulties he might have in answering the question. After
this brief digression – a characteristic feature of her questioning style –
she continued on with a reformulation of her earlier question, this time
asking "What are the conditions like?," a more specific and helpful
phrasing than her earlier: "Tell me about. . . ." She then produced two
more questions, illustrating the types of information which would be
appropriate, namely "hours" and "pay."

These elaborations could be described as being candidate-focused in
that they served on the one hand to reassure the candidate that the interviewer did not expect particularly insightful analysis and, on the other,
to define the scope of the question more clearly. They might also,

however, as has been claimed by Berwick and Ross (1996) and Ross (1996), have contributed to the difficulty of the interview in that, because of their complexity, such "probes" are likely to make candidates' talk more dependent on advanced listening skills.

In this instance, in fact, the candidate, Lim, did not appear to have any difficulty understanding the interviewer. He produced agreement tokens in relation to the two propositions: "I know you probably don't work" and "you're obviously a student still." Then, once Jean had finished speaking, he produced a series of turn holders, "er yeah er" which indicated that he had understood, recognized that he should take the floor, and was preparing to respond. However, when he did produce a response, rather than it being the general description of work conditions initially requested, it focused rather narrowly on answering the last of the questions: he described the length of a typical working day.

Ross (1998) found similar strategies in the speech of candidates in the OPI. He commented that such behavior is evidence of divergent frame interpretations. The behavior breaches Grice's maxim of quantity, leading to "uninformative answers that typically lead to repeated questioning on the same subject" (1998: 339). He argues:

> The context of the interview is understood by [some] candidates as one that bestows the speaking rights to the interviewer, while the candidate's role is to provide exact responses to the questions – no more, no less. ... Unfamiliarity with the speech event may also confuse some candidates as to what is expected from a cooperative interlocutor. (1998: 343)

Given the intent of her initial question – to elicit an extended piece of descriptive talk – Jean's follow-up to Lim's response was somewhat unexpected. Rather than repeating or reformulating the request to "talk about work" or otherwise letting Lim know that he had not treated the topic in enough depth and should continue on with the description, she acknowledged his response as valid by going on to produce a next question which took this narrow aspect of the topic, work hours, as the focus and elicited a single item of information. In effect, then, she ratified his answer but in doing so also closed off the opportunity for Lim to show that he could produce extended description, one of the assessment criteria. The interactional effect was that Lim produced very little descriptive speech in what was an interviewer-dominated sequence. Furthermore, the impression given by the interviewer through her abandonment of the initial prompt demands was that she did not believe the candidate was able to respond adequately.

Before turning to the raters' comments on Lim's performance, we will look at a further topic sequence taken from the same interview (Extract 2), in which Jean again sought to elicit an extended piece of description. She asked Lim to describe the population of Malaysia in terms of the distribution of income. As in the previous segment, before Lim had a chance to respond, she went on to elaborate on her question, explaining what she meant through a series of more focused but closed questions – that is, questions which do not require the candidate to produce original speech but (in this case) simply to select one of two alternatives offered.

Extract 2: Jean and Lim

```
J: mhm .hh ^going on from work a little bit, .hh (1.0) in Malaysia
   are there (0.6) you know wha- what's the distribution of income
   what I mean by that is that .hh are there some very poor people
   and some very rich, or a lot of middle class people, how- how
   is it based.                                                      5
L: e:r middle class (.) I think middle class er_
J: a lot of  [ middle class¿
L:           [a lot of middle class.
J: okay are there some very poor? or[m-
L:                              [poor erm [yeah] I- (.) I don't    10
   think so it just [no] (.) a small  [amount (.) of them very poor
J:                                     [oh right, .hh and what about
   very rich; are there some very rich people?
L: yah   [>quite a lot of very<
J:       [yeah so: SO: quite a big middle class (.) mainly. [yeah   15
   middle] (.) probably a bit like [°middle class°] Australia? You
   [yeah] know a large middle class? .hhh [middle class] okay .hh
   (.)/mhm/ ^what about if somebody erm (1.0) somebody <is poor
   and unemployed,>d- d'you have many unemployed?
```

There were a number of false starts and rephrasings in Jean's initial question, which indicated that she was formulating what she wanted to say as she was speaking. The subsequent questions appear to have been produced in response to a perceived need by Jean to "unpack" the meaning of the phrase "distribution of income." Yet again, however, Lim took the last question as his cue rather than the initial question; he responded by selecting one of the alternatives presented, "middle class."

Although Lim had selected one of the alternatives offered in Jean's question, he had not reproduced it in full, saying "middle class" rather than "a lot of middle class." By repeating "a lot of middle class?," Jean indicated that the previous response was not sufficiently elaborated.

Whether this was an indirect way of telling Lim that his response was inadequate or a genuine clarification strategy (i.e. did Lim mean a *small* middle class or a *large* middle class?), Lim appeared to take it as the latter. His echo of her words, "a lot of middle class," confirmed the factual supposition.

Although Jean had now received an answer as to which was the largest group in Malaysian society, she pressed on with the same topic, producing two further questions which, like the previous one, required Lim to do little more than confirm or disconfirm the supposition they presented, and which added no informational content to the topic. Jean closed the exchange down by producing a formulation, a summary of the preceding talk, adding to this a further comment of her own, that the distribution of population in Malaysia as described by Lim resembled that of Australia. Throughout this entire turn, Lim followed and agreed with what she was saying; he echoed her words and produced tokens of agreement at regular intervals in response to each of Jean's utterances.

From these two examples we see that the two speakers were at cross-purposes. In line with the interview guidelines, Jean attempted to get the candidate to produce descriptive talk. She did this by giving him a topic and suggesting ways to address it. Lim however, appeared to interpret the interviewer as asking him for specific factual information, which he gave piece by piece. Like the learners in Ross's (1998) study, he failed to understand (or, at least, respond to) the pragmatic intent of her whole turn, as a "starter for talk," responding instead to a single one of her questions, in each case the last question. What happened next is that Jean backed down from her initial expectations, engaging with the candidate at the level at which he had initially responded and reducing the interaction to a simple exchange of snippets of information.

Having now looked at some examples of the strategies employed by Jean to introduce and manage topics and elicit talk from the candidate, we turn to the verbal reports produced by the raters. We find that, in line with the overall assessment focus on effectiveness of communication and the ability to produce extended discourse, all four raters justified their scores in terms of the candidate's limited production and failure to respond adequately to the interviewer's questions.

Rater B evaluated Lim negatively, noting that his failure to produce occurred despite the attempts of the interviewer to elicit speech from him:

> Very hesitant, didn't say very much at all. I mean she gave him every opportunity on a number of subjects to come forth, and he just didn't. He responded with a word, maybe two. That was it. She worked very

hard to get as much out of him as possible, and he just didn't budge, didn't deliver really.

Rater D also shared the same perception:

> He wasn't forthcoming, so she really had to think of lots of strategies to get him to produce language and initially I think she started by giving him directions, giving him leads and he didn't take them up,

and Rater C similarly commented:

> What is it that makes him a 5? He didn't say enough. He didn't say enough good things. He didn't do enough sort of narrating. He didn't do any speculating. He didn't do any comparisons, really. He didn't do any of the difficult things. So on that, because he hardly said anything.

After they had given their overall assessment of the performances, the raters were asked also to replay the taped interview, this time commenting on particular aspects of the performance which were salient to their overall assessment. As they listened to the tape they stopped it at intervals in order to justify their scores with reference to specific exchanges. In relation to Extract 1 above, Rater A had this to say:

> She sort of got a bit stuck there because I think she felt she asked him a reasonable question and she gave him directions and he came forward with a very simple answer. Maybe she should have been silent and let him add more but I think she got the feeling he didn't have more to say and so she was trying to ask him more . . . because I felt her question was quite reasonable, and she gave him directions on how he could answer and he didn't do enough.

Rater B similarly interpreted the interviewer's dominance as a consequence of the candidate's inability to maintain the interaction himself:

> Yeah, that she has to keep feeding him these lines also. He's not really picking up and running with anything. She's talking about the distribution of wealth. He had every opportunity, and he just says *middle class*, you know, it's one word or one turn. He doesn't really extend on anything. She has to keep pushing, pushing, pushing to get him to talk.

Continuing on in the topical sequence introduced in Extract 2, we see (Extract 3, below) that Jean shifted the topic a little from the distribution of wealth to focus on unemployed people specifically. In this next extract she attempted to elicit a description from Lim of what happens to these people, posing the question: "What about if somebody is poor and unemployed?" After a brief digression in which she ascertained that unemployed people did not receive support from the government in Malaysia, she asked Lim, "So what happens to those people?" (line 7). Lim's response was minimal and relatively uninformative about how they cope with no financial support: "they just keep trying to find a job," and Jean next attempted to shift the topic from the general, abstract level to a more personally relevant level by asking Lim if he knew any unemployed people, presumably in the hopes that this question would set up a context in which a description might be more forthcoming. While a shift from abstract to specific is generally perceived as reducing the complexity or difficulty of the task (and is supported in the construct of IELTS as exemplified in the criteria), the strategy did not work in this case as Lim claimed not to know any unemployed people.

Extract 3

```
J: . . . . .^what about if somebody erm (1.0) somebody <is poor and
   unemployed,> d- d'you have many unemployed?
L: (1.0) [s-s-s- some yeah
J:        [is unemployment a pro'm? (.) .hh do they get unemployment
   benefits?                                                              5
L: >no<
J: no: mhm [yah .hh] mhm so what happens to those people.
L: they jus- (.) keep trying (.) to (.) >find a job.<
J: d'you know anyone who perhaps keeps trying and trying an (.)
   doesn't get a job?                                                    10
L: *er* nohhh huh [xxxx
J:                [no, no so most people do:: actually >get [yah >do
   get a job<] a work so< (.) unemployment's quite lo:w, is it?
L: quite low yah
J: yah: right .hh so the GOvernment doesn't give any suppo:rt. >no<     15
   ^what about people with things like (.) erm disabilities, (.) or
   people who . . .
```

After this second failure, Jean closed the topic down as she had done in the previous extract, by producing a "summary" of the exchange. The fact that her first summary statement was an inference which she had made on the basis of Lim's response (that people must be able to find jobs quickly) and that the second was a repetition of the single fact produced in the exchange (that the government does not support unemployed people) served to highlight the limited input from Lim on this topic. Again Lim responded to this summary with tokens of agreement (lines

12–14). Rater C commented that this tendency to make inferences or represent to the candidate what has already been stated is not conducive to the elicitation of candidate speech:

> She's giving him the answers. . . . He just picks up her last phrase. So she actually says to him, *Oh unemployment's quite low, is it?* You know, so what can he say to that except, *Yes, it's quite low*. You know, he's not getting much chance to-

In general, however, like the other raters she blamed the candidate rather than the interviewer for this state of affairs, commenting that:

> She's having trouble talking to him. That's always a sign that they're not too good. She's having trouble thinking of things to say to him and trying to work out where to go next. To me, I use that as a very good indicator. If I'm working hard in the interview, I know they're not too good. If the interview just flows, and you go out and you feel like "hey that wasn't hard work," that to me is a really good indicator that they're a good communicator. See that was his problem. He wasn't coming out with enough, and I think that's why she's saying so much because she's not getting him to talk. He's just, he's just not making generalizations and then moving into more specific information or anything, he's just answering her questions. It's like an interrogation almost, and so she's working hard. You can hear she's not finding this interview easy.

In Jean's interview, as noted earlier, there was a great deal of latching onto what the candidate said and overlapping with it. Overlap is known to be a very common feature in casual conversational interaction and is generally viewed as a collaborative strategy. In an interview, however, and particularly an interview designed to elicit from candidates a demonstration of their speaking ability, it might appear less appropriate in that the interviewer, by breaking in while the candidates are still speaking, is denying them the chance to further demonstrate their speaking skills. In addition, where the candidates know that they are to be judged on their linguistic demonstration, interruptions to this display might appear off-putting.

Extracts 4 to 6 present instances where Jean interrupted the candidate. In Extract 4, Jean did not allow the candidate to complete his comparison but interrupted him, contradicting what he has just said. In Extract 5, Jean interrupted with a clarification question (line 7) to which Lim responded and which, when he did not immediately return to his earlier response, triggered a new question from Jean (line 10). Similarly, in Extract 6, Jean interrupted Lim's response again, asking what he had meant by "very high."

Extract 4

```
J: .hh okay .hh ^Lim (1.0) I can- I know you are studying here at T-,
   (.) how are you finding it.
L: er quite good.
J: quite good? [yeah yeh
L:             [yeah because (1.0) not as tush (.6) not as tuk (.)      5
   sorry .hh it's quite- it's d- compared to my home country_ /ri:ght,/
   you take (.) less subject in here.
J: ^oh ri:ght [so-
L:            [cause I used to take eigh- ten subjects in my [home
   country                                                           10
J:                                                  [ BUT BUT
   it is in a different language,
L: that's [correct it's-
J:        [so: that- that- (.) @that's probably why:@ it's probably .hh
   you know EVerything in another language is surely harder .hh       15
   /yeah/
   where are you from.
```

Extract 5

```
J: . . . ^what about your family and your friends, what do they think
   about the fact that you want to do: mechanical engineering.
L: yeah my: fathers (.) like agree with me that (.9) because (1.0)
   some of my uncles a- are engineering, an:d my father's (.9) like
   (2.5) °*er*° (2.0) think that maybe engineering is good for me, as   5
   [I-
J: [but did you say your father's in engineer- [your fa-
L:                                             [ah no my uncles
   /uncles./ some of my uncles are engineering. /mhm,/ so:_
J: do you think he inspired you?                                       10
```

Extract 6

```
J: .hh ^what about tax rate. (.) do you know what the tax ra[te is ?
L:                                                          [tax rate
   (.) yeah (.) very high. the- [it's too- yah
J:                             [VERY high¿ er do you [yah] know what
   it is?
```

While these interruptions may be, as more than one rater commented, a strategy designed to help a student who was having trouble responding, by completing his responses or producing a new question where he appeared to be struggling, Jean ultimately did not allow him to produce expanded answers to the questions. Rater D commented:

> This student didn't really have much time to think. He was getting lots of yes/no questions and it made it- the structure of the interview I think didn't give him an opportunity to say as much as he possibly could have. The yes/no questions were a bit of a problem, I think, and interrupting him, not giving him thinking time to expand on what he might have been able to say . . .

Rater D commented also that she felt the interviewer's behavior inhibited the candidate from producing longer responses: "But again he was being- she was giving all the responses and I thought he's going to stop because he thinks she's ready to move on to the next bit."

In addition, the raters all commented that Jean tended to produce most of the input, presenting questions in such a way that all Lim needed to do was to select one of the alternatives (Extract 7, lines 3–4 and 12). As Rater C pointed out, such questions limit what candidates are able to do:

> What she was doing consistently was giving him both alternatives, like *Do you like it? Do you think Malaysia is developing well or do you think it's goi- ? Do you think Malaysia's got a lot of problems or do you think it's going well?* You know, like she gave him the (words?). So he was all the time just picking up her phrases. *Oh, I think it's doing well.* So she was putting words into his mouth. And so most of the interview was just him picking up phrases that she'd used and repeating them back to her. So I personally felt we didn't really get a chance to find out what that guy could do on that interview, that it was very limited in a sense.

Extract 7

```
J: oh right so .hh (.) yeah but they don't come in (.) people's houses
   and sort of live in a family they all (.) live separately[do they
L:                                                            [separately
   yeah
J: oh ri:ght okay that's quite different from Australia [hhh yeah]      5
   here. yeah Australia they sort of .hh do the opposite of that .HH
   ^um (.) that- that's quite interesting; ^d'you (.) ^d'you: um (.8)
   tsk see there are any problems with employment_ or industry:_ or:
   anything >that you think (.) you would like the government< to
   change¿ (.)or do you think at the moment it's qu- all working      10
   quite well.
```

```
L: <*er: I thi:nk that*> (1.3) all is quite well hh[hh yeah
J:                                                  [yeah it's well I
   s'pose with a large middle cla:ss: that's (.) quite quite wha- what
   most governments (.) h- hope will happen, .hh erm [yeah] that it      15
   probably is quite a good @id(h)ea to to do what they are doing.
```

Cath

Cath's speaking style is quite different from that of Jean. Whereas Jean's speech was relatively fast-paced and, through modulation and overlap, gave an impression of unplannedness and conversational engagement, Cath's speech rate was what could be described as "measured." It displayed features typical of *foreigner talk* such as a reduced rate of speech production, precise or over-enunciation, and stressing of important words (Ferguson, 1975).

Extract 8
```
C: thank you .hh u:m, (1.0) Lim, how long have you been in Australia¿
L: e:r (.5) >one and a half< months.
C: one and a half months [half yeah] ah good. u:m_ (1.0) where do you
   come from¿
L: er Malaysia, from Malaysia_ K.L. Malaysia                             5
C: Malaysia, (.) aha, (.) a:nd er have you got a family in Australia?
L: yes. I: (.) live with my sister and my brother
C: have they been here long?
L: ah yeah (.) my sister doing medicine in fifth year /o:h/ and my
   brother is graduate (.) also in medicine hh /@o:h (.) so in medicine  10
   too?@/ yeah.
```

The slow pace, use of fillers, and frequent pauses that characterized Cath's pre-question turns were indicative of pre-planning (see Extract 8). Such moves while they do not add to the talk, serve to hold the turn once the interviewer has indicated acceptance of the candidate response and allow her to plan her next question. In line 3, for example, Cath started her turn with an echo of the candidate's response. This was followed by an assessment ("ah good"), a filled pause ("um"), and a relatively long unfilled pause, before she produced her next question. The relative smoothness of the questions as they were ultimately produced contrasts with Jean's often convoluted syntax and false starts which indicated that her speech was relatively unplanned prior to production.

While Jean tended to both speak quickly and react quickly to Lim's responses, even to the extent of interrupting responses-in-progress, Cath, in contrast, not only spoke more slowly, with planning, but also tended to wait for an indication that the candidate had completed his turn before she took the floor. One consequence was that, although Cath's questions tended to be of the short-answer type (i.e. eliciting a simple and single item of information), Lim frequently added to his initial minimal responses. Examples of such elaborations are given in Extract 9.

Extract 9

```
C: you said you liked¿ /tennis/ °yes° /yeah/ and how long have you
   been playing tennis.
L: e:r I've been playing tennis (.) I play tennis: fo:r_ (.) six years,
   (1.0) >but I< not very (.) good at play(h)ing tennis, (.) I- (1.2)
   preferring (.) basketball.                                            5
C: basketball? /yeah./ so that's your other (.) sport; /sport, yeah/
   mhm, and do you play it- have you played it here yet?
L: (1.0) yeah e:r just (.) last Saturday, in (.) e:r (.) Dr W- house
   (1.4) we (1.4) we went- we went there for a picnic lunch, (.5) and
   (.) I played my (.) basket- my school mates sorry.                    10
```

In this extract, Lim responded to Cath's question appropriately by telling her how long he had been playing tennis. When Cath did not take up the turn at this potential turn-transition point (see Sacks *et al.*, 1974), a pause ensued (line 4, bolded). Eventually Lim took the floor again, elaborating on his answer by adding some information about how well he played ("I not very good at playing tennis") and a justification for his lack of skill ("I preferring basketball").

In the next turn Cath produced a further short-answer eliciting question: "Have you played it here yet?" (line 7). Again we see that she did not take up the turn immediately after Lim responded, with the consequence that Lim took the floor again after a relatively long pause (line 9, bolded). In Jean's interview there were, as noted previously, relatively few inter-turn pauses; Jean's speech tended to latch onto or overlap Lim's. Cath's style was much more like that of formal interviewing, in which the interviewer indicates through her silence that the floor still belongs to the interviewee. In fact, given her relatively slow rate of speech overall, it could simply be that Cath was more tolerant of longer pauses, perhaps recognizing that the candidate required time to gather his thoughts and plan his speech. Whatever the case, her actions allowed the candidate to re-take the floor, something that happened a number of times in her interview (Extracts 10, 11, and 12):

Extract 10

C: is that something that you: learnt from your family, or- anybody
   in your family collects stamps?
L: yes all my- all my family's members collect stamps (.7) so I also
   like. (1.4) like m- my fathe:r's collects (.) a lot (.6) <u>during</u>
   erm (.8) when he is young so that sh- he gave me (.) all his (.)   5
   all his stamps.

Extract 11

L: ... and (.) (it's) that's why (.6) I (.) (I) going to (.4) do
   engineering when (I'm) a student.
C: is there anyone in the family who (.) <u>is</u> an engineer?
L: yeah; my uncle. (1.0) one of my uncles (is) a- (.) mechanical
   engineering.   5

Extract 12

C: and er, would you think that erm — how do you think that (.4) your
   <u>study</u> (.) is going to <u>help</u> you when you go back.
L: (1.4) y- you- my studies (.) in: Mel- er in Australia: will
   >(finish) my< (.) it will (.) increase my (.) <u>chance</u>; (.9) *my*-
   (.7) my chance of (1.0) applying (.) a job in: Malaysia, (.8) and   5
   (1.4) I can learn (.) >quite a lot< in the M- University because
   (.) M- University- M- University is famous for (.7) engineering
   and (1.7) °*like*° other science subjects (.) so maybe I can learn
   more xxxx

In one instance towards the end of the interview (Extract 13), Lim
produced a relatively long response. When we examine it in detail, we
find that there were several points at which Cath could have reclaimed
the floor but didn't (bolded pauses), with the result that Lim went on to
produce a substantial piece of argument.

Extract 13

C: °yes,° okay; so is ^there anything else you want to study besides
   engineering? any other field that- you're- interested in?
L: ah (1.2) I was study- (.) I was- (1.0) thinking of studying
   pharmacy, (1.3) cause- (.) my- (.) sister and (.7) quite a lot of
   my cousins (.) study (1.0) medicine; (.) so if- (.) if I (.8) if   5
   I study: (.) pharmacy: (.) it's easy for me to (.) get a (.) xxxx
   (2.0) it's easy for me to: (3.0) earn some more money because hh
   my: (.) cousins can rec- recommend yah (.) patients to me(h) hh
   (.) so it's easy hh for me hh (.) to earns a lot

```
C: so you think it would be easy to get (.) a living. /yah/ ^how    10
   about engineering; is that- would that be easy to get a living in
   Malaysia?
L: yeah. °°(but)°° (.5) but it's not as: good as: (.) pharmacy: (.5)
   because (.) in Malaysia, pharmacists I think (.9) arou:nd_ (.7) a
   small number_ (1.0) in Malaysia °pharmacists° (.) (normally) I    15
   study pharmacy, I can (1.0) I can find- I can (.) f:ind (.) good
   job, (1.0) and work a lot. (.9) in Malaysia.
```

Three of the four raters commented specifically on this exchange, all positively:

Rater E

Yeah, I suppose again he's managing to get out quite a complex discussion there about the advantages and disadvantages of pharmacy. It's taking him a long time to get it out, but it's reasonably sophisticated, even if I don't sort of ethically approve that you can go into pharmacy because you can make a lot of money because your relatives who are in medicine can recommend patients.

Rater F

This is one of the last impressions that I had, that wasn't too bad, you know, I could have studied pharmacy because pharmacists make a lot of money. So that sort of expression was quite good.

Rater G

But then towards the end of it when he was asked to speculate about why he wanted to be an engineer and then he could have taken up pharmacy da di-da di-da he was able to talk about those fairly well. . . . Those last few bits where he talks about the advantages of being a pharmacist over being – he manages to get that out, he manages to get the language for it.

In a final extract, Extract 14, we find an instance of a double question where a question designed to elicit an extended response is followed by a closed, confirmation-seeking one. Just as he did in the interview with Jean (Extracts 1 and 2), Lim responded initially to the last question only. However, unlike Jean, Cath did not take up the turn immediately, and a pause ensued (line 3, bolded). Lim continued on, ultimately responding to the original question with a piece of extended description.

Extract 14

```
L: @not sure yet; o:kay,@ can you tell me: about your family? You
   probably have family at home too?
```

```
C: yeah, (.9) my parents, >oh sorry< my: father is a (.) business man,
   and my [°mhm°] mother is (.) housewife. /°mhm,°/ er I have three
   sisters, (1.0) they are all (.) older than me; (.7) and (1.0) my        5
   old- my elder sister, (1.0) is: (.) is an accountant, and my secon-
   er second sister is in now (.) in Australia; >staying with me,< (.)
   and my third sister is now (.) studying (.) >in K.L.< Malaysia.
```

So how did the raters respond to Lim's performance in his interview with Cath? The following extracts show that he was seen not only as producing adequate answers, but also as being responsive to the interviewer – a willing and active communicator. The description contrasts sharply with that produced in response to Lim's performance in the interview with Jean.

Rater G

Well, I mean he answers her correctly, he comprehends, he- the delivery flows. It's hesitant and that is against him obviously, and there are quite a few grammatical inaccuracies but – and sometimes pronunciation – but I think in the situation, he would be able to cope. Why? Because he can comprehend. He can produce fairly quickly a necessary response.

Rater H attributed his responsiveness to the encouragement of the interviewer:

Rater H

Straightaway she sets the tone like "I'm going to ask you questions now, and because this is an interview, you have to answer them." Like, "I'm not your friend, I'm not going to have a chat to you." And I think she sets up for a good interview just with those first few questions by the tone in her voice, like, I expect an answer to this, and she gets them.

Discussion

The data shown here illustrate the ways in which two interviewers employed quite distinct personal interviewing styles. Although, as has been found to be the case generally in oral interviews, both interviewers controlled the interaction in terms of selecting topics and asking the questions, Jean's interactional style could be characterized as conversational or collaborative, whereas Cath was much more interviewer-like (see the comment by Rater H above).

With Jean, Lim had little opportunity to elaborate on his answers. Much of the speech he produced was "reactive," echoing the interviewer's utterances, such as those in her multi-utterance questioning turns and formulations. The result was that his opportunities to produce creative speech were curtailed, and he therefore appeared to be limited in his productive ability.

Jean's lengthy questioning turns proved also to be problematic. Lim appeared to misinterpret the pragmatic intention of Jean's attempts to suggest how he might respond, with the result that he tended to respond inappropriately. Jean's attempts to continue the talk also failed, with the result that the topic failed to elicit much speech from the candidate.

Cath, in contrast to Jean, had a measured delivery. Although her questions did not always explicitly elicit an extended response, the fact that she reacted slowly as well as speaking slowly allowed Lim to develop his answers, elaborating on initial comments. Where the raters commented on this aspect of Cath's interviewing style, it was perceived as appropriate interviewer behavior in that it allowed candidates the opportunity to demonstrate their ability. Rater H commented:

> She leaves plenty of time for him to talk. She's just silent (laughs) letting him get over the gaps. ... I think the fact that she leaves a silence and he has to fix it means he's got more chance of showing that he's a 6.

The consequence of these different interviewing styles and their impact on the candidate's performance is that raters' perceptions of Lim's competence in the two interviews were quite different, resulting in different ratings. In the interview with Jean, Lim's failure to produce lengthy responses led to him being perceived as unresponsive. The fact that many of the questions required him only to "echo" the interviewer's words by selecting one of the alternatives presented and the fact that the interviewer presented a number of statements which simply required confirmation, led to him being seen as reactive – reacting to rather than initiating speech. His apparent pragmatic misunderstanding was interpreted as both unwillingness and inability. In the interview with Cath, in contrast, the fact that he was able to elaborate on his initial answers meant that he appeared a responsive and willing communicator.

The analysis presented here of both the interview discourse and the raters' comments on the performances shows that, despite training, interviewers may differ dramatically in the ways they carry out the task of interviewing, and that these differences, far from being trivial, may affect the quality of the candidate's performance to the extent that he or she is perceived as differently competent when interviewed by one interviewer than when interviewed by another. This finding raises the question of fairness to candidates and points to the need for effective and regular monitoring of interviewer conduct.

However, a more fundamental problem involves the validity of the conversational interview as a measure of candidates' second language competence. Current theoretical perspectives on interaction point to a fundamental problem in attempting to assess the proficiency of a learner through dialogic interaction, something that is all the more problematic the broader the construct of second language competence is. As we have seen here, in line with the communicative and interactional orientation of the assessment, the raters interpret Lim's interactional behavior in the one interview as "willing" and on the other as "unresponsive" and "reactive." While they do acknowledge the interviewer's role in constructing the candidates' behavior, their training does not provide them with the means to deal with this complication, and they have no alternative but to remove it from the equation when making their judgment, based as it is on a model of individual competence. The dilemma for test developers is how, on the one hand, to retain the conversational interaction which forms the basis of claims to validity for oral interviews, while at the same time ensuring that candidates are judged solely on what they are capable of, rather than what the interviewer allows or encourages them to do.

Conclusion

The aim of this book is to examine how research on speaking can inform second language instruction. Although the study described here is concerned with a formal, public test, there are nevertheless insights which can be drawn from the study and applied within the classroom context, whether or not the teacher is preparing students for formal tests.

Firstly, where learners are preparing to take formal tests which include an oral interview, the evidence here suggests that learners should be trained not simply to produce linguistically accurate responses, but to "construct" themselves as willing interlocutors. This entails providing expanded responses to what might appear to be simple requests for simple items of information. In the current climate of "communicative competence" as the goal of instruction and the construct underpinning assessments of proficiency, learners are judged not only on the linguistic qualities of their speech but on their interactional skills. In order to demonstrate *interactional* competence it seems that learners need to show that they can take the initiative as interlocutors regardless of the apparent expectations of the interviewer.

Secondly, if teachers themselves are required to make judgments of students' oral communicative competence in a second or foreign language, whether through an interview or based on their "in class" speaking performance, then they need to be aware that their (or other student interlocutors') style for prompting speech and maintaining the interaction can influence the quality of the students performance. What would seem advisable in a classroom assessment context is to base learner assessments on multiple interactions with a range of different interlocutors in order to obtain a fair measure of each individual's overall communicative competence. By doing so teachers can acknowledge the problems inherent in making an assessment of a single individual's competence through their involvement in dialogic interaction, while at the same time acknowledging that such assessments must ultimately be made if we are to effectively monitor learner progress in relation to current conceptualizations of what it means to be an effective communicator.

Note

1. The oral interview described here was replaced in 2001 with a more structured interview in which interviews follow a scripted interview outline using specified questions and wording.

References

Atkinson, J. M. and Heritage, J. (1984) *Structures of Social Action: Studies in Conversation Analysis*. Cambridge: Cambridge University Press.

Banerjee, J. and Luoma, S. (1997) Qualitative approaches to test validation. In C. Clapham and D. Corson (eds) *Encylopaedia of Language and Education, Volume 7: Language Testing and Assessment* (pp. 275–287). Dordrecht, The Netherlands: Kluwer.

Berry, V. (1997) Gender and personality as factors of interlocutor variability in oral performance tests. Paper presented at Nineteenth Language Testing Research Colloquium, Orlando, Florida.

Berwick, R. and Ross, S. (1996) Cross-cultural pragmatics in oral proficiency interview strategies. In M. Milanovic and N. Saville (eds) *Performance Testing, Cognition and Assessment: Selected Papers from the 15th Language Testing Research Colloquium, Cambridge and Arnhem* (pp. 34–54). Cambridge: Cambridge University Press and University of Cambridge Local Examinations Syndicate.

Brown, A. (2003) Interviewer variation and the co-construction of speaking proficiency. *Language Testing* 20 (1), 1–25.

Brown, A. and Lumley, T. (1997) Interviewer variability in specific-purpose language performance tests. In V. Kohonen, A. Huhta, L. Kurki-Suonio, and S. Luoma (eds) *Current Developments and Alternatives in Language Assessment: Proceedings of LTRC 96* (pp. 137–150). Jyväskylä, Finland: University of Jyväskylä and University of Tampere.

Brown, A., Iwashita, N., McNamara, T., and O'Hagan, S. (2002). An examination of rater orientations and test-taker performance on English for academic purposes speaking tasks. Unpublished report submitted to Educational Testing Service, Princeton, NJ.

Cafarella, C. (1994) Assessor accommodation in the V.C.E. Italian oral test. *Australian Review of Applied Linguistics* 20 (1), 21–41.

Drew, P. and Heritage, J. (1992) *Talk at Work: Interaction in Institutional Settings.* Cambridge: Cambridge University Press.

Egbert, M. M. (1998) Miscommunication in language proficiency interviews of first-year German students: A comparison with natural conversation. In R. Young and A. W. He (eds) *Talking and Testing: Discourse Approaches to the Assessment of Oral Proficiency* (pp. 147–169). Amsterdam: John Benjamins.

Ferguson, C. (1975) Towards a characterization of English foreigner talk. *Anthropological Linguistics* 17, 1–14.

Hall, J. K. (1993) The role of oral practices in interaction with implications for learning another language. *Applied Linguistics* 14 (3), 145–166.

He, A. W. and Young, R. (1998) Language proficiency interviews: A discourse approach. In R. Young and A. W. He (eds) *Talking and Testing: Discourse Approaches to the Assessment of Oral Proficiency* (pp. 1–24). Amsterdam: John Benjamins.

Jacoby, S. and Ochs, E. (1995) Co-construction: An introduction. *Research on Language and Social Interaction* 28 (3), 171–183.

Kim, K. and Suh, K. (1998) Confirmation sequences as interactional resources in Korean language proficiency interviews. In R. Young and A. W. He (eds) *Talking and Testing: Discourse Approaches to the Assessment of Oral Proficiency* (pp. 297–332). Amsterdam: John Benjamins.

Kunnan, A. J. (1998) Approaches to validation in language assessment. In A. J. Kunnan (ed.) *Validation in Language Assessment: Selected Papers from the 17th Language Testing Research Colloquium, Long Beach* (pp. 1–16). Mahwah, NJ: Lawrence Erlbaum.

Lantolf, J. and Appel, G. (1998) *Vygotskian Approaches to Second Language Research.* Norwood, NJ: Ablex.

Lazaraton, A. (1992) A conversation analysis of structure and interaction in the language interview. Unpublished doctoral dissertation, University of California, Los Angeles.

Lazaraton, A. (1996a) Interlocutor support in oral proficiency interviews: The case of CASE. *Language Testing* 13 (2), 151–172.

Lazaraton, A. (1996b) A qualitative approach to monitoring examiner conduct in the Cambridge assessment of spoken English (CASE). In M. Milanovic and N. Saville (eds) *Performance Testing, Cognition and Assessment: Selected Papers from the 15th Language Testing Research Colloquium* (pp. 18–33). Cambridge: Cambridge University Press.

Lazaraton, A. (2002) *A Qualitative Approach to the Validation of Oral Language Tests. Studies in Language Testing 14.* Cambridge: UCLES/Cambridge University Press.

McNamara, T. (1997) "Interaction" in second language performance assessment: Whose performance? *Applied Linguistics* 18 (4), 444–466.

McNamara, T., Hill, K., and May, L. (2002) Discourse and assessment. *Annual Review of Applied Linguistics* 22, 221–242.

Messick, S. (1989) Validity. In R. Linn (ed.) *Educational Measurement* (3rd edn) (pp. 13–104). New York: Macmillan.

Morton, J., Wigglesworth, G., and Williams, D. (1997) Approaches to the evaluation of interviewer performance in oral interaction tests. In G. Brindley and G. Wigglesworth (eds) *Access: Issues in English Language Test Design and Delivery* (pp. 175–196). Sydney: National Centre for English Language Teaching and Research.

O'Loughlin, K. (2001) *The Equivalence of Direct and Semi-direct Speaking Tests.* Cambridge: Cambridge University Press and University of Cambridge Local Examinations Syndicate.

O'Loughlin, K. (2002) The impact of gender in oral proficiency testing. *Language Testing* 19 (2), 169–192.

Perrett, G. (1990) The language testing interview: A reappraisal. In J. H. A. L. de Jong and D. K. Stevenson (eds) *Individualising the Assessment of Language Abilities* (pp. 225–237). Clevedon: Multilingual Matters.

Psathas, G. (1995) *Conversation Analysis: The Study of Talk-in-interaction.* Thousand Oaks, CA: Sage.

Reed, D. J. and Halleck, G. B. (1997) Probing above the ceiling in oral interviews: What's up there? In V. Kohonen, A. Huhta, L. Kurki-Suonio, and S. Luoma (eds) *Current Developments and Alternatives in Language Assessment: Proceedings of LTRC 96* (pp. 225–238). Jyväskylä, Finland: University of Jyväskylä and University of Tampere.

Ross, S. (1996) Formulae and inter-interviewer variation in oral proficiency interviewer discourse. *Prospect* 11 (3), 3–16.

Ross, S. (1998) Divergent frame interpretations in language proficiency interview interaction. In R. Young and A. W. He (eds) *Talking and Testing: Discourse Approaches to the Assessment of Oral Proficiency* (pp. 333–353). Amsterdam: John Benjamins.

Ross, S. and Berwick, R. (1992) The discourse of accommodation in oral proficiency interviews. *Studies in Second Language Acquisition* 14 (2), 159–176.

Sacks, H. (1992a) *Lectures on Conversation* (Vol. 1) (G. Jefferson, ed.). Cambridge, MA: Blackwell.

Sacks, H. (1992b) *Lectures on Conversation* (Vol. 2) (G. Jefferson, ed.). Cambridge, MA: Blackwell.

Sacks, H., Schegloff, E. A., and Jefferson, G. (1974) A simplest systematics for the organization of turn-taking in conversation. *Language* 50 (4), 696–735.

Tannen, D. (1984) *Conversational Style: Analyzing Talk Among Friends.* Norwood, NJ: Ablex.

UCLES (1997a) *International English Language Testing System: The IELTS Handbook.* Cambridge: University of Cambridge Local Examinations Syndicate.

UCLES (1997b) *IELTS Examiner Training Materials.* Cambridge: University of Cambridge Local Examinations Syndicate.

van Lier, L. (1989) Reeling, writhing, drawling, stretching and fainting in coils: Oral proficiency interviews as conversations. *TESOL Quarterly* 23 (3), 480–508.

Vygotsky, L. S. (1978) *Mind in Society: The Development of Higher Psychological Processes* (M. Cole, V. John-Steiner, S. Scribner, and E. Souberman, eds). Cambridge, MA: Harvard University Press.

Wigglesworth, G. (1997) An investigation of planning time and proficiency level on oral test discourse. *Language Testing* 14 (1), 85–106.

Young, R. (1995) Conversational styles in language proficiency interviews. *Language Learning* 45 (1), 3–42.

Young, R. (1999) Sociolinguistic approaches to SLA. *Annual Review of Applied Linguistics* 19, 105–132.

Young, R. and He, A. W. (1998) *Talking and Testing: Discourse Approaches to the Assessment of Oral Proficiency.* Amsterdam: John Benjamins.

Young, R. and Milanovic, M. (1992) Discourse variation in oral proficiency interviews. *Studies in Second Language Acquisition* 14 (4), 403–424.

Chapter 12

Difficulty and Practicality in Tests of Interlanguage Pragmatics

CARSTEN ROEVER

Assessment of second language pragmatic knowledge is a growing but complex area of second language assessment. Two particularly central challenges for test design in interlanguage pragmatics are item difficulty and practicality of administration and scoring. This chapter reviews findings on factors influencing item difficulty for different types of pragmatic items, and discusses ways of increasing practicality for productive item types. It concludes with pedagogical recommendations and an agenda for future research.

Introduction

The assessment of language learners' pragmatic knowledge in the second language has only recently drawn the attention it deserves (e.g. Bachman, 2000; Hudson *et al.*, 1995; Roever, 2001), but is still far from a mainstream concern in language testing.[1] At this point there are no established and widely used tests of pragmatics available, which is somewhat surprising, given that pragmatic knowledge and ability is part of the widely accepted models of communicative competence (Bachman, 1990; Bachman & Palmer, 1996; Canale, 1983; Canale & Swain, 1980). While there are probably multiple causes for the under-representation of measurements of pragmatics among language tests, I will focus on two issues which are ripe for investigation and, if solved, could help propel test design for pragmatics forward: the practicality and the difficulty of pragmatics tests. First, I will discuss the construct of second language pragmatic competence in general and show how it relates to item difficulty and practicality. I will then discuss some recent tests of interlanguage pragmatics and glean some insights from them about the factors that influence the difficulty of pragmatics tasks. Finally, I will discuss ways of increasing the practicality of tasks and mention some areas of future research.

Construct, Practicality, and Difficulty

To measure a learner's pragmatic competence presumes a clear definition of the construct "pragmatic competence," so that items can be designed to produce evidence of the construct's strength in an individual learner. This is not unproblematic for pragmatics which, as Leech (1983) points out, straddles the fence between linguistics and sociology. According to Leech, pragmatic knowledge, whether in one's first or second language, consists of two components: *pragmalinguistic* and *sociopragmatic* knowledge. The pragmalinguistic component encompasses conventions of means, which are strategies for realizing communicative intentions, and conventions of forms (Clark, 1979), which are the linguistic tokens necessary to implement these strategies in communication. For example, to perform a request in English, a speaker could use conventional indirectness (a convention of means), and one convention of form that can be used to express conventional indirectness is a question with a conditional – for example, "Could I have another roll?"

The sociopragmatic component of pragmatic competence encompasses knowledge of social norms, in other words "what you do, when, and to whom" (Fraser *et al.*, 1981), including knowledge of mutual rights and obligations, taboos, and conventional courses of action (Thomas, 1983), and the effect of context variables as well as the interpersonal variables of power differential, social distance, and degree of imposition as defined by Brown and Levinson (1987). To be pragmatically competent, learners must map their sociopragmatic and pragmalinguistic knowledge onto each other, and be able to use their knowledge online under the constraints of a communicative situation.

The sociopragmatic component of pragmatics makes it fundamentally situation-dependent. In other words, language learners cannot perform their pragmatic knowledge without a situational context, or at least such performance would not allow any inferences to be drawn with regard to the accuracy of the learners' pragmalinguistic and sociopragmatic mapping. This means that tests of pragmatic competence must establish context sufficiently, but such a requirement makes test design a very complex task.

Nonetheless, it is unclear what amount of contextual information is sufficient for learners to understand the situation fully and unambiguously and subsequently display their competence. Also, how best to present contextual information is unclear. Long, detailed prompts, as Billmyer and Varghese (2000) would propose using, not only take a long time to read and comprehend but also may overtax the learner's developing reading ability, thereby introducing construct-irrelevant variance. Rich, thickly descriptive visual scenarios in the form of video prompts may seem an attractive option, but, aside from our utter lack of knowledge of their strengths and weaknesses, they are also prohibitively expensive to create and administer, which raises a notorious issue in the assessment of pragmatics: practicality.

Bachman and Palmer (1996) describe the practicality of a test as the ratio between the resources available and the resources needed. Simply put, the more expensive a test is, the less practical it is. In reality, the less practical a test is, the less likely it is to be used. While practicality has often been treated as the ugly stepchild of validity, it is in fact directly related to considerations of the consequences of test use. As Ebel (1964) points out in evaluating the consequential validity of a test, we also have to take into account the consequences of *not* administering the test. This perspective adds urgency to the need for more practical tests of pragmatics, and, while the question of how to establish context sufficiently and efficiently remains intractable at this point, other practicality issues can be tackled with our present-day knowledge.

One important practicality issue is the prevalence of productive item types, such as discourse completion items and role-plays, which are notoriously time-consuming and expensive to administer and score. Streamlining administration and scoring of productive item types should allow for more items, reduce scoring times, and generally positively impact validity. I will suggest some ways to accomplish this later in this chapter.

A second issue concerns the difficulty of items. In a linear test, which delivers the same items to all test takers, item difficulty must be known so that all difficulty levels that are relevant to a population of examinees will be represented, and the test can render valid scores across the ability spectrum. In an adaptive test, which gauges the test taker's ability level and delivers items around that level, difficulty is a central concern in item selection. From a practical point of view, findings on item difficulty are useful for item generation, since generation is much facilitated once new items can be built to specifications that will reasonably assure a certain difficulty level.[2]

So the challenge in constructing tests of interlanguage pragmatics lies in the tension between the need for an accurate measurement of a complex, context-dependent construct on the one hand, and the problems of estimating task difficulty and increasing the test's practicality on the other. In the next section, I will review some recent assessment studies in interlanguage pragmatics to provide an empirical basis for discussions of difficulty and practicality.

Background: Recent Tests of Interlanguage Pragmatics

Not many efforts at assessing second language learners' pragmatic knowledge have been reported in the literature. The following discussion will refer to three major studies: Bouton's test of ESL implicature (Bouton, 1988, 1994, 1999), Hudson *et al.*'s test of ESL sociopragmatics (1995) and its spin-offs (Yamashita, 1996; Yoshitake, 1997), and my own test of ESL/ EFL pragmalinguistics (Roever, 2001).

Bouton (1988, 1994, 1999) has published extensively on his work in assessing international students' comprehension of two types of implicature, which he calls idiosyncratic implicature and formulaic implicature. Idiosyncratic implicature is common conversational implicature, which is characterized by an utterance appealing to the listener's ability to draw inferences, rather than conveying information directly, for example:

A: "Has the mail come yet?"
B: "It's only eleven."

Clearly B's utterance is not a response to A's question, which would require a yes/no response. However, A's knowledge about the circumstances of the mail delivery (which commonly arrives after eleven o'clock) will allow her to interpret B's statement as a negative response.

Bouton named his second category "formulaic implicature," and it incorporates indirect criticism and the famous Pope Q ("Is the Pope Catholic?") and its variants. Formulaic implicature follows the same basic principles as idiosyncratic implicature but differs in that it is more patterned, which makes it easier to decode for listeners who know the pattern but nearly impossible for those who do not.

Bouton uses a multiple-choice test of 33 items and, since his first round of testing in 1986, has tested several hundred students and conducted follow-up studies. He found that idiosyncratic implicature is easier, learned over time but not easily teachable, whereas formulaic implicature is more difficult, not acquired over time but very much teachable.

Hudson *et al.* (1992, 1995) undertook a major project, focused on testing sociopragmatic appropriateness in producing the speech acts request, apology, and refusal. They limited their target population to Japanese learners of English as a second language and they employed a variety of instruments: written discourse completion tests (DCTs), multiple-choice DCTs, oral (language lab) DCTs, and role-plays. The DCT is the most popular instrument in speech act research (Kasper & Rose, forthcoming) and deserves some explanation at this point. A DCT minimally consists of a situational prompt and a gap for the respondent to enter his/her response. Optionally, the gap can be followed by a rejoinder, for example:

```
You are in a deli with your friend Kevin to pick up a sandwich
for lunch. When it's your turn to pay you realize that you left
your wallet at the office and don't have any money on you. What
do you say to Kevin?

You: _____

Kevin: "Sure, no problem. Will $10 be enough?"
```

A DCT can also be in multiple-choice format with possible answer options instead of a gap.

Hudson *et al.* describe the careful empirical development of the test in detail, and Hudson (2001) provides some statistical analyses of their pilot run, which was hampered by the homogeneity and small size of their sample of 25 learners. Yoshitake (1997) replicated the test with 25 EFL learners in Japan, and Yamashita (1996) adapted the test and used it with 47 native English-speaking learners of Japanese as a second language. While Yoshitake's sample suffered from similar problems as in Hudson *et al.*, Yamashita's group was larger and included test takers with more varied abilities. Yamashita reports high reliabilities for all test sections with the exception of the multiple-choice DCT. Brown (2001) provides a convenient summary of Yamashita and Yoshitake's findings, and also discusses the practical advantages and disadvantages of each component of the test battery.

Last, I developed and validated a web-based test battery of pragmalinguistic knowledge, which incorporated a multiple-choice section assessing knowledge of idiosyncratic and formulaic implicature, a multiple-choice assessment of situational routines, and a productive DCT with apology, request, and refusal items (Roever, 2001). A group of 267 ESL and EFL learners took the standard version of the test, and small samples took experimental versions, and provided verbal protocols and NS baseline data. Reliabilities for all sections were high and learners' English proficiency was the main factor accounting for their speech act and implicature scores, whereas exposure to English was the driving force behind their knowledge of routines. Evidence in favor of construct validity included expert judgments, comparisons between groups with different characteristics, verbal protocols, and scores above 95% by the NS baseline group.

The above studies offer some insights into sources of item difficulty, which will be discussed in more detail in the following section.

Difficulty of Pragmatics Tasks

Classical test theory defines the difficulty of an item as the proportion of test takers answering the item correctly compared to the total number of test takers (Nunnally & Bernstein, 1994) – the fewer test takers know the answer to an item, the more difficult the item. Item response theory (IRT) relates test takers' ability directly to item difficulty, in that high ability test takers will be able to answer easy items and (some or most) difficult items, whereas low ability test takers will only be able to answer (some) easy items but none or very few difficult items (for a readable introduction to IRT, cf. McNamara, 1996). This reciprocal relationship between item difficulty and test taker ability shows that items are not inherently difficult or easy, but that their difficulty arises from an interaction between item characteristics and test takers' knowledge (or lack thereof). Identifying what makes items difficult can lead to the identification of ability hierarchies in learners, which would provide valuable empirical developmental information for interlanguage pragmatics research.

The practical relevance of item difficulty relates to test construction. A linear test (where every test taker receives the same questions) must contain items of varying difficulty levels to allow measurement across the entire ability spectrum. An adaptive test (where questions are computer-selected based on estimates of a test taker's ability) relies on the availability of item difficulty information to allow the algorithm to select items appropriate for a given test taker.

It is a challenging task to attempt to identify tangible insights into the reasons for pragmatic item difficulty on the basis of the three studies discussed in the previous section. It would of course be preferable to base such an analysis on a large number of studies, but these are the only studies that have been conducted in this area so far. Also, these studies assess somewhat different components of pragmatic knowledge: Hudson *et al.* assessed sociopragmatic knowledge of appropriateness – in other words, do learners know what is appropriate to say in a given situation? Bouton and myself assessed pragmalinguistic knowledge, which focuses on the correct linguistic realization and interpretation of speech intentions. So convergent findings from these studies have to be treated as tendencies that encourage further research, rather than as unassailable pearls of wisdom.

Implicature

Just like Bouton (1999), I found that formulaic implicature was more difficult than idiosyncratic implicature (Roever, 2001), but the effect size of implicature type was not very large ($d = 0.248$). Both Bouton and I tested interpretation of indirect criticism and the Pope Q as formulaic implicature types, and we both found that indirect criticism was more difficult for test takers than the Pope Q. This could be due to the fact that Pope Q-type questions can be solved by pure logical inference, once test takers get beyond the initial confusion of encountering a response that is completely unrelated to the question. I caught an inside glimpse of this inferencing process in the verbal protocol provided by my L1 Chinese-speaking test taker Mingrong, as she responded to the following item:

```
106: Maria and Frank are working on a class project together
but they won't be able to finish it by the deadline.
Maria: "Do you think Dr. Gibson is going to lower our grade if
we hand it in late?"
Frank: "Do fish swim?"

What does Frank probably mean?

1. He thinks they should change the topic of their project.
2. He thinks their grade will not be affected.
3. He did not understand Maria's question.
4. He thinks they will get a lower grade.
```

Mingrong said (in Chinese):

Oh it means if fish can swim this is bull shit of course fish can swim so uh he must uh yeah that's right they'll get a D grade.

Another explanation to which Bouton (1999) alludes is the greater conspicuousness of the Pope Q as a pragmatically motivated utterance as compared to indirect criticism. The Pope Q blatantly flouts the Gricean maxim of relation, which requires that a response be obviously relevant to the preceding question. Indirect criticism, on the other hand, is related to preceding utterance but praises facetiously a secondary aspect of the object of critique as in the following example, the most difficult implicature item in my test:

```
105: Jose and Tanya are professors at a college. They are talking
about a student, Derek.
Jose: "How did you like Derek's essay?"
Tanya: "I thought it was well-typed."

What does Tanya probably mean?

1. She did not like Derek's essay.
2. She likes it if students hand in their work type-written.
3. She thought the topic Derek had chosen was interesting.
4. She doesn't really remember Derek's essay.
```

To recognize Tanya's utterance as indirect criticism, test takers must have sufficient knowledge of US (academic) culture to realize that neatness of appearance is not the primary criterion faculty members use in evaluating the quality of a student's writing.

The difficulty of implicature items seems to be greater for items which:

- test formulaic implicature;
- require knowledge of cultural patterns;
- are not prima facie recognizable as containing an implicature.

A caveat is necessary here. From a construct perspective, it is important to ensure that assessment of knowledge of cultural patterns is part of the construct. It is hard to imagine how any pragmatic test could be constructed free of cultural patterns, but their presence must be made explicit in the construct to avoid simply testing world knowledge: the Pope Q in its original form ("Is the Pope Catholic?") requires a very specific piece of world knowledge, which not all test takers may possess. For example, in my data the difference in performance among German and Japanese test takers of the same proficiency level was significantly different on the original Pope Q ($p < 0.001$), which required knowledge about the religious role of the Pope, but not on the modified Pope Q shown above ("Do fish swim?") (Roever, 2001). From a fairness perspective, the importance of certain pieces of world knowledge such as the role of the Pope should be carefully evaluated, and replacement of items that rely very heavily on highly specific pieces of knowledge should be considered.

Speech acts

Again, one has to be careful in comparing studies as different as my own and the ones using Hudson *et al.*'s instruments, but some interesting tendencies and differences can be outlined with regard to difficulty. In my test, the two most difficult items were request items, and request and apology items together constituted 50% of the more difficult items. Refusal items on the other hand proved much easier.

Not so for Hudson *et al.* In their test battery, refusals were the most difficult speech act type and apologies the easiest, although differences were not very large (Hudson, 2001). Requests were not significantly different from either of the other speech acts. An important source of difficulty Hudson *et al.* identified was the testing condition: their language lab condition, where test takers responded orally to aural situation prompts, produced significantly lower scores than the written DCT condition or the role-play condition. Hudson (2001) suggests that the language lab condition may have been made more difficult by the absence of planning time (which the written DCT condition affords) and raters' less kindly attitudes to disembodied voices (as compared to images of people in the role-play condition). If there is indeed an effect of planning time, Hudson's language lab condition was actually measuring online performance under time pressure, whereas scores from the written DCT reflect offline knowledge. This is consistent with the lower scores under the language lab condition, since online performance burdens the test takers' processor more than a condition that allows time for reflection. However, the real effects of planning time are difficult to identify since they may be confounded with a rater effect.

In a small-scale methodological study as part of my test validation, I found no significant differences between written and spoken speech act responses, but my test takers were allowed the same time for responding under both conditions, and often took a few seconds to compose a response under the oral condition.

It is certainly psycholinguistically plausible that absence of planning time will increase cognitive load and thereby make it harder for test takers to produce acceptable responses. However, the delivery of the prompt as aural input in Hudson *et al.*'s study could also be a source of difficulty, particularly given that their test taker population consisted entirely of L1 Japanese speakers who are often reported to struggle more to understand spoken English, which requires real-time processing, than written English.

A source of speech act difficulty that both Hudson *et al.* and I found was degree of imposition. Degree of imposition is the cost for the hearer of acceding to a speaker's request, the weight of the offensive action for which the speaker is apologizing, or the cost for the hearer of having a request refused. For example, asking a friend for a glass of water while visiting their home is a small imposition, but asking to borrow their house for a night to have a college frat party is a much larger imposition. In my test, high-imposition items were significantly more difficult than low-imposition items, but the size of the difference was moderate ($d = .295$). This is not surprising, since my test was not focused on sociopragmatic appropriateness. Hudson found strong difficulty differences caused by degree of imposition in his DCT and language lab conditions, but curiously not for the role-play condition. Hudson (2001) did not find any significant differences for the variables power and social distance, which were not included in my test.

The reason for greater difficulty associated with high-imposition items is that they require more of an effort in order to save face and may overtax the learners' processing capabilities, so that they are either not undertaken at all or are undertaken unsuccessfully. Like any pragmatic failure (Thomas, 1983), this lack of success may be pragmalinguistic, which explains the effect found in my test, or sociopragmatic, which explains the effect seen in Hudson *et al.*'s data. Examples of pragmalinguistic failure include use of request strategies that do not have requestive force in the target language, situationally inadequate routines, or misunderstanding of implicatures. Sociopragmatic failure is contextually inappropriate language, usually utterances which are not polite enough, although the utterance may be correct and comprehensible.

Hudson (2001) does not discuss the absence of an effect of imposition in Hudson *et al.*'s role-play data, but it is possible that learners managed to do the necessary face saving by means other than purely linguistic ones – for example, by showing deference through smiling or tone of voice.

Routines

It is perhaps most difficult to speculate on the causes of difficulty in items assessing knowledge of routines because my study is the only one which included this item type. From my correlational analyses of test taker background and scores, it appears that exposure to exemplars is the strongest influence on knowledge of routines. Exposure to exemplars, however, means nothing other than frequency of encountering a certain routine: the more frequent a routine, the easier it should be. While there are no frequency measures of routines in spoken language, a comparison between the three most difficult and the three easiest routines in my study supports this impressionistically. The three easiest routines in my study were:

"Nice to meet you." [introduction]

"Hello." [telephone]

"Can I leave a message?" [telephone]

The three most difficult routines were:

"Here you go." [supermarket]

"Excuse me, do you have the time?" [stranger]

"Do you think you could make it?" [party invitation]

A relationship between prevalence in the input and learners' knowledge of routines is a matter of speculation but appears at least possible.

In summary, the picture on difficulty for pragmatics items appears fairly complex. The feature in question, the item type, and the kind of knowledge that the item accesses all interact to make an item easy or difficult for a specific test taker. More research into difficulty factors is essential to identify such factors with greater accuracy. At the same time, test practicality is a central concern because it ultimately determines how likely it is that a certain test will be used. Practicality and ways of increasing it will be discussed in the following section.

Practicality, Validity, and Response Format

There are various kinds of response formats for pragmatic assessments: multiple-choice tests were used in both Bouton's and my own study of implicature, and in my test of routines. In my test, I used traditional, written discourse completion tests (DCTs) for the speech act section, as did Hudson *et al.*, who also made use of spoken DCTs (their "language lab DCT"), multiple-choice questions, and role-plays. Different response formats differ in their practicality and their appropriateness for a given testing purpose.

Multiple-choice items

Multiple-choice items consist of an item stem, which in a test of pragmatic ability commonly contains contextual information, and three to five response options, of which only one is correct. Because the correct answer is present in the item itself, these items require recognition, not active recall or construction of the correct answer as productive item types would. This format facilitates guessing, since test takers can eliminate clearly wrong response options and then select one of the remaining ones without actually knowing with certainty what the correct answer is. At the same time, this selection process allows testers to manipulate the difficulty of items by providing highly plausible response options to make the item more difficult. This is particularly easy to do with routines, where distractors that resemble routines in the test takers' L1 can be utilized. Also, distractors can be used which sound more or less similar to the correct answer or actually occur, just not in the context described in the stem. Compare an easier item version (1) and a presumably more difficult one (2):

```
(1)   Jane is at the beach and wants to know what time it is.
She sees a man with a watch.
```

```
What would Jane probably say?
```

1. "Excuse me, can you say the time?"
2. "Excuse me, how late is it?"
3. "Excuse me, what's your watch show?"
4. <u>"Excuse me, do you have the time?"</u>

```
(2)   Jane is at the beach and wants to know what time it is.
She sees a man with a watch.
```

```
What would Jane probably say?
```

1. "Excuse me, do you have my time?"
2. "Excuse me, do you have this time?"
3. "Excuse me, do you have some time?"
4. <u>"Excuse me, do you have the time?"</u>

The distractors in version (2) are probably similar enough to confuse even a native speaker or at least require very close reading. In piloting the second item above, I found that my personal favorite distractor "Can you tell the time?" was often chosen by native speakers who misread it as "Can you tell *me* the time?," which is of course perfectly correct. This illustrates the absolute necessity of piloting any item type, since it is impossible for a test developer to predict how test takers will react to a given item.

It should be clear that multiple-choice items work well for routines, especially ones that test takers are not likely to have to produce, so that a productive test might underestimate the true state of their knowledge. A drawback with any paper-and-pencil test or a computer-based test which uses written text as in my test, is that situational routines are not usually encountered in writing, but rather heard in spoken input. While test takers might recognize a routine when it is spoken, they might not recognize it in writing, particularly if they have stored it as an unanalyzed chunk. However, the impact of this item delivery factor is an empirical matter that has not been explored yet.

This particular problem is avoided in multiple-choice tests of implicature, where the response options are interpretations of the utterance containing the implicature. It is probably more difficult to vary item difficulty through more or less plausible response options, since plausibility of interpretation depends on how much an interpretation matches test takers' background knowledge. Response options can also exploit nonrecognition of the implicature, but where an implicature requires fundamental world knowledge to be understood (like with the original Pope Q), absence of such world knowledge makes all response options equally (im)plausible.

The multiple-choice format is definitely the most appropriate format for implicature items, but it is definitely not the best format for speech act items. In designing multiple-choice items for their sociopragmatically oriented test, Hudson *et al.* (1995) report problems creating response options that are clearly incorrect: they found it difficult to implement lack of politeness in their options while still keeping the distractors plausible. Yamashita reports a similar problem for the Japanese version, and, indeed, in Yamashita's (1996) and Yoshitake's (1997) uses of the instrument, the multiple-choice sections had the lowest reliabilities. This may be an intractable problem for tests of sociopragmatics for several reasons. Most importantly, politeness is not a black-and-white, all-or-nothing phenomenon. In fact, many shadings exist along a continuum between polite and impolite responses, and native speakers' standards of what constitutes politeness or impoliteness can vary dramatically in the absence of outright insults. In other words, while there are several ways to ask for a light, "Sir, are you the owner of a match?" is not one of them, and therefore qualifies as a distractor for this routine. But as an example of a requestive speech act, we could ask whether it is clearly polite or impolite to say to a neutral stranger "Got a light?," "Excuse me, would you have a light?," "I'm sorry to bother you but could I possibly trouble you for a light?"

Another issue with regards to politeness is that suprasegmentals and extra-linguistic features can have a strong impact on the politeness of an utterance. A mocking tone, a haughty expression, or a challenging posture can imbue a superficially polite utterance with the force of an unbearable insult. Incorporating such features in a test requires a much higher level of technical sophistication than has been used so far.

Finally, the personal history between the interlocutors can also strongly impact the politeness level of an utterance. Specifying their relationship in detail, however, can make prompts unrealistically long.

These problems are particularly damaging for the construct validity of productive tests with a sociopragmatic orientation, but there are viable options for increasing validity and practicality for pragmalinguistically oriented speech act tests. Since testing of speech acts by means of discourse completion tests is one of the most common approaches to pragmatics assessment, I will discuss this type of instrument in some detail below.

Testing speech acts productively

Any productive test is less practical than a pure multiple-choice test, because such a test requires more time for item completion, completion time varies depending on the respondents' general linguistic ability and inclination to write an extended answer, and scoring generally has to be done by human raters. The longer completion times negatively impact validity by limiting the number of items that can be administered and thereby narrowing the content domain and lowering test reliability. The need for human scorers affects practicality by increasing administration expenses and can also impact validity by introducing construct-irrelevant variance through less-than-perfect ratings.

Both problems cannot be entirely solved, but they can be ameliorated by restricting the range and breadth of possible responses, thereby limiting how much test takers can reasonably write and facilitating raters' decision making. For tests of pragmalinguistics, such a restriction can be achieved through the use of rejoinders. A rejoinder is an utterance from the imaginary interlocutor that follows the gap in which the test takers enter their response – for example, this apology item in my test (Roever, 2001):

```
Ella borrowed a recent copy of TIME Magazine from her friend
Sean but she accidentally spilled a cup of coffee all over it.
She is returning the magazine to Sean.

Ella: _____

Sean: "No, don't worry about replacing it, I read it already."
```

Note that the rejoinder in the above example is constructed to elicit at least one supportive move from test takers, in addition to the apology token, which the situation itself demands: in order for the rejoinder to be a true response, the gap must contain an offer of repair – an apology alone is not sufficient. This greatly simplifies the raters' task because raters know which strategies are minimally required to award a point to the test taker response. In the absence of a rejoinder, it would be unclear what constitutes a sufficient response: an apology token alone, an apology plus one or more supportive moves (offer of repair, promise of non-recurrence), or even no apology at all. The judgment would be entirely left to the raters' discretion, thereby allowing individual differences between raters to unduly affect ratings.

A criticism leveled against rejoinders in DCT items concerns their effect on the authenticity of test taker responses, since in real-world communication one can only guess but not know for sure how the interlocutor will respond. It was for that reason that Hudson *et al.* (1995) removed rejoinders from the pilot version of their assessment DCT. Similarly, Johnston *et al.* (1998) suggest not using rejoinders in research DCTs, but they then go on to warn that the resultant lack of interlocutor uptake can also affect responses since one can expect uptake in real-world communication. It would be very strange if an interlocutor did not respond to a heartfelt apology, and in a rejoinder-less test, test takers may interpret the lack of uptake in unpredictable ways that may influence their responses.

In fact, this may be a case where research and assessment instruments serve different purposes. Research instruments are intended to engage respondents' natural preferences and ideally elicit responses similar or identical to what participants would provide in real-world communication. Assessment instruments on the other hand are intended to engage knowledge, and the tester's definition of the construct under investigation determines what exactly that knowledge should be. Simply put, testers need not care what test takers would prefer to say, but rather what they are able to say. From this perspective, rejoinders are perfectly justifiable, because they assist in engaging construct-relevant knowledge.

It should be noted that, even with rejoinders in pragmalinguistic tests, raters do not become automatons. While I achieved an interrater reliability of .96 after only a brief training of one hour, disagreements between raters existed but were mostly limited to issues of politeness. Even though raters had been instructed not to consider politeness in their ratings except where responses were grossly offensive or ridiculously overpolite, they expressed strong (and often divergent) feelings about the politeness of some test taker responses. With the help of gentle reminders by the researcher they did, however, manage to re-orient themselves to the pragmalinguistic focus of the rating.

The raters' reactions to politeness issues do foreshadow the problems that a test of sociopragmatics would face, whether or not it contains rejoinders. In fact, it is difficult to imagine how rejoinders would help tests of sociopragmatic appropriateness unless knowledge of different levels of politeness and impoliteness is part of the construct and the rejoinder indicates (via the imaginary interlocutor's pleased/neutral/offended reaction) which politeness level is expected.

Pedagogical Implications

All the preceding findings were based on tests of pragmatics administered outside of the classroom context, involving the testing of large numbers of learners (at least in Bouton's test and my own). This does not imply that classroom-based testing of pragmatics is impossible. In fact, some of the findings discussed above can be readily applied to the classroom context.

In the first instance, a decision must be made as to what level of competence is to be assessed: are we testing offline knowledge or online performance? Testing offline knowledge shows what students know, but they may not (yet) be able to use that knowledge in communication. Testing online performance shows what students can actually do with the language and gives a more realistic impression of how they would perform in the target situation. However, it may underestimate the extent of their knowledge, which may become available for use in due course. Testing online performance gives a snapshot of what students can do at the time of the test, while testing offline knowledge gives a fuzzier and less definite outlook of what they might be able to do in the future. The key practical difference between the two is that testing of online performance requires that there be very little or no planning time, just like one cannot take a timeout in conversation to carefully put together a sentence. If students can think about their answer and fiddle with it under little or no time pressure, offline knowledge is being tested.

The second consideration concerns testing productive vs. receptive abilities. Do we want to find out what students can say or what they can understand? This consideration plays out somewhat differently for implicatures, routines, and speech acts.

As a rule of thumb, implicatures are usually only tested receptively because it is difficult to design tasks that force students to produce implicatures. However, it is not impossible: making blunt statements more indirect is a type of implicature and can be easily practiced and tested. The more cultural knowledge an implicature requires, the more difficult it is likely to be.

The differentiation between testing productive and receptive abilities is probably most relevant for routines, depending on whether students are likely to have to produce them or will just hear them. For receptive testing of routines, students can either be given a multiple-choice test and asked to select the routine that fits the situation ("What would you/X say in this situation?") or to select the situation that fits the routine ("In what situation would you hear the following?"). Generally, rarer situations or routines will be more difficult than common ones, and learners who have never lived in the target culture will find all highly situational routines very difficult. For productive testing of routines, written or preferably oral DCT-type instruments can be designed, describing a situation and interlocutors.

Speech acts are usually tested productively, either orally or in writing with a DCT. It is not advisable at this time to try receptive testing of speech acts with multiple-choice instruments since the design of plausible distractors is still somewhat of a mystery. In addition, testing socioprag-matics should be limited to low-stakes testing because native speakers' ideas of what is appropriate and what is inappropriate vary too much (outside the extremes of unforgivable rudeness and laughable over-politeness) to allow testing with the precision necessary to support high-stakes inferences. As a general rule, the greater the degree of impo-sition, the more complex the learner's utterance will have to be, and, accordingly, the more difficult the task will be.

Outlook

The above is an outline of what can be distilled from the few studies on assessment of interlanguage pragmatics which exist at the present time. More assessment studies over a wide range of languages are sorely needed to gain a better understanding of the possibilities and challenges of the test instruments we use. In particular, creativity may be necessary to design instruments that test sociopragmatics reliably and without expending an excess of time and money.

It would also be very helpful to gain an understanding of how test takers at various ability levels approach various kinds of pragmatics assessment tasks. Developing a knowledge base concerning this question could take assessment of pragmatics a long way towards the targeted and controlled creation of items of various difficulty levels without the obfus-cating influence of overly long prompts or irrelevant/missing important information.

Ultimately, findings from the assessment of interlanguage pragmatics can contribute to a comprehensive theory of pragmatic development in second language learners, which in turn would allow the construction of more well-founded tests. Integrating such pragmatics assessments in comprehensive test batteries will render a more complete picture of test takers' second language competence as a whole.

Notes

1. I am using "testing" or "assessment" in the strict sense to denote efforts at measurements that have real-world consequences for the test takers. This excludes measurements undertaken for research purposes only. I will have more to say about the differences between assessment instruments and research instruments later in this chapter.
2. Knowledge about difficulty can also help generate hypotheses on learners' task processing and their cognitive representation and control of pragmatic knowledge (Bialystok, 1993).

References

Bachman, L. F. (1990) *Fundamental Considerations in Language Testing*. Oxford: Oxford University Press.

Bachman, L. F. (2000) Modern language testing at the turn of the century: Assuring that what we count counts. *Language Testing* 17 (1), 1–42.

Bachman, L. F. and Palmer, A. (1996) *Language Testing in Practice*. Oxford: Oxford University Press.

Bialystok, E. (1993) Symbolic representation and attentional control in pragmatic competence. In G. Kasper and S. Blum-Kulka (eds) *Interlanguage Pragmatics* (pp. 43–59). New York: Oxford University Press.

Billmyer, K. and Varghese, M. (2000) Investigating instrument-based pragmatic variability: Effects of enhancing discourse completion tests. *Applied Linguistics* 21 (4), 517–552.

Bouton, L. (1988) A cross-cultural study of ability to interpret implicatures in English. *World Englishes* 17, 183–196.

Bouton, L. (1994) Conversational implicature in the second language: Learned slowly when not deliberately taught. *Journal of Pragmatics* 22, 157–167.

Bouton, L. (1999) The amenability of implicature to focused classroom instruction. Paper presented at TESOL 1999, New York.

Brown, J. D. (2001) Six types of pragmatics tests in two different contexts. In K. Rose and G. Kasper (eds) *Pragmatics in Language Teaching* (pp. 301–325). New York: Cambridge University Press.

Brown, P. and Levinson, S. D. (1987) *Politeness: Some Universals in Language Usage*. Cambridge: Cambridge University Press.

Canale, M. (1983) From communicative competence to communicative language pedagogy. In J. Richards and R. Schmidt (eds) *Language and Communication* (pp. 2–27). London: Longman.

Canale, M. and Swain, M. (1980) Theoretical bases of communicative approaches to second language teaching and testing. *Applied Linguistics* 1 (1), 1–47.

Clark, H. H. (1979) Responding to indirect speech acts. *Cognitive Psychology* 11, 430–477.

Ebel, R. L. (1964) The social consequences of educational testing. *Proceedings of the 1963 Invitational Conference on Testing Problems* (pp. 130–143). Princeton, NJ: Educational Testing Service.

Fraser, B., Rintell, E. and Walters, J. (1981) An approach to conducting research on the acquisition of pragmatic competence in a second language. In D. Larsen-Freeman (ed.) *Discourse Analysis* (pp. 75–81). Rowley, MA: Newbury House.

Hudson, T. (2001) Indicators for pragmatic instruction: Some quantitative tools. In K. Rose and G. Kasper (eds) *Pragmatics in Language Teaching* (pp. 283–300). New York: Cambridge University Press.

Hudson, T., Detmer, E., and Brown, J. D. (1992) *A Framework for Testing Cross-cultural Pragmatics* (Technical Report #2). Honolulu: University of Hawai'i, Second Language Teaching and Curriculum Center.

Hudson, T., Detmer, E., and Brown, J. D. (1995) *Developing Prototypic Measures of Cross-cultural Pragmatics* (Technical Report #7). Honolulu: University of Hawai'i, Second Language Teaching and Curriculum Center.

Johnston, B., Kasper, G., and Ross, S. (1998) Effect of rejoinders in production questionnaires. *Applied Linguistics* 19 (2), 157–182.

Kasper, G. and Rose, K. R. (forthcoming) *Research Methods in Interlanguage Pragmatics*. Manuscript in preparation.

Leech, G. (1983) *Principles of Pragmatics*. London: Longman.

McNamara, T. (1996) *Measuring Second Language Performance*. London: Longman.

Nunnally, J. C. and Bernstein, I. H. (1994) *Psychometric Theory*. New York: McGraw-Hill.

Roever, C. (2001) A web-based test of interlanguage pragmalinguistic knowledge: Speech acts, routines, implicatures. Unpublished Ph.D. dissertation, University of Hawai'i at Manoa.

Thomas, J. (1983) Cross-cultural pragmatic failure. *Applied Linguistics* 4 (2), 91–112.

Yamashita, S. O. (1996) *Six Measures of JSL Pragmatics* (Technical Report #14). Honolulu: University of Hawai'i, Second Language Teaching and Curriculum Center.

Yoshitake, S. S. (1997) Measuring interlanguage pragmatic competence of Japanese students of English as a foreign language: A multi-test framework evaluation. Unpublished doctoral dissertation, Columbia Pacific University, Novata, CA.

Chapter 13

Assessing Speech Acts in a Second Language

ANDREW D. COHEN

This chapter sketches both earlier and more recent efforts to assess speech act performance and then considers contextual parameters in designing speech act measures, focusing specifically on delineating the setting. Next I look at the issue of authenticity in speech act data, and deal with the effects of both task requirements and of respondents' characteristics on speech act performance. Finally, I discuss the possible roles of verbal report as a means for validating both respondent and rater performance in speech act assessment.

Introduction

Along with a gradual increase in efforts at assessing pragmatic ability in recent years, there have emerged various paradigms for how to conduct the assessment. *Pragmatic ability* has been referred to as the ability to deal with "meaning as communicated by a speaker (or writer) and interpreted by a listener (or reader) ... [and to interpret] people's intended meanings, their assumptions, their purposes or goals, and the kinds of actions (for example, requests) that they are performing when they speak" (Yule, 1996: 3–4). Since the assessment of second language (L2) pragmatics has tended to focus on speech acts, this chapter likewise limits itself to speech acts.

A *speech act* is an utterance which serves as a functional unit in communication. Utterances have two kinds of meaning, their literal or *propositional* meaning in an utterance (e.g. "Where was I when that cell phone rudely interrupted me?" as uttered by a speaker who was just distracted away from his talk) and their functional or *illocutionary* meaning (i.e. the effect that the utterance or written text has on the reader or listener, in the cell phone instance serving as a complaint with the remedy that the participant turn it off so there will not be another similar interruption).

A *speech act set* refers to the set of functional strategies typically used by native speakers of the target language to perform a given speech act (Olshtain & Cohen, 1983). Generally speaking, any of the strategies in a speech act set might be recognized as the speech act in question, depending on the situation and the cultural group involved. So, the indirect request to shut off the phone – "That cell phone ring just distracted me" – could function on its own as a complaint or perhaps would be coupled with other strategies within the same speech act set, namely, a threat: "If you don't turn that cell phone off, I will ask you to leave the talk," and possibly a justification, "It's unfair to the others."

In this chapter, I first look at early and more recent measures of speech act ability. Next, context parameters that have come up or could come up in the design of speech act measures are considered. I then give particular attention to one contextual parameter, namely, the setting for the speech act. Fourth, I discuss what authenticity in speech act data collection might mean and its relative importance in the effort to describe complex speech behavior. Fifth, I consider the effects of the task requirements and of the respondents' characteristics of the resulting performance. Finally, I look at the possible roles of verbal report as a means for validating the performance of both respondents and of raters in speech act assessment. The ultimate question that is pondered in the chapter is whether it is possible to construct a language assessment measure that measures speech act performance accurately.

Historical Background

Early efforts at assessing speech acts in a second language

While descriptions of interlanguage pragmatic behavior such as speech acts began to appear as early as the 1960s, it was in the late 1970s that efforts were initiated to obtain more empirical information about key speech acts such as apologizing, requesting, complimenting, and complaining (see Fraser *et al.*, 1980). The following is a sample prompt from Fraser *et al.* in their early efforts to collect data on the speech act of "requests" from adult Spanish speakers responding in both Spanish as a native language (L1) and English L2, and from English speakers in their L1:

> **Parking Meter Situation**: You have just parked your car in front of the building where you have an appointment for a job interview in five minutes. You reach into your pocket for change for the parking

meter and find you have only a dollar bill. A meter maid is fast approaching. An older woman dressed as a waitress gets out of the car in front of you. You approach her to ask for change. What do you say to her to get her to give you change? (Fraser *et al.*, 1980: 82)

Spurred on by Fraser's pioneering efforts, the 1980s witnessed a shift from an intuitively based, anecdotal description of speech acts to an empirical one (e.g. Farhady, 1980; Cohen & Olshtain, 1981; Blum-Kulka, 1982; Raffaldini, 1988). Such empirically based research, encompassing both quantitative and qualitative approaches, focused on the perception and production of speech acts by learners of a second or foreign language[1] (in most cases, English L2), at varying stages of language proficiency, and in different social interactions. This work had as a principle goal to establish both cross-language and language-specific norms of speech act behavior, in an effort to better understand and evaluate L2 development.

An early effort at assessing speech act sets that this author was engaged in along with Elite Olshtain (Cohen & Olshtain, 1981) originated out of our frustration at the impressionistic and imprecise manner in which *sociocultural*[2] and *sociolinguistic*[3] abilities were being assessed. The challenge was to identify for each speech act the set of strategies typically used by native speakers of the target language. So, for example, in American English, the expression of apology may be a sufficient strategy for smoothing over ruffled feathers in an e-mail exchange with a friend: "I'm really sorry for that senseless e-mail I sent you." Likewise, the strategy of offering an explanation or an excuse, "The bus was late," when an employee arrives late for a meeting in Israel, may be accepted by the boss as enough of an apology, since buses are known to arrive late and consequently employees are only partially responsible for getting to meetings on time.

The instrument used for this study constituted one of the first discourse completion tasks for assessing adult L2 language learners' performance. The measure was also used to collect baseline data from natives of English and of Hebrew. The following are three of the apology situations from that measure (Cohen & Olshtain, 1981):

1. You completely forget a crucial meeting at the office with your boss. An hour later you call him to apologize. The problem is that this is the second time you've forgotten such a meeting. Your boss gets on the line and asks, "What happened to you?" You:

2. You forget a get-together with a friend. You call him to apologize. This is already the second time you've forgotten such a meeting. Your friend asks over the phone: "What happened?" You:

3. You call from work to find out how things are at home and your kid reminds you that you forgot to take him shopping, as you had promised. And this is the second time that this has happened. Your kid says over the phone, "Oh, you forgot again and you promised!" You:

In that preliminary work, nonnatives were assigned a point for each instance where they used a speech act strategy in a given situation where the findings showed that the group as a whole underused this strategy in comparison to native speakers. The nonnatives were also assigned a point in instances of "intensifying an expression of regret" as natives did, again where the nonnative group as a whole did not.

Another early effort at developing an assessment measure of L2 pragmatic ability was that of Farhady (1980), who constructed a multiple-choice measure of speech act ability in English L2 for his doctoral dissertation at UCLA. He devised a functional L2 test that had multiple-choice items that were both *stylistically* (linguistically) and *culturally* appropriate, and those that were unacceptable on one or the other grounds.

Toward the end of the 1980s, a study appeared which documented what Olshtain and I had observed at the beginning of the decade, namely, that tests like the Oral Proficiency Interview (OPI) were not measuring much in the way of sociolinguistic ability (Raffaldini, 1988). The study claimed that the American Council on the Teaching of Foreign Languages (ACTFL)/Educational Testing Service (ETS) OPI had failed to measure important aspects of communicative ability, such as being persuasive and sociable, or displaying emotions such as annoyance. Raffaldini viewed the interchanges as artificial because they were not directed toward a particular outcome. She developed both multiple-choice and oral situation tests to tap these areas, and tried them out on 60 American university students back from a year of learning French abroad. A comparison of these tests with the OPI showed that, whereas the OPI evaluated numerous aspects of grammatical competence and certain aspects of discourse competence (e.g. grammatical and lexical features in cohesive discourse), it did not assess what she referred to as *sociolinguistic competence* (which actually encompassed both sociocultural and sociolinguistic abilities, as defined in this chapter; cf. notes 2 and 3).

Raffaldini asserted that the "Situation Tests" which she developed did tap the area of sociolinguistic competence. Her multiple-choice test was aimed at assessing what respondents felt they should say in a given situation. Drawing on Canale and Swain's categories for communicative competence (1980), she rated the oral test responses according to: (1)

discourse competence: how well the discourse function was expressed and the factual information was conveyed in both a cohesive and coherent manner; (2) *sociolinguistic competence*: the sociolinguistic appropriateness and tone of the response; and (3) *grammatical competence*: the accuracy of linguistic structures, lexical precision, and overall fluency. The conclusion was that these tests assessed more areas of language proficiency in a wider range of language-use situations than the OPI. The following are two sample situations from Raffaldini's *Oral Situation Test* (1988):

> *Tone:* persuasive; *Stimulus:* You will be leaving France in a few weeks and all the students in the program would like to get together for a final party. The only place big enough is the house where you are living. You ask the parents if you can have the party there. You say:

> *Tone:* annoyed; *Stimulus:* The parents of the family with whom you are living have gone away for the day and left you in charge of their little boy. He went out to play and disappeared for quite a while. You went out looking for him but couldn't find him. When he finally returns you are upset at what he has done and tell him not to do it again. You say:

Given the series of empirical speech act studies that were conducted in the 1980s, it was possible by the beginning of the 1990s to review a growing literature on speech acts. However, the focus of the studies has primarily not been that of developing speech assessment measures, but rather one of conducting research in order to describe speech act behavior. This turns out to be an important distinction since, as is made clear below, we arrive at the twenty-first century without being able to point to that many current measures for assessing speech act ability. This dichotomy between measures that are meant for research as opposed to those intended for assessment of learners' general proficiency or achievement in a given course of instruction has been the focus of attention in recent years – for example, a series of papers discussing the interfaces between second language acquisition (SLA) and language testing research appeared in the late 1990s (Bachman & Cohen, 1998). Nonetheless, speech act measures continue to be mostly for research purposes rather than for the assessment of instructional outcomes.

With regard to the research on speech acts, in what was then the most extensive literature review available on the topic of research methods for studying speech acts, Kasper and Dahl (1991) described the measures for collection of research data in 39 studies of interlanguage pragmatics and the acquisition of L2 speech act knowledge. Data collection instruments were distinguished according to: (a) whether prompts called for closed, guided, or open-ended responses; and (b) whether the prompts tapped speech act comprehension or production. The authors questioned the validity of each type of data collection method in terms of its adequacy in approximating authentic performance of linguistic ability. They provided a taxonomy of measures starting at the "perception side" – that is, from the vantage point of the recipient of the speech act. These measures called for ratings, multiple-choice responses, and interview tasks. Such measures usually involved both looking at respondents' reactions to videotaped role-play, to screen plays (from TV series), or to written descriptions of speech act situations, and collecting these reactions by means of written questionnaires or verbal report interviews.

The Kasper and Dahl (1991) taxonomy also included measures on the "production side" – that is, where the deliverer of the speech act was (1) simply observed in the process of engaging in authentic discourse; (2) had to fill out a written discourse completion; or (3) had to conduct oral role-play. As measures of speech act production, investigators used observation of naturally occurring data when the desired speech act data were amenable to such observation. In addition, they made use of both open and closed discourse completion tasks, role-play, and verbal report interviews to get "behind the scenes" information about the production of the speech acts. With regard to verbal report, respondents were asked to reconstruct retrospectively (while viewing their own videotaped speech act performance) the processes that they went through and the strategies that they selected in performing the given speech acts (Cohen & Olshtain, 1993; Cohen, 1998: 238–256). More will be said about verbal report below.

The very complexity of certain speech acts such as requesting, complaining, or apologizing provided researchers with a daunting challenge. Ultimately researchers found that in order to describe speech act production in a rigorous way, for example, it was necessary to use a multi-method approach since a single approach was not deemed adequate for assessing the entirety of the behavior in question. So, the challenge was to effectively combine different approaches to description of the same speech act among both native and nonnative speakers of a language. Wolfson (1989) and her colleagues stressed the importance of collecting naturally occurring data through observation of both L1 and L2 speech act behavior, and they illustrated this by collecting data on, for example, complimenting. They felt that such data constituted an important source for hypotheses about how speech acts are actually performed. They argued that these natural data could form the basis and then elicited data could be added through role-play simulations and other means.

One problem with this approach was that it limited the scope of data collection both in terms of the speech acts that could readily be investigated and whether the investigation was within one language or across languages. In fact, it was often not possible, not feasible, or not easy to collect naturally occurring data from the same interlocutors in the L1 and the L2. Consequently, elicitation tasks attained a level of popularity that has continued to the present time. The following are some of the early formats for collecting simulated data, again primarily for the purpose of research, not that of assessing learners' general proficiency in speech acts or their achievement at dealing with them in a given course of instruction. The first was an open-ended oral or written completion task, consisting of a situation description:

> This is not the first time that your neighbor has played loud music late at night, and you have to get up early the next morning. Role-play the part of the irate person who knocks on the door of the noise maker. I will play the role of the neighbor, an avid music lover who is also partially deaf.

The second was a discourse situation description plus the remark of an interlocutor which was to be responded to:

> You promised to return a textbook to your classmate within a day or two, after xeroxing a chapter. You held onto it for almost two weeks. Classmate: I'm really upset about the book because I needed it to prepare for last week's class.
> You:

The third was like the second but with one or more rejoinders that the respondent needed to take into consideration (Blum-Kulka, 1982):

> You arranged to meet a friend in order to study together for an exam. You arrive half an hour late for the meeting.
> Friend (annoyed): I've been waiting at least half an hour for you!
> You:
>
> ---
> Friend: Well, I was standing here waiting. I could have been doing something else.
> You:
>
> ---
> Friend: Still, it's pretty annoying. Try to come on time next time.

The development of tasks such as these allowed researchers to focus on specific speech act realizations and allowed them to manipulate the social and situational variables. If investigators were concerned with the impact of the speech act on the recipient (referred to as its *prelocutionary force*), then they used questionnaires to get at the perception of videotaped speech act interactions. Likewise, they could follow up with an interview in order to provide further insights regarding the production or perception of naturally occurring data, role-play data, or discourse-completion data.

Let us now consider more recent efforts at designing instruments for collecting speech act data, both with a focus on gathering research data and, importantly, with an eye to possible applications to the classroom.

More recent efforts at assessing speech act ability

More recently, the field has evolved such that there are now more rigorous batteries of instruments for assessing speech act ability. While these batteries have primarily been used for research purposes, the potential use of portions of such instruments in language classrooms is open for investigation. An important consideration is one of feasibility, since some of the subtests may be too labor intensive to make them practical for the classroom.

The most rigorous set of studies of speech act perception and production were those conducted at the University of Hawai'i (Hudson *et al.*, 1992, 1995). The speech act measures that they devised were on a continuum from totally free to totally cued, focusing on requests, refusals, and apologies as their speech acts of focus because there was a robust cross-cultural literature. The coding scheme for analyzing refusals was a revision of both the scheme developed by Blum-Kulka *et al.* (1989: 37–70) and that by Beebe and colleagues (Beebe & Takahashi, 1989; Beebe *et al.*, 1990). The power of the speaker vis-à-vis the listener, the social distance between the speaker and the listener with respect to familiarity and solidarity, and the degree of imposition caused by the speech act situation were the three sociocultural variables of concern because these three had emerged as independent and culturally sensitive variables in pilot work. The responses were rated for: (1) ability to use the correct speech act; (2) typicality of expressions; (3) appropriateness of amount of speech and information given; (4) level of formality; (5) directness; and (6) politeness.

While pilot results for native and advanced L2 speakers generally showed that the two groups came out similar in the more commonly used strategies, the researchers were dissatisfied that a native-speaker standard was being used to judge nonnative-speaker performance. In fact, they considered it problematic to arrive at a so-called "standard" native-speaking model. In addition, they encountered three kinds of problems with their prototype measures: (1) at times the tasks elicited the wrong speech act; (2) at times the respondents opted out rather than performing any speech act; and (3) the respondents sometimes misinterpreted the relationships of relative power, social distance, and absolute ranking of imposition (Hudson *et al.*, 1995: 14). In addition, the researchers called attention to the need to avoid testing for acting ability (Hudson *et al.*, 1995: 49).

What ultimately emerged from the pilot work at the University of Hawai'i were six measures: *written discourse completion task, multiple-choice discourse completion test, oral discourse completion task, discourse role-play task, discourse self-assessment task,* and *role-play self-assessment* (through rating their own performance viewed on videotape) (Brown, 2001). Brown notes that these prototype speech act tests that he designed and constructed along with his two colleagues (Hudson *et al.*, 1992, 1995) were tried out in two doctoral studies – an English version of the battery with 25 EFL students at a university in Tokyo (Yoshitake, 1997) and a translated and culturally adapted Japanese version with English-speaking learners of Japanese at four universities, two in Japan ($N=34$) and two in the US ($N=13$) (Yamashita, 1996).

The battery took about three hours for paid volunteer students to complete. The English and the Japanese versions of the tests were largely mirror images of each other, although the situations in the Japanese version were altered slightly so that they would be culturally appropriate. The following is a description of the instruments that were used in both studies. These instruments included both direct and indirect measures of the speech acts, and both open-response and selected-response type tests:

(1) *Self-assessment of performance by situation*: the description was given in the L1 and the respondents were asked to think to themselves about what they would most likely say in the target language in each situation. With this in mind, they were then asked to rate themselves on a five-point scale, placing themselves on a continuum for having what they would say being completely appropriate on the plus side to having it be very unsatisfactory on the minus side. For example, if the respondent knew how to request that an item be lifted out of a case for closer examination, then s/he would rate him/herself a 4 or a 5, depending.

> "You are shopping for your friend's birthday and see something in a display case. You want to look at it more closely. A sales-clerk comes over to you."
> Rating: I think what I would say in this situation would be . . .
>   very unsatisfactory 1 – 2 – 3 – 4 – 5 completely appropriate

(2) *Listening lab oral production test*: the participants listened to brief tape-recorded descriptions of situations and then had to tape-record their open-ended response for each situation. The following is an example of a request that the respondent was asked to make:

> "You are on an airplane. It is dinner time. The flight attendant sets your food on your tray. You need a napkin."

The requesting behavior in this situation and the speech act behavior in the other situations were rated by three natives on scales for (a) the appropriateness of the speech act for the given situation, (b) the use of formulaic expressions (typical speech, gambits), (c) the appropriateness of the amount of speech and/or information for the given situation, and the appropriateness of (d) the level of formality, (e) degree of directness, and (f) the level of politeness for the given situation.

(3) *Written open discourse completion test*: the respondents produced in writing what they thought they would say in a given situation. These responses were also rated by three natives on the six categories used for the oral production test.

(4) *Videotaped oral role-plays*: for each scenario, respondents were provided descriptions about *who, when, where,* and *with whom* they were to conduct the role-play, which including performing three different speech acts (e.g. an apology, a request, and a refusal). Also, the three speech act situations, each calling for a different speech act in the scenario, were listed in numerical fashion so that the participants would know what they were to say next. Some key words were provided in the target language. Role-plays were conducted with a native speaker of the target language and two to three minutes of preparation time were given. Three native raters rated each role-play response on a five-point scale from very unsatisfactory to completely appropriate.

> E.g. "You go to apply for a new job in a small company at 11:30.
>
> (1) You see and greet the personnel manager but accidentally startle him and he drops some papers on the floor.
> (2) You need to schedule an interview in a morning because you currently work in the afternoons.
> (3) After arranging a morning interview, the personnel manager suggests you come with him on a tour around the company now. But you have to go back to work by 1:00 today."

(5) *Self-assessment of the video-taped role-play:* participants rated their own role-play videotape immediately upon finishing the role-plays to rate the appropriateness of each situation on the same five-point scale.

(6) *Multiple-choice discourse completion test*: the respondents selected their answer from three possible responses for each situation. This measure was administered last so as not to give respondents ideas for how to answer the other subtests.

The results for the English and Japanese versions of the speech act test batteries differed to some extent across languages. Five of the six subtest measures were found to be reasonably reliable. The only subtest that was unreliable – in both language versions – was the multiple-choice one. It proved to be the easiest in the EFL battery, with speculation that it was because Japanese respondents are used to doing these kinds of tests (Brown, 2001). In the piloting of the EFL multiple-choice subtest of speech act behavior, several native Japanese-speaking respondents had reported to the researcher "that they were very frustrated because there seemed to be no correct answer to select in many situations" (Yamashita, 1996: 57). For example, in some of the situations, the natives indicated that they would have wanted to use the strategies of *showing dismay* ("What do I do?") or *hinting* ("Uh, well, there is more to be said but . . ."), and that these were not included as options on the multiple-choice subtest. The researcher concluded that inappropriate options may have caused the low reliability of the Japanese version, which was in fact a translation of the English one. So, not surprisingly, the Japanese version came out with short sentences, similar to the English one. Yet on both the open discourse completion and listening lab production tasks, Japanese respondents produced longer utterances (than they were given on the multiple-choice items), involving strategies such as showing dismay or hinting in the situations where the imposition was great and were they were in a subordinate position in terms of power.

Along with the information on reliability or the lack thereof, Brown (2001) also reported validity information for the test batteries. For example, he assessed the *construct validity* of the instrument, namely, the degree to which the various subtests in the speech acts battery permitted inferences about the underlying traits (in this case, the ability to perform apologies, requests, and refusals). He used as his measure of construct validity the factor loadings for the various subtests, as resulting from factor analysis. He found that the subtests did not correlate highly with each other, which he interpreted as meaning that they were measuring different things. In this case, he argued that it was desirable for the subtests to be measuring different things.

The three measures in the Yamashita study (1996) that assessed language production – the written discourse completion task, the audio-taped language lab discourse completion task, and the role-play of scenarios – were found to produce different results for the three different speech acts (Hudson, 2001). Refusals were found to be rated lower than apologies and requests, a finding which Hudson interpreted as indicating that refusals were more difficult to negotiate. Apologies were found to be the easiest speech act to perform and a possible explanation given for this finding was that they were seen as more formulaic. Regarding the difficulty of the several language production tasks, role-plays were found to be the easiest and the language lab production test the most difficult.

Now that we have looked at one of the more recent speech act batteries, let us turn to the issue of contextual parameters and consider how each of these parameters may influence the speech act assessment process.

Contextual Parameters for Speech Act Assessment

In this section we consider contextual factors that could have some bearing on speech act performance and consequently are worthy of attention. These factors would apply to speech act measures intended not only for research, but also for those measures intended to be used in assessing speech act performance in the classroom.

In his book on assessing language for specific purposes (Douglas, 2000) and to some extent in his chapter for this volume, Douglas reminds us of the continued relevance of the contextual parameters established by Hymes (1974) over 25 years ago, noting that these parameters still have keen relevance to current assessment needs as well: *setting, participants, purposes, form and content, tone, language, norms of interaction,* and *genre.* Douglas then updates these parameters with regard to assessment for specific purposes, basing some of his suggestions on the work of Kramsch (1993: 94ff). I would note that certain features of these eight parameters also have relevance to the assessment of speech act ability, which is in some ways a "specific purpose," although the same speech act may undoubtedly be performed similarly across situations (e.g. apologizing to a patient in the hospital or to a client in a welfare office or to a patron in a movie theater).

With regard to *setting,* Douglas underscores the importance of providing detailed description in the prompt, realistic drawings or photographs, and even sound effects through audiovisual backup. In addition, information about the time of day (or night), day of the week, or season might be valuable. (More will be said about "setting" in the next section.) As concerns the *participants*, Douglas encourages the test developer to identify the participants clearly and in some detail – as professor, fellow student, close friend, colleague, or whatever. He adds that information about age, gender, and personality might also be relevant, depending on the type of inferences one wished to make about language ability. He suggests that the behavior of the recipient(s) of the communication (in our case, speech acts) could be varied, as well. For example, the test task could be addressed to a listener who constantly asks for clarification, one who shows interest by asking questions, one who shows boredom, and so on. Finally, he notes that the number of participants is relevant, since performance may vary depending on whether an individual or a large group is being addressed, for example.

With respect to the *purposes* for the interaction, Douglas recommends that the specific purpose for carrying out a task needs to be made clear in the prompt – beyond the obvious testing purpose of eliciting a performance for evaluation. With regard to *form and content*, the researcher needs to select topics for speech act situations that will "work." What this means is selecting situations that will not offend the respondents, such as attempting to use a babysitting situation with Japanese respondents for whom the practice may be so uncommon that they would not know how to deal with it. In addition, the test constructors need to select rhetorical forms that are appropriate to use for the language prompts or interactions in the given situation. As Douglas points out, the rhetorical form of the message is often as important as the content, and should reflect the norms of the target language use situation. Concerning *tone*, the use of anger, irony, humor, or sarcasm may play a significant role in the situation, and the respondent could be asked to pay attention to tone in either performing a speech act (as Raffaldini, 1988, had indicated in her earlier work) or in reacting to one. The test constructor might wish to consider how fair it is to include tone as a feature in the assessment, given the difficulty that nonnatives may have in perceiving its use correctly.

Regarding *language*, Douglas rightly notes that the input for the given task can vary in channel (whether aural or visual) and responses can vary in modality (whether written or spoken), and both can vary as to vehicle (whether live or taped), language/dialect (whether in the target or in the native language), and register (whether in an academic or technical or register or not). Not only can respondents be asked to carry out the same or similar tasks in two modalities so as to get a fuller picture of their speech act abilities, but also language features can be combined in tasks: test takers can, for example, be instructed to write out their responses and then to present them orally from notes. In addition, the language to be perceived or produced in a speech act task could call for knowledge of specific dialects, registers, formulaic and sometimes idiomatic expressions, as well as appropriate references to culturally specific material. The respondents may need to rate speech samples for naturalness (in perception tasks) or for how natural they sound in that situation (in production tasks).

With respect to *norms of interaction*, Douglas underscores the importance of providing sufficient information about setting and participants so that respondents would be able to make appropriate decisions about norms of interaction. The assumption is that test takers would be expected to perform differently (in terms of forms of address, turn taking routines, interruptions, and politeness forms) when the interlocutor is a professor rather than a fellow student, or when speaking to a medical colleague rather than a patient. Needless to say, these distinctions may be so fine-tuned that teachers may be reluctant to teach these distinctions and to assess for them. Likewise, perhaps only the most advanced of L2 students might actually adjust their speech act performance to conform to the norms of interaction in the given context.

Finally, concerning *genre*, speech act situations are usually restricted to oral and written interactions between two people, but they may reflect a carefully planned telephone or oral complaint to a superior in a corporation, or a casually uttered apology to a complete stranger in a crowded train station. Actually, it may be the task of the respondent to preserve the oral genre, even though the task calls for using written language as a measure of *projected speech*.

In the next section we take a closer look at the contextual parameter of setting.

Delineating the Setting in Speech Act Studies

Experience has shown that, among the contextual parameters listed above, the specific contextual situation or setting is an especially crucial one. Zuskin (1993a), for example, noted that, while the communicative objectives of discourse completion tasks (DCT) as a speech acts measuring tool may be in line with pragmatic principles, she contended that their contextual aspects required better development in order to convey more about the interlocutors' relationship (status and positional identities). She designed a study in which the focus was on the perception of speech act realizations by native and nonnative speakers, and in which the situations were contextualized through videotaped vignettes which served as prompts in place of written prompts (Zuskin, 1993b). The native and nonnative respondents were asked to interpret the interactions in 12 DCT vignettes involving apologies, requests, refusals, and complaints (e.g. "a female college student complaining to a female neighbor about her inability to study because of the neighbor's loud party music"). The respondents rated each vignette according to three sociolinguistic criteria: (1) the degree of *status inequality* between the main two characters in the scene; (2) the degree of *formality* designated by the situation; and (3) the degree of *imposition* on the interlocutor who was expected to produce a specific speech act.

Quantitative and qualitative data were collected from 63 native-English-speaking respondents and from 103 nonnative-speaking respondents at the University of New Mexico. The study examined the overlap between grammatical and sociolinguistic proficiency and the extent to which male–female subcultural norms influence perceptions about politeness. The study found gender differences on three of the vignettes and significant differences between natives and nonnatives on the imposition scale for several vignettes. The researcher concluded as follows:

> By enriching the test with cues more effectively delivered with video technology – cues such as gestures, facial expressions, pitch changes and stress patterns – the crucial connection of past L1 sociocultural experiences with L2 communicative interactions in the here and now can be made. . . . The video based version DCT used in this work offers viewers more information on which to base their sociolinguistic judgments. (Zuskin, 1993a: 87–88)

In cases where video prompts would be infeasible for a host of possible reasons, then other researchers would highlight the advantages of enhancing the written prompts. Varghese and Billmyer (1996), for example, found that the amount of detail in the prompt for request situations on the DCT made a significant difference in the nature of the response. This study of requesting behavior involved 55 native speakers of American English, with one group getting a version with information on the requestive goal, social distance, and social dominance; another group getting the same *plus* the gender of the interlocutor, the role relationship, the length of acquaintance, the frequency of their interaction, whether the relationship was optional, and a description of the setting; and a third group getting the same *extended* prompt as well as being asked to reflect on each situation for 30 seconds before responding.

Varghese and Billmyer found that, while the *head act request strategy* was not affected by extra information and wait time, the extended prompt yielded benefits: (1) the mean length of the request act was two to three times greater in the second and third versions than in the first; (2) there were two to three times more *supportive moves* (e.g. an aggravating or miti-gating utterance) in the last two versions; and (3) there was also three times more use of alerters (i.e. warning the hearer of an upcoming speech act) in the last two versions. The interpretation of the researchers was that a typical DCT situation does not bring out the real dynamics of natural interaction between members of a group because respondents are addressing an anonymous fictional character and there is no motivation to establish or preserve a relationship. Yet, as Roever (Chapter 12, this volume) points out, long prompts may be difficult to construct and then equally difficult for the respondents to read through.

A compromise between the videotaped prompt and an enhanced written one would be, for example, a picture or slide. Lyster (1994) used this approach in order to assess sociolinguistic competence among French immersion students. The study looked at the effect of having three French immersion teachers teach *sociostylistic variation* (e.g. the *tu–vous* distinc-tion) for five weeks to their eighth-graders during French language arts. The pre-post measures included an oral production test which involved having the students view slides of people in specific contexts and then perform five different speech acts (requesting or giving directions, requesting help in math, offering to help carry books) in a formal context (with unknown adults, with the school librarian, and with a math teacher) and in an informal context (with peers). The findings showed improvement in the experimental group's ability in oral production to appropriately and accurately use *vous* in formal situations.

While any enhancement may make the task more authentic, we must remember it is still a task attempting to simulate reality. With regard to videotaped prompts, for example, Douglas (2000: 275) made the following comment:

> . . . delivery of videotaped scenes of a teacher at work in a classroom or of a supervisor talking to an employee on a shop floor are no doubt an improvement over formats in which test takers are instructed to imagine the same situations, but such input delivery formats should not be considered to be substitutes for the real thing. The problem here is not so much a matter of unrealistic testing techniques as it is one of caution in the interpretations that are made based on performance on tests enhanced by technology. This is clearly a validity issue.

By the same token, however, Kasper (1999: 73) reminds us that "inau-thentic" does not necessarily meaning "invalid," since it depends on how judiciously the data are collected. And this is a most important message to remember, since most forms of language assessment are by their very nature a departure from unelicited, natural language production.

In Pursuit of Authentic Data

It is unquestionably a challenge to collect data approximating authentic performance of linguistic actions (Kasper & Dahl, 1991) and especially to assess spoken speech act performance in an L2 (for more on this, see Roever, Chapter 12 this volume). Kasper (1999: 74) cautions about the get-your-data-and-run type of authentic data collection; even in observation of naturally occurring data, there is the possibility of an initial reaction to the presence of the data collector (remembering Labov, 1972, and the observer's paradox). In the pursuit of Wolfson *et al.*'s (1989) call for the collection of naturally occurring data, daunting problems have been encountered. For example, Murillo *et al.* (1991) detailed how difficult it was for them to unobtrusively collect provoked apologies. Still, there are examples of naturalistic data having been collected over time, with positive results. For instance, Bardovi-Harlig and Hartford (1996) successfully collected extensive naturalistic[4] data from academic advising sessions.

Duff and Li (2000) highlighted the importance of extended observation and of notebook research, underscoring Wolfson's claim that, to get a genuine understanding of a speech act, ethnographically gathered data are needed. Li (1998) focused on requesting among five Chinese women who had immigrated to the US, and found that requests needed to be looked at over time because of their complexity. She noted that, while stakes might generally be low in classroom requests, real-world stakes could be much higher – for example, the request for a second opinion at a hospital or the request to speak to a supervisor. Li found the experiences of one of these women, Ming, to be especially insightful (Li, 2000). Data on Ming were recorded through audiotaping of daily interactions, the researcher's journaling, the participant's journaling, ESL essays, and formal and informal oral interviews. Ming was observed to use very indirect request patterns which Li attributed to her upbringing in China. Her indirectness made it difficult for interlocutors to know whether she was requesting anything. Critical incidents with Ming included her requesting information about a job, information on what to say in an interview, help at work, and adequate working space.

In the next section we look at two factors that have been seen to have an impact on the speech act data, namely, the influence of the task itself on the responses and also the effects of characteristics of the respondents.

Again, while the emphasis in the literature has clearly been on data collected for research purposes, the characteristics of the task and of the given respondents are bound to influence the results from speech act measures used for language assessment purposes as well.

The Effect of Task Requirements and of Respondents' Characteristics on Performance

A question that prevails with any language assessment measure, and all the more so with pragmatic measures that produce variable data under the best of circumstances, is the extent to which the data collected are to some extent an artifact of the task itself. That is why Brown (2001) and Hudson (2001) were both interested in comparing results across subtests and across languages, and, as indicated above, they found some differences that were, in fact, attributable to the particular instrument itself. Recall, for example, that they found their multiple-choice subtest to be a different kind of activity from the other tasks and considerably easier for the Japanese EFL respondents.

Let us explore the issue of differences across tasks a bit more closely now. In contrasting an *open-ended speech act production questionnaire* with a *multiple-choice questionnaire*, Kasper (1999: 85) noted that open-ended speech production requires that the respondents perform a sometimes challenging search of their memory and then select the appropriate forms from a wide array of possible solutions. Multiple-choice tasks, on the other hand, call only for evaluating a small number of presented alternatives against the respondents' memory structures for such speech events.

Another comparison that Kasper makes is between open role-play and written response. While *open role-plays* approximate authentic interactions in that there is the full operation of turn-taking, sequencing of moves, and negotiation of meaning, *written response* may allow for perhaps more thoughtful response, possibly more indicative of a speaker's competence (Kasper & Dahl, 1991: 228–229). Also pointing out the merits of written response, Beebe and Cummings (1996) noted that, while written discourse completion tasks do not have the repetitions, the number of turns, the length of responses, the emotional depth, and other features of natural speech, they do provide a good sense of the stereotypical shape of the speech act through rapid collection of large amounts of data, which can furnish both the researcher with an initial classification of strategies. These data could likewise be informative to the classroom teacher/tester who wants a snapshot sense of whether the respondent can capture this routinized behavior on paper. In an effort to render the DCT's more reflective of authentic exchanges, Bardovi-Harlig and Hartford (1993) would recommend that they be designed so that they have more conversational turns in the tasks.

Not only do we need to take into account the features of the speech act tasks themselves, but also the characteristics of the given respondents. Respondents may perform differently on given speech act tasks, depending on their age, gender, sociocultural background, socioeconomic status (SES), learning style preferences, or test-taking strategy preferences. For example, older respondents as well as those with higher SES may use certain conventional politeness strategies that are less prevalent among younger respondents (e.g. "would you be so kind as to . . ."). Females may be more indirect in requests to males than they are to females. It may also be the case that respondents with a more extroverted style are more comfortable doing oral role-play than are more introverted learners. Likewise, the introverts may prefer rating speech acts for appropriateness more than having to produce them in writing themselves. Finally, for some respondents, their test-taking strategies would include a minimalist approach under any circumstances – to generate only the data that they absolutely have to, and not to embellish their speech act response even though it might elucidate what they were intending to say. Then there are others who might take a shotgun approach to oral output on open-ended tasks – namely, to say as much as they possibly can, with the hope that "the correct answer" is going to be contained somewhere in their response.

In the final section we consider a potentially valuable tool for gathering data from respondents and raters on the rationale for their responses and their ratings respectively, namely, the use of verbal report.

Verbal Report as a Means for Validating Both Respondent and Rater Performance in Speech Act Assessment

After the more traditional means of determining reliability and validity of speech act measures have been calculated, there may also be some value in using verbal report as a complement the other forms of data – as a means of triangulation. Kasper and Dahl (1991) called attention to the usefulness of *retrospective verbal report*[5] for better determining the nature of possible transfer from L1 norms of speech behavior in nonnative L2 speech act performance. In fact, a series of studies have employed retrospective verbal report out of a concern for cross-cultural inquiry (Frescura, 1993; Cohen & Tarone, 1994; Arent, 1996; Tateyama *et al.*, 1997;

Nakahama, 1998). In addition, a few studies (e.g. Cohen & Olshtain (1993) and to some extent Robinson (1992) and Widjaja (1997)) have used retrospective verbal report to reconstruct psycholinguistic processes that the speakers utilized in an effort to produce the given speech acts in given situations. These kinds of data can be instrumental in better understanding the products of such elicitation techniques. We may learn what the respondents actually perceived about each situation (e.g. what they perceived about the relative role status of the interlocutors) and how their perceptions influenced their responses, what they wanted to say vs. what they actually said, how they planned out their responses, and what they thought of the social event of going through the tasks altogether.

In addition to finding out more about how learners respond to speech act tasks, there may be value in collecting verbal report from the raters. Since a portion of those measures used to assess speech act ability call for ratings by trained raters, it must be noted that the act of rating involves a difficult balancing act at best. Raters must interpret and apply the assessment criteria in a way that is true to the test's underlying framework of speech act ability and also in a way that they are able to reconcile with their own intuitions (Reed & Cohen, 2001). Moreover, raters must perform this difficult balancing act in as consistent a manner as possible. Research has shown, for example, that whether raters are native speakers of the language may influence what they rate for and how harsh they are in their ratings. In addition, the gender of the rater and the personality fit between the rater and the respondents may be a factor.

Verbal report from raters may provide a better understanding of how raters actually react to and evaluate samples of performance, whether consistent with, or at variance with, a test's explicit criteria. If these data are collected in a highly responsible way (see Cohen, 1998: 34–39, 49–61), verbal report data could be a beneficial source of complementary data in a number of contexts: while raters discuss the criteria during initial collaborative sessions to establish potential criteria; during training, while they rate alone or with a partner; and again later, while they are reconsidering taped performances and negotiating ratings with other stakeholders in the assessment measure.

Conclusions

This chapter has attempted not only to review and describe the kinds of assessment measures available for measuring speech act performance, but also to highlight some of the challenges associated with this work (as does Roever in Chapter 12, this volume). Thanks especially to the work of researchers such as Hudson *et al.* (1995), we have a relatively extensive panoply of options for assessing speech acts as a manifestation of language pragmatics. In addition, extensive descriptions of some of the more complex speech acts are now available. For example, at the University of Minnesota's Center for Advanced Research on Language Acquisition (CARLA), a website has been set up where information on speech acts (so far, apologizing, complaining, complimenting, thanking, and refusing) has been painstakingly distilled from analysis of numerous studies available in the literature (carla.acad.umn.edu/speechacts/teaching.html). While this material is intended for teachers and researchers, units for learner self-access are now available for intermediate learners of Japanese (www.iles.umn.edu/introtospeechacts/) and future work will entail developing units for learners of Spanish.

Despite the greater access than ever before to information about speech acts, the question still arises as to whether we know enough about them at this point in time to be able to adequately assess their performance in an L2 classroom setting. The problem is that sociocultural and sociolinguistic behavior are by their very nature variable. Thus, there will be few "right" and "wrong" answers in comparing L2 to L1 responses, but rather tendencies in one direction or another. Based on a review of the apology literature, for example, Meier (1998) came to the conclusion that there existed a less than unified picture of "facts" about apology behavior. She noted that there were conflicting claims regarding the distribution of strategies, the degree of mitigation effected by account types, the co-occurrence of strategy types, the effect of the severity of the offense, the effect of gender, and the effect of the interlocutor relationship. She thus concluded that attempts to provide a summary description of apology behavior in English based on such lack of consensus could only be arbitrary, vague, or disjointed.

While Meier (1998) may have been overstating her case, she raised an important issue as to how much knowledge it is necessary to have about a certain language behavior in order to assess it. The burden is both on the SLA researchers to fine-tune our descriptions of speech acts, as well as on teachers and test constructors to create assessment measures that are sensitive to acceptable measurement paradigms as spelled out in this chapter.

The variable nature of speech act behavior has made tested outcomes less reliable and valid than those for more circumscribed language performance and helps explain why such measures do not abound in the field. Hudson (2001) would recommend, for example, that more research be conducted to address the variability of native-speaker performance since this is the benchmark against which we are judging nonnative speech act performance. The very fact that the field of language pragmatics continues to develop means that paradigms continue to shift and consequently language assessment measures must be constructed consistent with the newly emerging patterns. So, the question remains as to whether it is possible to construct a language assessment measure that accurately determines success at performance of speech acts. And in a truly socio-linguistic fashion, we would have to respond, "It depends."

Since this volume is on how research on L2 speaking can inform class-room instruction, we must ask the hard-nosed question as to how the information in this chapter can inform the classroom teacher. Do teachers of an L2 have the relative luxury that a doctoral student has to spend inordinate hours designing, constructing, and administering large batteries of pragmatic assessment measures, such as those designed in Hawai'i by Yamashita? What would be the purpose of introducing into a classroom setting the highly rigorous and comprehensive measures such as Yamashita's battery? Would it serve for classroom instruction? Hudson (2001) cautions that the six measures in their battery, for example, should be used at this stage for research and not to make decisions about the pragmatic ability of language learners in pedagogical settings.

My own inclination is to encourage classroom teachers to engage in the assessment of speech acts. Their measures may not be rigorous in a research sense, but there may be real value in classroom assessment of this kind. For one thing, it indicates to the learners that the performance of speech acts such as requesting, apologizing, and complaining is of enough significance to warrant attention on tests. Even if the teacher's criteria for assessing the performance are not elaborate as in a research study, the point is made to the students that the behavior being assessed is worthy of such assessment. The students themselves could engage in the evaluation process so that the responsibility is shared. The teacher and the students together can check to see if the appropriate sociocultural strategies within the speech act set have been selected and whether the appropriate sociolinguistic forms have been enlisted in the response.

So let us end this chapter with a few tips both for teachers and students, based on the points in this chapter:

(1) Keep the speech act situations realistic (for the learner group) and engaging.
(2) Check for key aspects of performance such as:
    (a) the sociocultural appropriateness of the strategies in the given situation (that is, whether a given strategy is appropriate in a given situation, such as asking an acquaintance how much her new car cost or how much she makes a month);

(b) the appropriateness of the sociolinguistic forms used with regard to level of formality (e.g. too informal, just right, or too formal), degree of politeness (e.g. suitably polite or lacking in markers of politeness for that situation in that language and culture), and amount of language used (e.g. too much, just right, or too little).

(3) Have a discussion afterwards with the students as to whether the setting was clear and as to the factors that most contributed to the students' responses.

(4) Use verbal reports to help in reconstructing why the students responded as they did.

Once teachers embrace this endeavor more than has commonly been the case, we will most likely have more entries for the above list. We will also have a better idea of just which speech act instruments make the most sense for the language classroom – for perception or production, in spoken or written performance, at more elementary or advanced proficiency levels, in second vs. foreign language environments, and so forth. What is certain is that more work needs to be done, but the rewards can be great in that L2 speech act performance may be crucial in increasingly global communication.

Notes

1. For the purposes of this chapter no distinction will be made between second and foreign language, though in reality there may be a significant difference. The former implies that the language is learned in an environment where it is spoken and the latter implies that this is not the case. Of course, in reality it depends to a large extent on the degree to which learners avail themselves of any opportunities to interact with native speakers of the language – so, for example, a second language environment may for some learners be like a foreign language one.

2. *Sociocultural ability* refers to knowledge about (1) whether the speech act can be performed at all, given the culture involved, the age and sex of the speakers, their social class and occupations, and their roles and status in the interaction; (2) whether the speech act is relevant in the situation; and (3) whether the correct amount of information has been conveyed (see Cohen, 1994, for more on this).

3. *Sociolinguistic ability* refers to whether the linguistic forms (words, phrases, and sentences) used to express the intent of the speech act are acceptable in that situation (e.g. intensifying an apology for hurting someone physically with "really" to indicate regret, rather than with "very," which may be more an indication of etiquette).

4. It could be argued that, from the moment the participants sign a consent form to having the session audio-taped, the data are no longer "natural," but rather "naturalistic." Of course, it also could be argued that they may well forget about the taping and behave naturally.

5. *Retrospective verbal report* involves the inspection of specific, not generalized, language behavior, after the mental event is over (e.g. some 20 seconds or more later). Thus, it involves recollecting what was being thought at the time, unlike introspection, which occurs within the first 20 seconds of the mental event.

References

Arent, R. (1996) Sociopragmatic decisions regarding complaints by Chinese learners and NSs of American English. *Hong Kong Journal of Applied Linguistics* 1 (1), 125–147.

Bachman, L. F. and Cohen, A. D. (1998) *Interfaces Between Second Language Acquisition and Language Testing Research*. Cambridge: Cambridge University Press.

Bardovi-Harlig, K. and Hartford, B. S. (1993) Refining the DCT: Comparing open questionnaires and dialogue completion tasks. *Pragmatics and Language Learning* 4, 143–165.

Bardovi-Harlig, K. and Hartford, B. S. (1996) Input in an institutional setting. *Studies in Second Language Acquisition* 18 (2), 171–188.

Beebe, L. M. and Cummings, M. C. (1996) Natural speech act data versus written questionnaire data: How data collection method affects speech act performance. In S. M. Gass and J. Neu (eds) *Speech Acts Across Cultures* (pp. 65–86). Berlin: Mouton de Gruyter.

Beebe, L. M. and Takahashi, T. (1989) Sociolinguistic variation in face-threatening speech acts: Chastisement and disagreement. In M. R. Eisenstein (ed.) *The Dynamic Interlanguage: Empirical Studies in Second Language Variation* (pp. 199–218). New York: Plenum.

Beebe, L. M., Takahashi, T., and Uliss-Weltz, R. (1990) Pragmatic transfer in ESL refusals. In R. C. Scarcella, G. Andersen, and S. D. Krashen (eds) *Developing Communicative Competence in a Second Language* (pp. 55–73). New York: Newbury House.

Blum-Kulka, S. (1982) Learning to say what you mean in a second language: A study of the speech act performance of learners of Hebrew as a second language. *Applied Linguistics* 3 (1), 29–59.

Blum-Kulka, S., House-Edmondson, J., and Kasper, G. (eds) (1989) *Cross-cultural Pragmatics: Requests and Apologies*. Norwood, NJ: Ablex.

Brown, J. D. (2001) Pragmatics tests: Different purposes, different tests. In K. R. Rose and G. Kasper (eds) *Pragmatics in Language Teaching* (pp. 301–325). Cambridge: Cambridge University Press.

Canale, M. and Swain, M. (1980) Theoretical bases of communicative approaches to second language teaching and testing. *Applied Linguistics* 1 (1), 1–47.

Cohen, A. D. (1994) *Assessing Language Ability in the Classroom* (2nd edn). Boston: Newbury House/Heinle & Heinle.

Cohen, A. D. (1998) *Strategies in Learning and Using a Second Language*. Harlow: Longman.

Cohen, A. D. and Olshtain, E. (1981) Developing a measure of sociocultural competence: The case of apology. *Language Learning* 31 (1), 113–134.

Cohen, A. D. and Olshtain, E. (1993) The production of speech acts by EFL learners. *TESOL Quarterly* 27 (1), 33–56.

Cohen, A. D. and Tarone, E. (1994) The effects of training on written speech act behavior: Stating and changing an opinion. *MinneTESOL Journal* 12, 39–62.

Douglas, D. (2000) *Assessing Language for Specific Purposes*. Cambridge: Cambridge University Press.

Duff, P. and Li, D. (2000) Sociolinguistically contextualized approaches to IL pragmatics research. Paper presented at the Thirty-fourth Annual TESOL Convention, Vancouver, Canada, March.

Farhady, H. (1980) Justification, development, and validation of functional language testing. Ph.D. thesis, University of California, Los Angeles.

Fraser, B., Rintell, E., and Walters, J. (1980) An approach to conducting research on the acquisition of pragmatic competence in a second language. In D. Larsen-Freeman (ed.) *Discourse Analysis in Second Language Research* (pp. 75–91). Rowley, MA: Newbury House.

Frescura, M. A. (1993) A sociolinguistic comparison of "reactions to complaints": Italian L1 vs. English L1, Italian L2, and Italian as a community language. Unpublished doctoral dissertation, University of Toronto.

Hudson, T. (2001) Indicators for pragmatic instruction: Some quantitative tools. In K. R. Rose and G. Kasper (eds) *Pragmatics in Language Teaching* (pp. 283–300). Cambridge: Cambridge University Press.

Hudson, T., Detmer, E., and Brown, J. D. (1992) *A Framework for Testing Cross-cultural Pragmatics* (Technical Report #2). Honolulu, HI: Second Language Teaching and Curriculum Center, University of Hawai'i at Manoa.

Hudson, T., Detmer, E., and Brown, J. D. (1995) *Developing Prototypic Measures of Cross-cultural Pragmatics* (Technical Report #7). Honolulu, HI: Second Language Teaching and Curriculum Center, University of Hawai'i at Manoa.

Hymes, D. (1974) *Foundations in Sociolinguistics: An Ethnographic Approach*. Philadelphia, PA: University of Pennsylvania Press.

Kasper, G. (1999) Data collection in pragmatics research. *University of Hawai'i Working Papers in ESL* 18 (1), 71–107.

Kasper, G. and Dahl, M. (1991) Research methods in interlanguage pragmatics. *Studies in Second Language Acquisition* 13 (2), 215–247.

Kramsch, C. (1993) *Context and Culture in Language Teaching*. Oxford: Oxford University Press.

Labov, W. (1972) *Sociolinguistic Patterns*. Philadelphia, PA: University of Pennsylvania Press.

Li, D. (1998) Expressing needs and wants in a second language: An ethnographic study of Chinese immigrant women's requesting behavior. Unpublished doctoral dissertation, Teachers College, Columbia University, New York.

Li, D. (2000) The pragmatics of making requests in the L2 workplace: A case study of language socialization. *Canadian Modern Language Review* 57 (1), 58–87.

Lyster, R. (1994) The effect of functional-analytic teaching on aspects of French immersion students' sociolinguistic competence. *Applied Linguistics* 15 (3), 263–287.

Meier, A. J. (1998) Apologies: What do we know? *International Journal of Applied Linguistics* 8 (2), 215–231.

Murillo, E. A., Aguilar, H., and Meditz, A. (1991) Teaching speech act behavior through video: Apologies. Unpublished paper, Linguistics Department, Ohio University.

Nakahama, Y. (1998) Differing perceptions of politeness between Japanese and American learners of Japanese. *Southeast Review of Asian Studies* 20, 61–80.

Olshtain, E. and Cohen, A. D. (1983) Apology: A speech act set. In N. Wolfson and E. Judd (eds) *Sociolinguistics and Language Acquisition* (pp. 18–35). Rowley, MA: Newbury House.

Raffaldini, T. (1988) The use of situation tests as measures of communicative ability. *Studies in Second Language Acquisition* 10 (2), 197–216.

Reed, D. J. and Cohen, A. D. (2001). Revisiting raters and ratings in oral language assessment. In C. Elder, A. Brown, E. Grove, K. Hill, N. Iwashita, T. Lumley, T. McNamara, and K. O'Loughlin (eds) *Experimenting with Uncertainty: Essays in Honour of Alan Davies* (pp. 82–96). Studies in Language Testing 11. Cambridge: Cambridge University Press.

Robinson, M. (1992) Introspective methodology in interlanguage pragmatics research. In G. Kasper (ed.) *Pragmatics of Japanese as Native and Target Language* (Technical Report #3) (pp. 27–82). Honolulu, HI: Second Language Teaching and Curriculum Center, University of Hawai'i at Manoa.

Tateyama, Y., Kasper, G., Mui, L. P., Tay, H.-M., and Thananart, O. (1997) Explicit and implicit teaching of pragmatic routines. In L. R. Bouton (ed.) *Pragmatics and Language Learning* (pp. 163–177). Urbana, IL: Division of English as an International Language, Intensive English Institute, University of Illinois at Urbana-Champaign.

Varghese, M. and Billmyer, K. (1996) Investigating the structure of discourse completion tests. *Working Papers in Educational Linguistics* 12 (1), 39–58.

Widjaja, C. S. (1997) A study of date refusals: Taiwanese females vs. American females. *University of Hawai'i Working Papers in ESL* 15 (2), 1–43.

Wolfson, N. (1989) *Perspectives: Sociolinguistics and TESOL*. Cambridge, MA: Newbury House/HarperCollins.

Wolfson, N., Marmor, T., and Jones, S. (1989) Problems in the comparison of speech acts across cultures. In S. Blum-Kulka, J. House-Edmondson, and G. Kasper (eds) *Cross-cultural Pragmatics: Requests and Apologies* (pp. 174–196). Norwood, NJ: Ablex.

Yamashita, S. O. (1996) *Six Measures of JSL Pragmatics* (Technical Report #14). Honolulu, HI: Second Language Teaching and Curriculum Center, University of Hawai'i at Manoa.

Yoshitake, S. (1997) Interlanguage competence of Japanese students of English: A multi-test framework evaluation. Unpublished doctoral dissertation, Columbia Pacific University, San Rafael, California.

Yule, G. (1996) *Pragmatics*. Oxford: Oxford University Press.

Zuskin, R. D. (1993a) Assessing L2 sociolinguistic competence: In search of support from pragmatic theories. *Pragmatics and Language Learning* 4, 166–182.

Zuskin, R. D. (1993b) L2 learner interpretations of a video discourse completion test: Sociolinguistic inferences generated from context. Unpublished doctoral dissertation, the University of New Mexico.

Index

Authors

Subjects